Seminar Proceedings No. 28

SOUTHERN AFRICA AFTER APARTHEID

Regional Integration and External Resources

Edited by
Bertil Odén

Nordiska Afrikainstitutet, Uppsala, 1993
(The Scandinavian Institute of African Studies)

Indexing terms
Development aid
Economic integration
International relations
International trade
Regional cooperation
SADCC
Southern Africa

Cover picture: Adriaan Honcoop
Typesetting: Gun-Britt Nilsson
Copyediting: Sonja Johansson and Mai Palmberg
Language polishing: Alan Harkess

Printed in Sweden by
Bohusläningens Boktryckeri AB, Uddevalla 1993

ISSN 0281-0018
ISBN 91-7106-332-3

Contents

cont.

List of tables

Map

List of figures

Abbreviations

AAM	Anti-Apartheid Movement (England)
ACP	African, Caribbean and Pacific countries, signatories to the Lomé Conventions
ADPS	Asian Dialogue Partner System
AEC	African Economic Community
ADB	African Development Bank
ANC	African National Congress
APEC	Asia Pacific Economic Co-operation
ASEAN	Association of Southeast Asian Nations
BLNS	Botswana, Lesotho, Namibia, Swaziland
BLS	Botswana, Lesotho, Swaziland
CABEI	Central American Bank for Economic Integration
CACM	Central American Common Market
CCA	Common Customs Area
CCC	Central American Clearing House
CEAO	Communauté Economique de l'Afrique de l'Ouest
CET	Common External Tariff
CMA	Common Monetary Area
CODESA	Convention for a Democratic South Africa
CONSAS	Constellation of Southern African States
CSCE	Conference on Security and Cooperation in Europe
DAC	Development Assistance Committee (of the OECD)
DBSA	Development Bank of Southern Africa
EAC	East African Community
EAEG	East Asian Economic Group
EC	European Community
ECLA	Economic Commission for Latin America
ECOWAS	Economic Community of West African States
EERM	European Exchange Rate Mechanism
EMS	European Monetary System
ERM	Exchange Rate Mechanism
ESADB	Eastern and Southern African Development Bank
EU	European Union
FRELIMO	Frente de Libertação de Moçambique
GATT	General Agreement on Tariffs and Trade
GDP	Gross Domestic Product
GNP	Gross National Product
GSP	Generalised System of Preferences
IBRD	International Bank for Reconstruction and Development
IDA	International Development Association
IFI	International Financial Institutions
ILO	International Labour Organization
IMF	International Monetary Fund
IMPOD	Government agency for import of Third World products to Sweden
LAFTA	Latin American Free Trade Association
LAIA	Latin American Integration Association
LDC	Less Developed Countries
LNDC	Lesotho National Development Corporation
MDC	More Developed Countries
MFN	Most Favoured Nation
MPLA	Movimento Popular de Libertação de Angola
NGO	Non-Governmental Organization
NIC	Newly Industrialised Countries
OAU	Organization of African Unity
ODA	Official Development Assistance
OECD	Organization for Economic Cooperation and Development
OGL	Open General Licence
OPEC	Organization of Petroleum Exporting Countries
PAC	Pan-African Congress
PECC	Pacific Economic Cooperation Council
PTA	Preferential Trade Area for Eastern and Southern Africa
RENAMO	Resistência Nacional de Moçambique
RMA	Rand Monetary Area
SACU	Southern African Customs Union
SADC	Southern African Development Community
SADCC	Southern African Development Coordination Conference
SAP	Structural Adjustment Programme
SATS	South African Transport Services
SDR	Special Drawing Right
SIECA	Regional Secretariat for coordination of the integration process (Central America)
SUKAB	The Swedish Countertrade Company
TBVC	Transkei, Bophutatswana, Venda, Ciskei
TINET	PTA Programme for Trade Information
TNC	Transnational corporation
UAPTA	PTA Unit of Account
UN	United Nations
UNCTAD	United Nations Conference on Trade and Development
UNESCO	United Nations Educational, Scientific and Cultural Organization
UNIDO	United Nations Industry Development Organization
UNITA	União Nacional para Independencia Total de Angola
WFP	World Food Programme

SADCC member states and South Africa. Basic indicators 1990

Country	Population mid-1990 (mn)	Area (000 km²)	GNP/Cap 1990 (USD)	GDP 1990 (USD bn)	Life expectancy 1990 (years)
Angola	10.0	1,247	620	7.70	46
Botswana	1.3	582	2,040	2.70	67
Lesotho	1.8	30	530	0.34	56
Malawi	8.5	118	200	1.66	46
Mozambique	15.7	802	80	1.32	47
Namibia	1.8	824	1,030[b]	2.18[a]	57
Swaziland	0.8	17	810	0.81[a]	57
Tanzania	24.5	945	110	2.06	48
Zambia	8.1	753	420	3.12	50
Zimbabwe	9.8	391	640	5.31	61
SADCC total	82.3	5.708	336	27.20	
South Africa	35.9	1,221	2,530	90.72	62

Sources: World Bank: *World Development Report 1992*
    [a] Calculated from EIU data
    [b] Figure for 1989 in *Human Development Report 1992*

Membership in regional organisations

Country	Membership PTA[1]	SACU	CMA	SADCC[2]
Angola	*			*
Botswana		*		*
Lesotho	*	*	*	*
Malawi	*			*
Mozambique	*			*
Namibia	*	*	*	*
Swaziland	*	*	*	*
Tanzania	*			*
Zambia	*			*
Zimbabwe	*			*
South Africa		*	*	

[1] PTA also includes 10 countries in eastern Africa. Namibia became a member in January, 1993.
[2] The SADCC summit meeting in August 1992 decided to form a Southern Africa Development Community, SADC.

SOUTHERN AFRICA

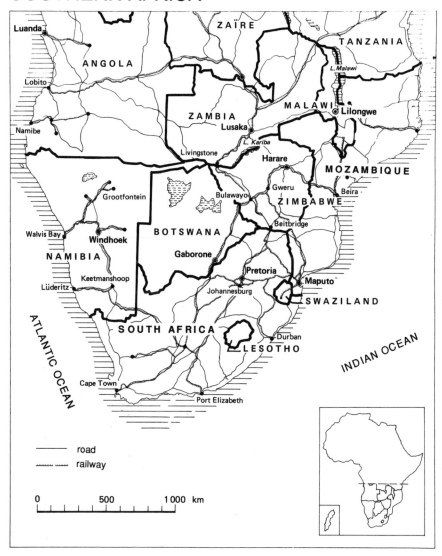

Luanda
Lobito
Namibe
ANGOLA
ZAÏRE
TANZANIA
L. Malawi
ZAMBIA
Lusaka
MALAWI
Lilongwe
Livingstone
L. Kariba
Harare
MOZAMBIQUE
Grootfontein
Bulawayo
Gweru
ZIMBABWE
Beira
Walvis Bay
Windhoek
BOTSWANA
Beitbridge
NAMIBIA
Gaborone
Keetmanshoop
Pretoria
Maputo
Lüderitz
Johannesburg
SWAZILAND
SOUTH AFRICA
Durban
LESOTHO
ATLANTIC OCEAN
Cape Town
Port Elizabeth
INDIAN OCEAN

——— road
········· railway

0   500   1 000   km

Preface

As part of its Africa Days in May 1992, Nordiska Afrikainstitutet (The Scandinavian Institute of African Studies) organised a seminar on *Southern Africa After Apartheid. Regional integration and external resources.* The planning of this seminar has involved close cooperation between the Scandinavian Institute of African Studies, Chr. Michelsen Institute in Bergen, Norway, and the Centre for Development Research in Copenhagen, Denmark.

The main objective of the seminar was to examine some of the issues related to alternative modes of regional integration and cooperation and their relevance to Southern Africa after apartheid in a post-cold-war world. In this context attention has also been paid to the role of external resources, especially development aid.

To carry out a multi-dimensional analysis, the seminar approached the topic from four different perspectives: integration theory, an issue oriented approach, an organisational approach and finally from the standpoint of external resources. The number of topics that may be considered under the heading of an "issue-oriented" approach is almost unlimited. All of them cannot be covered during one seminar, which means that a number of perspectives relevant to regional development are absent, such as gender, environment, and the role of economic restructuring at the national level. Focusing on certain aspects inevitably marginalizes others.

This volume contains an edited selection of the papers presented at the seminar following revision by the authors. Together they provide a multi-disciplinary, social science perspective on the issue of the development of the post-cold war and post-apartheid Southern Africa. It should be seen as a Nordic-Southern Africa contribution to the on-going international academic and aid agency discussion on the future of the Southern Africa region.

Special thanks to Gun-Britt Nilsson for her tireless and creative editing support and assistance.

Uppsala, October, 1992

Bertil Odén

Introduction

Bertil Odén

> Without integration, Africa will not merely be marginalised,
> it will be trivialised.
> *Salim Ahmed Salim, OAU Secretary General, 1992.*

Any research activity on the future of Southern Africa has to be carried out against the background of the far-reaching political changes that are under way in the region and at the level of the world system, especially in relation to the on-going process towards non-racialism and democracy in South Africa. Consideration will also have to be given to the collapse of the communist system in the former Soviet Union and the eastern part of Europe and the development towards a post-cold-war world order.

It is clear that the process in South Africa will be difficult and that we will probably see a number of temporary set-backs on the way. Compromises will be inevitable and the end result is uncertain. It might be "an ANC-led government without ANC policy" as one participant at the seminar expressed it. The prevailing impression that many in the present South African establishment believe that the on-going process will result in "business as usual", but with apartheid omitted from the legislative texts, points towards a potentially dangerous development. The discrepancies between the main actors in the South African negotiations are wide. Furthermore a serious backlash, delaying the process by years cannot be ruled out, as the events during the middle of 1992 showed.

Therefore it is important that for as long as a democratic government is not in place in South Africa, external players are careful and do not act as if it were. Premature lifting of some sanctions is a case in point. This does not imply that analysis of sequences and scenarios is superfluous. On the contrary, the various options for a future post-apartheid Southern Africa, their viability and realism have to be further analysed.

In the period between May 1992, when the seminar took place, and the publishing of this book, the SADCC Summit Meeting in August has agreed to form The Southern African Development Community, SADC, which in due time will replace SADCC. Some comments on the implications of this are made by Arne Tostensen in chapter 7. However, in the wake of ratification and preparation for the various activities of SADC, the SADCC activities will continue mainly along established lines. The perspectives and analysis in this book, concerned with the organisational set-up in the region will therefore still be of interest and the functional and theoretical perspectives are as relevant for SADC as for SADCC.

The chapters in this book follow the outline of the original seminar, which means they are divided into four categories, following the perspectives already mentioned; i.e. integration theory, issues, organisation and external resource-flows.

REGIONAL INTEGRATION THEORY—WHAT RELEVANCE FOR SOUTHERN AFRICA ?

Which theoretical framework is most applicable to the Southern Africa situation? Two papers presented at the seminar tried to examine this central question.

Tom Østergaard in his chapter *Classical Models of Regional Integration: What Relevance for Southern Africa?* carries out a critical review of the relevance of the classical models of regional integration to South Africa. He identifies and examines the market integration theory, the development integration model and the neo-functional model. His conclusion is that none of these three theories in its pure form is suitable for the Southern Africa situation, although elements in them might be useful and some eclectic combination might therefore be advisable. As a case he applies the theories to SADCC and concludes that SADCC cannot be considered a development integration scheme, and thus does not fit into any of the three models. He agrees with the suggestion that the SADCC approach should rather be characterized as "sectoral programming".

Experience demonstrates that regional integration is inherently complicated. For a number of reasons, it is particularly difficult in Southern Africa. As the economies are overwhelmingly geared to supplying raw materials to overseas markets, the current economic interaction among the countries of the region is limited. Furthermore, the countries are generally poor, the economies are stagnant, and class formation is limited. Finally, many of the countries are undergoing political crises and the states are still preoccupied with nation building.

Østergaard´s conclusion is that Southern Africa needs a less ambitious model of regional integration. The SADCC experience suggests the usefulness of adopting a much narrower scale of operation. The choice of activities should be guided primarily by the articulated needs from within the countries concerned. It should flow from the bottom and up.

In order to put regional cooperation efforts in Southern Africa into a comparative perspective, Hans C. Blomqvist et al. examine in their chapter *Some Experiences from Regional Cooperation between Third World Countries* the general theoretical and empirical evidence from other third world projects on regional economic integration. The potential gains from regional integration, specifically in terms of dynamic effects, are shown to be considerable from a theoretical point of view. Since favourable conditions for successful integration seldom prevail in LDCs, however, the integration schemes have generally not lived up to expectations. Small domestic markets and a high rate of protection against external competition have often encouraged trade diversion and limited the scope for expanding production efficiently. The problems of ensuring an equitable distribution of benefits between member countries have also complicated the integration process. Therefore it might be preferable for the LDCs to pursue cooperation gradually by means of e.g. partial sectoral integration and joint actions in international negotiations.

The three regional integration and cooperation schemes from other parts of the third world studied in the paper are: The Association of Southeast Asian Nations (ASEAN), the Central American Common Market (CACM), and the Latin American Free Trade Association (LAFTA).

In the discussion it was argued that the focus on the lack of markets might turn the discussion in a misleading direction as it shifts the focus from supply side issues. For good products, the market is there and the domestic market does not have to be very large. (Hongkong exports more than Sub-Saharan Africa together.) This means that the integration aim of forming large markets is dubious.

Accordingly both these initial chapters—from slightly different perspectives—conclude that from an integration theory point of view, Southern Africa might not derive any important benefits from the ambitious economic integration schemes, but may instead gain from less ambitious cooperation in specific areas. Blomqvist et al. even suggest that a general free trade strategy is preferable to any regional market model.

In any case, the theoretically oriented discussions show the complexity of economic regional integration. Market integration is definitively not sufficient on its own and the authors point to the high risk of polarization in a case where South Africa plays such a dominant part.

On the other hand, the theoretical conclusions disregard the fact that Southern Africa is for historical reasons already partially integrated in a number of important areas, including trade and labour. The practical task ahead is therefore how to adjust the present integration pattern, given the new global and regional circumstances.

ISSUE-ORIENTED PERSPECTIVES

A number of specific issues related to the post-apartheid region were discussed. One special category was the South African perspective which, due to its predominant role, will strongly influence regional development. Another dimension covered was the regional security issue, especially possible post-apartheid conflicts and measures to resolve them. The scope for financial and monetary cooperation was a third; and the efficiency of the regional transport network a fourth.

In his chapter *Emerging South African Perspectives on Regional Cooperation and Integration after Apartheid* Robert Davies argues that the question of post-apartheid regional cooperation and integration has to be seen against the background of a structural crisis in the pattern of regional interaction established during the apartheid era and of a counter tendency arising from the lowering of political barriers to South Africa's re-engagement with the region.

According to Davies, all major forces in South Africa now appear to agree that the post-apartheid period should see some form of closer regional cooperation and economic integration between all the countries of Southern Africa, including South Africa. However, the perceptions of regarding which mode of cooperation should be followed differ widely.

The present minority government and much of the corporate sector—the orthodox perspective—seem to view future cooperation as little more than a return to a somewhat modified version of the old (i.e. pre 1970s) "normality". In the short run this would boost South African trade and possibly allow for unhampered capital movement. The role of South Africa as the "natural gateway" to the whole region for overseas trade and investment is also put forward.

The main alternative perspective emerging within the democratic movement in South Africa is based on the view that regional trade and other economic relations need to be restructured as an integral part of a process of transforming the existing growth path. This is not just a matter of equity. This means that regional cooperation forms an important part in a project to change the present South African production structure in order to reduce its present dependence on exports of primary products.

Davies thus envisages a mutually beneficial, negotiated restructuring of regional economic relations, centring around a trade-off whereby South Africa gains greater access to regional markets and inputs in return for an agreement to cooperate with the rest of the region in restructuring key sectoral relationships.

As Østergaard also points out, this alternative scenario is close to the development integration model, which requires governmental commitment and societies where decisions at the top can trickle down to the players who should implement what is negotiated. Although this might not be the case in Southern Africa, as the present trend towards bilateral deals based on the extension of existing relations signals, it still might be the policy that internal players in the region as well as external ones could try to develop.

Some issues that did not clearly emerge in Davies' paper, were raised during the discussion, e.g. the alliances that could be built to support the alternative or "qualitative" scenario that the author prefers. Concern was also raised that they would be weak compared to the interests vested in the "quantitative" one. The geographical area for regional cooperation might also differ between various functions, such as water, electricity grid, transport and labour. A crucial issue would be the willingness and capacity of the governments in the region to put serious efforts into the "qualitative change scenario". If this political will is lacking, what moves should then be taken by those interested in that scenario?

The security and conflict resolution perspectives are discussed in the chapter *Towards Enhanced Regional Security in Southern Africa?* by Thomas Ohlson and Stephen J. Stedman. They identify four post-apartheid conflict issues at the level of individual state, namely those related to war termination and reconciliation, to inequitable distribution of resources, to monopoly of political power by a dominant party and to identity due to ethnicity. At the regional level, three security complex dimensions are emphasised; domestic consolidation, regional patterns of amity and enmity between states and the unequal distribution of economic resources and power.

Five scenarios for future security in Southern Africa are presented, in descending order of insecurity; Annihilation, Immature Anarchy, Hegemony, Security Regime and Security Community.

Ohlson and Stedman argue that what they call the Hegemony scenario, which is similar to a security version of Davies' "quantitative scenario", is the most likely. The authors then discuss the prerequisites and measures that are essential in order to move towards scenarios on their list which are more secure than the Hegemony one. They suggest a normative three-step solution to enhance security, stability and socio-economic development in Southern Africa:

1. Top priority must be placed on ending armed conflicts and helping to insure against their recurrence.
2. Domestic consolidation must be attained through the development of both capable states and vibrant civil societies.
3. Balanced regional cooperation in matters of socio-economic development and security must be expanded and institutionalised.

Ohlson and Stedman also point to the risk of the region slipping into still worse scenarios than the Hegemonic one. Some states might not be able to cope with internal conflicts. The challenge of marrying weak or nonexistent norms, value systems and expectations to capabilities via organizations and institutions is indeed a formidable one. The need to put internal (national) houses in order is crucial. If formal regional integration takes places before integration at the national level, this will only serve to perpetuate South African domination and lead to a volatile and highly unstable situation.

This discussion from a security point of view is compatible with the mainly economic/political one used by Robert Davies,

In their chapter on *Post-apartheid regional financial and monetary cooperation* Charles Harvey and Derek Hudson discuss possible modes of monetary arrangements, based on an analysis of recent developments of exchange rates and trade. The least formalised of the arrangements would be a continuation of the present system where most countries in the region maintain roughly real exchange rates against the South African rand, although with periodic fluctuations, and no form of consultation. The exemption is the cooperation between South Africa, Lesotho and Swaziland in the Common Monetary Area, CMA. Various alternatives are presented; some form of regular consultation on exchange rate policy; a more formalised mechanism which obliges members to maintain their currencies within narrow bands; and to peg to some non-regional currency or currency basket, which would be the strictest one.

The conclusion of the authors in this crucial but often overlooked field is that a more formal exchange rate mechanism for the countries of Southern Africa is a long way off, notwithstanding the enthusiasm of the Council of Ministers of the PTA and their SADCC counterpart. It would require the pre-existence of, among other things, an expectation of stable exchange rates within the group of countries concerned which requires low and stable rates of inflation; the actual setting of exchange rates more or less market determined; no exchange controls on current account transactions; sufficient liquid assets to be able to intervene; and greater macroeconomic policy coordination in general. None of these prerequisites can be foreseen, even in the medium term perspective.

The issue of development finance institutions for the region is also briefly discussed by Harvey and Hudson. From various quarters, it has been suggested that the Development Bank of Southern Africa, DBSA, could develop into a regional development bank. Its transformation would however imply the solution of a number of issues. The political question of membership of the so called independent bantustans, might be resolved if they were reincorporated into the new democratic South Africa. However, the bank is presently needed and organised for domestic development lending in South Africa.

The alternative to developing the DBSA would be a new development bank, but it could also be argued that development lending to the region could be channelled through the African Development Bank.

Oliver Saasa discusses *The Effectiveness of Regional Transport Network in the SADCC Region* the post-apartheid regional transport network against its historical background. He concludes that the SADCC links will have difficulties to compete with those of South Africa. He especially singles out the Tazara-Dar es Salaam route as a problem due to its low reliability, technical and managerial problems and the changed transport policy of the new Zambian government, supporting the southward routes. He also points out that part of Zambia's copper exports since 1991 use road/rail transport through Namibia and the harbour at Walvis Bay.

For the customers, issues such as cost-effectiveness, security of cargo and reliability of routes are crucial. Port-related elements explain most of the difference in user preferences; both the direct costs due to the tariff rate structure and the discounts that South African port authorities give their customers, as well as the level and quality of service. Software and management support will be needed in order to improve the competetiveness of the present SADCC routes. Regarding physical investments, the regional intra-transport network will require a higher priority.

ORGANISATION-ORIENTED ISSUES

The perspectives and roles of the three main regional organisations, SADCC, SACU and PTA, are analysed in the four subsequent chapters. Since the seminar, the SADCC summit meeting in August 1992 has decided to develop SADCC into the *Southern African Development Community, SADC*. The Treaty of the new organisation will come into force when it is ratified by seven of the ten SADCC members.

Consequently SADCC institutions will continue to exist during an intermediate period.

The new organisation is commented upon by Arne Tostensen in his What *Role for SADCC in the Post-Apartheid Era?* His chapter discusses some of the determinants of regional development and the relationship between the functions of regional cooperation and the institutional arrangements. He also analyses SADCC´s own responses to the new challenges and the issue of rationalising the existing regional arrangements such as SADCC, PTA, SACU and CMA. The concluding sections focus on the inherent tensions within regional integration between sub-national, national and supra-national levels and the problem of existing regional imbalances and disparities.

Tostensen suggests that SADCC has not so far analysed the new challenges sufficiently, especially the implications of possible South African membership. The SADC Treaty, which makes the organisation a legal entity eligible to negotiate and sign agreements is, according to Tostensen, characterized by its compromises. The degree of increasing power for the secretariat and the other SADCC structures ultimately depends on the political will of the member states. Tostensen fears that this will is weak, something which is symbolised by the trend towards bilateralisation of the region. However, this may be a difficult obstacle for future increased regional integration with SADC or any other organisation as an instrument. A new South African government, regardless of the relative strength of the ANC, will be heavily constrained in its efforts to implement a solidarity-style regional policy. Tostensen argues that short-term national interests will prevail in the post-apartheid regional *real-politik*.

Tostensen also argues, that with the increased convergence of issues upon which SADC(C) and PTA are embarking, it is absolutely necessary to focus on a rationalisation of the institutions. This is an issue for the member states. However, according to Tostensen, initiatives in this field will be supported by the donor community, and passivity will make them more reluctant.

Tostensen also comes close to the perspective of Davies' in the emphasis which he gives to the need to redress regional disparities. This argument applies *a fortiori* to a situation in which South Africa becomes a legitimate player. Two sorts of justification are relevant. First, the normative, to pursue equity and a fair distribution of costs and benefits. Second, equity issues are the core of the regional project.

In the following chapter, *SADCC; Future Challenges*, Emang Mothlabane Maphanyane from the SADCC Secretariat answers some of the criticism from different quarters felt by the organisation. The outcome is a more positive attitude towards the preparedness of SADCC to deal with the post-apartheid situation. After a brief summary of the SADCC 1992 theme document on regional integration, Maphanyane emphasizes three prerequisites for successful regional integration. Firstly the availability of trained and technically competent personnel is related to the need to build confidence among the people of the region in order to get rid of the over-reliance on outside experts. Secondly the success of regional integration depends on being able to go beyond governments in order to address the perceived interest of the majority of the people in the region. The third challenge is to mobilise increased regional resources for the implementation of the programmes from its present share of around 10 per cent, in order to reduce the dependence on external resources. It could be added as a comment that none of these prerequisites are easily achieved. Moreover, there are no hints as to how the challenges should be tackled.

Jan Isaksen discusses *Prospects for SACU after Apartheid*. As background, he describes the existing SACU-agreement, the South Africa and the BLSN countries in relation to the agreement. He also examines the experiences of changes to the agreement that have taken place, especially during the 1980′s. When SACU is discussed, the focus is normally on the trade and revenue sharing arrangements. Isaksen points out that there are other important dimensions of the agreement, such as transport clauses, the Customs Commission and subcommittees, which have provided the smaller countries with opportunities to discuss such matters with South Africa.

Isaksen shows the varied and rather shifting opinions on the role of SACU after apartheid. He suggests that new arrangements to provide fair competition between companies in the smaller states and South Africa will be required. At the same time, a number of changes of SACU can be envisaged, although it is impossible to predict their exact form. Isaksen sketches a "minimum" and a "maximum" change. The former would be a transformation of SACU to become a true international organisation which is not part of the administration of any of the members and/or changes to the compensation mechanism.

At the maximum end, the two main options could be called "widening" and "deepening" of SACU. The first option would draw one or more of the other SADCC states into SACU. Isaksen quotes rumours that Mozambique, Malawi and Zambia have informally expressed an interest in becoming members. This has to be linked to changed rules for compensation and also implies greater influence for other members than South Africa also in decisions on customs duties. For South

Africa the "domestic market" in terms of numbers of people would be almost doubled, although at present the average purchasing power is extremely low.

A widening of SADCC would have its repercussions on other regional groupings. PTA would face a de facto break up and would therefore probably resist the idea. SADCC in its present form would not necessarily have the same problem, but with higher integration aims, this might well be the case.

The deepening scenario would transform the customs union into an economic union including the free movement of not only goods, but also capital and labour. This implies using SACU to settle difficult migration issues. A free labour market would be to the benefit of the BLSN states, particularly Lesotho. This option would imply that SACU could be treated as one unit within both SADCC and PTA.

Arve Ofstad discusses *Will PTA be relevant in the Post-apartheid Era?* He starts with a short description of the PTA organisation and achievements so far and continues with some of the current problems of cooperation; mainly the lack of complementarities, high costs and relative prices, transport costs and inadequate transport, established interests and trading patterns, including dependency on donor policies (ODA finances over 50 per cent of all imports in at least 11 of the 18 PTA countries), finance and payments restrictions, uncertainties, and non-tariff barriers. The result is a low and declining official intra-trade share of the total trade of the PTA countries. It should, however, be noted that there are significant unofficial trade flows between some of the member states.

Ofstad examines whether South African trade with the PTA will benefit from PTA membership and discusses the trade implications for the PTA countries. His conclusion in brief is that the main factor that would improve South African trade with the rest of Africa is the lifting of sanctions; that the main markets for South African manufacturing exports have been SACU and Zimbabwe where South Africa already has preferential treatment; and that therefore there would be some, but probably modest, benefits of PTA membership. The main regional exporters among the PTA states are Kenya and Zimbabwe, which together export 70 per cent of all intra-PTA-exports. Their position will be changed since they will have to compete to a much larger extent with South African goods if that country should become a member of the PTA.

Another point raised by Ofstad is that while South Africa stands to gain from preferential trade arrangements, it still might be questioned whether PTA is the most useful framework for such arrangements. Kenya is the only non-SADCC country which is of much potential interest for South African exports. For Zimbabwe, the benefits of South African membership seem particularly problematic.

Can the very ambitious PTA plans in areas outside those related to trade be considered viable or just pipe-dreams? Would South African companies not benefit more from selective bilateral agreements with the few PTA countries of significant interest? Where will SADCC cooperation turn? Ofstad´s only clear conclusion is that the issue is complex.

THE ROLE OF EXTERNAL RESOURCES

In his chapter on *Factors Affecting Flows of External Capital to Post-apartheid Southern Africa* Bertil Odén begins with a background discussion of the external capital flows during the 1980s under the headings of direct investments, non-concessional loans and development assistance. After discussing the various factors affecting these and with an assumed "main-stream scenario" for the development in South Africa, his conclusions may be summarized as follows:

1. The disintegration of the Soviet Union and the collapse of the socialist system in Eastern Europe will on the whole reduce the political and economic interest in Southern Africa of OECD countries. However, two outside regions—Eastern Europe and South East Asia—will probably increase their interest in South Africa.
2. A short-term factor reducing OECD interest is the low economic growth in the industrialised countries, which lowers the demand for minerals and other raw materials. More serious are the technological innovations that will in the long-run also reduce the demand for minerals and metals.

The changes in South Africa also alter the context for regional cooperation in Southern Africa. Some of the trends evident in mid-1992 indicate *inter alia* the following developments due to regional and national factors:

1. In spite of the lifting of international sanctions both international and domestic companies will be reluctant to make major new investments in South Africa.
2. There is a great interest in developing further trade relations with South Africa from all quarters.
3. A gradually increasing inflow of loans can be expected from international capital markets to private and government borrowers in South Africa.

4. Significant South African borrowing from IFIs, mainly the World Bank and the ADB, provided the new government is prepared to follow IMF and World Bank conditions, and a certain inflow of ODA, mainly to support social sectors and activities to reduce the discriminating effects of the apartheid system.
5. Selective investments in SADCC countries by South Africa-based companies and farmers.
6. A reduced volume of ODA to the present SADCC region, and a continued lack of interest by OECD countries in direct investments and loans to the SADCC countries, with the possible exception of Angola, provided peace finally is reached.

For all categories of external capital discussed here, it can be assumed that successful regional integration will increase the external interest in Southern Africa.

In his chapter *Swedish Aid Priorities for Regional Development in Southern Africa* Jan Cedergren provides the perspective of an aid operator and adds further features to the recent changes on the regional scene.

According to Cedergren the new situation still justifies high aid volumes. The criteria for providing aid will however change in the new situation as it emerges. He suggests that political anti-apartheid criteria will be replaced by traditional aid criteria and conditionalities, which will affect the direction of aid. Moreover there are major reviews going on regarding many of the donor aid programmes to Southern Africa. There is continuous scope for bilateral aid to the weaker states in the region for donors who wish to support a more balanced regional development.

From this analytical perspective Cedergren presents a number of recommendations regarding future Swedish development aid e.g.:

1. Continued support should be given to assist poor countries to "put their house in order".
2. A special case can be made for substantial aid to resettlement, restructuring and rehabilitation in Angola and Mozambique, provided the process towards peace in these two countries is successful.
3. The special situation of South Africa ought to be a sufficient justification for aid in spite of the high GDP/capita. Two aid priorities should be kept in mind: support should be given in all possible terms to the fragile, emerging democracy and its institutions as well as to the acceleration of poverty alleviation.
4. SADCC's Programme of Action should receive continued support, with the emphasis shifting from project investment to management, maintenance, training and effective planning.

5. To promote a more balanced regional development and apply regional criteria in the appraisal of bilateral aid projects/programmes.

Finally Åke Magnusson in his chapter *Swedish Trade and Investment Links with Southern Africa* presents the trade and investment perspective of the Swedish private sector on the region. He begins with an overview of developments during the 1980s, sanctions introduced against South Africa, the slow economic growth in that country, economic crisis in most SADCC countries, which even without crises are minor markets for Swedish companies.

According to Magnusson, the volume and pattern of Swedish trade and investment links to Southern Africa in the future will be decided by a mix of factors: the actual rather than the stated intentions of economic policy and performance as well as the degree of political stability.

As the result of the last 15 years, the platform for Swedish business in Southern Africa is in bad shape. It is concentrated in one sector, mining equipment, which means a high dependency on the development of that sector in the region. Confidence in the investment climate is low and has to be improved by clear policy signals from governments. Political stability is uncertain in several countries. All these factors reduce the interest of Swedish companies in taking risks in Southern Africa.

The last 15 years have also reduced the competitiveness of Swedish companies in the South African market, and increased the strength of their South Africa-based competitors. Development in South Africa will be decisive for the interest of Swedish companies in the whole region, especially because they look upon South Africa as the gateway to the region. In this respect, Swedish business thus has the same perspective as their South African competitors and the present white establishment (c.f. Robert Davies' chapter).

After this "buffet menu" presenting the content of the book, let us proceed to the "full dishes" in the following chapters.

THEORY ORIENTED
PERSPECTIVES

1. Classical Models of Regional Integration—what Relevance for Southern Africa?

Tom Østergaard

The subject of economic integration in Africa is like a myth that won't die. Despite three decades of disappointing progress, African leaders continue to propagate the view that economic integration is an important device for fostering development.

With a few exceptions, all the major efforts of regional economic integration in Africa are inspired by the market integration model.[1] This is somewhat paradoxical given the vast literature suggesting the inapplicability of this European-derived model in the African setting.

Why, then, do so many African states pursue market integration? What are the expected advantages of regional integration?

The various models of regional integration are based on different motivations and perceptions of potential benefits. Not surprisingly, the common point of departure is the enlargement of space, from separate national territories to wider regional areas. In particular, emphasis has been placed on the expected advantages of creating a larger economic market. The earliest school of regional integration, the customs unions theory, emphasizes the gains from competition likely to result from creation of regional markets (Mikesell, 1963). Subsequently, development integration theories have focused less on the anticipated efficiency improvements from increased competition. Instead, they highlight the gains which may be derived from economies of scale in a regional setting (Hazlewood, 1967). During the 1960s, economic development was almost synonymous with industrialisation and the preferred strategy was import substitution industrialisation. Today, the debate is moving beyond the dichotomy between import substitution based and export oriented industrialisation, the former strategy is seen as an important step in the development of the latter, provided that it is properly regulated. It might also be argued that local industries based on the regional market probably stand a better change in the extra-regional export markets. Nevertheless, in most countries the import substitution strategy soon stranded because of insufficient domestic demand. Further industrial growth could be by-passed if the market was enlarged via regional integration (Tussie, 1982).

The creation of a wider market area is a positive motivation for integration. The corollary of this argument—discrimination against countries outside the regional scheme—may be seen as a negative reason for integration. The latter dimension is often more important than the former.

Trends in the international economy also act as a rationale for the formation of regional groupings. The creation of the European Economic Community presumably had an influence on the newly independent states of Africa. Olatunde Ojo (1985:142) states that it was argued that if countries like France and West Germany felt the need for regional integration, the need would be even greater for far smaller and underdeveloped countries. We may regard this as a positive demonstration effect of the EC. African states, however, have also acted in a manner akin to self-defence vis-a-vis the EC. Richard Pomfret (1986:112) argues that the EC has a primary responsibility for the proliferation of preferential trading arrangements among the developing countries because of its discriminatory trading arrangements with almost every country in the world. The following statement of the secretary general of the Preferential Trading Area for Eastern and Southern Africa (PTA) supports this argument: "In view of the economic integration process which is now taking place worldwide, it will be impossible for the small PTA states or African states to survive as independent political and economic units if they act individually" (cited in Martin, 1989:169). We may regard this self-defence reaction on the part of African states as a negative demonstration effect of the EC.

The concept of pan-Africanism has also been an important factor behind the formation of regional integration schemes in Africa. In the early 1960s, president Kwame Nkrumah wanted to institutionalize pan-Africanism by creating a "Continental Union Government", i.e. political integration before economic integration (Ojo, 1985). Whether they realized that everything else would not follow once the "political kingdom" had been attained, Nigeria wanted it the other way around. In any event pan-Africanism remains a powerful force, not least because of its emotional appeal among the African populace.

Finally, regional schemes are often formed in response to a common external enemy or threat (Etzioni, 1965). This was an important factor behind the Association of Southeast Asian Nations. The ASEAN was conceived as a mechanism for dialogue and negotiation to maintain regional stability in the face of the war in Vietnam (Buszynski, 1987). The perceived Soviet threat also had an influence in the formation of the EC. And in Southern Africa the apartheid regime in South Africa has been a decisive motive for regional integration.

This chapter focuses on the Southern African Development Coordination Conference. SADCC is one of those rare cases usually portrayed as a success story by international donors and the mass media. With a few exceptions, the scholarly literature has generally contributed to the praise of SADCC. In order to provide a basis on which to analyze SADCC, the bulk of the chapter discusses some of the major theoretical models of economic integration. The subsequent analysis demonstrates that SADCC does not fit into any of the models of regional integration. Moreover, it concludes that SADCC has not been as successful as it is often claimed. It is hoped that the entire exercise will provide general insights on regional integration in the post-apartheid era.

CLASSICAL MODELS OF REGIONAL INTEGRATION

While in practice some overlap often occurs between the different models, a division into three categories facilitates theoretical discussion. We shall discuss regional integration theory under the following headings: market integration, development integration and neo-functional integration.

Market integration

Initially the market integration theory[2] was referred to as "customs unions" theory. However, as that term applies to only one of the stages in the envisaged evolution from a free trade area to an economic union, it is more appropriate to speak of "market integration" because it more adequately captures this body of theories. Nevertheless, in keeping with the terminology of early market integration theorists, the term customs unions will be used when referring to the early literature.

Viner (1950) is recognized as the father of the customs unions theory. Before he put it in print, however, customs unions theory had a place in the oral tradition. Lipsey (1960:497) summarizes the pre-Vinerian reasoning as follows: "Free trade maximizes world welfare; a customs union reduces tariffs and is therefore a movement towards free trade; a customs union will, therefore, increase world welfare even if it does not lead to a world-welfare maximum." Viner showed this argument to be incorrect.

The model

Following Viner, the criterion of gain is whether a customs union on balance is "trade creating" or "trade diverting". Both result from removal of trade barriers between members of a union and—a cause of some confusion—*both* increase trade within the union. The two terms, however, refer to respectively gain and loss effects. "Trade creation" results from replacement of high cost domestic production by lower cost production from another member. This entails an economic expansion of one member country's (the lower cost) industry at the expense of another's (the higher cost) industry. "Trade diversion", on the other hand, represents a reduction in external trade resulting from diversion of one member country's demand from the rest of the world (assumed to be a lower cost producer) to a higher cost producer within the union. This entails an uneconomic diversion of output from the lowest cost producer outside the union to a member country's higher cost producer.

Balassa (1961) identified five levels at which discrimination (trade barriers) may be removed and, by implication, the ideal-types of market integration mentioned above. The integration process is anticipated to be linear from a free trade area to a political union; the market forces unleashed at one level will have a spill-over effect to the next level, so that its implementation becomes an economic necessity. At the lowest level there is a "free trade area" in which tariffs and quotas are eliminated among member states. A "customs union" goes a stage further. In addition to the elimination of internal tariffs and quotas, a customs union erects a common external tariff. The next level is a "common market" which combines the features of the customs union with the elimination of barriers against the free movement of labour and capital. One step further is an "economic union or community". Beyond the features of a common market, an economic union harmonizes economic policies among its members and sometimes adopts a common currency. The highest level of integration is political union such as in, for example, the United States of America.

The market integration theory has been widely criticized, both in regard to the inner logic of the theory itself and, in particular, in regard to its relevance for regional integration schemes in the Third World.

Problems of the model

Traditional customs unions theory suffers from a major logical difficulty. If the possibility is ruled out that integration may produce favourable changes in the terms-of-trade with the outside world, then, as Harry Johnson (1965:280) has argued, "These arguments (however) are equally arguments for unilateral tariff elimination, which would have the advantage of entailing no losses from trade diversion." The traditional theory does not adequately deal with these questions. In discussing these problems, Robson (1968:37) concludes

that "the basic arguments do not provide a rationale for the formation of regional customs unions.... Arguments for regional economic
groupings must therefore rest on a framework of analysis which either provides a rationale for protection as an aim of policy, or accepts
it." Robson's thesis about protection leads the discussion on to another theoretical model: development integration.[3]

The above criticism of the customs unions theory, however, needs
a bit of qualification. A substantial part of the debate about customs
unions took place between proponents of global free trade as the
immediate objective, and those who saw customs unions as a step
towards this. Those in favour of customs unions argued that while a
customs union would interfere with the trade flows of the member
states, it would also result in increased dynamism within the union.
Eventually, they argued, this would lead to greater trade with the rest
of the world and a reduction of the common external trade barriers.
They also stressed that the starting point in most cases was not a free
trade situation, but one of widespread protectionism among the participating states. A customs union would at least start the process
towards free trade by reducing protection among the member states.
The criticism referred to above seem to have addressed an ideal situation. With the benefit of hindsight, the European situation has revealed that the two perspectives are not necessarily in absolute opposition to one another.

The usefulness of the customs unions theory has also been questioned on the grounds of its assumptions. Robson (1968:27) points out
that in its simplest form, the theory makes the same basic assumptions as the static theory of comparative advantage. It thus deals with
a situation in which:

— Inputs of factors of production, the state of technical knowledge,
  tastes and forms of economic organization are all treated as constant or autonomous variables.
— Trade within each country is assumed to be perfectly competitive.
— Full employment is implied.
— Problems of adjustment in connection with the formation of a customs union are disregarded.

These assumptions are a far cry from reality. They do not apply in the
advanced market economies, on the basis of which the theory was
developed, and they apply even less in the underdeveloped economies of Africa. The assumptions were actually questioned at an early
stage by one of the pioneers of the customs unions theory, Lipsey
(1960:501), who stated that "Viner's implicit assumption that com-

modities are consumed in fixed proportions independent of the structure of relative prices is indeed a very special one. A customs union
necessarily changes relative prices and, in general, we should expect
this to lead to some substitution between commodities." It would not
be difficult to find dozens of examples to illustrate the inapplicability of the above assumptions.

Robson (1968:40) raises another criticism against the customs unions theory. He argues that the theory needs qualification because it
takes no account of the way in which potential benefits from integration may be distributed. While it is correct that the theory does
not explicitly address this issue, it is implied that every member will
gain on the basis of their comparative advantage and that all will be
better off with the union than without it. All experience shows, however, that this is not a viable manner in which to distribute benefits
from market integration. Where disparities exist among members of
an integration scheme, the "spread" effects of increased economic
activity will be less important to the poorer areas than the "backwash" effect of the attraction of resources from the poorer to the richer
areas (Myrdal, 1957).

Irrespective of the type of integration scheme, each member state
carefully assesses its participation in terms of the benefits which
accrue to it. Factors such as nationalism, the nature of the leadership,
and the role of interest groups will directly affect the cooperation of
governments on a regional level. These are completely overlooked in
the traditional customs unions theory. The relationship between the
objectives agreed upon at the regional level, and the commitment and
capability to implement such decisions at the national level represents, in my view, the most crucial variable in any regional integration scheme.

Given the difficulties internal to the theory of customs unions, it is
not surprising that scholars have warned against its relevance for
regional integration schemes in the Third World. As already indicated, the paradox lies in the many practical attempts at implementing
market integration in the Third World.

As already mentioned the static assumptions, on which the traditional theory of customs unions is based, are irrelevant in the Third
World. The reader need only glance at the assumptions outlined
above in order to agree with my assertion. Let us take the criticism
beyond the assault on the inadequate assumptions.

In their seminal article, "Toward a general theory of customs unions for developing countries", Cooper and Massell (1965:475) concluded that the potential gain from a customs union would be larger
if neither country dominated the other in industrial production. In

other words no country would have a comparative advantage in all or most industries. Throughout the Third World, however, one or a few of the members of a regional scheme have dominated the other members. This was certainly the case in the now defunct East African Community, the Federation of Rhodesia and Nyasaland, the Southern African Customs Union, and the Andean Pact, to name but a few. In every case the "backwash" effect mentioned above concentrated benefits in the most industrialized member countries, simultaneously creating "poles of stagnation" in the less developed partner states.

John Ravenhill (1980:46) makes a central observation in regard to the relevance of customs unions theory in the Third World: "Benefits from the creation of free trade areas arise only when tariffs have been a major impediment to inter-territorial trade. Among most LDCs, and in Africa in particular, this is rarely the case. The problem is not so much a matter of tariff barriers but of the inability of states to produce the goods which satisfy the import needs of their neighbours." While this quotation refers to free trade areas and not customs unions, it is not beside the point. An intra-regional free trade area is part and parcel of a customs union, and the envisaged dynamism of a customs union derives both from the freeing of internal trade and the common external protection.

Moreover, as Robson (1968:32–33) has pointed out, the effects of a customs union will also depend on the sensitiveness of the trade pattern to tariff changes and the extent of differences in relative prices at which protected products are produced. Third World countries tend to have large external trade and very little trade between each other. Despite a decade's efforts to expand intra-regional trade, ECOWAS, SADCC and PTA member states continue to conduct only 4–7 per cent of their total trade with fellow member states. Furthermore, the bulk of Third World exports are primary products not generally produced under protection and the majority of imports are intermediate and capital goods not produced locally. Apart from protected industrial production, which in the Third World is relatively small, customs unions are therefore unlikely to bring immediate gains in the Third World.

Development integration

The development integration model was gradually developed in response to the shortcomings of traditional customs unions theory. Whether or not it is fair to claim that it represents a separate theory, the development integration model encompasses various ways in which economic integration may be implemented more in tune with the peculiarities obtaining in the Third World: That are different economic size and political systems of member countries, and different levels of industrialization.

The experience of the East African Community (1967–1977) provided one concrete impetus for the shift of attention among scholars away from customs unions theory to development integration. This demonstrated that while trade diversion did occur, higher growth and development also took place than would otherwise have been the case (Ojo, 1985). Following this line of reasoning, theorists such as Nurkse, Myrdal, Prebish and Seers argued that there was a need to consider changes other than purely marginal ones operating within the existing structure; the problem is one of fostering structural transformation of the economies (Robson, 1968). This view is what Robson calls the "dynamic" approach, which, on closer examination, looks similar to the development integration model.

In essence, the development integration model does not focus on efficiency maximization of existing capacity. Instead, since most Third World countries have little productive capacity to start with, it focuses on how to stimulate the creation of that productive capacity in the first place. Hence, the development integration model links the theory of integration with the theory of development. Due to the emphasis on impediments embedded in Third World economies and their relations with the developed countries, the development integration model seems to fit within the larger tradition of structuralist analysis.

The model

According to a study by the Chr. Michelsen Institute (1986), the main characteristic of the development integration model is the conscious intervention by the regional partners to promote cooperation and interdependence. As noted above, political union is the final stage in the linear evolution of market integration. In development integration, however, political cooperation at a high level is a prerequisite for implementation (Axline, 1977:25). While this does not require that member states are centrally planned and directed, it does imply a higher degree of state intervention than in the market integration model. A second feature is the efforts to secure an equitable distribution of the benefits from regional integration. As this involves redistributive measures of a compensatory or corrective nature, the development integration model is structurally more complex than the market integration model. Some development integration schemes also address the condition of extra-regional dependence which they perceive to be one of the principal obstacles to integration and development. Such schemes usually attempt to implement a regional policy regulating foreign investment.[4]

At the lowest level, the distributional problem is addressed via compensatory measures. When certain agreements have been reached regarding a common external tariff, a transfer tax system may be introduced to allow less developed member countries to impose limited tariffs on imports from a partner state. Theoretically, the transfer tax mechanism ought to lead to the expansion in the less developed member countries of those industries for which the maximum permitted degree of protection would be sufficient to offset the cost advantages in the more developed member states (Robson, 1968).

Compensatory measures may also take the form of budgetary transfers, calculated on the basis of the cost of trade diversion (which is very complex) or the lost customs revenues (Chr. Michelsen Institute, 1986). This type of compensation works fairly well in the case of the Southern African Customs Union (SACU) and the Communauté Economique de L'Afrique de l'Ouest (CEAO).

At a higher level of regional integration, the distributional problem is dealt with through corrective measures. Briefly, these include planned regional industrial development that favours the less developed countries (LDCs). Industrial programming of this sort may allocate basic industries to each country on the basis of comparative advantage. These industries are then designed to supply the needs of the regional market under various conditions of protection. Corrective measures also include funds or regional development banks that give priority to loans to the LDCs; provisions that allow the LDCs longer time than the rest to abolish tariff reductions; and the creation of common fiscal incentives to investment which, however, permit the LDCs to offer especially favourable terms.

While the development integration model appears superior to the market integration model, it requires a much higher level of commitment within and among member states. Hence, it has proven to be equally, if not more, difficult to implement in practice. A quick survey of some of the compensatory and corrective measures illustrates the problems with the development integration model.

Problems of the model

The experience from the East African Community demonstrates that transfer taxes did not solve the problem of uneven gains from integration. Moreover, in the East African Community, the transfer tax system may actually have encouraged uneconomic duplication of previous investments (Hazlewood, 1985).

The situation in the Southern African Customs Union indicates that budgetary transfers do not offset the unequal distribution of benefits. Due to a compensatory formula strongly in their favour, Botswana, Lesotho and Swaziland receive relatively substantial customs revenues from their membership in SACU. Nevertheless industrial investments, both from within the union and from overseas, have invariably flowed to South Africa, by far the most developed member of SACU. (The issues related to SACU are analysed by Jan Isaksen in chapter 9.)

As these examples indicate, compensatory measures cannot obviously rectify the problem of uneven economic development. Apart from the positive effect that foreign investments may have on the balance of payments, the establishment of new industries generate employment and various multiplier effects: improved local skills, technology, and infrastructure. This may in turn serve to attract further investment. Therefore, a satisfactory long-term solution to the distributional problem may be achieved only through corrective measures.

Among corrective measures the most effective, at least in theory, is planned regional industrial development. However, as industrial location is perceived by the participants as the zero-sum condition, this represents the most significant and most divisive issue in the integration process.[5]

The attitude of member states in the negotiation of a regional industrial plan depends to a great extent on the relative strengths of their economies (Ndlela, 1987). The needs of industrialists vary from country to country and they will try to influence their governments to pursue regional policies that suit their particular interests. Axline (1977:12–13) argues that more developed countries (MDCs) in a group are likely to pursue an "expansive" strategy, aiming principally at an absolute increase in gains among member states, whereas LDCs are more prone to favour a "distributive" strategy, which determine in advance the distribution of any gains from integration. Basically, the MDCs and LDCs take these positions due to an awareness that in the absence of a regional industrial plan, benefits will accrue mainly to the MDCs.

Reaching agreement on a regional industrial plan is therefore no easy task. It is complicated by the interests of those national politicians who are responsible for the regional negotiations. Peter Vale (1982:33) correctly states that "the political practitioner has always to be conscious of the necessity to balance a commitment to the common (integrative) endeavour against the need to account to his constituency—local or national." More specifically, John Ravenhill (1979:229) states that "regional integration is frequently without enthusiastic domestic proponents: for politicians concerned with their national constituencies there are few rewards at the regional level, at least in the short term—the time horizon with which they must of necessity be concerned." In short, national politicians are reluctant to give up immediate national interests in favour of the regional agenda.[6]

If agreements are nevertheless reached on the allocation of industries within a region, they are usually not carried out in practice. In a recent survey of economic integration in Africa, Omotunde Johnson (1991:10) argues forthrightly that when national politicians cannot get what they want through industrial planning negotiations, "they are likely to ignore any integration agreement they may have signed." Economic nationalism as discussed above is only part of the explanation. As Bingu Wa Mutharika (1981) has pointed out, the implementing institutions in the member states are geared to national, not regional, goals.[7] Furthermore, large organizations function according to individual, time-tested, patterns which do not automatically change with a signature on a regional industrial agreement. National bureaucrats often lack understanding of the content and scope of decisions on regional industrial programs (Vargas-Hidalgo, 1979). Red tape and inefficient administrative structures further mediate against implementation of regional agreements.

The record of efforts to implement regional plans of industrial development also shows that the question of finance seems to be ignored. In reality, industries cannot be allocated at the politicians' negotiating table.

Regional planners of industrial development also tend to ignore that in many parts of the world foreign transnational corporations (TNCs) play an important role.[8] TNCs may promote regional integration of the market type if the national markets are fairly small *and* if such firms were not involved, through parallel foreign direct investments, in these countries prior to regional cooperation. In most cases, TNCs will welcome regional market integration because it provides a larger market for their products. However, if a TNC has subsidiaries with parallel (repetitive) activities in some of the national host markets, it is likely to oppose integration. Ravenhill (1979) suggests that the reason for this is that TNCs typically operate under licensing arrangements which grant them a supply monopoly of a particular commodity.

Ravenhill (1985) therefore argues that TNCs already established within the region tend to oppose industrial planning. They prefer instead to trade with the parent corporation and reap monopoly profits in each of the protected national markets. In general, TNCs resist measures—such as government intervention in the field of industrial planning—which hinder the free operation of their subsidiaries (Axline 1977; Vaitsos 1978).

As foreign direct investment is rather limited in Africa, other types of external actors need to be considered as well. Via disbursements of development aid and loans, various donors and lending institutions have exerted a considerable influence on some of the regional integration schemes in Africa. As the discussion later on will demonstrate, SADCC is an example in which bilateral donors have played a decisive role. Bilateral donors were also very positive towards the East African Community. The World Bank, along with the OECD and the EC, have also been strong advocates of regional integration in Africa. Given the ever increasing importance of the nationally-oriented structural adjustment programmes, the World Bank is likely to have a great influence in regard to the regional integration schemes in which individual states participate.[9] In line with the thrust of the structural adjustment programmes, the World Bank promotes a type of regional integration that emphasizes cooperation in specific functional areas, as well as the creation of supportive environment for private capital.[10] Although it is beyond the scope of the present chapter, it would be interesting to explore to what extent the World Bank's obligatory support of regional integration in policy statements is translated into practice.

In addition to attempts at industrial programming, less controversial corrective measures include funds and regional development banks.[11] In the East African Community, a development bank was set up to promote industrial development through financial and technical assistance. It was designed to give priority to industrial development in the relatively less developed partner states, and to finance projects that would make the economies of the member states increasingly complementary in the industrial field (Robson 1968). The effectiveness of this bank proved to be insignificant because of the limited scale of its activities. In any event, as Hazlewood (1985) argues, without some measure of agreement between the member states on a pattern of industrial specialization, a regional development bank cannot alone be expected to act as a catalyst for complementary industrial development. This should not be taken to mean that development banks have no potential as a corrective vehicle. The experience of the regional development funds within the EC illustrates that investments may be promoted in the peripheral areas of an economic community through such devices.

Finally, provisions to allow LDC members of a group longer time than the rest to abolish tariff reductions are not likely to solve the problem. The same is the case with the granting of exemptions to LDC members to a possible, regional investment code. This is because factors other than protection determine whether investors decide to locate an industrial investment in a given country. What is more important is the business environment, government attitude and markets. Above all, investors are concerned about the political safety of their investments.[12]

From the above it may be noted that while in theory the development integration model appears superior to the pure market integration model, it is beset with practical problems of implementation. Some of these problems might be avoided if the so-called neo-functional model is pursued.

Neo-functional integration

As the name implies, neo-functionalism has its roots in the functional theories of regional integration. The functionalist doctrine was a reaction to the devastating experience of World War II. David Mitrany, its leading advocate, held the view that it was necessary to construct an international system to solve the fundamental problem of security.[13] Rather than constructing an institutionalized supranational system, as the federalists wanted,[14] Mitrany argued that concrete areas should be identified in which states would see an immediate benefit from cooperation. International organizations should be established to promote transnational activities around basic functional needs such as transportation, health and welfare, trade and production. The expectation was that a transnational complex of economic and social organizations would develop over time. Such a network would serve to reduce the risk of aggression and war. As a result of the process of building international functional links, Mitrany envisaged that there would be an ultimate shift of loyalty and sovereignty from states to international organizations.[15]

The main problem with Mitrany's model was probably its assumption of separability of politics and economics in the functions of the state. As indicated above, Mitrany thought political divisions could be neutralized under a spreading web of international economic and social activities. In practice, however, it is difficult to divorce economic and social issues from political problems among states. As Claude (cited in Olaniyan 1989/90:10) maintains, states cannot be induced to join hands in functional endeavours before they have settled the outstanding political and security issues which divide them. In most developing countries, the separation of politics from economics is even more unlikely due to the weak class formation and limited role of interest groups.

The model

Concurrently with the development of the European Coal and Steel Community (the forerunner to the EC), Ernst B. Haas formulated in the 1950s a modified version of Mitrany's functionalism. In contrast to the latter, the neo-functional theory developed by Haas did not operate with a separation of politics from economics. As Panild (1989) has pointed out, the neo-functional theory represented an ingenious combination of the method of functionalism with the ultimate objective of the federalists.

The neo-functional theory borrowed the postulates of actor perception and behaviour held to be characteristic of pluralistically organized nation states (Haas, 1971:19). According to Nye (1971:195) the important actors in the neo-functional integration process were not seen to be governments, but various interest groups and integrationist-technocrats.

Like the functionalists, neo-functionalists held the view that international cooperation should be initiated in the technical, or basic functional areas mentioned above. They differed, however, in their belief that once success was attained in these areas, it would result in a spillover to other areas. The spillover mechanism, the dynamics of the model, works as follows. Once sector cooperation has been achieved in one area, the resulting sector imbalance, or *engrenage*, will create pressures for the initiation of integrative activities in other areas to offset the imbalance. One force likely to work in this direction is the expanding group expectations among industrialists, dealers and trade unions (Haas, 1958:313).

The integration in functional areas simultaneously results in various political spillover effects. The changing regional situation emerging from the sector imbalances referred to above requires that the political actors redefine their common tasks. As functional sectors merge at the regional level, a concern naturally develops over the political techniques that would be appropriate for the control of new and larger problems. The integration momentum may also be taken a step further by what Nye (1971:202) refers to as "cultivated spillover". This takes place when politicians or technocrats within a region form coalitions to deliberately promote increased integration on the basis of ideologically motivated projections and political possibilities. Ultimately, as Haas (1958:289) put it, those groups which have long-term positive expectations will look to supranationalism to achieve their goals. Panild (1989:443) adds that interest groups will cease to place their demands at the national level when they realize that their demands are met more effectively at the regional, or supranational, level.

As Haarløv (1988:23) has pointed out, neo-functional integration has an advantage over the market integration and development integration models because its sector-by-sector approach minimizes the problem of cost and benefit distribution among member states. It also circumvents the problems inherent in the ceding of powers from the national level to supranational institutions. The strong Euro-centric nature of the neo-functional model, however, limits its applicability to other parts of the world.

Problems of the model

Haas (1971:24) himself has emphasized the transferability problem of the neo-functional model. The problem emerges because the model is embedded in the modern, pluralistically organized, industrial societies of Western Europe. The crucial variable, present in Western Europe but weak or absent in most African countries, is modern associational pluralism, i.e. functionally specific, universalistic, achievement-oriented groups, such as interest groups and political parties. Haas (1971:14–15) argues in a straightforward manner that integration in Africa has been largely symbolic. Among his reasons he states that "the absence of pluralism makes the formation of voluntary groups on a regional basis very difficult".[16]

Nye (1971) adds some detail to the above argument. He states that the absence or weakness of modern associational groups make integration more difficult by depriving regional bureaucrats of potential allies. Interest groups and political parties can in principle free government decision makers to make integrative decisions by making it politically legitimate to make regional, rather than nationally focused, decisions. The absence of modern associational groups has one further negative implication: it deprives governments of useful channels of information in the formation of economic policy.

As Ravenhill (1980: 48–50) correctly points out low levels of economic development precludes the emergence of interest groups, the major force in the neo-functional integration process. He argues that the absence of interest groups makes the African heads of states the supreme decision making authority. Therefore, regional integration in Africa often stands and falls with the maintenance of cordial relationships between the personalities concerned. Regional integration is nowhere fully insulated from the instabilities of domestic politics and contentious inter-state disputes. This problem, however, is generally pronounced in African integration schemes.

Implications of the theoretical models

The foregoing three sub-sections have laid out and discussed some of the major mainstream models of regional integration: market integration, development integration and neo-functional integration. How can that exercise guide our analysis of SADCC? At the same time as the theoretical models are inspired by the European experience, they are also characterized by its special context. It is obvious, therefore, that these models in their totality cannot be transferred to the African setting. This is almost banal. What matters is whether the inspiration that the models after all do provide can help those who are cognisant of the particular conditions obtaining in Africa.

What are the main issues of relevance that emerge from the three theoretical models? The market integration model is too narrowly focused on the elimination of intra-regional barriers against the market mechanisms. Moreover, its static assumptions are completely unrealistic in the African context. The development integration model, on the other hand, often fails to work because the high level political cooperation—which is a prerequisite for its implementation—typically fails to trickle down through the layers of society. The heads of states cannot guarantee that their governments, private sector entities and populace act in a manner that fulfil the regional objectives that they agree upon. African states are perhaps too weakly integrated nationally to offset the centrifugal forces inherent in a regional scheme among developing countries at uneven levels of economic development. The neo-functional model holds more promise. In its pure, European-derived form, however, the neo-functional model is carried by national and regional interest groups which are not yet pervasive in most of Africa. Neo-functional integration is, so to speak, integration from below. This might well be the only truly viable basis on which to foster regional integration. The challenge is whether that basis can somehow be "engineered" into existence.

In order to refine these general conclusions, we now turn our attention to SADCC. When launched in 1980, SADCC rejected the market integration model. Its long-term aspirations instead approximated the development integration model. In view of the activities of the organization, however, observers have portrayed SADCC as an example of neo-functional integration.

THE SOUTHERN AFRICAN DEVELOPMENT COORDINATION CONFERENCE

How can SADCC be characterized vis-a-vis the models of regional integration discussed above? The term market integration has already been ruled out. SADCC would appear to fit into the development integration paradigm. The objective of "genuine and equitable regional integration", the emphasis on coordination of production, the high level political cooperation and the overall developmental thrust of SADCC all point in this direction. But the international economy and the economic relations between the member states mediated against the implementation of a development integration scheme. During the 1980s, the world economy experienced severe recession which, along with the South African destabilization campaign, had a profound effect on the SADCC economies. The SADCC states also started from a tradition of limited economic interaction. Ever since SADCC was launched, intra-regional trade has not exceeded 5 per cent of the total international trade of the member states. In short, circumstances made it difficult for SADCC to pursue a development integration scheme. Thus, as the following shows, SADCC does not score highly on any of the essential characteristics of this model.

Firstly, the conscious effort to promote closer interdependence among the SADCC members seems to have been rather minimal. The rehabilitation of the regional infrastructure is one possible exception. It is a qualified exception, however, because the effort has been concentrated largely on the transport corridors linking the interior with the sea ports and overseas markets. In other words, the emphasis has been on a revitalization of the colonial trade routes, rather than inter-country transport networks. Whereas this may be criticized, it also made good sense to begin with the transport corridors as a means to counter the decline in regional exports. Moreover, these projects have been funded almost exclusively by foreign donors.

Secondly, only a symbolic effort has been made to secure an equitable distribution of the benefits from the regional cooperation. SADCC sought to ensure this by decentralizing its sectoral activities, as shown above. It is apparent that the bulk of the SADCC projects, in terms of funds invested, have been implemented in Mozambique and Tanzania. Interestingly, however, this has not caused the other SADCC states to complain. The explanation is probably, again, that the funding for the projects comes not from a collective pool of the member's own resources, but from external donors. A distributional crisis is emerging, however, in the area of intra-regional trade. Zimbabwe has a large and growing trade surplus with its SADCC neighbours; Zimbabwe accounts for well over half of the intra-regional trade and its exports to the region exceed imports by more than 100 percent (Østergaard, 1989b:79). This is clearly untenable in the long run, and it is doubtful that SADCC-promoted activities in other areas will be sufficient to offset the "bambazonke"—take it all—feeling among some of Zimbabwe's neighbours.[17]

Thirdly, SADCC distinguishes itself from other regional schemes in Africa on account of its emphasis on coordination of production. Yet, in practice, nothing has been achieved in this regard. SADCC has promoted only a handful of industrial projects in the areas of agricultural implements, tractor assembly, paper and fertilizer manufacturing. In every case, however, these were national projects that could as well have been implemented without the intervention of SADCC.[18] Generally speaking, the industrial sector throughout the region is characterized by duplication and overlapping production. After two years of preparatory work the SADCC Council of Ministers in 1989 approved a new regional industrial strategy. It was so vague and ambitious, however, that implementation has not yet begun. SADCC has been completely unsuccessful in promoting the coordinated development of the productive sectors of the region (Østergaard, 1990).

On the basis of the above, SADCC cannot be considered a development integration scheme. As mentioned earlier, several observers have described SADCC as an example of functional or neo-functional integration. When reading Tostensen (1982), Zehender (1983) and Haarløv (1988) it seems as if the concepts of functionalism and neo-functionalism have been lumped together and referred to as "functionalist" integration. Unfortunately, this confuses the analysis of SADCC. As shown previously, functionalism operates on the assumption that politics can be separated from economics, and it regards governments as the main actors in the integration process. Neo-functionalism, on the other hand, assumes that politics and economics cannot be separated and sees interest groups as the main actors. Several arguments can be advanced to explain why it is misleading to label SADCC as a "functionalist" scheme.

Firstly, SADCC cannot be considered a "functionalist" scheme merely because it focuses on concrete projects in basic functional needs such as transportation. The key motivation behind the *functional* model was to create a network of transnational economic and social organizations *in order* to reduce the risk of aggression and war among the member states. This motivation is entirely absent in the objectives of SADCC.

Secondly, the absence in SADCC of a formal treaty or a supra-national organization does not make SADCC a "functionalist" scheme. The implicit reasoning would appear to have been that as SADCC has neither of these characteristics, it must be "functionalist". The lack of these features off-hand disqualifies SADCC as a market integration scheme or a development integration scheme. Given SADCC's project orientation, it is tempting to call SADCC a "functionalist" venture.

Thirdly, as the essence of the *neo-functional* model is interest groups, SADCC would not therefore appear to provide an example of this model. The political leaders are the driving force in SADCC and decision-making is overwhelmingly the prerogative of heads of states, ministers and senior government officials. National policies vis-a-vis SADCC are formulated largely without the intervention of interest groups, irrespective of whether they are national bourgeoisies or grassroots movements.

In short, SADCC does not fit into any of the models discussed in this chapter. Judged by its activities, SADCC may be said to have borrowed a number of elements from both development integration and functional integration. Chitala (1987:13) has appropriately characterized SADCC's approach as "sectoral programming". This approach is limited to a particular sector of activity in which the objective is to deepen rather than widen the integration movement.

CONCLUSION

SADCC's approach to regional integration can be criticized on several counts. Nevertheless, integration still has a tremendous appeal among the leaders of Southern Africa, the business community and foreign interests. The search for appropriate models of integration must therefore continue. What can we conclude on the basis of the above?

Experience demonstrates that regional integration is inherently complicated. For a number of reasons, it is particularly difficult in Southern Africa. As the economies are overwhelmingly geared to supplying raw materials to overseas markets, the current economic interaction among the countries of the region is frivolous. Furthermore, the countries are generally poor, the economies are stagnant, and class formation is limited. Finally, many of the countries are undergoing political crises and the states are still preoccupied with nation-building.

Southern Africa needs a less ambitious model of regional integration. The SADCC experience suggests the usefulness of adopting a much narrower scope of operation. Moreover, it indicates that the choice of activities should be guided primarily by the articulated needs from within the countries concerned. Regional integration must be *carried* by the social and economic actors of the countries involved; it must flow from the bottom upwards.

The need to enlarge markets in Southern Africa is beyond debate. Some sort of market integration is therefore necessary. What is called for is not uncontrolled market mechanisms. Trade and financial barriers must be brought down gradually. Parallel with this development, the most significant duty of any future regional organization should be to lessen the imbalances among the countries involved. When the starting point is one of great asymmetry, it is unrealistic to expect the achievement of complete balance. Nevertheless, it must be an explicit objective to strive to reduce relative imbalances—on specified parameters—as much as possible.

Agreements must be reached on the elements on which the member states wish to seek greater balance. When this is achieved, useful inspiration might be gathered from the experience of the Regional Funds of the EC, and from other regional integration schemes, especially in the Third World.

Whatever happens when a democratic South Africa enters the scene, it seems certain that regional integration will be on the agenda. South African companies are keen to expand exports to the SADCC countries which hope for improved access to South African capital, technology and know-how. The SADCC experience indicates, however, that less tangible factors motivate government leaders to take an interest in regional integration. Beyond the concrete benefits that are expected by the corporate sector, government leaders everywhere have a need to display statesmanship. Building regional organizations provides an excellent opportunity for such a display. Moreover, this can be a cost-effective way for government leaders to win status and prestige. The illusion of having a regional integration scheme is a reward in itself.

NOTES

1. One exception is the Southern African Development Coordination Conference (SADCC), which is discussed in detail in section 3 of this chapter. The East African Community (EAC) was formally a customs union, but in reality it was more than this. Under the EAC, a large number of common service institutions were created.
2. Market integration theory falls under the heading of economic theory. In Africa, however, the whole question of regional integration is possibly more "politicized" than in a developed country context.
3. See section below.
4. During the 1970s Lynn Mytelka developed a useful framework of models of integration which emphasized the extra-regional dimension.
5. See for example Mytelka (1973:247), Ojo (1985:164), Potholm and Fredland (1980:200).

6. During the ECOWAS Summit in 1988 the Togolese president warned that the delay in the implementation of the ECOWAS programme had its origin in the reluctance of some of the member countries' heads of State to give up national interests in favor of the community. See Julius and Nkiru Okolo (1991:242).
7. Bingu Wa Mutharika in 1990 assumed the post as secretary general of the Preferential Trade Area for Eastern and Southern Africa (PTA).
8. For a discussion of this, see Østergaard (1989a)
9. Rather surprisingly the role of the World Bank vis-à-vis regional integration schemes has not figured as a subject of thorough analysis in the literature.
10. See Chapter seven in World Bank (1989a).
11. Note that there is a difference between development banks and development funds. The former operate on a profitability criteria, while the latter are geared to more long-term developmental considerations.
12. For a discussion of what motivates foreign investors, see Martin Landsberg (1979) and Alan Whiteside (1987).
13. See David Mitrany's seminal essay, "A Working Peace System", written in 1943. The essay has been published under the above title by Quardrangle Books, Chicago, in 1966.
14. For a discussion of the federalist position, see Friedrich (1968).
15. The above presentation of functionalism is based mainly on Panild (1989) and Olaniyan (1989/90).
16. Despite the Euro-centric nature of the model, some of the African regional schemes, notably the East African Community and SADCC, have been characterized by attempts to address basic functional needs.
17. During the years of the Federation of Rhodesia and Nyasaland, when Zimbabwe developed at the expense of Zambia and Malawi, Salisbury (now Harare) was called "bambazonke"—meaning "take it all".
18. See Østergaard (1989b) for a detailed discussion of SADCC's approach to industrial development.

2. Some Experiences from Regional Cooperation between Third World Countries

Hans C. Blomqvist, Christian Lindholm, Mats Lundahl and Sven Schauman

The expansion of trade between less developed countries (LDCs) has been rapid during the last two decades. Nevertheless, currently less than one-third of total exports of the less developed countries as a group has its destination within that group (GATT, 1990:5). In many LDCs facing protectionism, declining terms-of-trade and limited domestic markets, economists and politicians alike argue for more intra-regional trade and economic cooperation agreements between LDCs (Nafziger, 1990:411). Sometimes economic cooperation also seems to be seen almost as an end in itself, promoting in some indeterminate sense the interests of the countries involved (Wong, 1985).

The purpose of the present chapter is to examine the experience of some other efforts of regional economic integration and cooperation in the Third World, so as to put the Southern African discussion in a wider perspective. The slowdown in economic growth rates in the more developed countries (MDCs) during the last couple of decades limits the room for expansion via exports for the LDCs as a group, although not necessarily for an individual country (Lewis, 1980). Expanding intra-LDC trade can thus be seen as a way of circumventing the problems concerning the trade with MDCs, but the LDCs themselves have traditionally retained high trade barriers, which has hindered South–South trade and obstructed the integration efforts between them. Recently, however, the political climate has turned in favor of less protectionism in several LDCs, and this has provided an incentive for expanding intra-regional trade. Lower barriers between LDCs are expected to bring larger markets, increased economies of scale, faster technological development and a greater diversification of exports (Hogendorn, 1987:427).

Thanks are due to the participants of the seminar on "Southern Africa after Apartheid: Regional Integration and External Resources", especially to Stefan de Vylder, for constructive comments. We are also obliged to John Rogers for checking the English of the chapter.

In the literature a clear distinction is not always made between the concepts of integration and economic cooperation. In the present chapter, following Balassa (Balassa & Stoutjesdijk, 1975; Balassa, 1988:43), *integration* denotes the absence or abolition of discrimination between domestic and foreign goods, services, and factors of production. *Cooperation* again can denote any form of concerted action in order to enhance the common interests of the nations involved. According to this definition, all international organizations and agreements, including those aiming at integration, can be regarded as a form of cooperation. Emphasis is put on the rationales and consequences of integration.

Even if the term economic integration is given a more precise meaning, integration may take place on many different levels, ranging anywhere from the mere existence of some preferential trade relations between two countries to a complete merger of the national economies. Economic integration as a strategy for development has a fairly short historic background. Except for the Southern African Customs Union (SACU) which goes back all the way to the 1890s, the first integration schemes in LDCs were begun during the 1950s and 1960s when the Latin American countries embarked on the path of closer cooperation.

Economic and political changes have revitalized the discussion of cooperation among the LDCs, including the nations in Southern Africa. More sophisticated economic integration is still a somewhat unrealistic alternative in LDCs. We will therefore focus on the consequences of free intra-regional trade within free trade areas or customs unions, while also paying some attention to the possibilities emerging from other forms of economic cooperation between countries. Furthermore, the chapter attempts to evaluate the experiences and summarize the lessons from some of the major cooperation and integration schemes between LDCs, namely the Association of Southeast Asian Nations (ASEAN), the Central American Common Market (CACM), and the Latin American Free Trade Area (LAFTA).

THEORETICAL ASPECTS OF ECONOMIC COOPERATION
BETWEEN LDCs

The theoretical and philosophical background for the discussion on economic *integration* among LDCs emerged in the early 1950s as a result of the so-called Latin American structuralist paradigm on the one hand, and the classical customs union theory, propounded by Viner (Viner, 1950), on the other. More recently, the integration process in Europe is also likely to have been a source of inspiration.

The early structuralism provided arguments based on the conviction that the prevailing world trade system inherently tends to exploit the LDCs and perpetuate their poverty. It was even emphasized in this context that development in some parts of the world necessitates underdevelopment in other parts of the world (Blomqvist & Lundahl, 1992:48). Later, the model provided by the on-going integration in Europe has had considerable influence (Cf. e.g. Curry, 1991). Radical changes in trade relations were called for. The LDCs were encouraged to break loose from the dependence on the MDCs and to promote development through closer regional cooperation (Cf. Johnson, 1967:25–32 and Hunt, 1989:141–143). The prospects for exports of primary goods were considered unfavorable, and the import barriers in the MDCs were allegedly discouraging exports of manufactured goods. Consequently, industrialization through import substitution and economic integration appeared attractive policy options for many LDCs. Concerted efforts at improving the position of the LDCs as a group in the world economy were also necessary, according to this view, and materialized e.g. in the propositions put forth by UNCTAD from the 1960s on.

In his seminal contribution, Viner studied the comparative static effects of a customs union on trade flows, resource allocation and welfare. According to his analysis, the welfare results of a customs union depends on whether *trade creation* (the replacement of higher-cost domestic production by lower-cost imports from partner countries) or *trade diversion* (replacement of lower-cost imports from third countries by higher-cost imports from member countries) dominates. Viner's analysis was subsequently modified by Meade (Meade, 1955), who separated the production and consumption effects of a customs union, and Lipsey (Lipsey, 1957, 1960), who connected the theory of customs unions to the theory of "second best" and defined the factors influencing the welfare effects of economic integration.

All in all, however, the traditional static effects may account for only a small part of the total consequences of economic integration. The *dynamic* effects of integration are usually considered the principal rationale for economic integration (See e.g. Balassa, 1961, Part II, Cordon, 1972, and El-Agraa & Jones, 1981, Ch. 6). These effects refer to a number of long-term consequences of free-trade arrangements affecting the growth rate of GDP, such as economies of scale, enhanced competition and efficiency, intra-industry specialization, and intensified investment activities. However, as these effects are difficult to analyze within the framework of traditional economic models, they have aroused widespread debate and controversy.

In the general case of *cooperation*, benefits emerge in principle from joint production of supranational *public goods*, e.g. research and education projects, environmental policies, infrastructure, defense, and health care. Cooperation of this kind is in many cases economically desirable and even necessary, but often encounters obstacles due to conflicts about the distribution of costs and benefits or lack of incentives for the single country.

In terms of international *political economy*, the basic reason for the existence of supranational organizations is that they produce an "output" that the member countries cannot or will not produce, or can produce only less efficiently. The "product" of an organization should thus be—as already noted—a public good from the point of view of the member countries. (Note the parallel to the relation between the individual and the state within a country.) The decision to join an organization is an outcome of the national interest, however, not of the benefits of the grouping as a whole. Hence, even if an organization is beneficial from the point of view of all members, taken together, it may not be formed (or survive) if the single members are not convinced about the national gains accruing to them. Related to this is the *free rider problem*: the contribution of a country to a common budget may not be proportional to its gains, because the individual member may have an incentive to stop contributing to cover the production costs before the optimal production for the group as a whole is reached (Olson, 1965; Olson & Zeckhauser, 1966). This problem frequently results in an unproportional influence in international organizations (as compared to their pecuniary contribution to the organization) of small countries (Cf. Langhammer, 1991).

The problem with evaluating the performance of an organization is that its "output" is usually ill defined and difficult to measure (Cf. Frey, 1984:151). Partly for that reason, the bureaucracy in an organization is hard to control, which may impose an increasing dead-weight loss to be deducted from the "output" of the organization. Considering these general problems, it is accordingly very hard to assess the distribution of the net gain between the countries.

Finally, since international organizations may have more than one objective (say, internal trade liberalization, collective bargaining with non-members, and cooperation in regional industrialization) and the members may have different priorities, Arrow's impossibility theorem (Arrow, 1950) may apply (Cf. Langhammer, 1991). This means that it may not be possible to arrive at a collective preference function that allows for a transitive ordering of the alternatives without imposing the choice externally or dictating it.

PRECONDITIONS FOR AND OBSTACLES TO SUCCESSFUL REGIONAL INTEGRATION

Several conditions determine whether economic integration will be successful or not. It has been proposed that the welfare effects of a customs union will depend on the relative importance of the consumption of goods produced domestically and goods imported from non-member countries prior to the establishment of the union (Balassa, 1988:4). According to this argument, the relative strength of trade creation and trade diversion will determine if a customs union has the potential to be successful. The likelihood that a customs union will generate positive welfare effects is greater, the larger the share of regional goods and the smaller the share of imported goods from non-member countries in total expenditure is before establishing the union. Since the share of extra-regional imports is large for many LDCs, the risk for trade diversion is often imminent.

The bigger the internal market, the greater the potential positive welfare effects of the customs union. Gains may arise from the increased opportunities for reallocation of production due to the larger market size. The price elasticities of supply and demand will also affect the welfare of the member countries. If the elasticities of demand in the member countries are high, consumption will increase significantly as a result of reduced trade barriers between members. If the elasticity of supply is high, production within the union will rise as a result of the increased demand (Hogendorn, 1987:427). The higher the pre-union tariffs, the greater will be the possibility of trade creation and welfare gains. The lower the external tariff, the smaller the risk of trade diversion.

Economic integration was primarily intended to promote industrialization by extending import substitution on a regional scale. At an early stage, it was recognized that the opportunities for successful import substitution on a national scale were limited due to the small size of the domestic markets. In many LDCs, domestic demand and exports are too low to enable efficient production. By removing trade barriers through integration, the market may be enlarged, which would enable the creation of dynamic gains in the form of economies of scale. The achievement of increased production at a lower cost may especially benefit infant industries which are not yet competitive enough for the world markets. The regional market would thus serve as a "training ground" for later success on extra-regional markets. The establishment of new industries as a result of free intra-regional trade and protection against extra-regional imports almost inevitably gives rise to trade diversion. This could only be defended on the grounds that the cost reductions that emerge are large enough to render the industry internationally competitive (Johnson, 1967:210).

The potential gains from this strategy are, however, uncertain, as the internal domestic market might still be too small. Consequently, inefficient industries may easily become dependent on foreign imports of input factors and develop a bias against extra-regional exports. In such a case, the dependence on primary exports may, in fact, increase.

Differences in production structures among members of a customs union may affect the success of the union. The more competitive the production structures of the member countries are and the more they substitute for each other, the greater the likelihood that the customs union will increase welfare. Substitutability provides room for both inter- and intra-industrial specialization, which facilitates the exploitation of scale economies. Such specialization almost inevitably presupposes closing down some existing capacity, however, which is bound to cause political difficulties (Lewis, 1980).

Enhanced competition and potential trade creation are likely to lead to an increase in investment activities in the member countries. The scope for new investments from the rest of the world is also considerable, since the elimination of trade restrictions creates new opportunities and may increase discrimination against foreign producers' exports to the region, thus making it more attractive for foreign companies to establish production within the integrated area (Chacholiades, 1981:271).

Economic integration or cooperation might also lead to an improvement in the region's terms-of-trade, provided that the supply of exports from the union is reduced, the demand for extra-regional imports declines, or the collective bargaining power of the members vis-à-vis the rest of the world improves. Since a group of LDCs seldom constitutes a major part of the world market for their imports or exports, and as the risk of retaliation from other economic groupings is considerable, this possibility is not particularly realistic. The discipline and coordination needed for improving and maintaining bargaining power are also unlikely to hold in the long run, OPEC being a case in point.

Transportation costs may affect the welfare outcome of a customs union. The higher the transportation costs between the members of the union, the harder it is to gain from economic integration. Trade-facilitating investments in transport infrastructure may, however, be another outcome of an integration (or cooperation) agreement. Such investment may not be profitable for a single country, but may produce a net welfare gain for the whole grouping. Nevertheless, it seems

that transport costs, on balance, are becoming less and less significant since they are much lower today than they used to be (Cf. Lewis,
1980).

To summarize, the necessary preconditions for successful economic integration seldom prevail in LDCs. A large number of problems
obviously exist which might hinder the integration efforts of developing countries. Below we point out a few additional obstacles to successful integration.

Existing *political differences* between nations is one of the first problems that integrating countries encounter. Many of the LDCs are
still in the process of finding their national identity; therefore it is
common that developing nations will strongly guard against any
sacrifice of their newly won sovereignty, and borders will consequently gain in importance (Langhammer & Hiemenz, 1990:14).
Tariffs in LDCs are often important sources of government revenue
and the administrative requirements of a union might exceed the
present capacity. These factors will hardly facilitate free trade and
a successful integration scheme between developing countries and
the essential coordination of national policies will not be accomplished.

One of the most important sources of conflict in the process of integration among developing countries is the problem involving inter-
country distribution. Free trade tends to accentuate inequalities in
the process of regional cooperation among developing countries
(Lewis, 1980; Vaitsos, 1978). This is the so-called *polarization effect*.
Differences between partner countries concerning the income and
industrialization level will in both the short and long run lead to a
polarization in favor of the relatively more advanced nations. The
less developed a member country is, the smaller are the comparative
static trade effects as well as the dynamic production effects. In particular, low pre-union levels of industrialization and lack of capital
act as obstacles to the realization of dynamic gains. Income transfers, which are usually difficult to accomplish due to political disparities, are needed as the benefits and costs of the integration do
not accrue evenly to the member countries. This has been a substantial problem in many integration schemes (see e.g. the section on
the CACM). Accordingly, the relations between the member countries easily deteriorate, and other useful forms of cooperation may
not take place either.

The rest of this chapter contains a brief discussion on the achievements and problems of three regional integration and cooperation
schemes: ASEAN, CACM, and LAFTA.

ASEAN

The Association of Southeast Asian Nations (ASEAN) was founded in 1967 by Indonesia, Malaysia, the Philippines, Singapore, and Thailand. Brunei joined the organization in 1984. The administrative apparatus consists only of a secretariat in Jakarta, which has a coordinating, rather than decision-making role. Decision-making in ASEAN can best be characterized by the term "consensus" (Cf. Wong, 1985).

The four large member countries have traditionally been major exporters of primary goods. However, during the last few decades industrialization has been rapid. Singapore has maintained its historical role as the trade and service centre of the region. Despite being neighbors, the ASEAN countries are extremely disparate in almost every possible sense. This should, *a priori*, be a negative factor as far as both integration and other forms of economic cooperation are concerned.

It is evident from Table 2.1, that the ASEAN countries—with the possible exception of the Philippines—have been very successful by

Table 2.1. *Main economic indicators for the ASEAN countries*

Country	Popu-lation (mill.)	GDP (USDbn)	GNP growth (%)	GNP/ capita (USD)	Gross invest./ GDP (%)	Total external debt (USDbn)	Total external debt/ GDP (%)	Inflation (%)	Income distr Poorest 40%/ Richest 20%
	1989	1989	1965–89	1989	1989	1989	(%)	1980–89	
Brunei	0.3	4.2	n.a.	17,000[1]	n.a.	n.a.	n.a.	–5.1	n.a
Indonesia	178.2	94.0	4.4	500	35	53.1	57	8.3	0.5 (1987)
Malaysia	17.4	37.5	4	2,160	30	18.6	50	1.5	0.3 (1987)
Philippines	60.0	44.4	1.6	710	19	28.9	66	14.8	0.3 (1985)
Singapore	2.7	28.4	7	10,450	35	4.6	16	1.5	0.3 (1982–3)
Thailand	55.4	69.7	4.2	1,220	31	23.5	37	3.2	0.3 (1975–6)
Low and Middle Income Countries[1]		2.5		800	26	..[2]	..[2]	53.7	..[2]

[1] Weighted average
[2] 1988
n.a. non-available data
Sources: World Bank,*World Development Report*, various issues, New York, Oxford University Press. Wagner, Norbert, 1989, "The Market Economics of Southeast Asia. Market Forces on the Rise?", *Southeast Asian Affairs 1989*, Vol. 16, pp. 37–50. OECD, 1991, *External Debt Statistics*, Paris.

international standards. A high rate of growth has co-existed with moderate international indebtedness and a remarkably equal distribution of income. This successful development makes ASEAN an exception among the regional economic organizations in the Third World. How much of this impressive performance is actually due to the benefits from ASEAN is, however, less clear.

ASEAN is neither a customs union nor a free trade area (although the latter is on the long-term agenda [Blomqvist, 1992]). As a matter of fact, ASEAN has consistently tended to avoid the term integration, preferring the vaguer "cooperation" label (Wong, 1985). The main goals of the organization were originally to a great extent political and security-related (Cf. e.g. Naya & Plummer, 1991). This should not be too surprising against the background of the political turmoil in the region in the mid-1960s. At least ASEAN seems to have been useful in settling many problems of that type. This is certainly a valuable achievement, and may also have indirectly generated economic benefits.

At the outset the specific forms of economic cooperation remained fairly vague. However they became more focused in the 1970s, primarily as a result of the publication in 1974 of a UN report (the so-called Robinson Report) suggesting preferential trade liberalization on a limited scale, complemented by a coordinated policy of inter-industry specialization (Arndt & Garnaut, 1979; Langhammer, 1991). Many of the specific cooperation programs embarked upon later emanate from the recommendations of this report.

In the economic area, ASEAN has been primarily active within five different programs (Langhammer, 1991; Naya & Plummer, 1991). Of these instruments of cooperation, only the Preferential Trading Arrangement is a direct device for integration.

The ASEAN Industrial Projects (AIP), which aimed at providing the governments with an instrument to assign *new* government-initiated industrial projects to different member countries, have for the most part failed, partly due to the difficulties inherent in industrial targeting in general, but also because there is no compelling reason why such targeting should be carried out at the regional instead of the national level. Furthermore the ASEAN Industrial Complementation (AIC) projects, which are primarily directed at *intra-industry* specialization in the private sector, have been disappointing. In this program it was the task of the ASEAN Chamber of Commerce to identify and promote suitable cooperation programs, as well as to work as an intermediary between the governments and the private enterprises (Wong, 1985). The institutional mechanisms for the program are both elaborate and complicated, which may provide a partial explanation for the poor performance. The basic reason, however, seems to be that with the exception of the existing trade barriers, there is no reason why the markets are not able to deal with this issue themselves. Government intervention was used here as a substitute for the elimination of trade barriers.

The ASEAN Industrial Joint Ventures (AIJV) program was also based on specific manipulation of trade barriers in order to make cooperation otherwise not deemed profitable more attractive. (The AIJV products qualify for tariff preferences in all ASEAN countries.) The idea was partly to avoid the broad engagement of countries required in the AIC—two partners would be enough—and to facilitate cooperation in smaller ventures. The bureaucracy involved is also much less elaborate (Wong, 1985). Quite a few projects of this category have been approved. On the whole, however, ASEAN firms seem to prefer joint ventures with partners from outside the region (Naya & Plummer, 1991).

The Preferential Trading Arrangement (PTA) is the integration instrument proper in the economic-political arsenal of ASEAN. It is also crucial for the workability of the industrial cooperation schemes (AIP, AIC, and AIJV) described above. The PTA nevertheless seems to have produced mixed results, apparently because of a limited coverage and low tariff cuts (25 percent). Recently, however, the tariffs on most traded goods were lowered by 50 percent (Naya & Plummer, 1991). The poor results may be also partly attributable to non-tariff barriers. As shown in Table 2.2, the importance of intra-regional trade is almost negligible and no clear time trend can be discerned. Hence, a concerted action in order to increase the share of intra-regional trade would cause significant trade diversion.

The fairly substantial degree of foreign ownership of manufacturing industry in ASEAN may also be an important reason for the small share of intra-regional trade. These industries are often verti-

Table 2.2. *Intra-regional trade between the ASEAN countries, 1970–1989*

	Share of total trade (%)	Share of total trade (%)
1970	12(6)	12(5)
1979	9(3)	12(4)
1989	12(4)	9(4)

Note: Figures excluding Singapore in parentheses.
Source: IMF, *Direction of Trade,* various issues.

cally integrated with the home country's industry. The high degree of intra-industry trade between ASEAN and Japan, on the one hand, and ASEAN and the NICs, on the other hand, (as demonstrated by Langhammer, 1989) is an indication of this development.

The picture changes considerably when Singapore is included. The figures demonstrate very clearly the pivotal role of Singapore in the region. The reason for this is hardly ASEAN as such, however, but the traditional role of Singapore as an entrepôt center for the region.

A successful development of the PTA into a free trade area would be dependent on whether the intra-regional trade is on the increase within the present system, indicating increasing interdependence and intra-industry complementarity between the countries. As we have seen, there are no such signs. The fact that intra-regional trade is fairly insignificant indicates that the total potential gain is likely to be small. The other precondition concerns the distribution of the gains of integration. As mentioned earlier, this has frequently been a crucial reason for the failure of many integration schemes. What tends to happen is that the more developed members of the organization reap most of the benefits, thereby causing severe political friction.

The Asian Dialogue Partner System (ADPS) encourages the governments to find questions of mutual interest to raise in discussions with the trade partners. The ADPS provides a useful forum for discussions between the ASEAN member countries and its major trade partners, the US, the EC, Japan, Australia, and New Zealand. According to Langhammer (1991), this is a truly supranational public good which cannot be satisfied individually by each country on its own. The dialogue is important not least due to the indisputable fact that ASEAN has profited from a relatively free international trade, and that the present threat of a more protectionist international trade climate is extremely unwelcome for the members of this organization.

Today ASEAN faces several profound challenges. One strategic decision which will have to be made is whether to widen membership to Indo-China. A decision will also have to be made about how the organization should develop its internal cooperation programs. A large number of new members, in this case much poorer members, are likely to further aggravate the possibilities for successful cooperation. A third problem is the role of ASEAN in the context of other economic groupings (or proposed groupings) in Asia-Pacific, such as APEC (Asia Pacific Economic Cooperation), PECC (Pacific Economic Cooperation Council) and EAEG (East Asian Economic Group) (Cf. Blomqvist, 1992; Langhammer, 1991).

On balance, it may seem that ASEAN as an organization has not accomplished many tangible results. However, taking into account the great diversity of the members the results are nevertheless quite respectable, although the main achievements may not be in the realm of economic integration.

CACM

The Central American Common Market (CACM), formed in 1960, comprised five Central American countries: Costa Rica, El Salvador, Guatemala, Honduras and Nicaragua. (Partly due to its special political status, Panama has remained outside the CACM, but has showed a continuous and increasing interest in the union.) The term "common market" is somewhat misleading, since the CACM never comprised free movement of labor or capital; the organization might thus more accurately be described as a customs union or even a free trade area.

The birth of the CACM may be regarded as a result of the historical and cultural unity of Central America on the one hand, and the drive towards integration provided by the Economic Commission for Latin America (ECLA) on the other hand. ECLA propagated in the 1950s a model of import-substituting industrialization (*desarrollo hacia dentro*) based on the ideological background described earlier in this chapter. The interest in import substitution gained additional strength from the fact that the world price of traditional Central American export products (mainly coffee and sugar) had started to decline after the Korean war. Realizing that the size of the individual Central American republics rendered efficient industrialization through import substitution impossible, ECLA called for a regional approach by means of economic integration (Bulmer-Thomas, 1982:236–237).

The fundamental goal for the integration scheme was to accelerate industrialization in Central America. The long-term objective was, however, not introverted development. Along the lines of the "training ground" argument, it was thought that greater participation in the world economy could be attained when the new industries had gained sufficient competitiveness (Blomqvist & Lindholm, 1992). The goal was to be achieved by using three main policy instruments: free trade in industrial products, a common external tariff (CET) on imports from third countries, and various fiscal incentives for industrial firms.

The freeing of intra-regional trade was carried out quickly and efficiently. By the end of the 1960s, 95 percent of all formerly dutiable trade was duty-free, which undoubtedly contributed to the favorable initial performance of the CACM. The CET raised the nominal and effective rate of protection on consumer goods substantially, and lowered the rate on capital goods (Willmore, 1976:398; Bulmer-Thomas, 1987:79). This naturally provided strong incentives for local production of consumer goods and encouraged external imports of capital goods, which is normally the case with import-substituting industrialization. This development was further supported by generous fiscal incentives from individual countries in an effort to attract new investments. As a result, firms were able to import their capital and intermediate products duty free.

Several regional organizations, including the Regional Secretariat (SIECA) for coordination of the integration process, the Central American Bank for Economic Integration (CABEI) for financing of infrastructure projects, and the Central American Clearing House (CCC) for the settlement of intra-regional trade obligations, were also established. Although important, these regional institutions were nevertheless unable to provide a solution to the problems and tensions that already started to emerge in the CACM during the 1960s.

The CACM has often been regarded as the most successful and sophisticated example of economic integration ever in the Third World due to the impressive macroeconomic development of these countries in the 1960s and early 1970s. The initial situation was, however, far from favorable. Intra-regional trade was negligible before 1960, the industrial base was insignificant and the Central American economies were in general complementary rather than competitive to each other. Hence, in terms of classical customs union theory, the risk of trade diversion was considerable, whereas the scope for trade creation was small (Bulmer-Thomas, 1982:238).

The growth rates attained by the CACM countries in the 1960s were high by international standards. Real GDP grew by an annual rate of 5.7 percent and manufacturing by 8.4 percent between 1960 and 1970 (Willmore, 1989:50). (See Table 2.3 for some basic data on the macroeconomic performance of the states forming the CACM.) The contribution by the CACM to the GDP growth rate is debatable; according to different estimates between 10 percent and 25 percent of the total GDP growth stemmed from integration. Due to the mechanisms and goals of the CACM, however, the increase in manufacturing output might be largely attributable to the union (Bulmer-Thomas, 1982:245). The rapid growth continued in the 1970s, although the rates were less impressive than in the 1960s (GDP 5.3 percent, manufacturing 6.0 percent). As manufacturing grew faster than GDP, the ratio of manufacturing output to GDP increased continuously, reaching a peak of 18 percent for the region in 1980 (Blomqvist & Lindholm, 1992).

Table 2.3. *Main economic indicators for the CACM countries, 1989*

Country	Popu-lation (mill.)	GDP (USDbn)	GDP growth (%)		GNP/ capita (USD)	Gross investm./ GDP (%)	Total ext. debt (USDbn)	Total ext. debt/ GDP (%)	Inflation (%)
	1989	1989	1965–80	1980–89	1989	1989	1989	1989	1980–89
Costa Rica	2.7	5.2	6.3	2.8	1,780	24	4.5	86	24.8
El Salvador	5.1	5.9	4.3	0.6	1,070	16	1.9	32	16.8
Honduras	5.0	4.3	5.0	2.3	900	13	3.4	78	4.7
Guatemala	8.9	8.2	5.9	0.4	910	14	2.6	32	13.4
Nicaragua	3.7	3.4	2.5	−1.6	n.a.	n.a	9.2	268	n.a.

n.a. non-available data
Source: World Bank, *World Development Report 1991*, New York, Oxford University Press.

Intra-regional trade increased rapidly due to the freeing of trade. 26 percent of the total trade in the CACM countries was intra-regional in 1970. The expansion of intra-CACM trade was achieved mainly at the expense of the USA, whose share of total trade dropped from 60–70 percent in the 1950s to less than 40 percent in 1968 (Bulmer-Thomas, 1982:243). A large part of the intra-regional trade was of the intra-industry type and consisted of non-durable consumer goods, while capital goods and durable consumer goods were overwhelmingly imported from third countries. In absolute terms, intra-CACM trade continued to grow until 1980, but in relative terms (as a percentage of total trade) it started to decline after 1970, suggesting a gradual loss of dynamism in the regional market from that date.

Most of the studies on the welfare impact of the CACM have confirmed that the comparative static trade effects of integration were negative, as assumed, but that the positive dynamic effects of the union were considerable (See Cline, 1978). All five countries seem to have gained from the CACM, but in varying degrees. The actual (or imagined) unequal distribution of gains led to growing tensions within the CACM, resulting in the departure of Honduras from the union in 1970.

This event marked the beginning of the virtual stagnation of the union. Under the surface, distortions and problems were building up, which finally led to the total collapse of the CACM in the 1980s. The breakdown could, in fact, have been triggered already by the first oil crisis, but a fortunate simultaneous increase in the prices of traditional Central American export goods postponed the disaster. The second oil crisis, rising international interest rates and political upheaval in Nicaragua and El Salvador in 1979–80 were, however, fatal for the Central American integration process. The terms-of-trade of the CACM countries deteriorated drastically, leading to a sharp increase in the foreign debt. The increased social unrest and deteriorating economic outlook contributed to capital flight, stagnating production and declining income levels. Intra-regional trade diminished rapidly; in 1980 intra-CACM exports amounted to USD 1129 million, falling six years later to only USD 420 million (Fuentes, 1989:107). Large payment arrears accumulated between the member countries, and the free intra-regional trade was replaced by tariffs, quotas and trade embargoes. By the mid-1980s, the CACM had turned into a mere paper organization.

While the external shocks undoubtedly accounted for a great part of the failure of the CACM, it is obvious that the inherent weaknesses of the integration scheme also played a significant role. The chosen strategy of industrialization through import substitution created a strong bias against external exports of manufactured goods and distorted the structure of external imports towards capital and intermediate goods, while favoring local production of consumer goods. Thus, the industrial sector grew increasingly dependent on the foreign exchange generated by the traditional export of agricultural products. Reducing imports in a situation of balance-of-payments difficulties caused severe problems for local industrial production. Consequently, import substitution increased rather than decreased the dependence on external imports (Blomqvist & Lindholm, 1992).

It is easy to understand why the external price shocks had such a serious impact on the Central American economies. Deteriorating terms-of-trade resulted in decreased external imports of inputs vital for the local industries, which reduced manufacturing output. At the same time, declining income levels and balance-of-payments problems reduced the demand for consumer goods and generated considerable cuts in intra-regional imports. A vicious circle emerged, launched by external factors and the dependence of the intra-regional trade and local industry on extra-regional trade.

Finally, it is also evident that industrialization in the CACM was skin-deep and never reached more than the "easy" stage of production of non-durable consumer goods. The growth potential of such production is fairly limited, which explains why the common market started to lose its dynamism in the 1970s. A deepening of import substitution to capital goods was hampered by the structure of the CET and the incentives offered by the local authorities. Moreover it is also more demanding to carry out (Cf. Colman & Nixson, 1986:293).

In general terms the CACM has not lived up to expectations, although it made a positive contribution to development during the 1960s and early 1970s. The original model of the CACM undoubtedly needs major modifications. The return of political stability and a modest economic recovery have provided a basis for a new start, which has in fact been reflected in an increased interest in a revitalized and enlarged Central American community (*The Economist*, August 24, 1991). Whether this will be translated into practical action, however, remains to be seen. Costa Rica, for example, has embarked on a strategy of promotion of non-traditional exports, whose main markets are outside Central America (Lundahl, 1990).

LAFTA

The Latin American Free Trade Association (LAFTA) was founded by Argentina, Brazil, Chile, Mexico, Paraguay, Peru, and Uruguay in 1960 (Colombia and Ecuador joined LAFTA in 1961, Venezuela in 1966 and Bolivia in 1967). Some basic macroeconomic statistics for the member countries are given in Table 2.4. The organization was replaced in 1980 by the Latin American Integration Association (LAIA). Two essential motives regarding the effects of integration initiated the foundation of LAFTA. First, import substitution was seen as a

Table 2.4. *Main economic indicators for the LAFTA countries, 1989*

Country	Popu-lation (million)	GNP (USDbn)	GDP growth, (%)		GDP/ capita (USD)	Gross investm./ GDP (%)	Total ext. debt (USDbn)	Total ext. debt/ GDP (%)	Inflation (%)
	1989	1989	1965–80	1980–89	1989	1989	1989	1989	1980–89
Argentina	31.9	53.1	3.4	−0.3	2,160	12	64.7	120	335
Bolivia	7.1	4.5	4.4	−0.9	620	13	4.4	96	392
Brazil	147.3	319.2	9.0	3.0	2,540	22	111.3	35	228
Chile	13.0	25.3	1.9	2.7	1,770	20	18.2	72	21
Colombia	32.3	39.4	5.7	3.5	1,200	20	16.9	43	24
Ecuador	10.3	10.4	8.8	1.9	1,020	22	11.3	109	34
Mexico	84.6	200.7	5.5	0.7	2,010	17	95.6	48	73
Paraguay	4.2	4.1	7.0	2.2	1,030	21	2.5	60	23
Peru	21.2	28.6	3.9	0.4	1,010	20	19.9	69	160
Uruguay	3.1	7.2	2.4	0.1	2,620	9	3.8	52	59
Venezuela	19.2	43.8	3.7	1.0	2,450	13	33.1	76	16

Source: World Bank, *World Development Report 1991*, New York, Oxford University Press.

strategy to counteract deteriorating terms-of-trade and dependence on imports of capital goods from industrialized countries. Secondly, the larger and more industrialized countries of LAFTA, namely Argentina, Brazil and Mexico, sought new local markets for their industrial products which were not yet competitive on the world market. The latter motive was dominant and consequently caused intra-regional inequalities and distributional conflicts between the member states (the intra-regional exports of Argentina, Brazil and Mexico accounted for 46 percent of the Latin American total in 1960 and for 66 percent in 1973 (Vaitsos, 1978). The lack of an adequate compensation scheme, which would have remunerated the smaller net importing countries, eventually obliterated the proposed LAFTA free trade area (Langhammer & Hiemenz, 1990:22).

Although there is not much empirical evidence available on the effects of LAFTA, some information is available from the development of the share of intra-LAFTA trade in the total trade of LAFTA. Intra-union trade as a percentage of total exports in LAFTA was 7.7 percent in 1960 and 10.2 percent in 1970 (World Development Report, 1991:107). The figures might suggest that the creation of LAFTA had a positive effect on intra-regional trade, but in fact the main reason for growing intra-regional trade in that time period was rising world market prices for commodities traded (Langhammer & Hiemenz, 1990:23).

The lack of major achievements within LAFTA may be explained from the standpoint of the prevailing key local social forces and their motives. In the larger countries (Argentina, Brazil and Mexico) there was no industrial group interested in either a more competitive larger Latin American market or one where the government could intervene and allocate activities and plants at the local level. The medium-sized countries (specifically Chile and Colombia) were sceptical about their ability to compete with exports from the larger and more developed countries in an open and competitive regional market, and therefore tried to propose a common industrial policy, which was consistently opposed by the bigger countries. The smallest and least developed countries (especially Bolivia, Ecuador and Paraguay) sought arrangements where they could have preferential treatment in the markets of the bigger countries. Simultaneously the non-traditional industries in the smallest countries were faced by resistance from the traditional agricultural or mining sectors and from the importers. Accordingly, there was a lack of consistency in the approach to. Consequently, no major local industrial group within LAFTA was in favor of effective trade liberalization (Vaitsos, 1978).

A decisive question is whether trade creation or trade diversion has been the predominant source of growth of intra-LAFTA trade. Studies seem to suggest that trade diversion has outweighed trade creation. Furthermore, as is the case in most studies, it has been concluded that the pure trade creation process of LAFTA failed to decentralize trade flows in processed goods among all member countries, and failed to provide an effective "training ground" for products which were not competitive on the world market (Langhammer & Hiemenz, 1990:25).

The principal reason for the failure of the LAFTA integration scheme was, however, as was pointed out earlier, the conflicts that arose in distributing the benefits and costs of integration among member countries. Industrial development, above all trade expansion, has been the basic motive for integration among developing countries. Consequently, integrating countries have seen the composition of flows of new goods relative to traditional goods as the crucial issue in the integration process. The industrial base and the level of industrial development were very heterogeneous in LAFTA, which gave the three largest, most developed countries an edge in their capacity to accommodate new industrial capacity (Vaitsos, 1978).

The dissatisfaction of the smaller countries in LAFTA, resulting from distributive conflicts and the lack of a development-oriented integration scheme including a model for compensating the misfavored members, eventually triggered the formation of the *Andean Pact* in 1969 by Bolivia, Colombia, Chile, Ecuador, and Peru (later joined also by Venezuela). The Andean pact aimed at deeper trade integration and regionally balanced industrialization, through regional investment plans and by common domestic policies. LAFTA could not successfully reap the benefits from an integration process, showing that the homogeneity of integrating countries is one of the preconditions for integration among developing countries to be successful. The Andean Pact has not been successful either, having been plagued by political and ideological differences between the member states. For example, Chile opted out in 1976 (Cf. e.g. Tironi, 1977).

CONCLUSIONS

The lessons from economic cooperation in the Third World which may be of relevance for Southern Africa are somewhat disappointing. Most significant schemes have aimed at some degree of integration. The experiences have been mainly negative. This may be partly due to the specific forms imposed on the schemes, although the general outlook does not seem very promising either. Three main conclusions may be drawn from the cases examined in the present context:

1. Economic integration does not seem to work in practice when the "natural" trading partners are found outside the integrated area. The incentives to trade within the area are then small. It is therefore difficult to promote the latter type of trade unless the tariffs towards non-member countries are very high. From a dynamic point of view, a competing industrial structure may be preferable to a complementary one, since a consequence of integration in the latter case may be diversion of trade from the most efficient producers.

   While the argument concerning industrial structures may not be very crucial in this case, due to the low level of industrialization in most of the Southern African countries, the low degree of intra-regional trade is certainly a problem. This fact is of particular relevance for South Africa, whose main markets for at least primary and agro-based products in the post-apartheid situation are likely to be found overseas rather than in poor neighboring African states. Possibly, integration could lead to increased exports of South African manufactured goods to the region. This is not, however, necessarily desirable. The manufacturing sector in South Africa, which has been protected since the 1920s, is a high-cost one. Trade diversion would ensue and impose a cost on the participating economies. Thus, promoting free trade appears to be a better strategy, since this would force South African manufacturing to reduce its costs.

2. When countries attempting to integrate their economies are not on a roughly comparable level of development before the integration effort begins, the result is likely to be polarization. Manufacturing industry in particular is likely to become increasingly concentrated in the already industrialized areas. The dynamic gains and losses from integration are likely to be unequally distributed, in favor of the more developed partners. (Again Arrow's impossibility theorem may apply. It may not be possible to distribute compensation in a way that can be agreed upon by all members.)

   This calls for some kind of compensation scheme of the type already in use in the Southern African Customs Union. However, as demonstrated by the experience of this group of states (Lundahl & Petersson, 1991, Ch. 10), this may give rise to controversy among the members.

3. Other forms of regional cooperation than integration may be easier to carry out, because they avoid some of the costs associated with integration: the sharing of infrastructure, educational facilities, international trade negotiations, etc. Such "public goods" may nevertheless be difficult to identify. It may be hard to reach an

agreement on how payments should be divided. Hence the dominant partners, notably South Africa, may attempt to impose their own views and preferences on the others. The best way to proceed may be through gradual and pragmatic development of specific cooperation projects without an outright aim at integration of markets. This line of thought by and large follows the philosophy of SADCC (Curry, 1991).

Thus, the inevitable conclusion to be drawn from the experience of ASEAN, CACM and LAFTA is that economic cooperation and integration among developing countries—including those of Southern Africa—may be a difficult and costly venture, in particular when the economies involved are not at the same level of development. This conclusion receives further support from the actual experience of the SACU (Lundahl & Petersson, 1991). In addition, as is well known, import substitution behind tariff walls, based on the national markets only, has strongly negative effects. Free trade with countries outside as well as inside the region may therefore be a superior alternative.

ISSUE ORIENTED
PERSPECTIVES

3. Emerging South African Perspectives on Regional Cooperation and Integration after Apartheid

Robert Davies

Developments in Southern Africa in the period since the battle of Cuito Cuanavale and in South Africa since February 1990 have placed the issue of the involvement of a democratic, non-racial South Africa in a programme of closer economic cooperation and integration with the rest of Southern Africa firmly on the agenda. Most of the "key players" inside South Africa—ranging from the present minority government and business community to the political organisations of the national liberation movement and the trade unions—are now on record as supporting some such move. At the same time organisations formed in the rest of the region, notably the Southern African Development Coordination Conference (SADCC) and the Eastern and Southern African Preferential Trade Area (PTA) are preparing themselves for a new relationship with a post-apartheid South Africa.

Despite the superficial appearance of consensus and some overlap in the use of language and terminology, significantly different perspectives have, in fact, emerged between different forces in South Africa on the terms, principles and approaches to govern a programme of closer regional economic cooperation and integration after apartheid. Future South African policy on this issue can thus be expected to depend to a considerable extent on the balance of forces established in the negotiation process now underway.

This chapter will critically examine some of the major perspectives emerging in South Africa on this issue. It will not offer a content analysis of the declared positions of key actors, nor will it discuss in any detail the merits or otherwise of the increasing number of specific proposals or models that have been put forward. Rather it will attempt to characterise the broad thrust of the main alternative approaches that are emerging against the background of an analysis of the current crisis in the pattern of interaction established in the period since the end of World War II. It will then, on this basis, evaluate the capacity or otherwise to produce policies capable of building a new pattern of relations between a post-apartheid South Africa and the rest of the region that is equitable, sustainable and growth orientated.

REGIONAL TRADE PATTERNS AND SOUTH AFRICA'S POST-WORLD WAR II GROWTH PATH

The current pattern of economic interaction between South Africa and the rest of Southern Africa was profoundly influenced by the overall accumulation or growth path of the South African economy. In the period following the end of World War II, South Africa's "growth path" was based on import substitution industrialisation orientated towards high income domestic consumption markets and financed by the export of primary products. Throughout the period, the manufacturing sector was the main engine of growth—contributing more to the Gross Domestic Product (GDP) than agriculture and mining combined. But, it was a sector dominated by the production of consumer goods for the upper income (white) domestic consumers and was highly dependent on imported machinery and other inputs paid for by foreign exchange earned through the export of primary products, mainly minerals, on world markets (Gelb, 1991).

Apart from producing acute domestic inequalities and an extreme vulnerability to the waning fortunes of a wasting gold mining industry, this path of accumulation also had a major impact on the shape of the trade relations that emerged between South Africa and the rest of the region. Import substitution industrialisation inevitably meant that South Africa's industrial sector produced a range of manufactured goods which were not competitive internationally. Although the production of manufactured goods was largely orientated to the domestic market and although mineral products and base metals (in which South Africa could be considered to have an international comparative advantage) continued to make up over a third of exports to African countries (other than members of the Southern African Customs Union—SACU) in the mid-1980s, exports of manufactured goods made a significant, albeit little noticed, contribution to South Africa's post-war manufacturing growth. A study conducted in the 1970s, for example, found that although the combined GDP of Botswana, Lesotho and Swaziland was at that time only 3 per cent that of South Africa, trade with these countries was responsible for 27 per cent of new value added and around 67,000 new jobs in South Africa's manufacturing sector (McFarland, 1983).

No comparable study for later years or a broader range of trading partners is known to exist, but available statistics point to a continuing disproportionate importance of regional and Sub-Saharan trade for manufactured exports. Figures for 1985, the last year when trade statistics were fully published, show that while trade with non-SACU African countries was responsible for only 4 per cent of total SACU exports, this trade accounted for 36 per cent of exports of machinery, 28 per cent of chemical products, 27 per cent of vehicles and transport equipment, 14 per cent of miscellaneous manufactured goods, 10 per cent of processed foods and considerable percentages of the total exports of other less important manufactured consumer goods (see Table 3.1). Many of these figures would, moreover, undoubtedly have been much higher had they referred to South African trade with all African countries (including other SACU members).

More recent figures confirm the continued importance of regional and sub-Saharan markets for South Africa's manufacturing sector. Thus while total trade with non-SACU African countries made up less than 10 per cent of total exports in 1990, this trade accounted for no less than 32 per cent of South Africa's manufactured exports. The upswing in this trade since the end of the 1980s is reported to have given an important boost to South Africa's steel, food, chemical and motor vehicle industries among others.[1] Commentators have also suggested that increasing sales to African countries made a major contribution to the sharp rise in exports of such "non-traditional" items as "plastic and rubber products" or "miscellaneous manufactured goods", which rose by 42 per cent and 41 per cent respectively between 1990 and 1991 (*The Star*, 28 January, 1992).

While southern, and to a lesser extent the rest of Africa, thus provided a significant market for a range of manufactured goods which would have been unlikely to have found export markets elsewhere, the protectionist policies followed as an integral part of the post-World War II growth strategy tended to restrict regional as well as extra-continental imports. This aspect is relatively well documented. Protectionist tariff policies first elaborated in the 1920s excluded a range of mainly agricultural products from neighbouring states; non-tariff barriers of various kinds were erected to prevent other SACU members using the official provisions of the agreement to export manufactured goods to South Africa; and even the politically—motivated trade agreement negotiated to provide support to the Smith regime in Zimbabwe in 1964 took pains to restrict imports of goods which might seriously compete with local manufactures (Hanlon, 1986, and Kumar, 1991).

This combination of relative uncompetitiveness and a protectionist stance towards regional imports shaped a pattern of trade character-

Robert Davies

Table 3.1. *Trade of SACU members with other African countries, 1985*
(Rand million)

Section of CCN nomenclature	Exports	Imports	Total exports of the section	Africa's % of total exports of the section
1. Live animals/ animal products	43.5	7.7	331.0	13
2. Vegetable products	78.9	38.5	868.9	9
3. Animal and vegetable fats	17.2	5.7	76.1	23
4. Prepared foodstuffs, beverages	79.7	91.7	808.3	10
5. Mineral products	288.4	21.0	4,996.0	6
6. Chemical products	262.1	9.5	930.7	28
7. Artificial resins, plastics	71.2	2.5	153.8	46
8. Skins, leather products	1.5	9.3	272.0	1
9. Wood products	13.8	20.1	106.5	13
10. Paper products	50.5	4.9	657.0	8
11. Textiles	51.8	83.6	1,044.8	5
12. Footwear	5.6	4.4	12.3	46
13. Stoneware	27.2	1.2	85.3	32
14. Precious metals, stones	1.4	52.3	2,607.1	0
15. Base metals	267.0	53.4	4,045.9	7
16. Machinery	189.3	20.0	529.6	36
17. Transport equipment	96.0	8.0	361.3	27
18. Optical and medical equipment	13.6	3.4	74.5	18
20. Miscellaneous manufactures	6.2	4.1	44.2	14
21. Works of art	0.0	0.7	23.0	0
22. Other unclassified	13.8	14.8	18,747.4	0
Total	1,579.0	457.0	36,775.8	4
(Total 1984)	(891.7)	(485.2)	(25,585.9)	(4)

Note: Totals may not add up precisely, due to rounding of section figures.
Source: Republic of South Africa, *Foreign Trade Statistics, Calender Year 1985,* Pretoria, Government Printer.

ised, at least in large part, by what Reginald Green has called the sell-ing of "overpriced South African exports for hard currency" (Green, 1991).

A constant feature of this trade over many decades has been a large, and indeed increasing, gap between visible exports and imports.

South African exports have not been matched by reciprocal imports of goods from the rest of Africa with the result that a large and widening deficit on the balance of trade has been recorded. Official figures, for example, show that exports from SACU to non-SACU African countries were 3.4 times the level of imports in 1985. By 1990 this ratio had widened to 5.7:1.[2]

This deficit in visible trade has historically been partly financed by invisible earnings from the provision by the rest of the region of various services to support the accumulation process in South Africa. As is well known, South Africa's gold mining industry was developed on the basis of cheap migrant labour, drawn not only from South Africa's "homelands" but also from neighbouring states. Indeed, for most of its history the South African mining industry had a majority non-South African labour force and even today draws more than a third of its workers from beyond South Africa's borders. Remittances from migrant workers were one important source of invisible earnings for many countries. Revenue from transport services and more recently from hydro-power and water projects have also been significant. However, overwhelmingly and increasingly purchases from South Africa have had to be paid for from foreign exchange earned by other countries from the sale of their primary products on world markets.

THE IMPACT OF THE POST-1970s CRISIS

The multiple crisis, affecting the whole of Southern Africa in the period since the mid-1970s, has significantly impacted on several of the key variables making up the above described regional trade equation. First, there has been a decline in rates of investment in South Africa's manufacturing sector leading to a probable decrease in the competitivity of many of its products. Between 1983 and 1987 real investment in manufacturing declined by 12.8 per cent per annum and although the manufacturing sector led a modest recovery in investment recorded between 1987 and 1990, overall rates of investment remain only around 2/3 the levels of the early 1970s (Senhadji & Walton, 1991). Establishing the precise impact of this on the competitivity of manufacturing exports to the region is more difficult. However, there has been an increase in the average age of plant and equipment in the sector and various estimates have been made suggesting that the prices of some South African manufactured goods sold in the region may now now be as much as 15–25 per cent higher than the f.o.b. prices of comparable goods from elsewhere.[3] Certainly, there are signs of preparations in some parts of the region for a shift away from from South African to cheaper global suppliers, notwithstanding the non-price advantages which South African suppliers continue to enjoy, such as lower transport costs and shorter delivery times (due to closer proximity) or easier credit terms offered to customers (financed by government export promotion guarantees and subsidies).

The period since the mid-1970s has, secondly, seen South Africa progressively withdrawing from two important relations in which it had historically been present as a buyer—migrant labour and transport services. This severely limited potential growth, and in several cases led to an actual decline, in invisible earnings from services supplied to South Africa. In the case of migrant labour, the proportion of "foreign" workers in the South African mine labour force (the largest employer of foreign migrant workers) declined from over 60 per cent in 1975 to around 40 per cent by the end of the 1980s with the absolute number falling from 220,000 in 1975 to 186,000 in 1989.[4] In transport, the period saw both a decline in South Africa's use of facilities in other regional states, and witnessed an attempt by South African Transport Services (SATS) to divert traffic from landlocked countries which had historically used the services of other regional states. South African traffic through Maputo was cut to around 15 per cent of pre-independence levels while regional traffic passing through South African ports increased to one-and-a-half times the level of 1981/2 by 1984/5 (*Financial Mail*, 15 August 1986). In the case of Mozambique, the country most affected by both these trends, remittances from migrant workers declined from USD 64.5 million in 1981 to USD 58 million in 1987—before rising slightly to USD 70 million in 1988. Earnings from transport services (provided both to other SADCC countries and South Africa) fell from USD 82 million in 1981 to USD 42 million in 1989 (World Bank, 1990a). In both cases the level of 1981 represented a significant decrease from 1975.

The 1980s were, thirdly, for Southern Africa, like the rest of sub-Saharan Africa, a "lost decade" for development, characterised by economic stagnation, worsening terms-of-trade and growing indebtedness, whose effects were exacerbated by the devastating impact of Pretoria's policies of aggression and destabilisation. Foreign exchange receipts declined sharply, drastically reducing the capacity of many countries to import (World Bank, 1989a, and UN, 1991).

The combined effect of all of these factors has been to place a severe strain on the established trade relationship between South Africa and the rest of the region: goods whose competitiveness was tending to decline were being offered in markets where the foreign exchange needed to buy them was becoming increasingly scarce.

The wave of escalating aggression and destabilisation unleashed in the late 1970s and 1980s can be recognised, in part, as an attempt by Pretoria to re-assert its hegemony in the face of this "scissors crisis". One of the objectives underlying destabilisation was clearly to preserve essential elements of the established patterns of regional economic relations intact, while permitting a highly partisan restructuring of others. Launched in response to set-backs to its proposals to draw neighbouring states into a new hegemonic alliance (CONSAS) and directed most particularly at those states and projects seen as most challenging to its designs, destabilisation did have the effect of impeding efforts by the rest of the region to reduce dependence on South Africa and diversify. The deepening transport dependence, which resulted from the sabotage of alternative facilities in Angola and Mozambique, for example, not only boosted the earnings of South Africa's ports and railways, it also tended to increase the non-price advantages of South African goods and thus tie landlocked countries into an enhanced trade dependence on South Africa. Destabilisation, however, eventually produced its own contradiction. By the end of the decade any potential benefits created for South African exporters by undercutting efforts to diversify were more than offset by the negative impact on the capacity of regional states to import. At the same time, South Africa's growing need for physical inputs— water and electricity—from the rest of the region became increasingly apparent.

A growing recognition on part of sections of South Africa's business community that some form of re-stabilisation of the regional economy was in South Africa's own interests can be identified as an important factor leading to the turn away from destabilisation policies in the late 1980s—although the resistance of regional states, the failure to resolve the domestic crisis of apartheid and the pressures generated by a rapidly changing international order were all more fundamental.

This shift, and more particularly Pretoria's involvement in negotiations leading to the independence of Namibia followed by the political developments in South Africa since February 1990, has introduced what might be termed an important counter tendency (from a South African point of view) to the effects of the continuing structural crisis of the post-World War II pattern of regional economic interaction. Post-Cuito Cuanavale and post-February 2, 1990 political developments have led to a progressive lowering of barriers to South Africa's acceptance in the region and wider continent and this has created unprecedented new opportunities both for an immediate increase in economic interaction and a growing involvement by state

and corporate officials as well as the liberation movements in dialogue with their regional counterparts about longer term -"post apartheid"-regional reconstruction. The effects of this are reflected, inter
alia in the trade figures, which show trade between South Africa and
the rest of Africa increasing by 40 per cent in 1989 and a further 22
per cent in 1990 (*Business Day*, 6 March 1991).

EMERGING PERSPECTIVES ON REGIONAL COOPERATION IN SOUTH AFRICA

The perspectives now emerging in South Africa on the question of
post-apartheid regional cooperation and integration have thus to be
seen against the background, first, of a structural crisis in the pattern
of regional interaction established and, second, of a more immediately felt counter tendency arising from the the lowering of political
barriers to South Africa's re-engagement with the region. Changes in
the international order—and more particularly the current trend
towards the formation of regional trading blocs both in the countries
of "the north" and in regions of "the south"—have also significantly
influenced perceptions.

Under these circumstances all major forces in South Africa now
appear to agree that a post-apartheid period should see some form
of closer regional cooperation and economic integration between all
the countries of Southern Africa, including South Africa. However,
significantly different perspectives have emerged over the approach,
terms and principles on which this should be built and, more particularly, over the extent to which qualitative transformation of established patterns is essential.

One perspective, not surprisingly embraced by many of those closest to the vested interests of the old order—including the present
minority government and much of the corporate sector—has tended
to view future cooperation as little more than a return to a somewhat
modified version of the old (pre-1970s) "normality". Past or existing
patterns of regional relations tend to be viewed rather uncritically
with the fundamental problem of the past often seen as little more
than the existence of political and regulatory barriers in other countries which prevented South Africa from playing its potential role as
"engine of growth" in the sub-continent. The progressive dropping
of political barriers is thus seen, at least in those quarters that take
Africa seriously, as potentially providing a significant boost to South
African trade. The more recent dropping by international donors and
funders of objections to the involvement by South African compani-

es in aid funded projects in neighbouring states is also seen as creating important additional opportunities and offering advice on how to tender more effectively for aid contracts has now become something of a growth industry in South Africa.[5] It should be noted, in parenthesis, that a more cautious or pessimistic sentiment also exists within the South African corporate "establishment". This tends to doubt that Africa can ever be of more than marginal importance for South Africa and favours concentrating on trying to project an image of South Africa as a "first world" player involved in global markets rather than a "third world" country relegated to regional markets.

The approach towards building closer cooperation and integration—at least in those quarters taking Africa seriously—tends largely to be seen in terms of the rest of the region consolidating the move towards lifting political barriers to doing business with South Africa with a more generalised liberalisation of regulatory systems in a way which will "open up" the region to South African exports and capital investment. Attempts to theorise from within this type of perspective, generally favour a a rather rapid move towards a regional common market allowing both free trade and unhampered capital movement.[6] In more practical terms, there are signs of some interest in trying to re-launch or re-structure SACU as basis of a free trade/free capital movement regional integration project. Apart from yielding benefits in its own right, involvement by the "new South Africa" in such a project also appears to be seen as a way of rebuilding relations with external forces on terms favourable to South Africa. The insistence on the need for unrestricted free movement of capital throughout the region appears, for example, to have much less to do with plans by South African companies to make investments in the region than a desire to reinforce South Africa's image as the "natural gateway" and partner for foreign investors in Southern Africa.

Much of this can be recognised as short term and self interested. It has been criticised as South Africa-centric and indifferent to concerns of the rest of the region about the acute imbalances in existing relations or to the appalling heritage left by destabilisation. It takes little or no account of the serious potential for polarisation that would arise in an integration project in which not only does one prospective partner have an economy more than three times that of ten others combined, but more importantly there are structural inequalities and patterns of domination/hegemony in existing relations. Such an approach is also rooted, implicitly if not explicitly, in a rather short term and over-politicised perspective on the crisis. The focus is on what was called above the counter-tendency—the immediate opportunities opening up as a result of the lifting of South Africa's pariah status—with little recognition given to the existence of an underlying structural crisis in the established path of regional economic interaction. As such it fails to offer any viable answer to the fundamental longer term problem of the increasing unsustainability of the existing model. By focusing myopically on the immediate, short term export "dividend" that the ending of pariah status may well provide, it fails adequately to recognise that this will not be consolidated into a longer term growing trade relation unless the rest of the region sees some benefit to itself in granting preferences to South African goods and unless South African exports become more competitive. Nor is the payments problem among prospective regional trading partners seriously addressed—except through hoping that international aid will provide some immediate boost. It cannot thus provide any satisfactory long term answers to many of the central questions of how to create a mutually beneficial, growth–orientated and sustainable pattern of regional cooperation and integration in a post-apartheid Southern Africa. Moreover, many of the specific schemes and proposals advanced within such a perspective, tend, whatever their professed intentions, to seek in practice to enhance South African hegemony. Notions of South Africa as the "locomotive of growth", the "natural entry point" to Southern Africa or the un-mandated representative of Southern Africa in a continental axis of "power point" countries have thus all unselfconsciously been put forward by proponents of this approach.

The alternative perspective, which is emerging within the democratic movement, is based on the view that regional trade and other economic relations need to be restructured as an integral part of a process of transforming the existing growth path. The restructuring of regional relations was initially seen largely as a matter of equity. The critique of the rest of the region about the detrimental impact of historic imbalances on their development and the devastation caused by destabilisation were seen as placing an obligation on a democratic South Africa to work with neighbouring countries in restructuring regional relations on a more equitable basis. There was also a recognition that South Africa could not hope to grow and develop while the rest of the region stagnated—particularly in a situation where clandestine migration was already swelling the ranks of South Africa's homeless and unemployed and where arms and drugs smuggling to South Africa were among the most lucrative forms of "unrecorded trade" taking place in the region.[7]

The reconstruction of regional economic relations on a new basis is, however, now increasingly also seen as an essential component of a new growth strategy. Current thinking within the South African democratic movement can perhaps be summed up as envisaging a mixture of "growth through redistribution" and "redistribution through growth". Redistribution is seen as essential to address pressing problems of poverty and inequality and redistributive projects are seen as potentially providing a significant impetus to growth along a new path giving greater priority to basic needs of the most impoverished and deprived. But there is also an increasing recognition that internally–oriented redistributive projects will not on their own be sufficient to place the economy onto a sustainable growth path. Externally-orientated policies aimed, in particular, at reducing the South African economy's current dependence on exports of primary products and increasing exports of manufactured goods are seen as also being essential.

Regional and sub-Saharan trade is increasingly recognised as having major strategic significance for any project aimed at promoting manufactured exports. The current disproportionate importance of African markets for exports of manufacturing goods has already been referred to above. Some of the products that would be encouraged as part of a policy of re-orientating domestic production towards basic needs—including building and construction material and consumer durables—could well find markets in other African countries. Africa could provide an important market for machinery and equipment—particularly mining technology. South Africa and the SADCC countries have many similarities and complementarities in the minerals sector: together they produce significant percentages of total world output of such mineral products as gold, manganese, platinum, diamonds, copper, nickel, ferro-chrome, cobalt, iron ore, asbestos, coal, chromite, zinc, tin, silver and lead, suggesting that there may be considerable scope for cooperation in minerals beneficiation projects aimed at increasing the value added of products sold in world markets.[8]

Growth and industrial development in South Africa could also be expected to boost demand for inputs from neighbouring countries such as water and hydro-power, and greater access to the South African market could provide several SADCC countries with a securer base on which to restructure their economies on a more productive and competitive basis.

These intersecting concrete needs and interests make it possible, in my view, to envisage a mutually beneficial, negotiated restructuring of regional economic relations after apartheid, which would address several of the key problems of the inequity and longer term unsustainability of existing relations. This would essentially centre around a trade off in which a democratic South Africa would be granted greater access to regional markets and inputs in return for agreeing to cooperate with the rest of the region in restructuring key sectoral relations in ways that both address existing imbalances and inequities and boost the income earning potential of other countries. The latter could, among other things, include:

1. Granting other countries greater access to the domestic South African market thus contributing towards bringing about a more equitable pattern of visible trade;
2. Accepting the need to grant favourable terms to regional suppliers of inputs like water and hydro-power;
3. Participating in a process of restructuring of regional transport relations in a way which acknowledges the need to address problems caused by distortion of historic transport flows and to promote a more rational utilisation of the region's transport infrastructure;
4. A democratic South Africa committing itself to finding mutually acceptable, regional solutions to problems arising from labour migration, based on an acknowledgment of the historic subordination and underdevelopment of labour reserve areas, the dependence this has created in neighbouring countries and the way in which problems caused by destabilisation have fueled the trend towards clandestine or "illegal" migration;
5. South Africa making some financial and other contribution to regional development programmes while accepting that the principle of prioritising the interests of the most impoverished and deprived countries and areas should govern the distribution of benefits;
6. All countries giving serious attention and priority to cooperating in mutually beneficial programmes, and most importantly investigating the possibilities for and implications of a minerals-based regional industrialisation strategy.

A negotiated re-structuring along these lines would address many of the factors underlying the unsustainability of the existing path of selling over-priced goods for foreign exchange—provided that access to regional markets was seen as a basis for tackling more effectively and not of avoiding the challenge of raising productivity and competitiveness across the region. It would also provide a suitable base for a programme of regional economic integration capable of countering the potential for acute polarisation. It would be mutually beneficial in the sense that all parties stood to make significant gains, but would simultaneously be rooted in a recognition of the need for a conscious redistribution of many of the benefits to the most impoverished and underdeveloped partners.

This relates to another major debate, at this point perhaps more developed in the rest of the region than it is in South Africa—what approach to building integration would be most appropriate for a post-apartheid Southern Africa? SADCC's recent theme document on integration identified three possible approaches:[9]

1. The neo-classical trade or market integration approach, focussing on the removal of tariff and non-tariff barriers to intra-regional trade and the creation in linear succession of a Preferential Trade Area, Free Trade Area, Customs Union, Common Market and Economic Union or Community.
2. The neo-functional or integration through project cooperation approach based on the view that conventional trade driven integration is inappropriate in regions characterised by underdevelopment and that cooperation in projects aimed at overcoming infrastructural and production based barriers to regional trade should have priority.
3. The development integration approach, also based on the view that laissez faire trade driven approaches will either not lead to effective integration or else will create unacceptable polarisation in underdeveloped regions. It stresses the need for both macro and micro coordination embracing production, infrastructure and trade; close political cooperation at an early stage of the integration process; the necessity to ensure an equitable balance of the benefits of integration and, in particular, to complement trade liberalisation measures with compensatory and corrective measures orientated particularly towards the least developed member countries.

While the South African democratic movement has scarcely even begun to debate these issues, the general thrust towards seeking to build closer cooperation and integration based on long term, structural transformation, consensus building with partners and democratic participation would suggest an initial preference for the development integration approach, also broadly supported in SADCC's Theme Document 1992.

CONCLUSION

As South Africa moves, hopefully, towards the establishment of a more representative, democratic government, two identifiable trends are underway in the region:

First, at the level of regional organisations like SADCC and within the South African democratic movement a search is underway for a formula to promote closer regional cooperation and integration based on principles of equity, interdependence and mutual benefit. While no agreed blueprint has yet emerged, it is generally acknowledged that this will have to involve major transformations in the existing pattern of regional relations.

The second trend, born of desperation on the part of neighbouring countries and/or expectations, partly fuelled by the present South African government's "new diplomacy", is towards bilateral deals based on a "pragmatic extension" of existing relations. This approach essentially involves prioritising short term advantage above long term considerations of transformation.

Any objective evaluation will have to acknowledge the existence of many factors favourable to the emergence of a scenario based more on pragmatic adjustment than on transformation. Such a scenario is being actively worked for by powerful forces among the current holders of economic power in Southern Africa. It is also being reinforced, whether consciously or unconsciously, by the actions of influential external parties. The pressure for a laissez faire approach to integration with its one sided emphasis on liberalisation and deregulation and its indifference to polarisation, the scarcely concealed eagerness of many donors to withdraw from aid commitments in SADCC countries the moment South Africa is accepted as a legitimate partner by the rest of the region, and the acceptance and indeed promotion of notions of South Africa as the "natural" entry point for aid and investment throughout the region can all be cited of examples.

And yet the simple positing of a "realistic" against a "normative" scenario does not adequately capture the dynamics of the issues at stake. This chapter has argued that the regional trading regime established in the post World War II period was not only unbalanced and inequitable, it is also enmeshed in a structural crisis. What is often posited as the "realistic" scenario does not in fact address itself to this reality and thus offers no credible answer to the question of how the crisis is to be resolved.

The end of apartheid will thus pose for South Africa a critical choice in its relations with its neighbours. It can continue, as it is under its present leadership, to pursue short term, partisan benefits, preying on the weaknesses, fears and expectations of the rest of the region. If it chooses to continue travelling along some version of this route it may derive certain short term economic benefits. But, these would be at the cost of the broader, longer term interests not only of the region as a whole, but of South Africa as well.

At the very least, the reproduction after apartheid of the existing unbalanced trade regime in which the income earning capacity of partners is not being enhanced will be trade in static markets. If, moreover, stagnation continues to be the lot of a significant part of the region and existing disparities are reproduced or even exacerbated in the future, South Africa can expect increasing clandestine migration across its extremely porous borders—with numerous consequences for domestic development programmes. More than this, the search for non–militaristic solutions to outstanding or potential future conflicts in the region and the creation of new development orientated security structures would become more difficult, in a context where no country in the region can expect to be immune from the effects of crises in other countries.

The only "realistic" alternative to such a scenario is for South Africa to join its neighbours in an honest search for solutions which are mutually beneficial—solutions which yield benefits for all, but which seek simultaneously to address the disparities and inequities in existing relations.

NOTES

1. *The Star* (*International Airmail Edition*), 8 February 1990, quoting then Trade Minister, Kent Durr.
2. For the 1985 figure see Table 3:1, the 1990 ratio is calculated from figures released to *Finansies en Tegniek* which show exports to non-SACU members of Rand 4,069,719,730 and imports of Rand 713,320,286.
3. On aging plant, see Kaplan (1987). The level of 15 per cent above world market f.o.b. prices is rumoured to be the "bench mark" figure of major business organisations in South Africa, the 25 per cent figure is apparently a calculation done for several SACU members mentioned in Green, op cit. A recent press report quoted "exporters" ranking "uncompetitive prices as the major obstacle to increased sales" of South African goods abroad, *Sunday Times: Business Times*, 16 February 1992, "Bully for exports, but it's tough".
4. Figures from *Chamber of Mines Annual Report*, Johannesburg, 1984, and SAIRR, 1990, p. 629.

5. On views from the South African business community on prospects for trade and the expectations of new opportunities through tendering for aid contracts see *Financial Mail* 31 January 1992 ("Trade with Africa: Don't presume too much!") and *Sunday Times: Business Times* 2 February 1992 reporting the launching by SAFTO with the support of the Department of Finance of a new initiative "to help SA companies crack the lucrative world development aid market".

6. For examples of such views, see H. P. de Villiers, Chairman Standard Bank Investment Corporation, "A Southern African Economic Community—A Pipedream or a Must?", mimeo, February 1990 and reports in *Financial Mail* 9 November 1990, *Cape Times* 13 November 1990, *Africa Business* October 1990 and *Cape Times* 16 March 1991.

7. Extracts from several speeches and documents of the democratic movement are reproduced in "Perspectives on Regional Co-operation from the Mass Democratic Movement in South Africa", *Backgrounder: A CSAS Resource Publication*, No. 3, Bellville, University of the Western Cape, December 1991.

8. See Jourdan (1989 and 1990). Paul Jourdan has also more recently argued that the "primacy of the minerals-energy complex", low cost energy, technological capacity and well-developed infrastructure provide a strong base for a regionally-oriented "resource based industrialisation strategy" (Jourdan, 1991b).

9. See SADCC (1992a), Mhlongo (1991) and Chr. Michelsen Institute/SADCC (1986). The three approaches are elaborated upon by Østergaard in chapter 1.

4. Towards Enhanced Regional Security in Southern Africa?

Thomas Ohlson and Stephen J. Stedman

Southern Africa is an exceptionally violent, conflict-ridden region. The dominant factors in producing conflict in Southern Africa have been settler colonialism and South Africa's system of apartheid and its brutal and multi-pronged attempt to dominate the surrounding region. The government of South Africa and the former colonial governments of the region used direct violence to maintain their political and economic subjugation of the peoples of the region. The incompatibility of values and the use of violence by the powerful produced a conflict complex within which conflict resolution has often come from pressure, force, and violence, rather than from moral reassessment. The legacies of that central conflict will be felt throughout the region for the foreseeable future. At the same time, the gradual disappearance of apartheid, the end of bipolarity on the global level as well as on-going political and economic changes in the region will bring about a re-emergence of older conflict issues as well as new ones.

Conflict, insecurity and underdevelopment are inextricably inter-linked in Southern Africa. The region as a whole and the individual countries are by the early 1990s in a precarious situation. In the process leading up to the current dramatic transformations, the political and economic manoeuvring space of governments has diminished dramatically. The aid dependence is higher than ever before, while global political dynamics, technological developments, aid fatigue and other factors are likely to reduce donor and investor interest in the region. The disappearance of formal structures of institutionalized racism and the end of the east–west conflict will not only bring good to the region. New conflict patterns in the region will come to the fore, and—even in the presence of the requisite political will—the ability within the region to deal with these conflicts is limited.

This chapter[1] first briefly analyses present and future conflict issues in the region. It goes on to outline scenarios of what a future Southern Africa might look like with reference to conflict, cooperation and security. It discusses the most likely and most preferable scenarios, respectively, and, finally, it describes which capabilities, norms, institutions and organizations would be conducive to producing the normatively preferred outcome.

One caveat is necessary. It is a commonplace that political and economic conditionalities and pressures, in general, and the content, direction and magnitude of the flow of investments, loans and grants from outside the region, in particular, will play an important role in defining the future shape of the regional security complex.[2] This chapter is not about those extra-regional forces. It is about internal regional processes into which external influences and flows will feed and try to affect.[3]

POST-APARTHEID CONFLICT ISSUES IN SOUTHERN AFRICA

The level and intensity of conflict, violent or non-violent, in the region will have a decisive impact on current national and regional transformation processes.[4] Conflict and perceptions of insecurity also constitute serious obstacles to socio-economic development and interstate cooperation. Beginning at the level of individual states, we discern the following *domestic conflict issues* within the countries of Southern Africa:[5]

— Conflicts over control of government or territory.
— Conflicts associated with war termination and reconciliation.
— Conflicts of participation caused by the monopoly of political power by a dominant party or racial group.
— Conflicts over inequitable distribution of resources.
— Conflicts over identity, due to ethnicity.

All these conflict issues in their various manifestations have one thing in common: they all have something to do with problems of legitimacy. As noted, the capabilities of Southern African states to end ongoing wars and resolve conflicts over participation, distribution and identity are under tremendous strain as a result of the impact of destabilization and war, crises of economic production and the need for reconciliation with white power in the region and international finance.

One of the consequences of the way in which regional and global actors have attempted to solve the basic conflict in the region is the introduction of market economies in the form of structural adjustment programmes, which are crudely implemented and which generate widespread criticism and even revolt among populations. This is not to say that political and economic change is not needed. On the contrary, participants and observers in this process agree to the necessity of economic reform. But it must be noted that economic liberalization through structural adjustment is a conflict generating pro-gramme, without a conflict resolution component.

Similarly, the idea that democracy in the Third World can be an institution for conflict resolution is a revival of liberal programmes from the 1960s that believed that "all good things go together."[6] But the history of multi-party democracy in the Third World is that it, like structural adjustment, generates conflict. Changes superimposed from outside may or may not be successfully internalized. The trans-formation of autocratic or racist regimes and one-party systems is a complicated process, riddled with dangers and uncertainties. Much time will be needed to gradually build up new forms of distribution, participation and legitimacy.

Economic adjustment and political democracy may be contradic-tory and incompatible programmes.[7] Those groups most hurt by eco-nomic liberalization may use democracy to reverse such policies. Ungovernability that arises from strikes and civil unrest against adjustment are as likely to lead to military interventions into politics and a return of authoritarianism, as orderly transitions to stable democracy. Questions of pace, sequence and timing are extremely important. This poses a tremendous challenge to the governments of the region.

Turning next to the regional level, regional security in Southern Africa is inextricably linked with the domestic security of its coun-tries. Classically, in international security studies, security is a prob-lem of relations between states. In Southern Africa, as in the rest of Africa, the basic unit of analysis—the state—cannot be taken for granted. The lack of strong states in the region implies that domestic conflicts cannot be contained within borders. There is a potential for internal violence to escalate into war between countries. By the early 1990s there are three different but interlinked *regional conflict clusters*, either manifest or latent, in Southern Africa:

1. *Overlay conflict:* that is, the continuation of conflict between states in the region due to the central, region-wide conflict between white minority rule and African liberation that has so dominated Southern Africa since the early 1960s. During the 1980s the major source of conflict in the region was the attempt by the government of South Africa to make the region safe for white domination at home. While that conflict is being transformed, it still plays a major role in that many of the current intra-regional conflict issues de-rive from or are to be considered spill-overs from that key conflict. For example: Mozambique is in conflict with South Africa over its continued support for RENAMO; Malawi's support for RENAMO

has brought it into conflict with both Mozambique and Zimbabwe; Zimbabwe is still undergoing destabilization; Angola still suffers from South African interference; and Namibia still has the issue of Walvis Bay to resolve with South Africa.

2. *Diffusion conflict:* that is, national conflicts within borders spreading across borders. This could take two forms. First, a re-escalation of violence throughout the region due to processes internal to South Africa. Conflict in the region will still be affected by events in South Africa. If the process of change stalls there, or falls victim to attack from within, then we should expect an upsurge in violence in South Africa, the continuation of large scale armed violence in Mozambique, and the potential of a return to a more active South African destabilization of the region in general. Second, violence as a result of political and economic crisis within the countries of Southern Africa and the potential for such violence to diffuse across borders. Every country in the region, with the probable exception of Botswana, suffers from a mix of legitimacy conflicts involving reconciliation of enemies, political participation, economic distribution and competing ethnic identities. Regional security in Southern Africa will depend on how its component states resolve those conflicts. The economic and political crises in the separate countries of the region have an enormous potential to spill over boundaries. For example, one single reversal of the democratization process could throw the entire region into turmoil. Or an economic collapse in one country could place a severe burden on its neighbours and lead to conflict. This potential is greatly heightened during 1992 by the worst drought in a century in Southern Africa, threatening up to 40 million people with starvation before the end of 1992.

3. *Asymmetry conflict:* apart from the above-mentioned two conflict clusters, there is another overarching and potentially explosive source of insecurity in Southern Africa. It has to do with basic regional asymmetries, that is, the grossly inequitable distribution of economic and military power between the states in the region.

Either one of these kinds of conflict—overlay, diffusion or the emergence of manifest violence in the region as a result of economic and military asymmetries—will exacerbate two other conflict issues that already tax the capacity of the region and its states: *refugees* and *migrant labour.*

There are upwards of 10 million refugees in Southern Africa if internal refugees, such as the so-called "deslocados" in Angola and Mozambique, are included. Others are living in refugee camps in neighbouring countries. Three concrete problems in connection with the latter category can be identified.

— The refugees pose a substantial economic burden to the host country.
— Refugee camps have traditionally constituted an important recruitment ground for those who have an interest in turning the refugees into weapons against their country of origin.
— Refugee camps are fertile grounds for the spread of dangerous diseases, such as AIDS.

In general, refugee camps are volatile social entities, consisting of individuals that have been forced to abandon their natural habitat. The refugees are cut off from the normal instruments of social communication and they have limited access to information; therefore, they can easily be manipulated. Due to the general distribution conflict that characterizes all the countries in Southern Africa, refugees often become a target for the anger of the population of the host country. Similarly, refugees are powerful cards in inter-state relations, especially when the country of origin have problems in receiving repatriates.

Second, there is the problem of mass migration and migrant labour. Unprecedented rural-urban migration in many countries amasses people without the means of subsistence in the cities and siphons off those with most resources and initiative away from the rural areas. There is also another, and potentially more dangerous dimension to the migration problem. Migrant labour has always been a central building block in the regional economy. Expectations regarding a better life away from home have thus been built up around the region. If or when South Africa gets a government that is considered representative and legitimate in the eyes of the rest of the region, a mass migration movement to that country may well follow. The explosive potential in such a situation is obvious. On the other hand, protective measures from South Africa against such flows may create similar problems and tensions.

An additional dimension of the migration problem concerns braindrain from the rest of the region to South Africa. Semi-skilled, skilled and professional people are increasingly seeking a new life in South Africa. A substantial outflow of such people from the neighbouring countries to South Africa would be economically disastrous to the home economies and a potential conflict issue between that country and South Africa. As Alan Whiteside has pointed out, the cross-border migration problem may turn out to be a double losing game, and a highly conflictual one, for the labour-supplying countries: first, the new brain-drain flow will subsidize growth in South Africa and, often, expatriates will have to be hired as replacements at higher costs while, second, the decline in the flow of less qualified migrant labour will reduce money inflow and create higher unemployment levels (Whiteside, 1991).

In sum, the region is ripe with real and potential conflict that may threaten a successful search for democracy, economic reconstruction, stability and security. The chapter now turns to identify some key factors within the region that will be crucial for the future of Southern Africa.

DYNAMICS AND CHANGE IN SOUTHERN AFRICA'S REGIONAL SECURITY COMPLEX

In any discussion of change one faces the challenge of distinguishing the significant from the trivial. Southern Africa is currently in a state of profound change, but no firm outcome has, as yet, emerged on the horizon. The old regional security complex is in some form of transition, but it is impossible to say positively whether the on-going changes will result in qualitatively different patterns of regional interaction. However, in order to stimulate debate, some possible future scenarios for Southern Africa are outlined in the next section. They represent cross-section snapshots of some key dimensions within the region that will be of importance for the future of the Southern African regional security complex.

The first dimension concerns *domestic consolidation*. To what extent have the individual states of Southern Africa region succeeded in establishing and maintaining a healthy state-society relationship? This concerns patterns of interaction between the state and civil society and which are determined by the norms and capabilities of each. Such issues are directly related to the problems that these states face concerning political and economic reform. In a broad sense, consolidation concerns the development and sustenance of legitimacy on the national level. In Southern Africa, consolidation will depend on the outcomes of the on-going processes of transition in the region, with the South African one being particularly crucial. Figure 4.1 focuses on the number of countries which have reached a level of domestic consolidation that allows for setting some national goals aside in favour of regional ones or, alternatively, produces a perception of at least partial compatibility between certain national and regional goals.

The second dimension concerns what Buzan calls *regional patterns of amity and enmity* (Buzan, 1991:213–215). It concerns the absence or presence of fear between the states in the region. It has to do with beliefs, perceptions, norms and formal rules that guide interaction in the region. The more that the norms and rules provide a sense of mutual identity, the more likely it is that the region develops mechanisms of interaction that can compensate for existing asymmetries, reduce the negative impact of certain "hard" asymmetries and give more weight to non-conflictual or even integrative asymmetries. The presence of such norms may also offer more legitimacy and formal authority to regional organizations. Amity/enmity goes from strong enmity at the one end to strong amity at the other. Both bilateral and region-wide patterns of hostility and friendship must be taken into account. The central focus is on the extent to which national and regional identities are compatible or harmonized.

The third dimension concerns how the region as a whole and the individual states within the region deal with the basic problems of *unequal distribution of economic resources and economic power*. What mechanisms and vehicles of economic cooperation and integration are developed to address economic imbalances between the states of the region, without confronting national goals with regional ones? Can those goals be modified and made more compatible? Outcomes with respect to economic power contain two dimensions: first, the scale ranges from no regional integration to competing integration schemes to full integration under a common scheme, including the factors that inhibit such interaction and, second, those schemes of regional integration that would be compatible with each scenario are also listed in Figure 4.1. These schemes, discussed in detail by Østergaard, are Market Integration (MI), Neo-Functional Integration (NFI), Development Integration (DI) and Functional Integration (FI) (Østergaard, 1991).

The final dimension in the scenarios is how the states, and the region as a whole, address issues related to the *inequitable distribution of military power* in the region. Will the region be capable to address in an orderly and gradual fashion existing imbalances, inequities and threats in the regional distribution of military power? The focus is on the actual distribution of military power, but also on the mechanisms developed to prevent inter-state military violence. Outcomes with respect to military power refer both to the level of military domination or hegemony in the region and the organizational fora to deal with matters related to military security and military threats that are created.

Thomas Ohlson and Stephen J. Stedman

Figure 4.1. *Linear scenarios for the Southern African regional security complex*

Outcome / Scenario	Domestic Consolidation	Regional Amity/Enmity Patterns	Solutions to Unequal Distribution of Economic Power	Solutions to Unequal Distribution of Military Power
Annihilation	None	• Criss-Cross Bilateral Enmity • No Regional Identity	• No Integration • Breakdown of Existing Schemes • Limited Exchange	• Fragmented • All Against All
Immature Anarchy	Low	• Polarized Enmity • National and Regional Identity Incompatible	• Competing Schemes (MI) *vs.* (NFI/DI) • Integration Dynamics Restrained by Conflict	• Fragmented/Unipolar • Alliances
Hegemony	Mixed	• Indifference • Indifference	• Competing Schemes NFI, (MI) • Integration Dynamics Restrained by Inequality and Low Incentives	• Unipolar • Bilateral Security Arrangements
Security Regime	High	• Polarized Amity • National and Regional Identity Compatible	• Common Scheme/Compatible Schemes NFI, MI, (DI) • Sector Integration within EC-type Framework	• Unipolar • Regional Security Coordination
Security Community	Total	• Criss-Cross Bilateral Amity • National and Regional Identity Harmonized "Regional Solidarity"	• Common Scheme/Compatible Schemes NFI, MI, DI, FI • Trading Bloc • Self-Sufficiency Without Autarchy	• Unipolar • Regional Security Integration

FIVE REGIONAL SECURITY SCENARIOS

Figure 4.1 sets out five possible scenarios for future security in Southern Africa. In descending order of insecurity we call them Annihilation, Immature Anarchy, Hegemony, Security Regime and Security Community.[8] The scenarios are constructed in a stylized fashion on the basis of an assumed linearity between the four dimensions outlined in the previous section. This is done for reasons of simplicity. In reality, of course, the actual configuration of Southern Africa's regional security complex will represent a mix of some of each.

The *Annihilation* scenario would, on the national level, induce the implementation of classical power politics, based on military force. An important objective for those in power will be to try to liquidate all forms of organized resistance. One can envisage, for example, the South African security establishment re-asserting itself and returning to massive destabilization inside South Africa and in the region through the instigating and fuelling of so-called black-on-black violence in order to maintain white minority domination in the region. Similarly, one can envisage the coming to power of brutal, repressive military regimes in the present SADCC member states, basing their power on ethnic or other sectarian loyalties and leading to the breakdown of the nation-state system as we know it today in the region. On-going processes towards economic restructuring and liberalization would be interrupted and substituted with power-based command economics to serve the self-interest of rulers or a corruptive "smash and grab" mentality, either of which would make impossible any kind of socio-economic development strategy. On the regional level, this scenario suggests criss-cross patterns of strong enmity with few, if any, friendly relations and without any organizational or institutional crisis-management capability on the inter-state level. While national identity in this scenario is weak, perceptions of a regional identity is non-existent. Everybody will be the enemy of everybody else and military power will be so fragmented or, alternative, so bogged down with domestic strife, that no-one will be able to assume and sustain a hegemonic role based on military force. Formal economic interaction will be limited (though cross-border informal relations may flourish) and there will be no institutionalized economic structures or organizations on the regional level. In this extreme and Orwellian-type scenario, Southern Africa will face, if not annihilation so at least an almost uncontrollable downward spiral of perennial conflict, insecurity, massive violence, starvation, misery and environmental collapse.

The *Immature Anarchy* scenario entails an open-ended transition process in South Africa: the threats to the process from the extreme right would be such that a Nationalist Party/ANC-based interim government finds itself in a fragile situation effectively leading to a suspended transition. Progress towards democracy is thus blocked, but collapse is avoided. Some other transitions in the region fail and armed hostilities between rivalling groups on the national level occur in some instances. Domestic consolidation is, on average, fragile. Regional amity/enmity relations are more polarized than in the previous scenario, allowing for some alliance-building and institutional management of contradictions and disputes. The distribution of military power is still fragmented in the sense that no state can fully dominate the region (in South Africa's case due to the internal situation). The level of economic integration will be low, due in part to the existence of competing schemes and, in part, since the dynamics towards integration that do exist will be hampered by the level of conflict in the regional system.

In the third scenario, *Hegemony*, we would see an extended period of transition in South Africa with the National Party and the ANC gradually moving the process forward. Some violence in the transition processes of other countries will occur, but the level of consolidation would be sufficient to keep the violence within bonds. Amity/enmity patterns in the region would be characterized by relative indifference. Norms and value systems would be competitive rather than compatible both within and between states. The basis for subordination of national goals in favour of regional ones would be weak. South Africa would dominate the region, in both military and economic terms. Security arrangements would be bilateral, rather than multilateral. In terms of economic integration one may envisage the outline of the classical centre-periphery situation with a regional dominant surrounded by weaker neighbours. Incentives to market-integration schemes would certainly exist, but would be hampered by competing schemes and legacies from the past. The fundamental inequities within each state in the region and between the regional dominant and neighbouring states would continue. Due to the basic indifference in amity/enmity patterns it is conceivable that economic cooperation becomes based in actor-propelled functional integration of a mutually beneficial kind in certain sectors and between small groups of, most often, neighbouring countries. This would then be at the expense of region-wide integration along the lines of any of the existing schemes (SACU, SADCC, PTA) or a combination of schemes. Classes, ethnic groups, economic sectors and geographical regions in "underdog" positions within states would tend to become increasingly marginalized. This, in turn, would create a favourable environment for the return of authoritarian types of government in order to maintain domestic stability. The regional system would tend to be conflict-prone due to an absence of significant corrective or compensatory measures and, by and large, a perpetuation (possibly even a deepening) of basic structures of domination and subordination. Due to the many unresolved conflicts and the protestations arising out of basic inequities, the system would be unstable.

Under a *Regional Security Regime* we would see completed transition processes throughout the region. Domestic consolidation would be modestly successful, albeit still with fragile state-society relations in the most conflict-ridden countries, e.g. South Africa, Mozambique and Angola. Amity would dominate over enmity in regional interaction, but uncertainties would remain about what unites and what separates. The legacies of the past are here contained, but not eliminated. States will actively seek to cooperate to get away from the security dilemma and avoid war, through action and through a lowering of threat perceptions. A regional identity would exist, in that states see the value of imposing mutual self-restraint based in self-interest in security matters. Economic integration would take place within the framework of a common scheme based on market forces, but with some compensatory and corrective measures built into it. At the heart of the economic integration process, driving it forward and constraining it at the same time, one would find neo-functional perceptions of common interest on sub-regional levels.

Finally, and at the other extreme of the axis, we have the *Regional Security Community*. Here, national transition processes are consolidated and regional states will consequently be characterized by healthy and developmental tensions between capable states and vibrant civil societies. On the regional level, amity is strong and omnipresent. National goals co-exist in dynamic tension with over-arching regional objectives, much like the state-society relationship on the national level. A regional identity is formed around common norms and perceptions, and becomes entrenched through the support from both actors on different levels and from institutional or other structural set-ups. In general, regional interaction of all types is characterized by solidarity, based on an appreciation of the long-term value of common beliefs and a shared, regional identity. High levels of mutual confidence, transparency and security integration characterizes the military security relations. Military violence as an option to solve disputes would not come easily, if at all, onto the agenda. Military and economic interaction patterns are in this scenario formalized through organizations based in treaty-type agreements. These organizations are seen to be legitimate and have substantial authority. Economic integration would be advanced and based in a common, region-wide scheme incorporating elements of market integration, development integration as well as functional components.

THE LIKELY AND THE PREFERRED

These five scenarios are outlined on the basis of various more or less conceivable processes *within the region*. This means that the relative importance of the factors that will determine which particular version or mix of scenarios that eventually comes true for Southern Africa has been somewhat distorted. In reality, whatever future scenario that comes about in Southern Africa will not only depend on the peoples and governments in Southern Africa itself and the choices they make. It will also—as was noted earlier—be affected by events, processes and decisions taken by the principal actors in the international system.

On the basis of of the above, we table three opinions. *First*, that Southern Africa by April 1992 (immediately after the whites-only referendum in South Africa) reveals characteristics similar to those outlined in the second scenario, the Immature Anarchy Scenario.

Second, by the turn of the century, the Southern African regional security complex is most likely at, or on its way to the Hegemony Scenario. There are no substantive indications that the region will move towards anything more "secure" than that. The amount of current conflict issues on both national and regional levels, the durable impact of past conflicts and legacies and new conflicts on the horizon militate against the security regime/security community scenarios. The low conflict resolution capabilities within and between states, as well as the chronic lack of material resources and major crises of production in almost all countries also constitute serious obstacles. In addition, there is no positive writing on the wall with respect to decisive extra-regional financial support to Southern Africa being engineered in the direction of balanced regional development and reductions in basic inequities between states.

Two additional factors suggest that the Hegemony Scenario is most likely in store for Southern Africa. First, that scenario requires little more than a positive continuation of present trends. It will require peace in Mozambique, stability in Angola and an relatively orderly transition in South Africa. Over and above these basic requirements, it will come about if everyone goes on doing just what they are doing. It thus has the advantage of momentum. Second, it also has the advantage of the support of a large number of powerful actors, including the major western governments, international financing institutions, leading donors, major economic and political interests in South Africa, and important actors within the SADCC member states.

Third, it can be argued that a majority of Southern Africans (and others) would agree that a process leading towards the Security Regime/ Security Community Scenarios would be preferable. The objectively speaking most likely outcome does not equal the normatively preferred. The rest of this chapter is devoted to the following question: what could be a suitable path, pacing and sequence of events of a process leading towards the normatively preferred outcome?

CONFLICT RESOLUTION, SECURITY AND DEVELOPMENT: A NORMATIVE VIEW

Arriving at normatively preferred steps and their sequence is fairly uncomplicated. Regional security can only be achieved if national and regional identities can be harmonized around shared perceptions of mutual benefit and if authoritative organizations can be set up on the regional level to implement mutually beneficial policies concerning regional interaction. A prerequisite for this to occur is that patterns of interaction within states are steered by common norms and shared expectations. Institutions and organizations on the national level must enjoy legitimacy from national citizens. Domestic consolidation is needed in order to enable countries to harmonize national and regional concerns or to set aside certain short-term national goals in favour of more long-term regional ones. This, in turn, is only possible if military violence within and between countries is no longer seen as a legitimate way of pursuing goals and resolving conflicts. Warring parties must be satisfied with negotiated outcomes, so as to accept to resolve outstanding or future conflicts of goals and interests through non-military means. The normative three-step solution to enhance security, stability and socio-economic development in Southern Africa is thus as follows:

1. Top priority must be placed on ending armed conflicts and helping to insure against their recurrence.
2. Domestic consolidation must be attained through the development of both capable states and thriving civil societies.
3. Balanced regional cooperation in matters of socio-economic development and security must be expanded and institutionalized.

Progress towards the Hegemony Scenario predicted above is by no means irreversible. It is easy to see how the inability of some of the states in the region to cope with new internal conflicts, combined with different international (in)actions, could push the region towards the brink once more. Events could conspire to abort a new Southern Africa and result in unprecedented death and destruction: a back-slipping that may head all the way back to the Annihilation Scenario. Developments in South Africa, Mozambique and Angola figure prominently in whether the region can distance itself from such an outcome, and demand that priority be given to ending armed violence in Mozambique, and keeping the fragile cease-fire in Angola. But if we must point to one factor in determining the likelihood of an outcome along the lines of the Annihilation Scenario, it would be the military question in South Africa. Anti-apartheid proponents throughout the region and beyond have come to fear the lack of accountability of the South African security forces, their central role in constructing and defending the apartheid system and the threat that those forces so far have posed to any settlement that drastically reduces white political and economic domination in the region.

If, on the other hand, the violence ends in Mozambique, if the potential for recurrent outbreaks of violence in Angola, South Africa and elsewhere in the region is reduced, and if the armed forces in South Africa are tamed, then the probability of the region moving towards the Annihilation Scenario will be much reduced. Then it becomes more likely that South Africa reaches an internal accommodation that will protect its business interests and those interests will to some limited degree turn to the region as a whole to further its profits. Such a turn will likely be embraced by some within the region, but it will be at the cost of freezing present inequities and exacerbating severe distribution conflicts in the different countries of the region. To counter the Hegemony Scenario, a different regional programme will have to be articulated.

The ending of apartheid in South Africa does not mean that the people of Southern Africa will achieve dignity, justice, and basic human rights. The ending of violence in Angola and Mozambique will not in and of itself provide security for the peoples of those countries. However, most would agree that these must be seen as first steps. But first steps towards what? A number of major obstacles must be overcome if the region is to reach beyond Hegemony. The gradual expiration of old conflicts has—as already noted—given rise to new ones in Southern Africa, and one should not be over-optimistic about the ability of states within the region and the region as a whole to resolve them.

It will be incumbent upon the countries of Southern Africa to put their own houses in order, if they are to create a more prosperous and just region. Open conflict between embattled states and nascent, phony, rejuvenated or threatened civil societies must be replaced by a healthy and creative tension between states that can govern and societies that are autonomous, and organized to defend their interests. An important point must be made here. We do not subscribe to a simplistic interpretation of the recommendations often presented to African governments by Northern donors and money lenders along the lines of "straightening out state-society relations".

Pluralist politics, independent trade unions and other autonomous social organizations such as we find in the North are, indeed, atypical in Africa. This may be unfortunate, but it is nevertheless true. However, in order to enjoy legitimacy, the social organizations within civil society must spring out of that society. They cannot be top-down constructions or in any other fashion imposed from outside society itself. Democracy-building is a time-consuming, fragile and easily reversible process that has to be built from bottom and up. Meanwhile, many of the social organizations now emerging in Southern Africa derive much of their present momentum from "traditional" society, that is, the society whose power structure and legitimacy solved conflicts and controlled participation and distribution in pre-colonial times. Colonial authorities often only partially did away with these structures, partly to guarantee stability and partly to gain a measure of legitimacy to the colonial rule. Post-colonial, nationalist governments in Southern Africa frequently took steps to eradicate these structures completely, seeing them as obsolete phenomena and incompatible with true independence, nation building and modernization. The type of conflict this gives rise to in the context of current political and economic transformations—and the necessity of reconciling some form of modernization paradigm with elements of such traditional structures—will probably pose far greater challenges to states and societies seeking to build peace and stability than the relatively more simple introduction of market economy and multi-partyism. To begin to accomplish this, three processes ought to take place at the national level:

— states and societies must no longer view each other as adversaries in a zero-sum battle where what one gains, the other loses;
— states must be strengthened to develop the capacity to regulate conflict, social relations and economic activity within their borders, thus creating conditions for both individual welfare and national growth and development; and

— societies must be strengthened in order to hold states accountable and to facilitate market-based, socio-economic development on the national level.

Conflict resolution in the region will not be furthered by the visceration of state institutions and the singular celebration of civil society or market forces. The problem for the countries of Southern Africa is not simply to develop states capable of governing or civil societies capable of serving as a watchdog on state power, but to do both simultaneously in a compressed amount of time. This, of course, is much easier said than done. For the democracies of western Europe the process took centuries, under much more favourable circumstances. In Southern Africa, the challenge of marrying often weak or nonexistent norms, value systems and expectations to capabilities via organizations and institutions of implementation—that are often equally non-existent—is a formidable one.

While the development of stronger states and societies in Southern Africa is a necessary condition for equitable development of the region, it is not sufficient. An added step must be taken: regional interaction, mainly in the economic arena, so that Southern Africa can negotiate and compete with the rest of the world on a better footing. This is not only a question of economics, but Southern African regional security as a whole will obviously depend very much on regional economic developments. The inability of the countries in the region to overcome crises of production will reinforce the violence-proneness of the region's security complex. It seems an error, from this perspective, to argue for any quick-paced regional integration. For one, given the basic structural inequality in the region between South Africa and its neighbours, any integration at this time will most likely exacerbate existing inequalities. Sequencing and pace are all-important. If the region becomes formally integrated before the countries of Southern Africa get their internal houses in order, the likelihood is that the integration will only serve to crystallize and perpetuate South African economic domination of the region. Furthermore, it may lead to a volatile and highly unstable situation in which region-wide economic integration is taking place simultaneously with fragmentization processes, and quite possibly even breakdowns, within individual states. Instead, regional cooperation should be a product of more equitable development, with every member state enjoying the gains from trade and other forms of economic interaction to be made in the region. Regional coordination will be a common good if there is horizontal accountability between the states of the region. This can only come as the countries of the region increase their internal legitimacy, and work together to increase their leverage with South Africa. This is true for whatever outcome unfolds within South Africa itself. The chain of regional cooperation and integration is only as strong as its weakest link.

What would be the appropriate vehicles for such a process of regional economic integration between countries that are domestically consolidated? It is necessary to acknowledge existing realities. A future democratic South Africa will almost certainly join SADCC. The ANC has declared its support for such a move, and SADCC's willingness to accept a "South Africa free of apartheid and the dream of economic and military hegemony" is public knowledge. Does this mean that SADCC will be the appropriate vehicle for promoting non-hegemonic regional cooperation after apartheid? Certainly, it will have a central role to play. The principles SADCC has espoused will be essential if a regional order is to be constructed which is genuinely cooperative and non-hegemonic. A democratic South Africa's entry into the organization would be a strong symbolic statement of its commitment to such principles. However, concerns have been expressed in the region that SADCC's current organizational character and role have not proved effective in promoting cooperative regionalism, even among existing members. The loose, lowest common denominator-type organizational structure is increasingly being seen as a major weakness. Ibbo Mandaza has argued that the absence of a firm EC-type treaty has deprived SADCC of any serious capacity to lead the kind of integrative and cooperative process to which it is in principle committed. He has also suggested that the current focus on project cooperation "...is more likely to enhance the vertical integration (of the SADCC member states) into the northern hemisphere than promote horizontal cooperation among the member states...mainly because the projects themselves are either northern-initiated or almost entirely northern donor-funded." (Mandaza, 1991). SADCC itself has now acknowledged many of these criticisms and is in the midst of a process aimed at transforming itself. Its significance in the future could well depend on how successful it is in bringing about in practice the transformations it has itself called for. Certainly, any programme of cooperative regionalism which included South Africa would have to involve much more than promoting project cooperation. It would need to involve an integrated set of agreements covering, at least, trade arrangements, investment and capital movement, transport, water and electricity supply, labour movement, the establishment of regional agencies to jointly manage common facilities as well as the promotion of cooperation in a number of other spheres.

What then of the PTA? Again, the PTA could make an important contribution. Its experience in promoting non-foreign exchange-based trade could potentially contribute significantly to rectifying imbalances in existing trade patterns with South Africa as well as to promoting greater trade among current members. However, there are also a number of features of the PTA which have raised doubts about its effectiveness. The range and kind of countries it embraces is seen as too diverse. Is this really the optimum grouping among whom to promote greater integration at this stage? Does the PTA not in reality lump together countries which have historically been and should, initially at least, continue to be regarded as part of two distinct groupings: Southern Africa and East Africa? More significantly, the PTA has no strong mechanism for linking trade to other issues.

As far as the SACU/CMA is concerned, as Gavin Maasdorp has pointed out, all that would be necessary to transform the present customs union into a common market would be to allow free movement of labour (Maasdorp, 1990). Greater integration would thus immediately benefit those countries already highly integrated with South Africa and potentially contribute to finding an equitable, regionally-focused approach to the issue of migrant labour. A transformed and more integrated SACU/CMA could thus potentially benefit the "inner periphery", but it is scarcely applicable to other countries in the region, where, as we have already argued, a premature integration would tend to exacerbate existing imbalances.

All of this suggests that while all of the existing organizations (at least if transformed) could potentially provide elements of a new co-operative regional order, the need is for something greater than the sum of the existing parts. An institutional framework appropriate to promoting non-hegemonic, regional cooperation and integration in a Southern Africa including a post-apartheid South Africa would have to embrace all of the functions of existing bodies and more. It would also need to incorporate mechanisms to promote non-militaristic forms of conflict resolution. Of the existing institutions in the region, it is SADCC which has shown most awareness of and sensitivity to these issues. Its current reappraisal and restructuring, coupled with its stated willingness to work more closely with the PTA and other organizations seeking to promote regional cooperation and integration, offer perhaps the best hope for the creation of an institutional mechanism through which an equitable, balanced and mutually beneficial new relationship between a post-apartheid South Africa and the rest of the region can be negotiated.

However, it is important to take account of the lessons from integration ventures in general and from the SADCC experience, in particular. Three of these lessons are of paramount importance.

1. Regional cooperation and integration along the normative lines above will fail, unless they are preceded by a resolution to "the national question" in the individual states. Domestic consolidation is a prerequisite, even though such consolidation under certain circumstances can be facilitated by cooperative or integrative measures.
2. While an integration framework must be constructed on the level of governments, exclusive top-down attempts at the preferred type of integration are likely to fail. There are no automatic "trickle down" effects from the political executive to the level of economic actors and interest groups. Once conceived, regional integration must, in Østergaard's words "... be carried by the social and economic actors of the countries involved; it must flow from the bottom and up." (Østergaard, 1991:31). The central problem here—i.e. from whom at the bottom?—again illustrates the importance of solving the national question.
3. While the need for some form of market integration to take place is evident, it is equally evident that the normatively preferred scenario outlined in this chapter will not come about through market forces alone. Gradual change, careful and engineered pacing and sequencing of measures, and reasonable mechanisms to address the imbalances so as to reduce existing asymmetries will require the full attention of political executives.

Gavin Maasdorp has suggested a number of conditions that—if fulfilled—would be conducive to such a process (Maasdorp, 1991b:15–16). They are:

— The establishment of a supranational authority with real powers, ceded to it by member governments.
— A preparedness to counteract the tendency of manufacturing industry to polarize in the most advanced country.
— Broad agreement between members on the fundamentals of economic policy.
— Political differences among members should be containable.

Last, but not least, *there must be something in it for all.* The perspectives and medium-term expectations of key actors and decision-makers in this last respect is probably the key to any move towards something better than the Hegemony Scenario. As argued earlier, the power of momentum discourages integration efforts that seek balanced and more equitable development; it instead favours an expansion of bilateral agreements along functional lines. In such interaction, mutual benefits are more readily identified and more rapidly available.

Finally, on the more general issue of cooperation in security matters—with an emphasis on military security—much can be done to eliminate the currently high levels of insecurity in Southern Africa. For some years now, a discussion has been under way between regional politicians, scholars and foreign policy experts in the donor community over the prospect of embarking on a series of multilateral talks along the lines of the Conference for Security and Cooperation in Europe, the so-called CSCE or Helsinki process. Security cooperation is, of course, nothing new to the present members of the Front Line States and SADCC. Furthermore, one should not overstate the CSCE comparison. In many respects, the CSCE is far too elaborate for anything Southern Africa needs. In other respects, many of the problems in the region are alien to the European scene. Regional experts will know best which issues must be dealt with. However, a process involving South Africa and based on common values and norms regarding such notions as transparency of military establishments and force levels, exchange of information, confidence-building and mutual trust has tremendous appeal from the point of view of ultimately reaching a security regime in Southern Africa.

The idea of having different "baskets" or "calabashes" within the overall framework of an essentially economics-oriented supranational authority is attractive. First, it would be an excellent instrument for confidence-building and increased transparency with respect to armed forces, the quality and quantity of military arsenals, actual and perceived threats and threat projections, etc. Second, it could provide a useful framework for regional conflict management and conflict resolution. Third, it could provide the framework for an orderly, planned, coordinated and mutually agreed regional disarmament process, involving reduced military spending, force level and hardware reductions, and conversion projects. Fourth, it could, with time, contribute to such institutionalization that could further a process of equity-based regional cooperation and integration over a wide range of issues, including, but not only, economic issues. Conversely, dealing with economic and security aspects of cooperation and integration in the same framework could—if progress is made in the economic arena—contribute to reduced threat perceptions and, thus, lead to quicker reassessments and redefinitions of national security needs.

The proviso with such security cooperation is, naturally, that it does not take place in a general environment characterized by hegemonic ambitions. Military security, from the normative perspective used here, is something that—just as in the case of mutual economic benefits—must be analyzed and dealt with together with others, not against them.

NOTES

1. This paper makes extensive use of material from two of the chapters in Ohlson & Stedman, 1993, forthcoming. That book and this paper also draw on contributions from Robert Davies of the University of the Western Cape.
2. Buzan defines a security complex as "a set of states whose major security perceptions and concerns are so interlinked that their national security problems cannot reasonably be analysed apart from one another", Buzan et al., 1990:13.
3. For a discussion of the impact of global dynamics on Southern Africa, see Ohlson & Stedman, 1992.
4. In this paper conflict is defined as broadly as possible, so as to cover the vast range of conflict in Southern Africa. Among other things, it includes manifest (violent) as well as latent (non-violent) conflict; conflicts over values, interests and resources; subjective (goal-oriented) and objective (structure-oriented) conflict. Following Wallensteen, conflict is seen as a social situation in which at least two parties try to acquire the same set of scarce material or immaterial resources at the same time; see Wallensteen, 1988:120.
5. A detailed examination of domestic conflict issues is made in Ohlson & Stedman, 1993, forthcoming (note 1). Identity and loyalty issues are also discussed by Tostensen in chapter 7.
6. For critiques of these programmes see Packenham, 1973, and Huntington, 1968.
7. For an analysis that is sceptical of the conjunction of economic adjustment and political democracy as a sustainable programme, see Sandbrook, 1990:673–702.
8. The concept "Immature Anarchy" is borrowed from Buzan. However, we give it a somewhat different meaning, with Buzan's original concept being closer to our Annihilation scenario, see Buzan, 1991, (note 9), p. 175. "Security Regime" comes from Jaster, 1982, and "Security Community" comes from Deutsch & Burrell, 1957.

5. Post-Apartheid Regional Financial and Monetary Cooperation

Charles Harvey and Derek Hudson

The ending of apartheid, already under way, raises the prospect of South Africa entering into the full range of normal international relations, including various forms of economic cooperation with its neighbours in Southern Africa.[1]

This chapter analyses the case for monetary cooperation, and the various ways in which it might develop.

Originally, the English-speaking countries in Southern Africa used British currency, or, later, their own currencies linked very strongly with British currency through the Sterling Area. The only country in the region which has not yet issued its own currency is Namibia, which is about to do so.

Since the delinking of domestic currencies from sterling, there have at times been large and disruptive fluctuations in exchange rates in the region. Moreover, governments have changed their exchange rate policy, for example changing from market-determined exchange rates to pegged rates or vice versa, without consulting their neighbours. Despite these large short term fluctuations, real bilateral exchange rates against the rand have been fairly constant in the medium and long term. Rates of exchange against non-regional currencies have been determined mainly by South African policy, again without consultation with South Africa's neighbours.

This chapter first explains the existing exchange rate arrangements in slightly more detail, examines how they have worked out in practice, and analyses their advantages and disadvantages.

It then sets out various ways in which they might be improved in the future. The options analysed are:

— continuation of the present system
— some form of regular consultation on exchange rate policy, in order to prevent disruptive shifts in nominal and real bilateral exchange rates, perhaps using existing institutions, perhaps through a new institution set up for this purpose
— a more formal exchange rate mechanism, perhaps along the lines of the European Exchange Rate Mechanism (ERM), which obliges

members to maintain their currencies within agreed narrow bands, and with adjustments to the central rates undertaken only very occasionally and after consultation

Cooperation in the management of exchange rate policy could be seen as giving an undue advantage to the more developed economies in the region, South Africa and to a lesser extent, Zimbabwe. One way of getting agreement of the less developed economies to monetary cooperation would be to have a regional development bank with a mandate that would include preference for the region's less developed areas.[2] The next section discusses the arguments for a regional development bank and what form it might take.

Finally, there may also be a case for cooperation in international payments. The Preferential Trade Area of Eastern and Southern Africa (PTA) has already set up a clearing house. The PTA Clearing House is described in a section, which also discusses the possibility of its being extended to include South Africa and Botswana, and performing a regional role.

Finally the conclusions of the chapter are summarised.

FORMAL COOPERATION AND INFORMAL LINKS

There are two forms of monetary link in the Southern African region at present: formal and informal. The main formal link is very extreme, basically a one-to-one link with the rand by three small neighbours of South Africa. A minor formal link is the PTA Clearing House, but it handles only a small proportion of regional trade. Moreover, South Africa and Botswana are not members of the PTA. The informal link is not cooperation, but de facto tracking of the rand in the medium and long term, in real terms, by most of the other currencies in the region.

Formal monetary arrangements

South African currency was used in what are now Botswana, Lesotho, Namibia and Swaziland from the nineteenth century. This arrangement was formalised in the Rand Monetary Area (RMA) Agreement in 1974. Lesotho and Swaziland issued their own currencies which circulated alongside the rand. They received a share of the income from rand estimated by an agreed formula to be in circulation in their countries (seignorage).[3] Botswana decided not to join the RMA; it created its own central bank and issued its own currency in 1976.

Namibia announced soon after independence its intention to do the same.

The RMA agreement was renegotiated in 1986. It was renamed as the Common Monetary Area (the new name was supposed to symbolise an attempt to put the agreement on a more equal footing). After independence Namibia remained a de facto member of the CMA until arrangements to leave could be completed.

Lesotho and Swaziland have so far maintained their currencies at par with the rand. Swaziland has negotiated the right to revalue or devalue against the rand, but has not exercised it. Lesotho and Swaziland agreed to have no exchange controls in the RMA and CMA, and to operate the same exchange controls vis-à-vis the rest of the world as South Africa.

A second, but much less significant, formal arrangement is that those countries in the region which are members of the PTA participate in the PTA Clearing House, which operates from Harare. The PTA Clearing House plays a rather small, and at present declining role, in payments for international trade between PTA members.

Informal monetary links

Informally, those countries in the region which are not members of the CMA have maintained fairly constant *real* exchange rates against the rand in the medium and long term, but with wide short term fluctuations at times. This tendency is probably a de facto recognition of the dominant size and importance of South Africa in the regional economy. South Africa is the dominant supplier of imports (74 to 95 per cent) to Botswana, Lesotho, Namibia and Swaziland, as shown in Table 5.1; supplies 20 to 30 per cent of imports to Malawi and Zambia; and probably supplies a higher proportion of imports to Zimbabwe than shown in the table. Exports to South Africa are less important, because most exports were primary commodities which were sold outside the region on world markets; Swaziland and Zimbabwe (and to a lesser extent Botswana) were partial exceptions.

In some cases, for example Botswana, the maintenance of a constant real exchange rate against the rand has been one of the explicit objectives of exchange rate policy, although not the only objective (Harvey 1992:8–11).

In other cases, for example Zambia, the currency diverged substantially from its past pattern of a constant real value against the rand for a short period, but reverted to its former level thereafter, without this having been an explicit policy objective.

Table 5.1. *South African trade with selected neighbouring countries,*
         excluding gold

	South African exports (USD million)		South Africa's market share (%)	
	1984	1989	1984	1989
Botswana	552	1,021	78	80
Lesotho[1]	474	556	95	95
Malawi	109	152	40	30
Namibia	685	671	90	75
Swaziland[1]	315	431	90	74
Zambia[2]	129	175	21	20
Zimbabwe[2]	184	62	19	6
SA non-gold exports	8,878	14,937		
Share of neighbours	28%	21%		

[1] Trade with South Africa in 1989 estimated from share in 1985.
[2] Trade with South Africa in 1989 estimated from share in 1988.
Sources: IMF, 1986, *Directions of Trade Statistics Yearbook.* IMF, 1990, *International Financial Statistics (IFS) Yearbook.* Government of Swaziland, *Annual Statistical Bulletin, 1985.* Lesotho Bureau of Statistics, *Statistical Yearbook 1988.* Government of Botswana, *Statistical Bulletin 1991.* EIU *Country Report: Namibia, Botswana, Lesotho, Swaziland,* 1990.

This strong tendency for regional currencies to remain fairly stable in real terms against the rand over long periods, with shorter term fluctuations, is shown in greater detail in Figures 5.1, 5.2 and 5.3.[4]

Figure 5.1 shows the narrow limits within which the real exchange rates of Botswana and Zimbabwe fluctuated against the rand during most of the 1970s and the 1980s. The recent very sharp nominal decline of the Zimbabwe dollar has caused it to fall substantially in real terms against the rand. It remains to be seen whether the fall will be sustained. The Zimbabwe government appeared unlikely, at the time of writing, to reduce its budget deficit significantly; if that is correct, then domestic inflation will quickly erode most if not all of the effects of nominal devaluation.The collapse of the Zimbabwe dollar (it fell by some 50 per cent against the United States dollar in 1991) may have been necessary as part of the Zimbabwe government's adjustment strategy, but it created enormous problems for other countries, especially Botswana. Some two thirds of Botswana's manufactured exports went to Zimbabwe in the 1980s, so the fall of the Zimbabwe dollar made it difficult and in many cases impossible for those exporters to compete in the Zimbabwe market. It would be desirable for

Figure 5.1. *South Africa real exchange rate, Zimbabwe, Botswana*

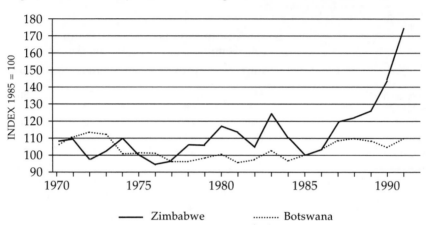

Note: an increase denotes a real appreciation of the rand against each currency, making
     South African exports less competitive by this measure.
Source: International Financial Statistics.

Botswana to diversify its markets for manufactured exports, but that
process needs more time than the speed of the Zimbabwe devaluation allowed.[5]

As can be seen in Figure 5.2, there was a sharp real depreciation of
the Zambian kwacha against the rand from 1985 to 1987, the period
when Zambia had a foreign exchange auction. However, the earlier
level of real bilateral exchange rates was quickly restored, by a combination of revaluation of the kwacha when the auction was abandoned and rapid inflation in Zambia.

The Malawi kwacha appreciated in real terms quite substantially
against the rand during the 1970s, but remained fairly steady in the
1980s. Although South Africa's share of the Malawi market fell in the
1980s, Malawi became more, not less dependent on South Africa
during this period because preferred transit routes to the sea were
cut off by the war in Mozambique. As a result Malawi had to use
South African transport routes for nearly all the country's international trade.

Figure 5.3 shows that when the rand depreciated sharply against
non-regional currencies in the early 1980s, Mozambique at first maintained the same nominal exchange rate against the United States dollar. As a result, Mozambique's real exchange rate rose steadily, against
all currencies including the rand. Mozambique did not devalue until

Figure 5.2. *South Africa real exchange rate, Zambia, Malawi*

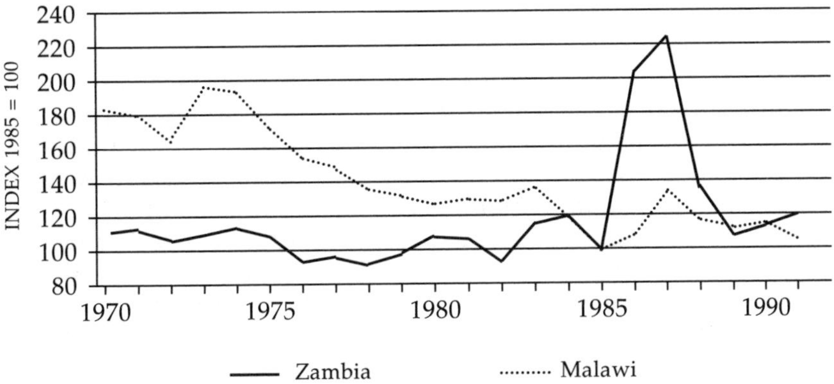

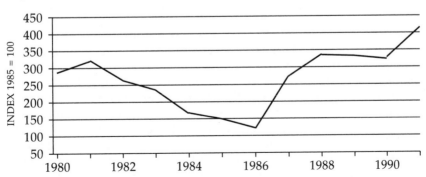

Source: International Financial Statistics.

1987, when the annual average cost of foreign exchange increased from MT 40.4 to MT 289.4, or by more than 800 per cent. This restored the earlier real exchange rate against the rand during the late 1980s, and in fact went further to give Mozambique a competitive advantage, by this measure.[6]

It would seem possible in principle that South Africa's neighbouring countries would be allowed to depreciate their currencies in real

Figure 5.3. *South Africa real exchange rate, Mozambique*

Source: Economic Intelligence Unit *Country profile: Mozambique* (various years).

terms against the rand, even though this has not happened to any great extent.[7] It is unlikely that the South African government would feel it necessary to retaliate against any one of its neighbours, in order to protect the competitive position of South African producers. None of South Africa's neighbours is large enough to force such a move by the South African government. It is not possible to give more than rough orders of magnitude of South Africa's direction of trade because published statistics are for the whole of the Southern African Customs Union. The potential error is large: official statistics show that about 4 per cent of South Africa's exports went to the rest of Africa in 1985 (after which no official direction of trade statistics at all have been published). On the other hand, South Africa's exports to seven of the countries in Southern Africa[8] in 1989, based on those countries' import statistics, were 21 per cent of South Africa's non-gold exports. This excludes any underrecording because of official sanctions policy and political embarrassment at being seen to trade with South Africa.

Even if the figure of 21 per cent is a low estimate, the market in any one of South Africa's neighbouring countries is too small to justify retaliatory devaluation by South Africa. The largest regional importer from South Africa in 1989 was Botswana, as shown in Table 5.1, but this amounted to only 7 per cent of South Africa's non-gold exports and 5 per cent of total exports. The industrial countries remained by far the most important markets for South African exports, taking more than half of non-gold exports. In addition, the continued importance of gold exports meant that South Africa's exchange rate policy had frequently to be used to maintain the profitability of the gold mines rather than to pursue other objectives (Kahn 1991).

In contrast, it seems unlikely that South Africa could achieve a lasting real depreciation of the rand against neighbouring currencies, because the neighbours would have to retaliate, if not at once, then within a year or two. South Africa is too important in most of the neighbours' foreign trade and payments for changes in bilateral exchange rates to be ignored for very long.

In addition to the problem of short term exchange rate fluctuations described above, the de facto link to the rand has meant that real exchange rates against non-regional currencies have been determined almost entirely by the policies of the South African government. As a result, the smaller economies have suffered from the effects of South African exchange rate policy where it has been wrong for the whole region, or where it has been right for South Africa but not for the other regional economies. In addition, even where changes in South

African exchange rate policy have been in the regional interest, the timing and speed of change have not necessarily suited all the countries affected.

For example, before its depreciation in the early 1980s, the rand was seriously overvalued against non-regional currencies. That meant that the currencies of other countries in the region were also overvalued, against non-regional currencies if not against the rand, with all the problems that that entailed. In addition the speed of the adjustment when it finally occurred created problems for other countries:

— imported inflation increased for those countries with high propensities to import from South Africa (see Table 5.1);
— the local cost of servicing foreign debt increased sharply, for both private and public sector borrowers;
— expatriate gratuities paid in local currency were suddenly reduced in value in the expatriate's home currency by significant amounts, which was unjust in itself and made foreign recruitment more difficult;
— and governments were unable, or were unable for some time, to capture a full share of the sharply increased profits of traditional exporters.[9]

The potential benefits, including a supply response to the sharply increased profitability of exporting outside the region, were slower to be realised.

South Africa's action was undertaken without consultation or thought to its consequences for the rest of Southern Africa; it may have been desirable for those countries in some long term sense to correct for overvaluation against non-regional currencies, but the speed of adjustment created some severe problems.

It does not necessarily follow that cooperation would be better than the present situation. Cooperation has its own costs; and might do no more than formalise the dominant position of South Africa in the region, without providing any real benefits to the smaller and weaker economies. On the other hand, the reduction of uncertainty in regional transaction, which would be achieved if exchange rate fluctuations could be reduced, would be of real value. There would appear to be a prima facie case, however, for investigating whether cooperation is a realistic political possibility, and for considering the form that such cooperation might take.

FORMS OF COOPERATION

Continuation of the present system

One option is that the present situation in Southern Africa could continue. It has been shown in the previous section, though, that there are serious disadvantages inherent in non-cooperation: a) large and disruptive short term fluctuations in nominal and real exchange rates within the region, and b) non-regional exchange rates determined by South Africa, without consultation or consideration of SADCC interests. In particular, the rand could again become overvalued without the neighbouring governments having any say in the matter. The post-apartheid South African authorities will be under great pressure to use government spending to try and achieve a wide range of political and social objectives. If this leads to budget deficits financed in an inflationary way, and is not offset by nominal depreciation, the rand would again become overvalued against the important non-regional currencies. The other countries in Southern Africa would then have to choose between maintaining a constant real rate against the rand, and maintaining competitive exchange rates against the rest of the world.

Inherent in the above analysis is the assumption that a new South African government, unencumbered by formal international obligations towards its neighbours, would be no different from its predecessor in acting in what it considered to be South Africa's own interests.[10]

On the other hand, it can be argued that regional cooperation on exchange rate management is impossibly difficult, that attempting to achieve it would not be successful, that the attempt would be costly in terms of the time of senior officials and in the ill-will generated by failure, and that the present "system" has yielded roughly constant real exchange rates in the medium and long term, de facto, at quite a low cost. Even such disruption as is currently being caused by the collapse of the Zimbabwe dollar could prove worthwhile, if it results in a recovery of Zimbabwe's capacity to import. It can also be argued that in the changed climate of opinion in the 1990s, it is unlikely that South Africa would allow its currency to become overvalued again, particularly if it is an active borrower from the World Bank and is influenced by World Bank advice as a result.

Regular consultation on exchange rate policy

An alternative would be an international agreement among the countries of Southern Africa requiring some sort of regular consultation on exchange rate policy, along the lines of the regular meetings of the technical committees of the Southern African Customs Union (SACU) or the monthly meetings of the OECD central bank governors at the Bank for International Settlements in Basel. The advantage of such regular meetings is not only the exchange of information and the potential for informal cooperation, but that the meetings take place without publicity precisely because they *are* regular. It is the nature of exchange rate management that any unusual behaviour among policy makers is likely to cause currency speculation; regular meetings would enable central bank governors to consult without publicity, in a situation where they would already be familiar with each other and with the issues.

If this process were successful, South Africa would become aware of, and might take some notice of, the impact of South Africa's exchange rate policies on SADCC interests. Similarly, the other members of the group would be in a position to consult over significant changes in their own exchange rate policies. This would be intended to prevent disruptive changes in exchange rates. For example, Zimbabwe might have given some warning to its neighbours of its intention to depreciate the Zimbabwe dollar, and might have moved less fast in order to allow the country's trading partners more time in which to adjust.[11]

There are various possible fora for such consultation. One possibility would be to use SADCC, provided that agreement is reached on South Africa's joining. Alternatively, the PTA has experience in negotiating reductions in tariffs, and might provide a suitable forum for negotiations on exchange rate policy.

The advantage of using SADCC is that it already exists and has an established secretariat. Civil servants, ministers and heads of state from member countries meet regularly, and are on reasonably good terms with each other. SADCC is able to work informally if necessary, which would suit what is being proposed under this option.

One problem of using SADCC is that Tanzania might see no point in linking its currency with the rand, even informally, since it has not traded at all with South Africa for many years. However, trade between South Africa and Tanzania is likely to develop rapidly; trade missions from South Africa have already visited Dar es Salaam. Alternatively, Tanzania could simply be excluded from cooperation on exchange rate management, which would be managed by a SADCC committee composed of the other member countries.

A second problem is that SADCC tried once before to get started on a study of the convertibility of its currencies, and found it a much more difficult subject than had at first been thought. That reflects reality. The potential beneficiaries of any monetary cooperation are not ready to give up the amount of control over their own economic policy instruments that cooperation would require; and their economies are far from the required degree of convergence in rates of inflation that would make cooperation relatively easy.

The other problem is that South Africa might not join SADCC. On the one hand, South Africa may not see any advantage in joining an organisation whose main objective has been to reduce its members' economic dependence on South Africa. On the other hand, existing SADCC members will remain worried about the economic, political and military strength of South Africa, even if a less hostile government is installed, because it is by far the most powerful country in the region. The existing members may want, therefore, to continue to plan their strategy towards South Africa in a SADCC without South Africa as a member.

The PTA has already expressed its strong support for the principles of monetary harmonisation among its own members. The monetary economics section of the PTA headquarters in Lusaka has been requested by the annual meeting of the PTA's Council of Ministers to find a way to achieve convertible currencies, stable exchange rates and no exchange controls, in order to enhance intra-PTA trade.

The ministers want answers from the PTA staff by December 1992, which appears wholly unrealistic. These objectives require several prerequisites. There would have to be a genuine desire, matched by considerable progress, among all the members of the PTA to reduce budget deficits and inflation. South Africa and Botswana are not at present members of the PTA; and there is an unresolved contradiction between the membership of Lesotho and Swaziland in both the PTA and SACU. So the future of SACU must be resolved before the PTA can be used as an instrument for monetary cooperation in Southern Africa.

It is interesting to note that the idea of merging SADCC and the PTA, first suggested by ex-president Kaunda of Zambia, is gradually gathering support. This would bring Botswana into the PTA, which would hopefully remove one serious source of friction between Botswana and Zimbabwe.[12] This has at times had significant consequences for trade and investment relations between the two countries. Trade is supposed to be governed by a 1956 Trade Agreement but recent years have seen import surcharges and disputes about rules of origin, and cross border investment from Zimbabwe to Botswana has been adversely affected by changes in Zimbabwean exchange control rules.[13]

A completely different idea would be to expand the functions of the Common Monetary Area, by creating two classes of membership and a broader set of goals. Full membership of the CMA would continue to be limited to those countries which had signed the original CMA Agreement. (Namibia would probably have left the CMA by then). Associate membership could be granted to countries which want to maintain a fairly stable exchange rate against the rand. It might appear that for this kind of arrangement to work, some superior status, even if unwritten, would have to be accorded to South Africa. This would be politically difficult for some countries. However, formal equality of status could be allowed to coexist with de facto recognition of the weight of the South African economy in the region; something similar has been reasonably successful in SACU and the existing CMA, and for that matter in the EC.

A European example of a type of associated status is the recent decision of some of the Nordic countries to peg their currencies to the ecu, even though they are not members of the European Monetary System (EMS), still less of the Exchange Rate Mechanism (ERM). Presumably, these Nordic countries believe that they can keep their inflation rates in line with those of the EMS/ERM countries, so that constant nominal exchange rates against the ecu will be consistent with the desired constant real exchange rates. There is also a strong implication that these Nordic countries are more concerned with their regional real exchange rates than with those against the US dollar and the Japanese yen. In fact, their relationship with the German mark, the unwritten senior partner of the EMS, is their most important concern. This is somewhat analogous to the position of the smaller economies in Southern Africa with respect to South Africa.

Whatever form of cooperation proves practicable, it is essential that the IMF and the World Bank be included. They have been the main influence on exchange rate policy in Mozambique, Zambia and Zimbabwe and are likely to extend that influence to other Southern African countries in the future. Yet the impact of their exchange rate recommendations on neighbouring countries has been virtually ignored. The Fund and the Bank should be obliged to consider the regional implications of their conditionality. Participation in a mechanism of regional co-operation would be one way of ensuring that they do so.

A more formal exchange rate mechanism

If it is correct, as argued above, that the countries of Southern Africa are not ready politically to cooperate more actively on monetary (or trade) issues, then it is even less likely that they can adopt a more formal system of exchange rate cooperation.

However, it can be argued that formal cooperation ought probably to be a longer term goal. It is not too soon therefore to start on establishing the legal framework. Some of the original statements of intent by the EC appeared at the time to be impossibly visionary, but they were necessary to start the slow process of movement towards their long term objectives.

Discussion of a more formal exchange rate mechanism for Southern Africa requires a brief look at the past history of some of the older and more formal exchange rate mechanisms in Southern Africa, as well as the relatively new ERM in Europe.

Monetary cooperation was not a problem when all the English speaking countries of Southern Africa were members of the Sterling Area. There were virtually no exchange control restrictions between member states; all the regional currencies had fixed nominal exchange rates against each other; borrowing pounds from the UK carried no exchange rate risk (nor did investing reserves in pounds); and no member state with its own bank notes could print unlimited quantities of them in order to finance a budget deficit, because all local banknotes had to be backed by solid assets in Britain and borrowing from a central bank was not possible. Inflation was low, so it was not likely that any one member of the Sterling Area would find its real exchange rate moving significantly against any other member's currency. Trade and travel were facilitated within the Area.

The major problem was that the British pound was overvalued against the US dollar for long periods. British decisions to devalue were long delayed, and were eventually made without considering the interests of the rest of the Sterling Area.

The French franc zone in Africa uses the CFA franc at a fixed exchange rate of CFA 50 = FRF 1. The right to borrow from the central bank is limited to 20 per cent of the previous year's tax revenue. Features of the zone include no exchange controls within the zone, the convertibility of the CFA Franc, and lower rates of inflation in CFA Franc zone countries than in the rest of Sub-Saharan Africa.

Although individual members of the CFA Franc zone have had annual inflation rates sharply different at times from inflation in France, overall their inflation has been lower than in the rest of Africa, and the macroeconomic policies required to achieve this have been shown not to have reduced the growth of GDP over what it otherwise would have been (Guillaumont et al, 1988). However, if individual CFA Franc zone members do need to devalue, they can only do so by leaving the zone.[14] As with the sterling area, CFA Franc countries have no influence on their exchange rates against other currencies they are determined by what happens to the French Franc.

The Common Monetary Area, previously called the Rand Monetary

Area also has real advantages, although, unlike the CFA Franc, the rand is not linked to a major international currency; nor is the rand freely convertible. Lesotho and Swaziland have been able to lower their real exchange rates against the rand, because their inflation rates have been slightly lower than South Africa's while they maintained fixed nominal rates of exchange against the rand.

The Central Bank of Swaziland has used its powers to keep the assets of Swazi banks invested inside Swaziland.[15] By this means, Swaziland has on occasion kept its domestic interest rates a little below those in South Africa. A small amount of interest rate variation within a currency zone is therefore possible.

The central banks of Lesotho and Swaziland have, over the years, negotiated the right not to have to keep all their foreign exchange reserves in rand. Because the rand has been weak against major non-regional currencies, they have made gains from holding non-rand assets rather than handing "their" revaluation gains over to South Africa.[16] In addition, the RMA Agreement made provision in 1974 for Lesotho and Swaziland to receive a share of the profits from the issue of rand, based on an agreed formula for estimating the amount of rand circulating in the two smaller member countries.[17] Swaziland withdrew from this arrangement in 1986 when the rand ceased to be legal tender in Swaziland, even though the rand continued to circulate; as noted above, it was officially accepted from tourists.

The gains to Lesotho and Swaziland of being in the CMA are those that derive from a stable rate of exchange with the rand, mainly reduced the risk in tourism, trade and capital flows between the member countries. It is worth asking whether Botswana, having chosen not to participate in the RMA, was better or worse off as a result. As it happens, Botswana is unusual among countries in Sub-Saharan Africa in the use that has been made of having an independent monetary system: the government has not abused its monetary independence by borrowing from the central bank;[18] and it has deliberately (and successfully) raised the nominal rate of exchange against the rand in order to have a lower rate of inflation than in South Africa, and has done this without raising its bilateral real exchange rate against the rand. Botswana's circumstances are so unusual that it would be wrong to generalise. In particular, Botswana's experience is probably not a guide to what will happen in Namibia; the prospects there are more worrying, because of the pressure on the government to spend more than is available from non-inflationary sources of finance.[19]

The experience of the CFA Franc zone and the CMA appears to show that there are some real advantages to foregoing some of the freedoms bestowed by having an independent central bank. It would almost certainly be more difficult to set up a formal monetary system involving several countries, than it was to continue an existing arrangement. Nevertheless, as already noted, it is worth starting now, rather than later, on setting up the formal arrangements.

DEVELOPMENT FINANCE INSTITUTIONS

There are a number of reasons for considering the establishment of a regional development bank:

— it could be used to favour projects in the region's least developed areas (as noted already, this could be a contribution to persuading some countries in the region to participate in a form of exchange rate cooperation)
— it would be a convenient way of chanelling donor finance to projects, especially projects involving more than one member country
— it could develop a valuable concentration of regional expertise
— if well-managed and successful, it would be able to borrow in regional and non-regional markets, and thus improve the quantity as well as the quality of development finance available.

On the other hand, the record of development banks in Africa, and in other developing countries is poor (Harvey, 1991: 271–83; World Bank 1989b: Ch 4, Ch 7). It would be essential, therefore, to establish an effective and efficient bank, either by building up an existing institution with a good reputation in such a way as not to undermine its efficiency, or by establishing a new bank with as many built-in safeguards as possible against it going the way of so many other development banks.

Two candidates which already exist are a) the Development Bank of Southern Africa (DBSA) which operates almost entirely within South Africa, in spite of its name, and b) the Eastern and Southern African Development Bank (ESADB) which has its headquarters in Bujumbura, Burundi. The DBSA has a good reputation (see below); the ESADB is at present more international in character but has less of a track record, and would have to set up a regional subsidiary for Southern Africa. It is probably not ready to do this; the following discussion concerns only the DBSA.

The most important argument in favour of expanding the role of the DBSA is its reputation for good management: being careful with its money, and demanding a high standard of performance from the organisations to which it lends. This was confirmed by a recent (internal) review.

On the other hand, there is a growing feeling at DBSA that staff need to devote more attention to continuous counselling of DBSA's clients, especially during the lifetime of any outstanding loan to the client. The DBSA management is being requested to allow a larger share of the budget to be spent on technical assistance to the DBSA's clients. This suggests that all may not be quite as well as implied in the previous paragraph.

If DBSA is "internationalised", with representatives of all member governments on its board, and additional branches in member countries, it may be difficult to sustain the strongly professional and technocratic operating record, and protect it from the political pressures that have ruined some other development banks.

At the moment, DBSA is almost exclusively a South African institution. It was formed in 1983 by the governments of South Africa and the four "independent Homelands" (Transkei, Ciskei, Bophutatswana and Venda) whose independence is not recognised by any other country. The four homeland members would either have to drop out, or be formally reincorporated into South Africa, before any other country would join DBSA, even though its constitution says that membership is open to all the countries of Southern Africa. DBSA management is fully aware that the initiative, to expand its role in the region, must come from those countries and not from the DBSA or the South African Government.

DBSA lends mainly to local-level development banks and non-government organisations (NGOs) that then onlend directly to customers, and to second-level governments, almost exclusively in South Africa. It has made one loan to the Lesotho National Development Corporation (LNDC) and one to a lending agency in Mozambique.

At present the DBSA gets all its finance from the South African government. If DBSA were to seek new sources of funding, from IBRD and ADB, from regional governments, or from international financial markets, it would have to develop new expertise. In particular, it would have to devise policies to handle the exchange rate risk of borrowing and lending in different currencies; at present both sides of the balance sheet are denominated in rand. Inability to handle this risk has made some development bank in Africa insolvent.[20]

A possible new institution

Another possibility would be to create a new institution, with or without some sort of link with DBSA, but probably with its headquarters outside South Africa. This might make it more acceptable to those countries which might be reluctant to accept a South African institution.

An expanded DBSA, or a new institution, should have:

(i)   agreed rules as to the allocation of credit between South Africa and the other countries;
(ii)   a mechanism for handling exchange rate risk;
(iii) some more flexible lending instruments than conventional loans, e.g. loans with repayments linked to project income, equity-type finance with limited rights of ownership or control.

The various ways of handling exchange rate risk in cross-border development banking are mostly unsatisfactory. If the government guarantees all risk on the bank's liabilities, the bank is encouraged to borrow hard currencies at low rates of interest knowing that the government will pay the (expected) cost of depreciation against the currencies borrowed. If the risk is passed to the bank's clients, they will find it hard to meet sudden large increases in debt service which arise from the large and sudden devaluations which have occurred in the region. On the other hand, if the government guarantees ultimate borrowers against exchange rate risk, the borrower is subsidised because inflation should increase the borrower's profits or income by the domestic rate of inflation; only devaluation greater than the inflation differential, between the domestic currency and the currency originally borrowed, exposes the borrower to risk that might be argued to be unacceptable. Similarly, if the development bank borrows in foreign currency and lends in domestic currency, thus taking the risk itself, it is both subsidising the bank's clients and taking an unmanageable risk—one that has made some development banks insolvent as noted already above.

This problem is not easily resolved, and has been badly handled historically; many development banks have behaved as if currencies were still stable against each other as in the 1950s and 1960s.

A very high proportion of development finance, both national and international, has been in the form of loans. Yet loans have fixed schedules of debt service, while projects, and developing country economies, have variable income from which to pay debt service. The need of projects in Africa (and elsewhere) for more flexible forms of finance as well as loans has also been badly handled (Harvey, 1983: 99–114). Projects which cannot repay either default on debt service payments, or have to reschedule their debts which is costly and damaging to their future ability to borrow. A regional development bank should therefore establish more flexible forms of lending, as well as providing a mix of equity and loan finance, from its own resources or by seeking co-finance in the form of equity.

INTERNATIONAL CLEARING MECHANISMS

The PTA Clearing House

The basic rules of the PTA Clearing House (CH) are quite simple:

(i) any trade transaction between two members of the PTA may be settled through the CH;

(ii) importers pay for their imports in local currency to a domestic bank;

(iii) exporters are paid for exports in their local currency by a bank in their country;

(iv) in order to account for this, the CH values the transaction in UAPTAs (one unit of account of the PTA = one SDR), according to that day's exchange rate of the currency of the transaction against the UAPTA; it then enters a credit in the books of the exporting country and a debit in the books of the importing country;

(v) after a two month trading period, the CH adds up the credits and debits of each member state, and produces a net plus or minus position for each member;

(vi) the debtor members must settle their debts with the CH, in hard currency, within two weeks of the end of the two month accounting period; this is normally achieved by calculating the USD equivalent of the SDR denominated debt, and transferring the appropriate number of dollars;

(vii) the CH then distributes the total hard currency that has been received, to the creditor members.

The basic concept behind the CH is of course that hard currency is not needed for each separate transaction, only for settling the net position after two and a half months. The importer cannot pay the exporter in the importer's domestic currency, because the local PTA currencies are in general not convertible. The exporter would not be able to use the importer's currency. The CH's primary goal is to supply liquidity to intra-PTA trade, by first utilising domestic currency as far as that will work, then resorting to hard currency at the last stage only.

If trade were evenly balanced among all the PTA members, then it would be purely random as to which countries ended up with net credit and debit balances, after each two month period. In practice, however, Zimbabwe tends to have a favourable net position; to that extent, Zimbabwe is giving a modest amount of trade credit to its fellow PTA members. This may be an acceptable price for Zimbabwe to pay, if the credit increases its exports above what they otherwise would be.

As things stand, less than half the eligible intra-PTA transactions do in fact pass through the CH at present. This is in spite of considerable publicity by banks, chambers of commerce, etc., and urging by central banks to use it. For example, Zambia preferred to be paid in US dollars when it exported electricity to Zimbabwe, in the hope that it might be paid faster that way. Somewhat perversely, the reverse may have been true.

It is an interesting question whether Southern Africa as a whole would benefit from a more broadly based clearing house. If South Africa and Botswana were to join a newly combined SADCC/PTA, South Africa would be the country with the largest net favourable trade balance, in place of Zimbabwe, and South Africa would thus be supplying some trade credit to the region. The risk to South Africa would probably be less than the current risk taken in extending credit to the weaker economies in the region on a bilateral basis; and the trade gains might appear to offset the cost.

As a footnote, the effect of large scale supply of aid in support of imports to some of the weaker economies in the region should be noted. For example, Mozambique imports more than five times what it exports; Tanzania imports are two and a half times greater than exports. The extent of aid for imports has produced a kind of balance of payments equilibrium. At the same time, however, large budget deficits have to be financed in large part by the banking system. The previous terrible shortage of (cheap if you can get it) foreign exchange has been replaced by a relatively plentiful supply of (much more expensive after devaluation) foreign exchange, while the private sector is being crowded out of access to bank credit. In some countries, therefore, it is local currency that is in short supply to finance imports, not the foreign currency.

CONCLUSIONS

The world is swinging back to wanting more stable exchange rates, after having abandoned them in the early 1970s. The advantages of floating are now seen as being matched and often exceeded by disadvantages.

However, the era of fixed exchange rates (with only very occasional realignments) ended because it was unsustainable when inflation rates diverged substantially. Establishing stable rates of exchange again will not be possible in Southern Africa until rates of inflation have converged. Discussion of monetary integration, although fashionable, is not therefore practicable at present in Southern Africa.

The CMA has worked well because Lesotho and Swaziland cannot borrow from their central banks and because the South African Reserve Bank has not lent to the Lesotho and Swaziland governments. The latter can only borrow on a significant scale, therefore, if they can convince commercially-oriented banks of their ability to service any borrowing. As a consequence, inflation rates in Lesotho and Swaziland have been much the same as in South Africa (in fact slightly lower) and the CMA has not been put under unmanageable strain. It is possible for a country or a local government to get into serious financial trouble without access to borrowing from a central bank (for example, Liberia, or New York City) but it is more difficult and depends on the foolishness of banks as well as the foolishness of governments.

Realistically, therefore, full monetary cooperation in Southern Africa is not possible at the present. Inflation rates are too divergent. Moreover, governments do not appear to be ready to give up their newly won symbols of independence: control over certain instruments of economic policy and the opportunity to finance budget deficits by money creation.

It has been argued above that even limited cooperation, for example to consult over and slow down the more violent exchange rate changes so as to give more time for trading partners to adjust, will be difficult to achieve. That does not exclude other forms of cooperation. There are possibilities for building on the success of the DBSA for example, and converting it into a regional institution, although the work of a regional development bank would be made much easier if fluctuations in regional exchange rates could be reduced, and for extending the scope of the PTA Clearing House.

Meanwhile, if inflation rates converge in some regional economies, they could perhaps participate in limited forms of cooperation on an ad hoc basis, one by one. If that proved successful, others would want to join the system and it could gradually become more formalised. That is very roughly what has happened in the EC. It is not at all easy or inevitable, but it is possible. It may become easier to achieve as the cost of the alternatives, and the gains of monetary stability, internally and internationally, become more apparent. Given the long term nature of improved cooperation, it would do no harm, and might be genuinely useful, to embark on the process of setting out the long term objectives of monetary cooperation at this stage, so that the framework is in place when it is needed.

NOTES

1. The chapter mainly covers Botswana, Lesotho, Malawi, Namibia, South Africa, Swaziland, Zambia and Zimbabwe. Angola and Mozambique are treated in less depth because their economic situation has been so dominated by war.
2. The EEC's European Investment Bank plays such a role.
3. Swaziland stopped receiving this income in 1986 when the rand ceased to be legal tender in Swaziland.
4. Note that Figures 5.1, 5.2 and 5.3 use different scales.
5. It should be noted that manufacturing employed three times as many people as mining in Botswana by 1991, and that with mining exports not expected to grow significantly, manufacturing exports were Botswana's best hope for further rapid economic growth.
6. Note that official Mozambique statistics did not record any trade with South Africa until 1988. Recent official statistics show that South Africa's share of the Mozambique import market rose from 12 per cent to 23 per cent from 1984 to 1989 (National Planning Commission, 1990).
7. Note, however, that Lesotho and Swaziland have had lower rates of inflation (12.8 per cent and 11.9 per cent) than South Africa (14.1 per cent) in the 1980s, with constant nominal exchange rates (one-to-one) so that their bilateral real exchange rates fell against the rand.
8. Botswana, Lesotho, Malawi, Namibia, Swaziland, Zambia and Zimbabwe.
9. For example, it was not possible to increase the taxation of diamond mining in Botswana because it was determined by a negotiated agreement.
10. The impact on the neighbours could, by luck, be beneficial.
11. Member countries could also consult with each other on tariff and non tariff barriers (NTBs) to trade. In principle, this should occur through the existing bilateral cooperation councils; but they are often ineffective. It is possible, but by no means certain, that a multilateral agency would work better. The PTA might be a convenient place to study tariff and non-tariff barriers, since the PTA has had at least some success at finding ways to reduce some of the barriers to trade between its members.
12. For example, some senior civil servants in Zimbabwe appear to feel they have been snubbed by Botswana, resulting in intense irritation.
13. The rule in question says that a company in Zimbabwe may only invest in another country if the company has the majority of its shares held by residents of Zimbabwe.
14. Mali, for example, left the zone in 1962, and rejoined in 1968.
15. CMA exchange control rules cannot be used to prevent transfer of money from Swaziland to South Africa; but the banking acts can be used to require commercial banks to hold their assets in Swaziland.

16. This is what used to happen when South Africa's foreign exchange reserves effectively included those of Botswana, Lesotho, Namibia and Swaziland.
17. In the nature of things it is not possible to know what the note circulation is in a small part of a currency zone. The formula in the RMA Agreement would have overestimated by a substantial amount the note circulation in Botswana, which became known after the Pula was issued in 1976; the formula for estimating growth in currency in circulation was also generous (Harvey, 1985: 3–4).
18. The government has had such rapidly increasing mineral revenues that it has large positive balances at the Bank of Botswana.
19. Moreover, there are reports of government intentions to borrow from the central bank as soon as it is established.
20. It has not always been the fault of bank management: the government of Uganda guaranteed the borrowing of the Uganda Development Bank against the risk of devaluation of the Uganda shilling; this guarantee was unilaterally withdrawn after the shilling was devalued from 14 to 70 to the US dollar in 1987.

6. The Effectiveness of Regional Transport Networks in Southern Africa—some Post-Apartheid Perspectives

Oliver S. Saasa

Both SADCC and the PTA have recognised the importance of regional transport sector development and have, accordingly, assigned it a special place in their institutional set-ups. In particular, it is maintained that no meaningful commercial and trade interaction is possible without carefully conceived and coordinated regional transport network. SADCC members are perhaps more explicit in their commitment. The development of this sector has received top priority since 1980. The Transport and Communications Commission (SATCC) was created as the implementation body of the sub-region's transport policies.

There is little dispute among Southern African observers that the prospects of the post-apartheid Southern African region's transport network should be understood in the context of the following:

— the nature of the region's past relationship with South Africa;
— the unfolding geopolitical stability in the region, particularly with the emerging peace in Angola and Mozambique and the hope surrounding the on-going negotiated settlement in South Africa;
— the cost-effectiveness, efficiency, and reliability of the region's alternative trade routes, including those in South Africa; and
— the technical and managerial issues that have characterised the sub-region's transport systems and the manner in which they are addressed.

Against the above background, this chapter examines the problems and prospects of the Southern African region's transport sector during the post apartheid period. Conclusions will then be made as to whether the 1990s will witness continuity of change in the region's transport policies and strategies. Particular attention will be paid to the issue of integrating the South African transport network into the sub-region's overall transport framework.

A critical assessment of Southern African region's main transport routes will be made in the next section. Then follows an analysis of the position of the South African transport system, to indicate possible areas of cooperation in the post-apartheid period. Finally, some general conclusions are made regarding the post-apartheid situation in the region's transport sector.

SADCC REGION'S TRANSPORT SYSTEM

Dar es Salaam Port Transport System

The Dar es Salaam Port Transport System consists mainly of a) the port of Dar es Salaam; b) TAZARA; c) TANZAM Highway; and d) the Malawi corridor link. The construction of TAZARA started in October 1970 with Chinese technical assistance and was handed over in July 1976 to the Zambian and Tanzanian governments, the joint owners. The TANZAM Highway was also constructed before the foundation of SADCC.

It is worth noting that TAZARA's viability is being threatened by the prospects of peace in post-apartheid Southern Africa. The January 1992 SADCC review of the transport sector, for instance, revealed that total transit traffic handled by the Railway System declined in 1990 to about 710,000 tonnes as opposed to 775,000 the previous year. This was in spite of the fact that 13 new locomotives were acquired for TAZARA during this period. Additionally, total throughput at the port of Dar es Salaam also decreased to 3.6 million tonnes in 1990, as opposed to 4.0 million tonnes in 1989, a 9 per cent drop (SADCC, 1992b:6–7).

There are several factors that explain TAZARA and Dar es Salaam's decline in cargo handling. Firstly, the cost-effectiveness, efficiency and reliability of the Southern routes have posed a threat to the competitiveness of the Dar es Salaam system especially now that the sub-region is increasingly becoming receptive to the South African government. Secondly, the Dar es Salaam system's peculiar technical, administrative and managerial problems have made this route generally uncompetitive in the light of the growing challenge from the south.

Thirdly, the Zambian government's decision in 1991 to openly trade with South Africa necessarily creates potential for an increased volume of the country's trade using the South African routes. Fourthly, Zambia's generally poor economic performance in the past decade and in the foreseeable future suggests that the country's capacity to export and import will be constrained. This would necessarily have an effect on the country's main external trade routes, including the Dar es Salaam system.

Beira Transport System

The Beira corridor's hinterland countries comprise Zambia, Malawi, Zimbabwe, Botswana, Zaire and Mozambique. At present, the port of Beira is the nearest harbour for the majority of inland SADCC countries. Up to 1975, the Beira port handled most of Zimbabwe's and Malawi's external trade while considerable volumes of Zambian cargo also passed through this corridor.

Total port throughput declined to 1.3. million tonnes in 1986 compared to 3 million tonnes in 1975. The deterioration in port facilities and the insecurity that characterised the Beira corridor explained the decline. However, with the rehabilitation programme and improvements to the port management system, a steady growth in cargo handling has been registered in the post-1986 period. The positioning of 12,000-strong Zimbabwean troops along the Beira corridor significantly improved the security situation on the route.

More recently, the railway traffic on the Beira–Zimbabwe line maintained its growth momentum in 1990 with a 30 per cent increase to 651,000 tonnes over the previous year. The recent acquisition of five new diesel-electric mainline locomotives on the Beira route has enhanced traffic flow. Meanwhile, the Beira port's total throughput also increased in 1990 by 4 per cent to 1.83 million tonnes (SADCC, 1992b:6). Until recently, one of the main restricting factors in the effective use of Beira was the depth of the port. Dredging has, therefore, been undertaken to enable the port to accommodate fully laden third generation vessels of 42,500 tonnes. This has resulted in a reduction of additional freight costs caused by long ship-waiting time outside the harbour until high tides came. 1992 registered the greatest gains from the on-going rehabilitation programme for the Beira Port System. The new multi-purpose and container terminal was finally commissioned in April. The terminal's capacity is now 100,000 TEU's handled per annum, or three times its pre-April 1992 capacity. Before the rehabilitation and expansion programmes were undertaken, Beira had a port capacity of only 2.4. million tonnes. This increased to 4.8 million tonnes as of April 1992. Table 6.1 shows the annual port capacities of the main SADCC ports, including Beira.

It is expected that from mid–1993 when the new oil terminal at the port of Beira is ready, 1.5 million tonnes shall be added to the Beira Port's capacity. The performance of the Beira railway also shows very good signs of sustainability. SADCC reported in 1992 that "the transit time has been reduced to a minimum, the line is being served with reliable diesel-electric locomotives and no sabotage actions have been encountered for approximately one year.... Provided that the neces-

Table 6.1. *SADDC annual port capacities in January 1992*

Port	Million tonnes	(of which POL[1])
Maputo	8.0	–
Matola	5.9	1.0
Beira	4.8[2]	1.0
Nacala	1.8	0.5
Dar es Salaam	5.0	2.0
Lobito	2.8	1.0

[1] POL = Petroleum, Oils and Lubricants
[2] Beira annual port capacity increased to 4.8 million tonnes in April 1992.
Source: SADCC, 1992, Transport and communication, Maputo, p. 4.

sary locomotive power is available, capacity of the line—even with the present 12-hour operations per day—is well above the double of actual transport in traffic bound for Beira, and more than three times the actual traffic the other way" (SADCC, 1992b:20).

Notwithstanding the above positive trends in the Beira corridor, a number of constraints still continue to affect the transport system. Several port-related problems come to the fore in this respect.

Firstly, regular maintenance dredging of the Beira port to facilitate the sustainability of a certain port depth has been crippled by inadequate funds. Secondly, the corridor's railway–port interface has been constrained by security considerations that have reduced operations to day time only. It has been estimated that such restrictions have reduced the corridor's capacity to less than 60 per cent. Thirdly, poor line maintenance has led to frequent derailments on the Beira corridor, a phenomenon that has compromised exporters' and importers' confidence in the route. Fourthly, the port of Beira is constrained by inadequate basic equipment such as grabs and forklifts, a problem that has led to costly long cargo storage time at the port. Fifthly, the war situation in Mozambique has affected the security of cargo through pilferage and damage at both the port and during transit.

A number of operational problems have also been reported on the Beira Port Transport System. These include (a) the high spate of vandalism to wagons due to the war situation; (b) long turn-round time for wagons; (c) the high wagon transit time due to inadequate motive power.

Finally, there is absence of an effective marketing strategy for the purpose of popularising the Beira Transport System. While one notes the existence of two organisations which deal with private sector projects (i.e. the Austral Group in Mozambique and the Beira Corridor Group in Zimbabwe) and their having included on their mandate the task of marketing the image of the Beira Transport System, it is still recognised in SADCC that marketing strategy weaknesses are still real. A detailed marketing study for the Beira Transport System is under way.

Maputo Port Transport System

This port system includes the port of Matola and serves Mozambique, Swaziland, Zimbabwe, Zambia, Botswana, Malawi and Zaire. Until the 1970s, the Maputo transport route was of great significance to Zimbabwean, South African and Zambian export trade, mainly due to its possession of specially equipped berths that handled agricultural products and bulky minerals. However, the volume of cargo that was handled by the port declined considerably from 13 million tonnes in 1974 to 4.4 million tonnes in 1978 (SADCC, 1981). This declined further to 2.5 million tonnes in 1985. The reduction was explained mainly by South African decisions to reroute transports through South African ports. The 1976 decision by the FRELIMO Government in Mozambique to close the border with Rhodesia led to a further decline in the volume of cargo that was handled by Mozambique ports and transport network. Thus, at independence in 1980, as much as 90 per cent of Zimbabwe's trade passed through South Africa (*Africa Business*, October 1980).

When the Limpopo line was re-opened in 1980, its condition had deteriorated to such a level that only limited traffic (mainly from Zimbabwe) could be handled. The railway line was also attacked by RENAMO. The Maputo Port's infrastructure also deteriorated during the four-year border closure. Thus, in contrast to the port's capacity of approximately 20 million tonnes during the early 1970s, this has declined to only approximately 8 million tonnes by January 1992 (see Table 6.1).

The harbour of Walvis Bay

The Port of Walvis Bay is particularly important to Zambia as an alternative route to her West European trading partners. As a result, serious efforts are being made to improve this corridor's cost-effectiveness and dependability. In September 1990, Zambia Consolidated Copper Mines Ltd entered into a two-year contract with Transnamib which facilitated the former's transportation of 30,000 tonnes of its copper per month via Walvis Bay. Much of this volume is being diverted from the Dar es Salaam Port Transport System. It is estimated that the Port of Walvis Bay has a dry cargo capacity of 2.4 million tonnes.

A recent study on the competitiveness of Walvis Bay route vis-a-vis Durban and Dar es Salaam revealed several useful ideas regarding the potential competitiveness of Zambia's newest alternative trade route (Ngwenya et al., 1991). Firstly, it was established that Walvis Bay could compete with Durban for road destinations north of Livingstone and Lusaka. Given the shorter road distance to the Namibian Port, land transport rates should be cheaper on this route, *ceteris paribus*.

Secondly, transit times for sensitive cargo are important in the assessment of route competitiveness. For Zambian cargo originating from Western Europe and North America, it appears that Walvis Bay has a definite competitive advantage over Durban. This is because Walvis Bay has a sailing time advantage over Durban of some six days from Europe and the United States. This means that goods from these two sources could be in Lusaka via Walvis Bay *before* they could have docked in Durban.

The trans-shipment from road to railway systems on the Walvis Bay route could entail considerable interruption of cargo transit flow. The magnitude of the delays during trans-shipment would, however, depend on the road-rail interface efficiency.

Walvis Bay's competitive advantage is at present being compromised by the poor road conditions on both the Zambian and Namibian side. Both the Zambian and Namibian governments, under the auspices of SADCC, are embarking on the up-grading of the relevant road networks.

Lobito Port Transport System

The port of Lobito in Angola is one of the best natural harbours on the West African coast with a wide and deep entrance channel from the Atlantic Ocean. However, the Benguela Railway has remained closed to regional transit cargo movement due to insecurity in Angola. The signing by MPLA and UNITA in May 1991 of a peace agreement to end the war in Angola facilitated the initiation of the Lobito Port Transport system's rehabilitation programme within the SADCC context.

The objective of the ten-year rehabilitation and upgrading of the Lobito Port Transport System is to provide adequate capacity for the region's future transport needs. It is hoped that the Benguela Railway will increase its capacity to roughly 3 million tonnes per annum. It is expected that Zambia shall direct at least 20 per cent of her export/import trade with Western Europe and America to this route if it operates efficiently. Currently, port-related problems are many and, unless attended to, threaten to compromise the inland transport advantage that the route has over most of Zambia's other trade outlets.

SOUTH AFRICAN AND SADCC ROUTES: A COMPARATIVE ANALYSIS

When the economic/market criteria are used for either cargo routing or infrastructural investment, the South African transport system seems to possess a comparative advantage in several important respects. Firstly, South Africa compares favourably in the Southern African region in terms of its extensive railway network. Of the 39,000 kilometres railway track in Africa, 23,000 kilometres (approximately 60 per cent) are located in South Africa and Namibia. Southern Africa possesses 65 per cent of the rail track in the region; about 58 per cent of the road network; and 60 per cent (in numbers) of the international harbours. The SADCC region, on the other hand, has only about 13,000 kilometres of railway network. South Africa dominates actual cargo handling. For example, "South African Transport Services (SATS) rail network handles a combined traffic volume of 172 million tonnes annually, compared to the total combined annual traffic or SADCC railways of approximately 25 million tonnes. The national railways of Zimbabwe accounts for about 56 per cent of total SADCC rail traffic. In the port sector, the South African port of Durban alone handles an average of 24 million tonnes, which is more than the combined SADCC ports throughput of approximately 10 million tonnes" (Ngwenya et al., 1991:97).

Secondly, transport links in the Southern African sub-region ties the SADCC states closer to South Africa than to each other. Indeed, during the 1980 meeting in Lusaka which witnessed the creation of SADCC, there was a recognition that "the dominance of the Republic of South Africa has been reinforced and strengthened by its transport system". Most of SADCC's land-locked countries are geographically closer to SADCC than South African ports. Estimates for 1987 showed that, on average, 33 per cent of overseas traffic (by volume) of SADCC's six land-locked states used the South African routes/ ports. Table 6.2 shows the disaggregated figures. In recognition of the above reality which worked against the SADCC objective of reducing dependence on South Africa, the regional group's transport sector investment has always received the lion's share of all total SADCC

Table 6.2. *Distribution of SADCC overseas traffic by volume, 1987*
(million tonnes/year)

| Country | Total | via South African ports | via ports in SADCC countries | | | Total via SADCC |
			Mozambique	Tanzania	Angola	
Landlocked states:						
Botswana	0.1	0.1	–	–	–	–
Lesotho	0.1	0.1	–	–	–	–
Swaziland	0.8	0.4	0.4	–	–	0.4
Malawi	0.4	0.3	0.1	–	–	0.1
Zambia	1.7	–	0.1	1.6	–	1.7
Zimbabwe	2.4	0.9	1.5	–	–	1.5
Landlocked total	5.5	1.8	2.1	1.6	–	3.7
Coastal states:						
Angola	11.3	–	–	–	11.3	11.3
Mozambique	1.7	–	1.7	–	–	1.7
Tanzania	1.4	–	–	1.4	–	1.4
Coastal total	14.4	–	1.7	1.4	11.3	14.4
SADCC total	19.9	1.8	3.8	3.0	11.3	18.1

Notes: Volumes of less than 50,000 tonnes per year have not been included. Amounts
include both dry cargo and oil volumes.
Source: Hanlon, J., 1989, *SADCC in the 1990s: Development on the Frontline*, The Economist Intelligence Unit, Special Report No. 1158, London, p.135.

projects. In 1991, for example, transport and communications projects
accounted for USD 6.6 billion out of the SADCC total of USD 8.5 billion, which is equivalent to 77 per cent of the total value of SADCC
labelled projects in 1991 (SADCC, 1992c:32).

One emerging reality is that while it was easier for SADCC to assign
traffic to particular routes on political and/or security grounds, the
changing geopolitical and market atmosphere in Southern Africa suggests that extra-political factors are more likely to determine the
choice of routes. In fact, even before the positive political climate in
the sub-region emerged, it has been evident that, to a considerable
degree, it is actually freight forwarders who ultimately decide on
which route and mode of transport are optimal for the particular con-
signment. In the emerging deregulated regional market, the role of
the private sector forwarders is likely to significantly alter the SADCC
region's somewhat sheltered ports and transport networks. The fact
that most of the region's dominant forwarders (e.g. Manica Freight)
are subsidiaries of South African companies could indicate that

SADCC corridors are to face stiff competition in the post-apartheid period. Equally fundamental is the fact that forwarders commonly prefer to operate on routes that guarantee them loaded runs in both directions. This means that, at intra-regional trade level, one would expect that the limited trade among SADCC states, estimated at roughly 4–5 per cent of their total trade, would bias forwarders' operations towards routes that connect South Africa with SADCC countries considering the substantial trade interaction, real and potential, that exists between these countries and South Africa.

The procedure of clearing cargo has also influenced the choice of route adopted by importers and exporters. Contrary to the common practice world-wide of using the negotiable *Through Bill of Lading* for the purpose of port clearance, SADCC ports insist on the production of both this document and the *Ocean Bill of Lading*. Considering that the Ocean Bill of Lading is carried by the ship captain and that these have been known to get lost quite often, it is little wonder that some SADCC ports have failed to clear cargo due to lack of sufficient documentation, a phenomenon that partially explains the congestion at some of the SADCC ports, particularly Dar es Salaam. Simplification of clearing procedures is, therefore, vital in a competitive environment.

In 1978, South African ports computerised their clearing procedures. Indeed, with the introduction of advance cargo clearing, this has significantly reduced the turnaround time. The computerisation of cargo clearing has also meant that South African transport agents such as Rennies and Manica freight (who have offices in almost all SADCC ports) have managed not only to monopolise the forwarding business but also to provide a much more efficient transport service in Southern Africa. In a situation like this, it becomes extremely difficult for the relatively under-financed and under-skilled SADCC transport agents to compete favourably with their South African counterparts in a deregulated regional market. (Cf. Abrahamsson, 1989).

Against this background, a reliable, punctual, cost-effective, and regular traffic system in the SADCC region is essential for the group to successfully compete with the South African network. The introduction of a competitive and efficient door-to-door transport system similar to what exists in South Africa is, in this regard, important for SADCC.

The competitiveness of Southern African ports is also compromised by the mode of payment used for their services. SADCC ports insist on payment in convertible foreign exchange *before* cargo can be released. This has resulted in long cargo dwell time at the ports. This condition is largely explained by the stringent foreign exchange control regulations and hard currency difficulties that bedevil some of the regional countries, particularly Tanzania, Mozambique and Zambia. The process of obtaining foreign exchange is slow. It is here where South African ports possess one of the strongest advantages over their SADCC counterparts. In the South African transport system, cargo representatives settle port and other relate charges in local currency on behalf of cargo owners who are billed and asked to settle the amount at a later time in hard currency. This leads to a much faster settlement of charges and a resultant quick flow of consignments, a phenomenon that is an important consideration in the choice of routes by importers and exporters.

The competitiveness of transport routes is also crucially influenced by the tariff rate structure that is used. For transit traffic, rail tariffs are usually based on distance although in South Africa, contract rates are normally negotiated. At this level, (i.e. transit tariffs), there isn't a significant difference between South African and SADCC-based operators. On the other hand, marked differences between South African and SADCC systems exist at the level of port cargo handling rates. The levels of port tariffs are influenced by the port's degree of mechanisation; labour productivity and cost; the volume of port throughput; and the level of government subsidy. Earlier investigations revealed that while tariff rates for low volume cargo have been roughly the same for the entire Southern African region, important differences do exist for high volume commodities where South African port charges are much lower than those obtainable at SADCC regional ports (SATCC, August 1989). According to recent SADCC revelations, "...the cost of imports through Maputo and Beira is approximately USD 25 per tonne higher than through Durban according to the average tariff" (SADCC, 1989a). The high SADCC tariff rates are also influenced by the method used to compute them. Currently, about 60 per cent of SADCC countries' external traffic is containerised cargo. Instead of applying a box rate for all the containerised commodities handled irrespective of the value of the contents therein, SADCC ports determine the tariff on the basis of the value of the commodity in the container (i.e. the commodity rate). Many ports worldwide now charge box rates for all commodities. Although South African ports also use the commodity rate, they have established realistic ceilings. Besides, unlike their SADCC counterparts, South African shippers usually negotiate lower tariffs (contract rates) with customers who give them business guarantees. All these considerations have made South African rail and port tariffs, on average, lower than those in the SADCC transport systems.

There are other constraints that have compromised the efficiency levels of Southern African transport systems. Border formalities, for example, have seriously affected full utilisation of the region's transport corridors.

EPILOGUE: CONTINUITY OR CHANGE?

Since 1980, the main driving force in transport infrastructural development (which includes ports, railways and roads) has been the declared SADCC objective of reducing dependence on South Africa. Using the "corridor principle", the SADCC states placed a high priority on their rehabilitation and new development projects. Considering the background to the region's geopolitical situation vis-a-vis the detested apartheid system in South Africa and its condemnation by the international community; as well as taking into account the South African government's destabilisation policies in the regions, it is understandable that SADCC adopted this strategy in the past ten years.

Available evidence suggests that very little has been achieved in reducing dependence on both South Africa and the world as a whole. A lot of problems still remain unsolved in the region's major transport systems, particularly in the areas of capacity utilisation of installed infrastructural capacities; numerous port-related problems; managerial constraints; poor maintenance of equipment; inadequate rolling stock; limited access to development finance; generally poor record of co-ordination among the various transport sub-sectors; etc. Even more worrying in terms of the declared desire to reduce dependence has been the growing dependence on foreign funds not only in the area of transport and communications (which has more than 80 per cent external dependence) but in almost all the SADCC sectors. The net result has been that projects and programmes that fail to receive donor blessing and support usually fail to take off.

It seems apparent that the unfolding scenario in the region suggests a departure from regional transport policies that are dictated by political considerations to those that recognise the region's changing market conditions. The market criteria would, thus, reign over political ones during the 1990s and beyond not only in terms of the importer/exporters' choice of transport routes but, equally important, with respect to the pattern of infrastructural development in this sector.

Out of necessity, the fact that one of SADCC's *raison d'etre* (i.e. reduction of economic dependence "particularly, but not only, on the Republic of South Africa") has been overtaken by events means that, for the regional transport sector, South Africa shall be integrated into any future considerations of donor support to the entire region.

In practical terms, several issues ought to be addressed in post-apartheid Southern Africa in the area of transport. Firstly, there seems to be an urgent need to re-orient the Southern African region's transport sector beyond the current regional concerns to encompass both continental and intercontinental perspectives. Many of the sectors in the Southern African transport system are assuming a transnational/global character, e.g. the shipping and aviation industries. Considering the fact that external trade in Southern Africa has very strong extra-regional links, mainly located in the West, it is important that strong linkages with the existing transnational transport networks are developed. The failure up to now by most regional member countries to sign the 1984 Multi-modal Transport Convention testifies to the abnormality of the present trend.

Against the above background, it is important to recognise that in order to reduce ocean tariff rates, for example, regional states, especially within the context of SADCC, should institute negotiations with representatives of world leaders in the shipping business, particularly those that own conference lines operating to and from the region. These include BEACON (the representatives of the North East Conference line) and UNICORN who represent the South East Conference. The latter is a South African company which is owned by Safmarine. Negotiations with Safmarine would greatly enhance the competitiveness of the SADCC ocean rates considering the fact that almost all coastal vessels that ply between regional ports on the eastern coast and those of South Africa all belong to Safmarine. In addition, Safmarine owns the region's influential forwarding company, Manica Freight, which operates in all major SADCC ports and capitals.

SADCC cooperation with global/intercontinental leaders in shipping and forwarding is justified not only on grounds of the emerging regionalisation and globalisation of the international transport system but also due to the fact that the small, largely primary exporting economies in the region are highly integrated into the existing global transport links. Simply stated, the transport policies adopted by the Southern African region in the past ten years of SADCC existence aimed at circumventing South Africa to such a degree that the relationships between the region's prime movers in the transport sector are at present too weak to meaningfully confront the emerging transport market challenges of the 1990s and beyond.

There are quite extensive inter-personal and inter-company contacts at the informal level between SADCC and South African transport operators.These relationships seem to be better developed than those under formal SADCC arrangements. This is in spite of the fact that the region's policies towards South Africa tended to be quite restrictive with regard to the facilitation of such commercial interaction.

It is also worth noting that South African transport operators appear to be more prepared for the emerging post-apartheid transport regime than their regional counterparts. The former are already making well organised advances into the SADCC region trying to "hunt" for post-apartheid transport partners. Spoornet (South African railways), for example, has been sending representatives to SADCC countries to discuss possible areas of cooperation. Recently, Spoornet visited Zambia and reached an agreement with Zambia Railways for a joint facilitation of a fast cargo service between Zambia and South Africa. Such arrangements should be expected to increase considering the fact that, according to Spoornet Chief Executive, Barry Lessing, "... in 1988 financial year, South African Railways handled more than 6 million tonnes of regional cargo. At any one time, more than 8,000 units of rolling stock worth R 700 million are on the railways of other countries" (*Financial Mail*, November 1990).

In view of the above, regionalisation of the Southern African transport sector calls for enhanced cooperation among operators and authorities in the area. Almost all the railway authorities in the region are currently involved in cooperative railway operations. In 1983, a committee on conditions of carriage for international traffic was formed and all countries in the region, including South Africa, are involved. What appears to be most urgent now is the need to prepare for the formalisation of a meaningful regional transport strategy for Southern Africa particularly in the following areas:

— the consolidation of the already existing frameworks in the road and railway transport sub-sectors, namely, the PTA Road Transit Regime and the Memorandum of Understanding on Road Transport in the Common Customs Area (for the road sector); and the Inter-Railway Conference and the SATCC Working Group (for railways).
— the need to reform the public sector of the region's transport with a view to allowing the private entrepreneur to assume an upper hand in its management.

This should entail a serious effort towards deregulation in a way that involves a shift from restrictive government controls to competition-enhancing facilitative policies and structures. The incorporation and privatisation of many of the regional transport sector's operational functions is necessarily an integral part of this process. The transport sector is largely controlled by governments in the sub-region. In this vain, "the transformation of introverted transport parastatals into aggressive privatized or quasi-public independent business corporations may convert some of these companies into the most powerful business entities in the region with the capacity and the inclination to exploit market power in key market segments. These entities need to be regionally regulated to ensure that they do not become monopolistic in their behaviour. Equally, there is a need to encourage inter-modal transport development on a region-wide basis to ensure effective competition and efficient resource utilisation." (Mistry, 1992).

Lastly, what is urgently needed now is for the SADCC regional transport corridors to correct the transit route and port-related constraints to facilitate effective use of existing infrastructure. Some of the solutions require technical/administrative capacity improvements. With regard to this last aspect, it is important to note that SATCC has placed too much emphasis on hardware investments (e.g. roads and railways) and very little attention has been directed towards such supportive software investments as management support. Donor support to SATCC, for instance, has been concentrated more on the provision of infrastructure rather than on a well-conceived programme of training the required manpower.

In the above light, it is crucial to recognise that for SADCC countries to become competitive and operate efficiently in the emerging post-apartheid conditions where market forces will significantly influence the use of regional transport systems, it is important that more investment resources are directed towards institution-building by way of developing competent and appropriate professional know-how and administrative capacity. In the light of the above analysis, one is left with only one conclusion regarding Southern Africa's post-apartheid transport policies and strategies: *Change* rather than continuity shall prevail.

ORGANISATION ORIENTED PERSPECTIVES

7. What Role for SADC(C) in the Post-Apartheid Era?

Arne Tostensen

More than twelve years have elapsed since SADCC was formed. The Southern African region has changed in many respects since then and is still in a process of rapid change. As a result, the question arises whether the observed changes of the past and the anticipated future changes are of such a fundamental nature that the role of SADCC will need to change accordingly. There is no simple and clear-cut answer to that question due to a great number of uncertainties and ambiguities. Nevertheless, some tentative answers may be ventured.[1]

The major changes that have taken place in the late 1980s and early 1990s include a move towards liberalisation of the economies of the region, in large measure under pressure from outside but also emanating from social forces within the states in question. Concomitantly, a process towards democratisation has been set in train, brought about through a combination of external pressures and internal popular struggles. It remains to be seen how deep it runs and to what extent democratic rule will be consolidated. Thirdly, signs of donor fatigue have become apparent, compounded by a diversion of aid funds to Eastern and Central Europe at the expense of Southern Africa. Fourthly, the international context has become gradually more adverse for Southern Africa e.g. in terms of access to markets in the North. Fifthly, in the 1980s a majority of SADCC economies performed poorly. Finally, the process towards complete eradication of apartheid has led to the end of military and economic destabilisation by South Africa directed against neighbouring states. There is now the prospect of a post-apartheid era emerging with a new democratic South Africa as a legitimate and equal partner in regional affairs. Although these changes are manifest, their implications for the future remain ambiguous. Therein lies a challenge for analysts and pundits.

The first section of this chapter deals with certain determinants of regional developments, including the unfolding events in South Africa as well as the international context. The second section discusses the relationship between the functions of regional cooperation and the accompanying institutional arrangements to perform those functions. The third section focuses on SADCC's own response to the new challenges as reflected in proposals for a formalisation of the organisation. The fourth section addresses the issue of rationalising existing regional arrangements such as SADCC, PTA, SACU and CMA. The fifth section directs attention towards the tensions inherently involved in regional integration between sub-national, national and supra-national levels. The final section addresses the problem of existing regional imbalances and disparities. During the editing period, a postscript has been added on the decision by the SADCC summit meeting in August 1992 to transfer the organisation into a *Southern African Development Community*.

PRINCIPAL DETERMINANTS OF REGIONAL DEVELOPMENTS

Before going into the specifics of the region, one should be reminded of the international context within which developments in Southern Africa unfold.

The international context

The international context[2] represents a major determinant of policies and actions on the part of various agents in the region. It sets the scope for action and may seriously be narrowing the range of policy options available to governments and other social actors. What is more, the international context is not only a backdrop against which local processes evolve. What is normally considered the international context is a social structure with powerful actors pursuing certain goals, thus making that context a dynamic one to the point of direct intervention in the affairs of Southern Africa.

In the economic sphere, the international trade regime is at once established under GATT auspices but still undergoing change through multilateral negotiations; the international market forces produce fluctuations in prices and sometimes alter terms-of-trade adversely for the economies of SADCC. The Bretton Woods institutions intervene actively and directly in the policy-making of individual states through the conditionalities of structural adjustment packages. These are but a few examples of the dynamism of the international context.

Another aspect of the international context of particular importance to Southern Africa in the current economic crisis, is the stagnating volumes of aid accruing to SADCC member states. This trend is partly due to a general aid fatigue which in turn is caused by economic problems in major donor countries being forced to cut aid budgets. A contributing factor is a diversion of aid funds to Eastern and Central Europe following the demise of the communist regimes. This tends to take place at the expense of e.g. Southern Africa since total aid budgets have been reduced or remain at the same level as before. Southern Africa has come up against competitors for aid from parts of the world where previously there were none.

The nature of a post-apartheid regime in South Africa

A second major determinant of future developments will be the nature of the post-apartheid government of South Africa. The internal struggles currently being waged may be monitored but it is exceedingly difficult to predict their outcome (Tjønneland, 1992, and Maasdorp & Whiteside, 1992, particularly chapters 10 and 12). Nonetheless, those outcomes will to a large extent determine the nature of the post-apartheid regime. The precise nature of a new post-apartheid coalition government is, of course, not yet known in terms of its social bases and the concomitant set of policies it will pursue. One can only speculate in probabilities. In theory virtually anything is possible. This is not the place, however, to go into detailed analysis of the many actors in the present negotiation process. A qualified prediction would be, however, that the post-apartheid regime will represent a fairly broad coalition of largely social democratic forces. The question then arises as to the type of social democracy that could be expected. This would be ultimately determined by the relative strength of the forces at play.

One may deduce from past policies and performance what are the regional objectives of the social forces whose interests are represented by de Klerk.[3]

Regional export markets and investment outlets, unfettered by political considerations, are clearly in the interest of most business groups, albeit to varying degrees. Southern Africa has always been and still is an important outlet for South African goods and services. The need to retain these markets is reinforced by the fact that large sectors of the South African economy are not competitive on the world market. Proximity to the region and already established trade relations, despite sanctions, make markets close by all the more attractive.

After a long period of regional destabilisation which has caused material damage in neighbouring states to the tune of USD 60 billion over the period 1980–88, the prospects for South African exports would appear good if viewed cynically in terms of the destruction caused. Leading business circles see an opportunity in South Africa changing its policy *vis-à-vis* the region from destabilisation to restabilisation and reconstruction. If capital can be secured from South African and international sources, South African business would have a number of comparative advantages.[4] A further precondition for such a scenario emerging is the political acceptability and legitimacy of South African businesses in the region to be earned through playing a constructive role. Ideas of a "Marshall Plan" for the region has been mooted with the Development Bank of Southern Africa playing a major role as a financial vehicle. Grander schemes of a Southern African Community has also been floated in a number of circles. One possible scenario of post-apartheid regional relations might be, therefore, the resurrection of the Constellation of Southern Africa States (CONSAS) in a new guise, this time cleansed of its former racialist content, though not necessarily resulting from a grand design. How *likely* that scenario may be, is open to question, however.

South African interests would most likely not be concerned about the wider economic and political context, in terms of regional disparities, of such a possible resurrection of CONSAS. Existing disparities, which are partly a colonial legacy and have since become further accentuated, could thus be reinforced and entrenched. A policy designed to bring about such a structure of regional relations could justifiably be dubbed a neo-apartheid policy.[5] A new CONSAS, brought about more as a result of the "spontaneous" dynamics of markets and political games rather than by design, would not only mean continued gross disparities. The very concept is based on a divide-and-rule principle. South Africa would assume the key position in the constellation and being linked in bilateral relationships to each of the neighbouring states, the former assuming a dominant position relative to subordinate clients. In such a structure the smaller and dominant states would relate to the superordinate state directly and only bilaterally, precluded from collective action among themselves. A *bilateralisation* of regional relationships would ensue. Thus the smaller states of Southern Africa would be weakened *vis-à-vis* their mighty neighbour to the south.

The regional policies of the ANC

The principal actor at the other end of the spectrum is the ANC. The crux of the matter, as seen from the point of view of the region, is the extent to which the ANC and its adherents will have a strong voice in the new foreign policy of the majority regime.[6] Not much has been said officially about ANC's position on the future policy towards the Southern African region. The issue was briefly touched upon in a discussion paper at a workshop on *Economic Policy for a Post-Apartheid South Africa*, held in Harare from 28 April until 1 May 1990. Following another workshop in Harare in September 1990, the ANC issued in

1991 a revised discussion document on economic policy. Although this document does not represent an agreed policy, it does give substantive pointers as to the direction of ANC economic policy in a post-apartheid situation. The section on regional relations has been somewhat rephrased and extended (ANC, 1991, pp. 15-16). Part of it states:

> A future democratic government should actively seek to promote greater regional cooperation along new lines which would not be exploitative and which will correct imbalances in current relationships. The new state must be prepared to enter into negotiations with its neighbours to promote a dynamic and mutually beneficial form of co-operation and development. While all of us stand to benefit from such an arrangement, it should be recognised that creating a new non-exploitative form of regional cooperation will require prioritising the interests of the most impoverished of our neighbours in certain areas, according to the principles of affirmative action.

Similar views have been expressed by Nelson Mandela on behalf of the "Leadership collectives of the ANC and the PAC" at the 1991 Annual Consultative Conference of SADCC in Windhoek, and by Thabo Mbeki, head of the Department of International Affairs of the ANC. The 2–5 July 1991 ANC Conference reconfirmed that membership would be sought in such organisations as SADCC and PTA as well as the OAU, the ADB, the Lomé Convention, the Non-Aligned Movement, and that relations would be re-established on a new footing with the World Bank, the IMF and the UN.[7]

The above quotations and references express in optimistic terms the friendly sentiments of the ANC towards their black brothers and sisters further north. But one needs to move beyond generalities and good intentions to the basic hard choices. In a setting of *"post-apartheid realpolitik"* how realistic is it that those intentions may be put into practice? Assuming that the ANC will play a determining role in a future South African government, its constituency will undoubtedly be inside the country. Pressures will be mounting for public expenditure on job creation, health care, education and housing to dismantle *real apartheid*. In order to preserve its political legitimacy the ANC will want to move beyond the mere eradication of *legal apartheid* and use its position in a future government towards that end. Coalition partners of the government—be they on the right or the left—may add to those pressures, although for different reasons. In such circumstances, will the ANC succumb or stick to its good intentions? Will it be affordable to make expensive concessions to neighbouring states in order to develop new non-exploitative relationships? These are real problems that are likely to face a majority gov-

ernment in the short-term future. The present author is not at all convinced that an ANC-dominated post-apartheid government will deviate all that much from the economic policies of the present government towards the region. A rather narrowly perceived "national interest", however defined, is likely to carry the day.

Regional interdependencies

On the other hand, a post-apartheid regime will surely have an interest in establishing new relations and in being seen to be breaking with
past patterns of extreme dependency and exploitation. Economic relationships are no one-way streets. Dependencies do not run in one
direction only. The RSA is up to a point also dependent on the region
and will need the region in the future.[8] To a degree dependencies are,
therefore, mutual and may best be characterised as *inter-dependencies*,
which are at present extremely asymmetrical. Although the principal
constituencies and sources of legitimacy are to be found inside South
Africa, a majority regime can ill afford to antagonise neighbouring
states by carrying on business as usual. However, pressurised from
two sides a post-apartheid government will face a dilemma and be
compelled to perform a difficult balancing act.

The new majority regime will have many benefits to offer the region. Several SADCC countries can be expected to draw benefits from
expansion of trade and other economic relations with South Africa.
For instance, Mozambique will, provided RENAMO banditry ceases,
in the short and medium term clearly benefit from selling electricity
from its Cabora Bassa plant to South Africa. The use by industries in
the Transvaal of Maputo as an export port will give Mozambique considerable transit revenues. Likewise, Lesotho will gain from selling
water and electricity to South Africa from the Highland Water
Scheme. Namibia also has a potential for electricity exports to South
Africa. And Botswana's Sua Pan soda ash project would not be economically viable without an export outlet to South Africa. The examples could be multiplied. The critical question, however, concerns
which party will stand to gain most in *relative* terms and *over time*,
even if both parties will derive *some* benefit in an absolute sense in
the short run. One must guard against further entrenchment of asymmetries in relationships.

The single most important benefit flowing from democratisation is
the end of destabilisation. Although this is not really the result of a
change of *economic* policy, but rather one of foreign and military relations, it may have profound economic repercussions on the region.
Peace and security will obviate the need for wasteful defence spend-

ing which could be diverted to productive purposes instead. However, doubts have been raised in this regard. The elimination of apartheid will undoubtedly remove the principal source of military spending, but in the post-apartheid era old suppressed conflicts may reemerge and lead to tensions deemed to require a high level of military preparedness.

FUNCTIONS AND INSTITUTIONS OF INTEGRATION

Given the objective of closer regional integration between all countries of the region, including a democratic South Africa, based on equity in the sharing of costs and benefits, the discussion should ideally start with the functions to be performed and thereafter the appropriate mechanisms required to achieve that objective. The case for regional integration is as strong as ever. African organisations have on a number of occasions reiterated the need for continent-wide integration but recognising regional groupings as building blocs towards the final objective of pan-African unity (OAU, 1991). There has been no lack of grandiose schemes and visions. However, when it comes to strategy and the practicalities of implementation, there have been serious weaknesses and, in effect, a lack of firm commitment to the stated goals.

The problem Africa is facing today, and *ipso facto* also Southern Africa, is how to relate to the plethora of organisations with integrative objectives that have emerged historically. These organisations tend to be resilient with entrenched vested interests in the preservation of existing institutional frameworks as ends in themselves, rather than looking at the appropriate functions to be performed and designing institutional arrangements facilitating those functions towards the stated objective of integration. Regrettably, some such organisations are competitive and even incompatible in some cases rather than complementary. Others overlap in terms of functions and membership to the extent of duplication of effort leading to wasteful use of resources which are much scarcer in Africa than most other places. Cases in point are SADCC and PTA. Africa can ill afford that; better husbandry of resources is needed.

There is clearly an urgent need for reviewing thoroughly and comprehensively the multilateral regional arrangements in Southern Africa with a view to rationalising the existing structures to make them conducive to achieving the purported objectives of them all: closer regional integration. Whether the outcome would be an amalgamation of existing institutions or a realignment of constellations in terms of membership cannot be predicted in advance.

If vested interest are allowed to sabotage the streamlining of regional arrangements in order to better serve the common long-term objective of integration, external actors may wish to activate themselves
in this regard. Although SADCC has emphasized all along the need
to become collectively self-reliant in terms of financing and personnel, the painful fact remains that SADCC is still heavily dependent
on extra-regional assistance. To put it bluntly, if donor support were
to discontinue abruptly, the implementation of the Programme of
Action would come to a standstill very fast! SADCC organs are very
aware of this and it is a source of serious concern to all involved. But
given the present economic crisis in most SADCC member states, the
repeated calls for generating a larger share of the resources locally
remain a futile exercise in exorcism.

Reinforcing the general aid fatigue observed in recent years and
the relative marginalisation of Africa and Southern Africa in that
respect, the donor community's dissatisfaction with the present state
of affairs may lead to new conditionalities regarding regional relations and institutions. The forthcoming democratisation of South
Africa serves to underscore this point acutely. Hence, in the new circumstances that are emerging, the donor community may wish to
impose conditions on continued support for regional integration
efforts, e.g. a thorough reexamination of existing regional arrangements with a view to rationalisation of such organisations as SADCC,
PTA, SACU and CMA.

It should be borne in mind that donors are facing constituencies
which are increasingly critical not only of existing aid volumes but
also of the efficacy of aid policy implementation. Northern governments cannot, in a spirit of accountability, afford to ignore such pressures from voters. When aid funds are dwindling, stricter prioritisa-
tion moves upwards on the agenda. Efficiency criteria tend to be
emphasized and applied more scrupulously. Relating these trends to
the Southern Africa context, many bilateral and multilateral aid agencies, have initiated studies to provide them with a basis for overhaul-
ing policies and adjusting them to a regional post-apartheid situation.

On the other hand, apart from the resentment which the imposition of such a conditionality may cause on the part of Southern
Africans, an additional problem may arise with regard to the dura-
bility of whatever solution would result. External conditionalities
amounting to a form of coercion are never preferable mechanisms of
inducing change. If changes produced by external pressures are re-
sisted by those affected, instead of being home-grown, the sustainability of the desired change may be brought into jeopardy. However,
there appears to be sufficient recognition within the region that pres-

ent arrangements are sub-optimal to say the least. A certain desire does exist in political leadership circles to engage in a rationalisation exercise. However, there is also some apprehension. The donor community may, accordingly, adopt a soft stance on this issue. Instead of taking a tough line on conditionality, the donors may wish to see themselves as a mediator, broker or midwife in a process allowing ample time for thorough discussion and consensus-building across the region.

FORMALISING SADCC

Originally SADCC was set up as a loose association of states with a common denominator and a shared geography. The member states were otherwise very heterogeneous in terms of economic size, political systems, foreign orientation and internal policies, and cultural characteristics. The very name of the organisation as a "conference" attests to the looseness of its structure.

Its institutions were deliberately designed to *coordinate* joint action. No supra-national powers were conferred on any organ. In effect, each member state was given a virtual veto right because all decisions are to be taken by consensus.[9] Observers have seen this institutional approach as a novelty and the hallmark of SADCC as a regional grouping. It has been considered successful because it is non-bureaucratic and pragmatic. Arguably it has served SADCC well in its first decade.

After twelve years have elapsed the time is ripe for reassessing the adequacy of SADCC's institutional framework in the face of the challenges of the 1990s. The theme document from the 1990 Lusaka ACC raises the issue thus (SADCC, 1990, para 2.11:6)

> ...the 1989 Summit meeting instructed the Council of Ministers to *formalise the Organisation, and give it a legal status.* The aim is to enable SADCC to structurally, institutionally and operationally respond adequately and effectively to the challenges of the 1990s and beyond.

The challenges referred to are those posed by a higher level of regional integration. As an organisation SADCC was established by virtue of a Memorandum of Understanding, which also underscores the looseness and informality of its institutions. Following the directive of the Summit a small working group of eminent SADCC personalities was appointed in 1989 to assess the options and work out a proposal, originally meant for submission to the Summit in 1990.[10] The terms of reference included a review of the institutional structure as well as the formalisation of the organisation in terms of international law by an agreement, treaty or charter.

It should be recalled that in addition to the objective of reducing dependence on South Africa and other extra-regional forces, SADCC also aims at "the forging of links to create a genuine and equitable regional integration". It is noteworthy that such an objective can hardly be achieved through mechanisms of loose coordination alone. In other words, there is a contradiction between this ambitious objective and the institutional tools that SADCC has at its disposal at the moment. The acuteness of this contradiction has been brought into the open in recent years, particularly as the organisation has moved into cooperation in production which requires harmonisation of macro-economic policies such as taxation, exchange rate management, licensing and price controls (SADCC, 1992d, Draft Report, para 6). There is a growing realisation among the SADCC leadership and further down the ranks of officials that time has come

> ... to advance SADCC's mandate beyond the facilitation of investment projects by each country, to the promotion of regionally coordinated and rationalised macro-economic policies and programmes. (...) What is required is to ensure that the various organs have the expertise and the *authority* to advance the cause of regional cooperation.

Highlights of the formalisation Committee Report

As it were, the working party on formalisation took longer time than expected and reported only in March 1992. SADCC's own institutional response to the changing circumstances is thus expressed in the report and proposals of this working party.[11] The working party has consulted widely in the region and arrived at the conclusion that SADCC be formalised by way of a treaty and thus become a legal personality in terms of international law. The suggested new name is *Southern African Development Community*. In addition a new declaration is proposed to replace the Lusaka Declaration of 1980.

SADCC's status as a legal person means that the organisation will acquire "capacity and power to enter into contract, acquire, own or dispose of movable or immovable property and to sue and be sued." (Article 2 of the draft treaty). Notwithstanding this new formal status, the working party has through its other recommendations sought to strike a balance, on the one hand, between the informality and flexibility of the "old" SADCC, and, on the other, a desire to give the organisation the necessary clout to move faster and more determined towards the goal of regional integration than has been the case in the past.

Perhaps the most salient new feature is the envisaged strengthened role of the Secretariat as the principal executive institution of SADCC (Articles 12–13). It will be charged with close liaison "with Commissions, Committees, Technical Units and Sector Coordinating Units and monitor the performance of the various sectors to ensure conformity and harmony with agreed programmes and projects." As the Secretariat is responsible to the Summit whose decisions are binding on member states, this new role for the Secretariat is the practical expression of a new element of supra-nationality in the mode of operation of the organisation. Nevertheless, the Secretariat may not act independently on its own initiative without consultation with and the consent of the decision-making organs to which the Secretariat is answerable. It should be duly noted that once taken, all decisions by the Summit or the Council of Ministers will be *binding* on member states. In accordance with this thinking the Secretariat has been proposed to be accorded more authority and resources to ensure compliance and effective implementation.

To be able to discharge this duty, it is envisaged that the Secretariat will increase its staff. In addition the Secretariat will appoint staff members to be deployed at the Sector Coordinating Units (SCU). This addresses a major problem of communication and liaison between the Secretariat and the SCUs since SADCC's inception. Although the SCUs will remain national entities, such deployment of staff will undoubtedly give the Secretariat more authority.

Since SADCC is proposed to become a separate legal entity and some of its organs set to increase in size and scope of operation, the organisation's budget will become more important. Article 28 of the draft Treaty states that member states shall contribute equally to the budget. However, the operational costs of the SCUs will be borne by the respective member states in charge of the sector concerned. The "equality" of contribution may become a source of friction. Is it fair that Lesotho contribute a share equal to that of Zimbabwe? An alternative approach would be to differentiate according to a set of criteria, e.g. GDP per capita. On the other hand, to be fair, one would then also have to look at the other side of the equation: the distribution of benefits.

Will this formalisation, if adopted by the Summit, make any difference in reality? Legal superstructures reflect the political consensus prevailing at particular points of time. Hence, if intra-SADCC power relationships change significantly in the future, the codified mode of operation as laid down in the Treaty may face tensions. Institutional structure does make a difference.[12] Nevertheless, one should be mindful of the limits of enforcing decisions against the will of some member states, even when legal instruments of supra-national enforcement are available. Therefore, the continued emphasis on consensus in decision-making is important. It means that SADCC will fall short of transforming itself into a fully fledged supra-national institution, because supra-nationality involves decision-making by majority vote rather than by consensus. By implication, it would also mean that it will still be difficult for powerful member states to assert their particularistic interests through the use of supra-national structures.

DIFFERING APPROACHES TO REGIONAL INTEGRATION

SADCC has been associated with a so-called development or planned coordination approach to regional cooperation which involves some measure of state intervention to steer the process in certain directions and to ameliorate undesirable effects. By contrast, PTA has been associated with a market-based approach to regional collaboration, leaving it largely to market forces to produce integrative processes. Whereas it may be helpful to make these distinctions from an analytical point of view, they do not necessarily conform to reality, particularly when considered over the whole decade of the 1980s. A tendency towards a convergence of approach has been discernible in recent years, although vacillation between positions has to some extent occurred. However, PTA has definitely been more interventionist in practice from the very start through managed and gradual dismantling of tariff barriers to create a free trade area. Due to the non-convertibility of currencies, the PTA Clearing House mechanism is indeed a form of intervention by virtue of necessity. For its part SADCC has in the latter part of the 1980s increasingly adopted a policy of liberalisation of economic policies, perhaps most clearly articulated in the theme document for the 1990 Annual Consultative Conference in Lusaka (SADCC, 1990). National programmes of structural adjustment being implemented by a majority of the states in the region point in the same direction. Similar views have been reiterated in the theme document for the 1992 Conference in Maputo although in considerably muted form (SADCC, 1991). The latter document rather distances itself from the market-based laissez faire approach to integration and stresses instead planning and management of the integration process. It appears that the approach of economic liberalism which has been in vogue in much of the 1980s is waning.

The same document recognises the need for new institutional mechanisms of a supra-national nature to enable SADCC to take decisions binding on all member states if progress is to develop along those lines (Cf. Chapter 8). In some respects the theme document preempts the formalisation proposals and seems to point in basically the same direction. Such supra-national mechanisms already exist within PTA, but in this specific regard the document makes no reference to PTA. However, the document is in no way oblivious of the existence of PTA and points out that urgent attention needs to be given to the issue of overlapping membership and functions, and the potentially conflicting obligations and loyalties of countries which are members of more than one integration organisation. This applies to membership in SACU as well, which is incompatible with membership in PTA. An integrative project pursued by SADCC will have to address the question of relations with, or impact on, activities undertaken within the framework of PTA and SACU.

It is surprising, therefore, that the draft report on formalisation of SADCC only treats relations with PTA cursorily. It is astounding that the report simply states that "...SADCC Member States feel comfortable that these Organisations can continue to exist side by side without prejudice to their main objectives." But the report does make a plea for avoidance or minimisation of overlap, duplication and waste. Towards that end "...a constant watch should be kept on the SADCC/PTA relationships—including regular formal and informal contacts between the two Secretariats." (pp. 37–38). Those statements seem feeble indeed in view of the magnitude of the problems!

The formalisation report is also conspicuously vague on the prospects of South Africa becoming a member of SADCC. It merely expresses a number of wishes and hopes, particularly as regards *equitable and balanced* integration, implying a certain apprehension but falling short of attempts to tackle it head on.

It appears that the formalisation exercise, as expressed in the draft report, has been conducted as a matter entirely internal to SADCC without due regard for the rapidly changing external environment. To effectively curtail the thinking about SADCC's institutional framework to the organisation's internal development, largely ignoring the challenges posed by the forthcoming reintegration of South Africa into regional affairs as well as the several overlapping regional arrangements, does not augur well for the regional integration project in Southern Africa.

MULTIPLE IDENTITIES AND LOYALTIES

Underlying the structural and institutional problems evidently thwarting efforts to achieve a higher level of regional integration, is probably the persistence of multiple identities and loyalties on the part of regional leaders and citizens alike. Modern societies consist of layers or levels of social organisation. At the core are individuals who through kinship make up families as the basic unit. In turn, nuclear and extended families form larger communities such as clans and nationalities with a common denominator in terms of norms, language and culture as fundamentals of social organisation, and normally inhabiting a specific territory.[13]

The state formations which are encountered today are political and legal constructs, which have resulted historically from a combination of traditional alliances, struggles and colonial imposition of borders and systems of government. Through these state formations nationalities have, partly by their own volition and partly by external coercion, entered into association within the confines of the modern state as we know it. *Ipso facto* contemporary African states are almost invariably multi-national state formations, even though the degree of heterogeneity may vary. Ever since independence in the early 1960s the governments of these multi-national state formations have sought to create even larger entities, inspired by sentiments of pan-Africanism propounded by leaders like Kwame Nkrumah. The foremost all-African organisation which still carries that ambition is the Organisation of African Unity (OAU). A multitude of sub-continental organisations have also been formed towards the same end, SADCC and PTA among them.

It follows from the above that all members of society have, or are expected to have, developed identities and concomitant loyalties not only as a family members; as clansmen; as members of e.g. the Shona, Bemba or Herero nationalities; but also as Zimbabweans, Zambians and Namibians; as well as Southern Africans; as pan-Africans; or even as cosmopolitans for that matter. Their relative strength and depth differ rather much.

Further complicating the picture are identities and loyalties not based on kinship, culture or geography. In economic, political and social life individuals enter into relationships which place them in certain positions which in turn constitute bases of identity and loyalty: Class, profession, religion, party etc. Some of these cut across other identities and loyalties.

Individual South Africans to varying degrees carry these multiple identities and loyalties concurrently. They are not mutually exclusive and they are not necessarily contradictory. As in a Chinese box they coexist. However, in certain situations, sharp conflicts may arise, not because of mutual exclusivity, but rather because in certain circumstances, one level of identification and loyalty will take precedence over the others. Which one is likely to prevail is contextual and may change over time. Only empirical investigation in concrete situations may tell.

Linked to these identities and loyalties is the critical question of legitimacy which will ultimately determine social action. Feelings of legitimacy are not exclusively based on facts but perhaps equally on perceptions and consciousness. People are inclined to be reluctant to lend support to a particular object of identity and loyalty, e.g. the state, if they do not perceive it to be working for their benefit. The family is close at hand and personal experiences of support are likely to guarantee loyalty. The "imagined communities" of nationalities are somewhat more remote, but nevertheless remain at the forefront of people's consciousness.[14] The state is even more remote as a point of identification and loyalty. The sheer distance to its centres of decision-making and its lack of transparency tend to weaken ties to the grassroots. It is difficult for a citizen at the local community level to identify clearly how state decisions and their implementation will benefit her or him. All the same, citizenship is certainly a widespread identity of importance.

An ambitious project of regional integration, e.g. SADCC or PTA, widens even further the distance between the individual and the centres of decision-making. Unless they are very well informed and highly conscious, citizens will find it virtually impossible to understand how decisions and actions at the regional level affect their grassroots condition. There are too many layers in between to penetrate. Following on this line of reasoning it becomes apparent that the level of regional consciousness is very low and exceedingly difficult to build up. In other words regional ventures tend to lack constituencies beyond rather narrow circles of political leaders. SADCC and PTA have never been orientated towards the grassroots. Hence, active support from below is not forthcoming; legitimacy is lacking.

Identities and loyalties cutting across cultures and polities may better serve as a source of regional cohesion and support. Trade unions and professional societies have elsewhere been instrumental in breaking down or at least weakening narrow particularistic thinking. In Southern Africa with a history of considerable labour migration since the 1880s, such organisational expressions of regionalism take on a particular significance. Although they have not yet managed to develop a grassroots profile, both SADCC and PTA have arguably been instrumental in the 1980s in furthering the forging of a regional consciousness, principally among bureaucrats and professionals.

Nevertheless, there is every reason to believe that, when it comes to the crunch in times of economic crisis, the narrow "national interest" of member states will take precedence, even among the above-mentioned "regionalised" professionals and bureaucrats as well as among the top leaders and politicians who have previously pushed the regional project so fervently. The state formations of the region are still young and their processes of state-building are incomplete. After all state leaders will, as a result, be more attentive to their constituencies at home. Consequently, if a choice has to be made—which is more likely to happen in times of crisis when resources are in short supply—state leaders will tend to concentrate on their home bases. It is far more difficult to redistribute poverty than wealth and to think regionally in such a situation is asking for trouble with the voters (provided elections are held regularly).

The argument presented here is that regionalism is hardly the dominant outlook in any quarters in Southern Africa. However, there is nothing strange about this being the case. The youthfulness of state formations and the shortcomings in building state identities make it perhaps premature to expect enthusiasm for regional ventures. Southern African states may be seen to be finding themselves in a pre-regional phase where a lack of serious commitment to regional goals is in evidence. Quite apart from the institutional arrangements for regional integration, this lack of regional consciousness may be seen as one of the main stumbling blocks in the current situation.

REDRESSING REGIONAL DISPARITIES

Closely related to multiple levels of identity and loyalty and their corresponding legitimacies is the question of regional disparities. As noted above, the perceived legitimacy of political arrangements, regional or sub-regional, is based in the distribution of costs and benefits flowing from them to those lower down in the social hierarchy. At the outset, the founder members of SADCC—and even more so those of PTA—as well as Namibia as the recent newcomer are differentially endowed with resources. That is a fact which cannot be altered. However, in promoting regional integration, utmost care must be taken to avoid reinforcing existing disparities whether they result from natural resource endowment or from human-made power relationships evolved historically. This argument applies *a fortiori* to a situation in which post-apartheid South Africa becomes a legitimate player. The future reintegration of South Africa into regional affairs will widen the range of regional disparities considerably and tilt the balance even more in its favour.

When discussing regional disparities and the need for redressing them, a distinction should be made between two sorts of justification for such a view. First, there may be a normative case, in its own right, for pursuing equity and fair distribution of costs and benefits, even if it is difficult to determine what is fairness given the unequal points of departure.

Second, disregarding the question of fairness, the equity issues goes to the core of the regional project. Even if the economically and politically stronger partners in a regional integration venture may see it as perfectly fair that benefits accrue to them in proportion to their size, economic base, resource endowment etc. and that the costs are assessed as a flat rate, other members may differ. But that is beside the point. What matters is that the stronger partners refrain from exercising their clout even to the point of forfeiting some of the benefits and carrying a disproportionate share of the costs in the short run. In the longer view such a "benevolent" policy would still be in the interest of those stronger partners. If, alternatively, the stronger partners insist on a "just" distribution of costs and benefits from day one without making any concessions, the entire regional venture may be in jeopardy. In the event of a break-up even the stronger partners would stand to lose.

The accumulation and entrenchment of disparities may serve as a basis for mobilising support for withdrawal from such arrangements. The smaller and weaker partners may feel they are getting a raw deal and opt out to avoid what is perceived—justifiably or not—as oppression and exploitation by the stronger partners. It may work both ways, however. Stronger and larger partners may over time feel that they are carrying too much of the burden and reaping too little of the benefits; in effect subsidising the weaker partners. As a result, those with a generous resource endowment and a relatively more developed economic base may decide to go it alone.

Recent examples of the disintegration of unions and state formations in Central and Eastern Europe have been accompanied by nationalist sentiments being stirred up and tending towards chauvinism, sometimes with ghastly consequences, the end of which we have not yet seen. Narrow nationalism, particularism or parochialism of one sort or the other may serve as a rallying point for all kinds of dubious causes. Nationalism is at once a progressive and a retrogressive force. Its ambiguity can, in the African context be exemplified, on the one hand, in the anti-colonial struggles of nationalist coalitions, and, on the other, in the break-up of a number of state formations by secessionist movements.

For the sake of a regional venture in Southern Africa as a variable-sum game in which all partners benefit to some degree, instead of a zero-sum game in which one player's gain is the others' loss, it is vital that redistributive mechanisms be built into the institutional set-up and that the stronger partners be made to see that short-term concessional policies will produce greater deferred benefits over the longer term than will insistence on reaping as many benefits as possible immediately.

POSTSCRIPT SEPTEMBER 1992

On 17 August 1992 the Summit meeting of SADCC adopted three important documents intended to transform the organisation from a fairly loose assemblage of like-minded states into a firmer and better instrument for regional integration. The documents include:[15]

a. Towards the Southern African Development Community. A Declaration by the Heads of State or Government of Southern African States;
b. Treaty of the Southern African Development Community;
c. Protocol to the Treaty Establishing the Southern African Development Community on Immunities and Privileges.

The name of the organisation was also changed to *Southern African Development Community (SADC)*.

Below each document will be treated separately although the bulk of the discussion is centred on the Treaty as the most important one of the three.[16] Only the main alterations from the original proposals will be highlighted in this postscript and differences will be emphasized. Cross-references will be made, as appropriate, to the main body of text above.

The Declaration

This declaration, which in the future is likely to be referred to as the *Windhoek Declaration*, replaces the Lusaka Declaration. Recognising that Southern Africa has changed considerably since 1980 and is still undergoing rapid change, the new declaration takes cognizance of new points of reference and departure (pp. 1–3). Special reference is made to current processes of democratisation; the imminent eradication of the apartheid system and the subsequent reintegration of a non-racialist South Africa into the region; the prospects for regional peace; the end of the cold war; and lastly pan-African initiatives as set out in the Lagos Plan of Action of 1980 and the Abuja Treaty signed in 1991. SADC is seen as a regional building block for a continental community. However, there is no mention of Africa's marginalisation in global affairs and what it may mean to Southern Africa that trading blocs are emerging from which Africa is largely excluded. The assumption about regional peace may be also somewhat optimistic, at least it may take some time to appear.

One may add that the shift of regional leaders since 1980, whether they have been of a generational nature or brought about by changes of political constellations, has probably weakened the leadership cohesion at the top based on close inter-personal ties and affinities.

Like most declarations it sets ambitious objectives and makes commitments by the signatories towards achieving those objectives. In reviewing the SADCC experience over the past decade or so the Declaration is rather self-critical, particularly with regard to the modest progress made in reducing the region's economic dependence and in forging economic integration (pp. 4 and 8). Notwithstanding this refreshing self-criticism, the level of ambition of the new SADC venture is not lowered. On the contrary, it is arguably higher. Furthermore, the scope is widened to include aspects of foreign policy in general as well as concerns of governance and democracy, peace and security. It appears as if SADC has taken on board the mandate of the Frontline States. Broadly speaking the Declaration lists three objectives for which a framework of cooperation will be worked out (p. 5):

1. Deeper economic cooperation and integration, on the basis of balance, equity and mutual benefit, providing for cross-border investment and trade, and freer movement of factors of production, goods and services across national borders;
2. Common economic, political and social values and systems, enhancing enterprise and competitiveness, democracy and good governance, respect for the rule of law and the guarantee of human rights, popular participation and alleviation of poverty;
3. Strengthening regional solidarity, peace and security, in order for the people of the region to live and work together in peace and harmony.

It is noteworthy that SADCC's erstwhile objective of reducing dependence on South Africa has been deleted in the anticipation that a post-apartheid era will be ushered in shortly. A majority-ruled South Africa will obviate such clauses although the socio-economic legacy of legal apartheid will continue to persist in the region as well as inside that country. It is a legacy that needs to be redressed.[17] Key words like "balanced" and "equitable" integration are indicative of the awareness of this legacy among the signatories.

The objectives are not only very ambitious and comprehensive, but also vague and general as befitting a declaration which is basically a statement of intent. Admittedly it goes some way towards specifying the objectives but not very far in operationalising them and in spelling out the ways and means by which they are to be attained. As far as institutional framework is concerned, the Declaration recognises that (p. 10):

> Integration will require mechanisms capable of achieving the high level of political commitment necessary to shape the scope and scale of the process of integration. This implies strengthening the powers and capacity of regional decision-making, coordinating and executing bodies.

Conferring such powers and capacities onto regional bodies will inevitably involve ceding a measure of national sovereignty. Aware of the sensitivity of ceding sovereignty, the Declaration interestingly couches this in positive terms: "Regional decision-making also implies elements of change in the locus and context of exercising sovereignty, rather than a loss of sovereignty." (p. 10). Time will show to what extent the constituent members will subscribe to this view in actual practice.[18] But it is of historical significance that statements of this nature are being made in Southern Africa.

The Treaty

In purely technical terms the Treaty establishes a new organisation. But in actual fact its adoption represents rather an amendment of an existing organisation. Basically the Treaty ensures the continuation of SADCC with some significant modifications in objectives and mode of operation. It would be correct to say that the new Treaty, referred to as the *Treaty of Windhoek*, supersedes the Memorandum of Understanding, which had been the formal basis of SADCC until 17 August 1992.

Beyond the statements of intent, sentiment, commitment and strategy contained in the *Windhoek Declaration*, the Treaty is the legal instrument in terms of international law whereby the Declaration is to be implemented. A ratification procedure, which was not included in the original proposals, requires that two-thirds of the member states, i.e. seven out of the ten current members, ratify the Treaty before it may enter into force (Articles 7 and 41).

It makes interesting reading to compare the proposed draft text with that of the Treaty actually adopted. Although many of the changes are mere rearrangements of articles, there are some notable differences, some of which may have far-reaching ramifications.

The principles and objectives of SADC are very ambitious and comprehensive. These objectives follow from the Declaration but are stated somewhat more specifically in the Treaty. As in the Declaration there is no reference to reduction of dependence on South Africa as an objective. A post-apartheid era is almost taken for granted in which closer but balanced and equitable relations with a new South Africa are envisaged. No attempts are made, however, at operationalising the objectives. For instance, SADC shall (Article 5):

> harmonise political and socio-economic policies and plans of Member States; (...) [and] develop policies aimed at the progressive elimination of obstacles to the free movement of capital and labour, goods and services, and of the peoples of the Region generally, among Member States;

In effect, this means a fully-fledged economic union with free movement of the factors of production and harmonisation of economic policies. Given this high level of ambition it is noteworthy that no time horizon is indicated for the realisation of the multiplicity of objectives. Nor are there any suggestions as to the approach to integration which the organisation will adopt. These omissions may be interpreted to mean patience in terms of integration tempo and pragmatism in terms of approach, more or less along the lines of practice to date. But at any time the Summit will, of course, be at liberty to take decisions otherwise. It is likely that such issues were discussed at the Windhoek Summit and Council of Ministers' meetings, to which the public did not have access.

The Treaty lists seven areas of cooperation which are arranged differently from the current allocation of sectoral responsibilities to member states (Article 21):

a. food security, land and agriculture;
b. infrastructure and services;
c. industry, trade, investment and finance;
d. human resources development, science and technology;
e. natural resources and environment;
f. social welfare, information and culture; and
g. politics, diplomacy, international relations, peace and security.

These areas of cooperation subsume existing ones, but points (f) and (g) contain new elements. In the past social welfare (e.g. general education and health) has been seen as a domain for action at the national level. International relations in a broad sense represent a widening of the scope of the organisation to the effect that the erstwhile preserve of the Frontline States is taken on board. It should be noted that point (g) in the original proposal by the formalisation committee included only peace and security. The terms *politics, diplomacy, international relations* have been added subsequently.

The stated objectives are to be achieved through the implementation of programmes and projects within a conducive policy framework. The institutions of SADC will be charged with implementation in tandem with national institutions of the individual member states. Consequently, the appropriateness and efficiency of the institutional framework will be critical.

It is significant that the organisation has now, by virtue of the adoption of the Treaty, been formalised in terms of international law. SADC has become a legal person which may enter into contract, acquire, own and dispose of property, and to sue and be sued. In its new separate identity SADC may, provided consensus may be arrived at in the meetings of the Summit and the Council, act on behalf of its member states. Thus, SADC's organs would facilitate and promote a more determined and speedier process towards regional integration. Such were presumably the thinking of the formalisation committee. However, the powers proposed to be conferred on SADC's decision-making bodies have been modified in the articles of the adopted Treaty.

The authority accorded the Secretariat in the original proposals have been substantially curtailed.[19] This comes out most clearly in the relationship between the Secretariat and the Sector Coordinating Units (SCUs). Whereas the original proposals suggested that the Secretariat appoint and deploy staff at the various SCUs, the proposed articles 17 on Sectoral Ministerial Committees, 19 on SCUs and 20 on National and Sectoral Contact Points have been deleted altogether from the adopted Treaty.

It appears that the member states have, at the end of the day, found it risky to allow the Secretariat too widely discretionary powers to take initiatives on its own and too much authority to direct the organisation's total activities.

As a matter of formality it may be correct that the Sector Coordinating Units are excluded from the articles of the Treaty. Strictly speaking they are not part of the institutional framework of SADC. Although the SCUs are technically national units under the auspices of line ministries of those individual member states that are responsible for coordination of specific sectors, they are critical to the functioning of SADC as an organisation, of which they are a vital part organically if not legally. Against the backdrop that the weakness of the SCUs to date has been a recognised problem of major proportions for the progress of the organisation, it is surprising that the Treaty seems to fail to address this problem.

It is disturbing that the SCUs are neglected in the Treaty. As a matter of fact it is the work of the SCUs which in practice will determine the success or failure of SADC, unless they are all meant to be upgraded to Commissions shortly after the Treaty has been ratified and entered into force.

The main institutions of SADC will remain basically the same as those of SADCC. But there are some amendments regarding their mode of operation and an addition, a Tribunal. With respect to the Summit there is one significant alteration. Article 10 on the Summit reiterates that it will be the supreme policy-making institution of SADC. Its decisions shall be by consensus, *and shall be binding* (Article 10). The latter provision was included already in the proposal of the formalisation committee. To make this an explicit provision is something new, and signifies a movement towards supra-nationality of a kind. It drives home to the member states that the organisation is serious about enforcing consensus decisions.

Article 11 on the Council does not contain the same provision regarding *binding* consensus decisions, despite the fact that it was proposed by the formalisation committee It is probably meant to underscore the supreme authority of the Summit relative to the Council. However, in the day to day operation of the organisation the Council plays a more important role.

The Tribunal is a novelty. The loose nature of SADCC based on consensus decisions across the board did not require a mechanism for adjudication upon conflicts. Such conflicts were unlikely to arise. That situation is now seen to be changing. Although the principle of consensus decision-making is still upheld, the very formalisation of the organisation in terms of the Treaty and increased stress on enforcement of *binding* decision may cause conflicts to emerge with respect to the interpretation of legal provisions and concomitant decisions by organs of the organisation. Hence, the need for a Tribunal.

Disputes which may not be settled amicably may be referred to the Tribunal for adjudication. It is unclear whether the Tribunal will have authority to intervene in disputes even when they are not referred to it by either party or by any organ of SADC. The specifics of its composition, powers, functions and procedures shall be prescribed in a separate protocol adopted by the Summit.

The Summit and the Council may request advisory opinion from the Tribunal. But the rulings in disputes referred to the Tribunal shall be *final and binding* (Article 16). There is no recourse to appeal.

Another mechanism of enforcement is contained in Article 33 on sanctions. The inclusion of a provision like this suggests that the member states do not find it inconceivable that some of them may find binding decisions difficult to comply with, even when they are based on consensus at the outset. The sanctions mechanism represent the "stick" of the organisation, while its mode of operation is generally informed by consensus and good will. A Treaty involves legal obligations, and failure to fulfil them will provoke sanctions by the other members represented in the Summit.

There are two types of failure to meet obligations. One is the case when a member state is persistently inactive in furthering the cause of the organisation for no acceptable reason. The other is more serious, i.e. when a member state wilfully implements policies which undermine or run counter to the principles and objectives of the organisation.

The kind of sanctions that may be imposed are not specified in the Treaty. It shall be determined by the Summit on a case-by-case basis. The original proposal made specific reference to suspension of membership, but this has been deleted in the adopted Treaty. Presumably suspension of membership will be within the range of sanctions that may be applied in extreme cases.

As a consequence of SADC having become a legal person, mechanisms of assessing member states are necessary to balance the budget. Assessed funds are additional to other sources of funding which may be secured from regional or extra-regional sources. Whereas the original proposal suggested that the member states contribute equally to the budget, article 28 of the adopted Treaty states that contributions be differentiated as determined by the Council (See also the discussion of this issue in the main text above). Nothing is said, however, about the criteria to be applied in calculating the respective contributions.

It is not to be expected that the Treaty includes references to other specific organisations like the PTA. Article 24 of the Treaty only refers in general to relations with other states, regional and international organisations, e.g. the OAU, the UN and individual donors. One would have expected, though, that the relationship between the two main organisations of integration in Southern Africa would have been put on the agenda for discussion at the Summit given the overlap of membership. Whether this was in fact the case is not known to the public.

Whatever the case may be as far as internal discussion is concerned, the widening of the scope of SADC will undoubtedly further intensify competition and rivalry with the PTA. In the past it was possible to see some sort of division of labour between the two ventures, but now the process of convergence in functions and scope appears to have been made complete, except in membership. PTA still covers a wider geographical area, but in all other respects differences have been lessened.

Similarly, the formalisation of SADC is of little consequence with regard to the challenge posed by the advent of South Africa as a legitimate partner in regional affairs. More than anything else the adoption of the Treaty dodges the issue. In three respects, the new Treaty may have a bearing on SADC's relationship with a democratic South Africa.

Firstly, if and when South Africa becomes a member of SADC, the graduated assessment of members will probably mean a boost to the budget of the organisation. Virtually any criterion selected as a basis for assessment will mean a sizable contribution by South Africa.

Secondly, unlike the voting procedures of the Bretton Woods institutions where the voting powers of members are differentiated according to their contributions, South Africa will be only one member of SADC with one vote on an equal footing with the others. South Africa may, of course, exercise its implicit veto right by blocking consensus decisions, but once decisions have been made they will be binding on South Africa as well as on all the others. However, in real life the economic clout of South Africa may count more than formalities would suggest. On the other hand, the political and diplomatic cost to South Africa of failing to take a constructive attitude to regional collaboration might be substantial, even prohibitive. In that sense, the current SADC member states may be capable of pinning down their powerful southern neighbour.

Thirdly, the way in which SADC is now constituted may deter South Africa from seeking SADC membership and prompt a new government to opt for membership in PTA instead. The procedures of PTA by way of binding supra-national decision-making by majority vote may be found to be more attractive. Although PTA does not have graduated voting powers either, the economic clout of South Africa may arguably be expected to count more in PTA than in SADC.

The Protocol on Immunities and Privileges

The annexure of this protocol to the Treaty will undoubtedly go a long way towards facilitating the work of SADC and its personnel. Basically it confers on SADC a status similar to that of diplomatic missions, including exemptions from direct taxes, import, export and customs duties, as well as a right to hold currencies of any kind and to transfer such currencies unhindered.[20]

The adoption of the protocol is likely to make positions in SADC's institutions more attractive to prospective candidates throughout the region. SADC institutions will thus probably become more competitive vis-à-vis the private sector because tax exemptions will in some measure compensate for lower salary levels. Overall, the net effect for SADC may be recruitment of high calibre personnel, at least in the upper echelons to which the protocol applies.

Future scenario

Given the ratification procedure it may take considerable time until the new Treaty comes into force. It should be recalled that for some member states it took almost a decade before the Convention establishing SATCC was ratified. In the meanwhile SADC will continue to operate more or less as it has until today. Notwithstanding the speed of the ratification process, the formalisation process will not make all that much difference with regard to the two most intractable problems facing SADC in years ahead.

Firstly, the relationship between SADC and PTA remains an urgent matter to address. If anything, the recently adopted Treaty is likely to aggravate rivalries between the two organisations because their mandates have become increasingly alike.

Secondly, the region appears not to be facing up to the challenge of the post-apartheid era. The new SADC may be a better framework for dealing with these issues. But if past performance is anything to go by, it does not augur well for the future. And it does not follow from the Treaty that regional disparities will be redressed, be it with South Africa as a full member of SADC or not.

If these challenges continue to be evaded, the general aid fatigue of the international donor community may be reinforced in the medium term by a feeling of despondency on the part of aid agencies with regional prospects in Southern Africa.

NOTES

1. The author wishes to thank the participants at the workshop on "Southern Africa after Apartheid. Regional integration and external resources" for constructive comments and criticisms, in particular Emang Maphanyane who acted as a discussant.
2. This issue is further elaborated by Odén in chapter 11.
3. It is recognised that the identification of constellations of interest groups supportive of de Klerk's political coalition is a complex task, but it is beyond the scope of this chapter to go into such detail. For further details see Tjønneland, 1992, particularly chapter 4.

4. Although South Africa may be short of capital, it has a well functioning banking and financial system with access to overseas sources. If attractive investment projects can be found in Southern Africa it is conceivable that South African capital markets may act as a conduit for overseas investment capital to the region, perhaps in joint ventures with interests domiciled in South Africa.

5. This author first came across this apt term of "neo-apartheid" in Peter Vale, 1990, p. 11.

6. The ANC is, of course, no monolithic entity. But the present author prefers to desist from making speculations on the internal politics and struggles within the ANC and their possible outcomes.

7. See excerpts from conference resolutions in SouthScan, 12 July 1991, p. 235.

8. See e.g. the somewhat dated but still valid analyses of McFarland Jr., 1983, and Guelke, 1974. More recent works include Lewis Jr., 1990, chapter 4, and Libby, 1991. The two trump cards in the hands of SADCC countries in prospective negotiations include water and energy.

9. See the forthcoming book by Mandaza & Tostensen, on the genesis of SADCC and its institutional framework.

10. The group includes Kighoma A. Malima of Tanzania, Rui Baltasar of Mozambique, Kebby S.K. Musokotwane of Zambia and David M. Zamchiya of Zimbabwe.

11. See SADCC, 1992d, including appendices, annexes and protocols containing drafts.

12. For a theoretical discussion of the political importance of institutions see March & Olsen, 1989.

13. Concepts like ethnic group and tribe are also in common usage, but this author prefers to use the term nationality to denote what others derogatorily refer to as tribe or euphemistically as ethnic group.

14. See Anderson, 1983. He refers to nations or nationalities as "imagined communities". They are "... imagined because the members of even the smallest nation will never know most of their fellow-members, meet them, or even hear of them, yet in the minds of each lives the image of their communion." (p. 15).

15. The documents are not yet officially available in printed form. Page references are to the mimeographed versions distributed in Windhoek.

16. The author wishes to acknowledge with thanks the oral and written contributions to this discussion by Bertil Odén.

17. See section on regional disparities in the main text above.

18. See section on multiple identities and loyalties in the main text above.

19. Compare articles 12 and 13 in the original proposals with articles 14 and 15 of the adopted Treaty.

20. See various articles of the Protocol.

8. SADCC—Future Challenges

Emang Motlhabane Maphanyane

The future challenge for SADCC was established in Lusaka, Zambia, in 1980 when its founders decided on the following objectives for the organisation:

a. the reduction of economic dependence, particularly, but not only, on the Republic of South Africa;
b. the forging of links to create a genuine and equitable regional integration;
c. the mobilisation of resources to promote the implementation of national, interstate and regional policies;
d. concerted action to secure international cooperation within the framework of our strategy for economic liberation.

It is important to re-state these objectives because there has been a considerable attempt to see SADCC only as an anti-apartheid organisation by those outside the region and a vehicle for aid by those inside the region. Some outside the region have even gone further to suggest that since apartheid is soon to end, SADCC will have no role. Nevertheless, it will be clear from the original objectives of SADCC, that its founders saw it as a logical corollary to the political independence process which was then still unfolding in Southern Africa, and not as a contingency measure against the apartheid regime in South Africa. It will also be clear from these original objectives of SADCC that "equitable regional integration" was to be the final destination of SADCC. This is also contrary to the view expressed in certain quarters, that the current thrust by SADCC toward regional integration is an attempt to find a new role by the organisation in the light of the impending demise of apartheid.

Since its creation, SADCC has been through all the tribulations of Southern Africa. The organisation was born at a time of enormous upheavals in the region, arising from South African destabilisation and military aggression, the anti-apartheid struggle and South Africa's illegal occupation of Namibia.

Although the author is part of the SADCC Secretariat, the views expressed on this note do not necessarily represent those of the Secretariat.

Consequently, SADCC is part and parcel of the economic and political fabric of Southern Africa and will play a significant role in any future economic dispensation in the region.

The path that SADCC chose to follow was determined by the peculiar circumstances of Southern Africa. Chief among these were the emergence of new nation states, the continuing struggle for liberation, the threat of successive apartheid regimes imposing their will on the region, a history of the dependence of the region on South Africa and the colonial divide between English and Portuguese speaking Southern Africa. In addition, the economic and physical infrastructure within and between countries of the region was weak and much of what existed had been badly damaged in the liberation struggles. It is important to repeat these facts because much of the recent commentaries on SADCC have chosen to ignore them, although they decided the path SADCC would follow toward regional integration.

Nevertheless it was for these reasons that SADCC eschewed the conventional market integrationist path to regional integration. A gradualist approach was instead adopted which aimed at consensus and confidence building and avoidance of anything that would infringe on national sovereignty which had just been acquired often through a long and bitter and bloody struggle. It was the most sensible way to proceed in Southern Africa under the circumstances. Regional integration had to be a maturing process. Much of the recent comments on SADCC have been cast in a conventional mode and have consequently arrived at erroneous conclusions. For instance, it has been argued that since SADCC does not have a formal treaty and does not have a programme of market integration through trade, it is not a true vehicle of regional integration.

Deliberately and wisely, at the beginning, SADCC chose a Memorandum of Understanding as opposed to a treaty as a basis for cooperation. A modest agenda was also agreed, providing for the rehabilitation and the building of the region's economic and physical infrastructure. This explains the large programmes in agriculture, transport and communications and the energy sector. Also deliberately, the basis of cooperation was the discrete project. This had the effect of making the benefits of cooperation immediate and tangible, and also building confidence among member states.

As expected, it soon became obvious that the project approach had serious limitations. A coordinated policy framework was necessary for projects to achieve optimal results. This explains SADCC's decision to introduce sectoral planning and policy coordination. At the same time there was a realisation that greater investment and trade was necessary to underpin the viability of the huge investment in physical infrastructure that was taking place. Since intra-SADCC trade was a mere 5 per cent of total regional trade, the potential for cross-border investment and greater regional exports seemed obvious. This brought to the fore other contradictions of a macro-economic kind, particularly the valuation of national currencies and the widespread shortages of foreign exchange. To achieve greater policy coordination and promote investment and trade, higher instruments or regional cooperation were therefore necessary. Hence, the theme of the 1992 SADCC Annual Consultative Conference—SADCC Toward Economic Integration. The theme document outlines the case for regional integration and concludes as follows:

a. The experience of regional cooperation under SADCC, so far; and changing domestic, regional and global circumstances have made closer economic cooperation and integration an imperative for SADCC member countries. In many ways, the real question is not whether some form of regional integration arrangements will be attempted in Southern Africa, but rather on what principles and terms; and the extent to which the people of the region will be involved in shaping it.
b. Although the creation of a regional market under existing circumstances could lead to only a modest increase in intra-regional trade, its most important impact will be to spur new types of investment in more productive and competitive industries, to supply the regional and international markets.
c. A laissez faire approach to regional integration, in a region with gross disparities, would be inappropriate and tend to entrench existing inequities and imbalances.
d. A development integration approach, based largely on SADCC's current strategies, is appropriate for Southern Africa. However, such an approach must give priority to the integration of systems of investment, production and trade; including promoting the freer movement of capital, goods and labour, and people generally within the region, in order to create a true Southern African Community of nations.
e. The integration strategy for SADCC should allow for a degree of flexibility, for smaller groups of countries to move in some or all aspects of the process, at different paces. It should also recognise, and as far as possible, aim to harmonise with the goals, principles and efforts of other organisations, e.g. SACU, the PTA, etc.
f. The new situation in the region would also require new non-militaristic political and security arrangements, that would guarantee peace, stability and mutual security.

In Part I, the document discusses the background to the situation that Southern African countries and SADCC are facing. It briefly assesses the experiences of cooperation in SADCC so far, highlighting both the achievements and shortcomings. It then reviews the economic and political changes taking place in SADCC member State, in South Africa and in the wider world.

It would be clear that SADCC planners followed a staged approach to regional cooperation. This arose from the conviction that regional integration has to be a maturing process requiring painstaking confidence-building steps and the establishment of a regional identity. Contrary to the view of the organisation's detractors, the theme document was not an attempt by SADCC to find a new role for itself in the light of the impending demise of apartheid but a logical next step on the road to regional economic integration which SADCC had chosen for itself influenced by the peculiar circumstances of Southern Africa.

FOSTERING ECONOMIC DEVELOPMENT AND GROWTH

The purpose of any regional cooperation effort is the promotion of economic development and growth, represented by the improvement in the standard of living of the people it is intended to serve. This requires higher levels of investment, greater productivity and trade both within the region and internationally. The achievement of these goals is the foremost challenge facing SADCC today.

Southern Africa is a region well endowed with natural resources and great agricultural potential, but also a region of acute inequalities and differences in size, economic wealth and performance among its countries. SADCC member countries produce a significant proportion of the total world output of a number of mineral products, as illustrated by these 1988 figures: diamonds (18.7 per cent), cobalt (15.0 per cent), ferro-chrome (7.2 per cent), asbestos (4.8 per cent) and chromite (4.6 per cent). The value of SADCC's mineral production in 1989 was estimated at USD 3.6 billion. South Africa alone produces about two thirds of the world's platinum, 50 per cent of the world's vanadium, 36 per cent of chromite, one third of gold, 15 per cent of manganese, 10 per cent of uranium, and accounts for about 13 per cent of the world coal exports (Jourdan, 1989, 1990).

For the last two decades of independence, Southern Africa has been at war. Fortunately peace is returning to the region. Peace is not only a necessary condition for investment and trade, but the absence of hostilities frees resources previously committed to defence and security for development. It is, therefore, important for Southern Africa that the current efforts at finding solutions to the political conflict in Southern Africa succeed, particularly in Angola, Mozambique and South Africa.

The tragedy of any war is the destruction of communities and turning their inhabitants into displaced persons and refugees. In Southern Africa at least seven million people have been displaced by conflicts or turned into refugees. Unfortunately, their fate has not been sufficiently noticed in the media due to the conflict in Eastern Europe and the Horn of Africa. If Southern Africa is to return to normalcy, it is important that the displaced persons and refugees are assisted to return to their communities and productive lives. The resources required for this effort are well beyond the capacities of the countries involved and will take the concerted effort of the international community.

SADCC has stated on several occasions that inappropriate economic policies and the poor management of national affairs have been the principal cause of the rapid economic decline of the last two decades. The most affected SADCC member states have put in place policy reform measures to address the problem. The reforms have been aimed at attracting both domestic and foreign private investment.

The process is constrained by foreign exchange shortages which can only be alleviated through the inflow of foreign investment, aid and debt relief. The process is also constrained by the absence of the necessary investment financing institutions and mechanisms such as stock exchanges and the limited market possibilities.

Trade is necessary for development and economic growth. Given the dependence of the region on outside sources of supply and on the export of raw materials, the potential for the growth of intra-regional trade currently estimated at only five per cent of the region's total trade, is enormous. However, the constraints must be overcome. Chief among these are bureaucratic impediments, the non-convertibility of many of the national currencies and weak production and marketing infrastructure. The issue of currency convertibility will also be addressed in the context of the on-going policy reforms in the member states: macro-economic policy coordination, the increase in cross-border exchanges and investment.

PRE-REQUISITES FOR REGIONAL INTEGRATION

First and foremost, successful regional integration in Southern Africa will require trained and technically competent personnel in the member states and in the various SADCC organs, who also think regionally. This will require both training and proper discussion of the issues. SADCC hopes to achieve this through a programme of induction courses, formal technical training, workshops and attachments. A related aspect is the need to build confidence and a "can-do" attitude among the people of the region that they can do these things themselves. Currently, there is far too much over-reliance on outside experts and others to bring about regional integration. Consequently, much of the outside assistance has little impact on the region in terms of creating capacity. Instead, the resources and the experience flow out from the region.

For any regional integration to be successful, it has to reach beyond governments to touch the lives of the ordinary citizens and to be relevant to the primary agents of integration—the business community. In other words, for regional cooperation to be successful, it must address the perceived interest of the majority of the people of the region. Successful regional integration in Southern Africa will, therefore, require the establishment of appropriate regional institutions by which the people of the region can determine its content and direction.

The next major challenge facing SADCC is to mobilise regional resources for the implementation of its programmes. Currently only about 10 per cent of the resources required for the implementation of the SADCC Programme of Action comes from within the region. This will take both technical competence and a strong constituency for regional cooperation. Since resources are short, trade-offs and a strong political will be necessary. Hence, it is important that regional cooperation competes for resources on the basis of offering better alternatives as perceived by the general population. A formalised SADCC must address this issue and must seek to satisfy these conditions and create necessary structures and mechanisms for the mobilisation of the region's own resources. Such mechanisms should mobilize non-public resources and involve the private sector in the implementation of the regional programmes.

REGIONAL COOPERATION INCLUDING SOUTH AFRICA

Recently there has been much debate about relations in the region post-apartheid. The SADCC approach proceeds from the realisation that:

— existing relations with South Africa which are the creation of successive colonial and apartheid regimes are not acceptable to SADCC member states and will not be acceptable to a post-apartheid government. A case in point is the migrant labour system and elements of the Southern Africa Customs Union (SACU);

— South Africa needs the market of the region which currently absorb about 50 per cent of its non-mineral exports and its natural resources such as water, power, etc. The rest of the region need South Africa's large market, and its—in the regional context— advanced technology;

— a scenario of regional relations favoured by the current government in South Africa and by some quarters in the international community which see South Africa as a "regional power", a conduit of investment provider of goods and services to the rest of the region, is unacceptable and can never be sustained.

Sufficient community of interest therefore exists to work out a mutually beneficial arrangement acceptable to all the countries of the region. This process is currently under way.

SADCC AND OTHER REGIONAL ORGANISATIONS

Two other regional organisations exist side by side with SADCC in Southern Africa. The Preferential Trade Area for East and Southern Africa (PTA) and the Southern African Customs Union (SACU). In addition to this, there is a plethora of bilateral trade arrangements. The SADCC approach is not to require member states to choose between one or the other of these arrangements at this stage. Instead the approach is to allow them to work out an arrangement that best serves their interest. In this regard, the introduction of a post-apartheid government in South Africa is of paramount importance.

SADCC will seek to prepare its members to reach that goal which might be pivoted on SADCC with South Africa as a member, the SACU or the PTA, depending on which arrangements best serve the interests of the region's peoples.

CONCLUSIONS

SADCC has deliberately eschewed conventional approaches to economic integration and has also avoided the temptation of a complicated blue-print for the region. Instead SADCC has chosen to be guided by the peculiar and historical circumstances of Southern Africa in approaching the issue.

Southern Africa remains a developing region and hence the decision by SADCC to emphasize development integration which recognised both the need to maintain the on-going programmes to expand the region's physical and economic infrastructure alongside a programme of investment and market integration.

9. Prospects for SACU after Apartheid

Jan Isaksen

AN OUTLINE OF THE SACU AGREEMENT

The agreement entitled "Customs Union Agreement between the Governments of Botswana, Lesotho, South Africa and Swaziland" is dated December 1969. It is in some respects a continuation of an agreement of 1910 between the same four countries. The negotiations which led to the new agreement were largely a result of the advent of independent governments in the BLS (Botswana, Lesotho and Swaziland). The new governments considered the gains from the customs union to be unjustly distributed. The BLS were successful in achieving a better balance, including acceptance of a certain degree of protection to the BLS. The formula for the sharing of customs revenue changed, considerably to the advantage of BLS. In the first fiscal year under the new agreement, the BLS received roughly three times as much revenue as they would have received under the old one. In the preamble to the 1969 agreement, it is explicitly stated that the changes from the 1910 agreement aims "...to ensure in particular that these arrangements encourage the development of the less advanced members of the customs union and the diversification of their economies,...."

The text of the agreement consists of 22 articles and a memorandum of understanding. In addition there is also a secret memorandum of understanding which gives a more detailed explanation of the understanding of the parties, article by article.

The main elements of the agreement may be grouped under the following headings.

General provisions of trade

SACU is set up as a regular customs union covering the Common Customs Area (CCA), comprising South Africa and the BLNS (BLS + Namibia). The two main elements of such agreements—also included in SACU—are *firstly* the absence of duties and quantitative restrictions on trade within the area. This applies whether goods are produced inside the CCA or imported from outside. *Secondly*, goods imported from outside the CCA face a common external tariff. There are clauses that grant a drawback on such duties, but an automatic right to duty free imports into the CCA is only granted in case of goods needed for relief operations, imported under technical assistance agreement or other types of multilateral international agreements.

A member state has the right to prohibit or restrict imports for economic, social, cultural or other reasons but not to prohibit the importation of goods produced in the CCA for the purpose of protecting its own industries.

The marketing of agricultural products are covered by a special article of the agreement. Arrangements for agricultural marketing in any country shall be applied equally for products of another member country. The agreement envisages consultations between the parties for the improvement of agricultural marketing in the CCA.

Determination of customs and excise duties

In general, it is South Africa which determines the rates of duty which will be in force for the CCA as a whole. The only action South Africa needs to take to effect changes is to give the other parties "adequate" notice. The proviso on "adequate notice" does however not apply for changes for fiscal purposes or for interim measures for the assistance of local industries. In the cases where notice is given the BLNS have not considered it "adequate".

It is unique for SACU and noteworthy for a customs union that one of the parties decides unilaterally on the setting of duty rates. It is equally noteworthy that the agreement not only extends to the *determination* of excise and sales duties in all member states but also covers the laws relating to customs, excise and sales duties. While the reason for including the legal framework in the agreement was to achieve a common standard for the four countries the fact is however that different types of sales taxes and different rates exist in the member countries. This may well be considered as a breach of the agreement. South Africa led the way in doing so by introducing a General Sales Tax which was held outside the scope of the agreement. South Africa has recently introduced a Value Added Taxation system which is also outside the scope of SACU.

Protective measures for BLNS industries

In the agreement there is provision for two types of protective measures for industries in the BLNS. Firstly, the countries may impose duties on the importation of goods that compete on their domestic market with the products of their domestic so called "new industries". "New" in this context is defined as not having been established for more than eight years. The duty protection must be applied equally to goods produced in the other member countries and goods imported from outside the CCA, directly or via another member. The period of protection cannot exceed eight years. Consultation with the other members must take place before imposition of the protective duties.

Secondly, tariff assistance may be given for goods produced in Botswana, Lesotho or Swaziland and marketed throughout the CCA. Such assistance may be afforded to specified industries of major importance to the country in question and for a specified time period. The arrangement will need the concurrence of all the other contracting partners. The first level of protection is a "standstill" agreement meaning that the existing CCA duty on competing goods cannot be decreased without the consent of the government specifying that industry. For goods also subject to excise duties, the "standstill" relates to the difference between customs and excise duties which is called the margin of protection.

Whether the country may be granted a second and higher level of protection during the specified time period is entirely up to South Africa. The agreement only states that South Africa will give "sympathetic consideration" to increasing the level of duty, or the margin of protection, on competing goods. Furthermore, it may give "sympathetic consideration" to reducing the customs duties on imports of materials used directly in the production of the goods in question.

These clauses have only occasionally been used. However in several cases where one or another of the BLNS have made representations to South Africa for the application of protection in one of these ways, the response has been negative. Opposite examples have also occurred, a recent one being CCA wide protection promised to Botswana for its exploitation of the soda ash resources at Sua Pan.

Trade agreements with parties outside SACU

The rules governing outside trade agreements by any of the parties to SACU are fairly standard for customs unions. *First*, a country may not without the consent of the others enter into or amend an existing agreement such that it would amount to a concession on the duties in force in the CCA. (A "most favoured nation" clause). *Second*, if the other members consent to such a concessionary agreement, the member entering into it cannot transfer lower duty goods to other members without collecting for SACU the difference between the lower duty and the one in force within the CCA. *Third*, member countries may enter into outside trade agreements or amend existing ones only if they do not conflict in any way with the SACU agreement. Upon doing so they will have to supply copies of the agreement to the other partners.

Revenue sharing

All duties, plus specific and ad valorem excise duties collected throughout the CCA are paid quarterly into a so called revenue pool. The pool is held as part of the Consolidated Revenue Fund of South Africa.

The distribution from the pool takes place annually according to the formula set out below. Important ideas behind the formula are *first* that the allocation of revenues from the pool should be related to the value of the dutiable goods imported (for customs duties), produced or consumed (for excise duties) in the CCA. Therefore, the calculation of an overall rate of duty for the whole customs area is an important part of the formula. This overall rate is simply the CCA wide collections to the pool as a percentage of the values of the dutiable goods on which they are collected.

Second, it is considered that the BLNS derive considerable disadvantages from being SACU members and that they should be compensated accordingly. The overall rate set out above is therefore "enhanced" by the multiplication with a factor of 1.42. This "enhanced rate" is then applied to the total value of each of the BLNS imports, dutiable production and consumption to arrive at the payment due.

Third, changes in the agreement introduced in 1976 aimed at stabilizing the revenue share distributed to the BLNS. The enhanced duty rate was therefore given an absolute "floor" of 17 per cent and a "ceiling" of 23 per cent. Between the two extremities a certain mechanism was introduced for stabilization; The enhanced revenue rate as calculated above is adjusted by adding to it half the difference between the rate and 20. This means that an initial rate over 20 would get a negative adjustment, an initial rate under 20 would get a positive adjustment. If the rate after such adjustment would not fall within the 17–23 per cent band, it would be set to 23 per cent if over and to 17 per cent if under.

Fourth, the payment takes place over a period of roughly two years. This was apparently necessary at the time of the 1969 negotiations, as the trade statistics used for the formula calculation were severely delayed. The effect of the lag is to seriously erode the receipts of the

BLNS. In 1981 the Commission (see below) agreed to alter the formula to reduce considerably the lag. The agreement was however not ratified by the South African authorities.

Transport and transit

The members grant freedom of transport for goods to and from the areas of the other contracting partners. They may however impose conditions on transit for a number of reasons; health and security concerns, public morals, precautions against animal or plant diseases and to secure the adherence to multilateral international conventions. Members may refuse transport through their areas for the purpose of protecting national security interests.

Mutual non-discrimination in transport charges is also part of the agreement. *First*, transit of goods through any of the countries from or to non members will not be subject to discriminatory transport "rates", presumably to be interpreted as taxation on transport services. *Second*, in the case of publicly owned transport, tariffs or charges applicable for domestic transport shall also apply to transport to and from the other countries. *Third*, rules for non-discrimination extend also to the treatment of private transport operators for both passenger and goods transport. Transport operators from member countries will in any other member country receive a treatment no less favourable than that accorded to the operator registered in that country.

Consultative arrangements

The main consultative body is the Customs Union Commission. It is a committee of officials which may only discuss matters and report to their respective governments. For example in 1981, the Commission had agreed to certain changes in the revenue distribution formula which were never implemented because of the rejection at the political level in South Africa. The framework for the Commission given in the agreement is otherwise very general. It amounts to no more than an obligation to meet once a year and for discussing any matter arising out of the agreement. Ad hoc meetings may be demanded by any of the contracting partners.

The structure which has evolved is the following: The Commission meets before the end of October every year and a main item in the agenda is the agreement on the revenue shares for the next fiscal year. This fits in with the budgetary procedures of the parties. The venue of the meeting is rotated between the member countries.

The Commission has considered it practical to set up a number of sub committees. The only one meeting on a regular basis quarterly—is the Customs Technical Liaison Committee which is central to the technical work on revenue distribution. In addition there are two standing committees, the Trade and Industry Liaison Committee and the Transport Liaison Committee. Ad hoc committees have been appointed from time to time. Now and then, the ministers responsible for the various aspects of the agreement in the member states have met and discussed matters of mutual interest. This is not a feature envisaged by the agreement.

The agreement also contains clauses on bilateral consultations in the case of disorderly marketing or dumping, where the affected party is given the right to require from the other party that they shall consult at the earliest opportunity. Consultations are also prescribed from time to time on zoo-sanitary and phytosanitary matters.

Termination clause

If any of the members gives notice of withdrawal from the SACU, the agreement envisages consultations with the other parties on the date and conditions of the withdrawal. If an understanding is not reached, the agreement is deemed to remain in force twelve months from the day notice was given. There is no specific mention of the problems created by the lagged payments to BLNS in the context of a withdrawal.

BLNS AND SOUTH AFRICA EXPERIENCE WITH THE AGREEMENT

There are a number of analyses of the BLNS experience with SACU (see for example the list of references in Guma, 1990), several of them with the explicit aim of a cost benefit evaluation. If one was to assess the overall outcome of these analyses, it would most likely end in a "draw". The balance of costs and benefits will vary from country to country, from year to year and according to the particular aspect focused. Above all, however, the outcome depends on which alternative to SACU one considers.

Although the BLNS themselves have long had the balance between costs and benefits under observation, none of them have indicated that they have seriously examined the option of leaving SACU. Their choice has been to try and improve SACU from the inside. To some extent they have succeeded as for example with the floor/ceiling agreement in 1976.[1] Also, the BLS have used SACU in increasingly sophisticated ways.[2] In future, in spite of SA's present suspension of negotiations, BLNS will be likely to go on, attempting to improve their position.

The official BLNS conviction about a positive balance of benefits from SACU membership contrasts with academia's ambiguity on the matter. There are however a number of factors which serve to explain the contrast:

— The analyst may construct alternatives for South Africa's reactions if a withdrawal was sought. The policy makers would have to live with the uncertainties of the effects of very serious decisions, making them much less brave than the observers.
— The fact, insufficiently covered in most of the literature, that the ease of *supply* makes South Africa a superior source of many imports although in theory, one might show that cheaper sources exist.
— Academic contributions have been overwhelmingly concerned with trade and revenue sharing arrangements. They have therefore often excluded from the analysis, the advantages of e.g. the transport clauses, as well as the existence of the Customs Commission and sub committees which have provided the smaller countries with a platform for quasi diplomatic contacts with South Africa which was recognised (or at least not heavily criticized) by the international community.
— When considering the option of leaving SACU, the analysis has not properly accounted for uncertainties and the time dimension: For a decision maker in a BLNS Ministry of Finance[3] the losses, in terms of revenues, have appeared very large because they were certain to occur and were short term, whereas advantages, in terms of greater prospects for industrial development, would be considered uncertain and their occurrence was long/medium term. There is little doubt how the scales would tip for any minister of finance focusing on next or the next few years budget.
— Studies have largely overrated the potential of duty protection. Tiny economies like BLNS would hardly benefit from the instruments of protection that they would gain by leaving SACU. Scepticism about the virtue of such measures is widespread in the BLNS administrations. Moreover, as argued by Lewis and Sharpley (Lewis & Sharpley, 1988), the case of Botswana appears to illustrate that a number of non-duty based infant industry policy options inside SACU may work.
— Lastly, as hinted by many authors (See e.g. Maasdorp, 1991a) several analysts have taken on a negative predisposition to SACU

because of SA's apartheid policies. This has not only influenced authors. It has also come through in semi-official comments on SACU from BLNS' neighbours. The apartheid aspect has not been regarded irrelevant for the BLNS, but its prominence has, for them, been limited in relation to the economic pro SACU arguments.

The post apartheid era may bring an alignment of the points of view. Certainly the abhorrence for the apartheid system will no longer interfere with the "purely" economic issues (if such issues at all exist). Furthermore, the omission of SACU as a diplomatic device will not be as important as before. As an existing institution, it may serve as a platform for the various economic concerns of the countries in years immediately after the demise of apartheid.

Seen from the side of South Africa, the most prominent feature of its attitude to SACU has been its increasing complaint that the size of the revenue payments to BLNS. This has been followed up by the argument that the BLNS' preoccupation with the revenue distribution mechanism rather than economic cooperation and development has been inappropriate. (See e.g. McCarthy, 1986). Ideas from the South African side about a SACU using various forms of "development cooperation" with contributions from South Africa has been refuted for obvious political reasons, strongly by Botswana and Lesotho, less strongly by Swaziland.

The literature is largely in agreement that South Africa has had both political and economic advantages of the agreement. In political terms, the apartheid state has been able to argue internationally that it has "very cordial" economic relations with a number of African states. In economic terms there is McFarland's finding that supply to BLS markets accounted for about 20 per cent of the growth in manufacturing GDP in South Africa during the 1970s. (McFarland, 1981). For South Africa, like for the BLNS, pulling out of SACU has hardly been considered a desirable option.

SACU membership has however not been without controversy in South Africa. The Ministry of Finance has been concerned about the fiscal effect and long had a rather cool attitude to SACU. Since the emergence of the so called TBVC states (The South African "homelands", Transkei, Bophutatswana, Venda and Ciskei), the alleged serious drain on resources has, always included TBVC "shares" of the Customs Pool, although they are not *de jure* SACU members. The political advantages have caused the Ministry of Foreign Affairs to take a more positive view of the agreement.

THE POST-APARTHEID SITUATION

The elimination of apartheid and the introduction of democratic government in South Africa will not in itself dramatically change the basic economic relations between countries in the region. What may happen more rapidly is a change in the formal, institutional links between the countries. The SACU issue is part of the picture and cannot be considered in separation from possible future decisions made with regard to the other regional economic relations, be they multilateral or bilateral.

In each country, the *loci* of final decisions on external economic relations will be the governments, conclusions being reached through bureaucratic and political processes. Analyses from bureaucrats/consultants will focus on economic factors and strategic factors as well as the bureaucratic feasibility of various solutions. Prospects for the bargaining process and the country's bargaining power vis-à-vis the other potential partners will also figure.

The determination of foreign policy is usually carried out by relatively limited groups of politicians and bureaucrat. *Non-government organizations* chiefly from business and labour may wield a particularly strong influence. E.g. in the case of South Africa, post apartheid, the strong links between ANC and the unions are particularly likely to be important in decisions pertaining to regional labour migration.

Non national players are also important. Among them are international organizations world-wide EC, World Bank) as well as the regional ones (SADCC, PTA), and not least, bilateral donors and countries with strong commercial interests in the region.

The analysis below attempts to *first* characterize the basic interests of the various players in the politico-economic process, and *second*, under a medium term perspective, consider a few ways in which these basic constellations of interests may translate into concrete solutions.

The BLNS

The BLNS countries are not as similar as the use of a group acronym may indicate. *Namibia* probably differs most from the other members. R.H. Green argues that Namibia's economic links to South Africa are uneconomic or unnatural and created by the colonial administration for other than economic purposes. It is likely that factors like the access to the Atlantic and the nearness to Angola would make a cost benefit analysis of Namibia's SACU membership turn out less positive (or more negative) than a similar analysis for the other countries.

Botswana's stronger economic position would seem to make it less

SACU dependent than the other BLNS countries. The location of its economic centres are however much nearer to those of South Africa than is the case for Namibia. Furthermore, in the medium term, as signalled by Botswana's latest development plan, industrial development will have to be increasingly relied upon as the engine of the economy and relations with a democratic South Africa may therefore play an increasingly important role in the future.

Swaziland and Lesotho are very closely related to the South African economy (the latter to the extreme). It is hard to see that the post apartheid era should bring any changes (short medium or long term) in their need to let institutional arrangements reflect economic reality.

In conclusion, it is likely that Lesotho and Swaziland would be interested in preserving SACU, come what may and may even seek nearer integration, whereas the position of Botswana and Namibia would be more dependent on possible future changes to the agreement and what other options may appear. This indicates some degree of probability that SACU members attitudes to the grouping are slightly different and therefore that a split and change in membership would be possible.

It is unclear whether the BLNS had a common negotiating stance during the negotiations which were interrupted. If a new opening materializes they would presumably wish to change SACU in one, more or all of the following ways:

— Improve the compensation mechanism in order that it may be seen to give adequate compensation for the erosion in payment because of the two year lag, price raising effects, polarization effects and loss of fiscal discretion. This has been a reoccurring argument from BLNS and would be advanced whether negotiations take place with the present or the new democratic government.
— Greater involvement of BLNS; administratively in e.g the setting of duties and in other decision making by the Board of Trade and industries (presently administering SACU); Overall by creating a system for multilateral arbitration. Proposals along these lines have been floated by South Africa, through the McCarthy report (McCarthy, 1985) and refuted by the BLS. They would probably not be advanced by BLNS if negotiations took place under the present South Africa regime, but certainly in a post apartheid setting.
— Greater opportunities for infant industry protection and for protection of agricultural products.
— Mechanisms to decentralize industries to BLNS.

The latter proposals would probably be advanced in spite of BLNS' above mentioned scepticism to protective solutions. They might at least conveniently be used as a bargaining chip.

The preamble of the SACU agreement spells out a number of laudable aims with regard to free trade and the encouragement of the development of the less developed countries. Examples of such aims is the mention of consultation about marketing arrangements for agricultural commodities (Article 12) and about dumping (Article 17). The latter was until recently a little appreciated problem (See however Commonwealth Secretariat, 1991). Such arrangements have however been difficult to realise in the past, because of the greater cooperation between the BLNS and the apartheid state which they presumably would necessitate.

The greater realism of arrangements to give the BLNS a greater say in SACU affairs post apartheid may introduce a new factor in the negotiations and increase the chances for a balanced solution even if the financial compensation would have to be reduced. In forthcoming negotiations BLNS could refer to the spirit of the agreement and push for a redesign of the treaty which would make it an efficient instrument to reach its laudable objectives.

South Africa

South Africa's emphasis on economic relations with Africa as opposed to other developed or developing countries is not discussed here. In *Africa* South Africa, as a regional superpower in terms-of-trade and production, would be likely to focus on trade relations with the higher potential markets, many of them outside the South Africa subregion. The present government appears to respond to the "opening up of Africa" with bilateralism which is presumably favoured by business because of the higher speed with which government can initiate bilateral negotiations and make agreements. Multilateral deals are infinitely more complex and time consuming to arrange.

Based on present indications of ANC policies for regional economic relations, it is likely that an ANC led government would favour multilateral solutions. In as far as the ANC considers wider multilateral solutions than SACU, neither of the two "governments" would appear to have any special interest in SACU for the time being.

The South African government last year unilaterally suspended the on-going negotiations with the BLNS. Among the reasons that were given was the incompatibility of SACU with the present South Africa low duty, export oriented trade policies which certainly under the present SACU compensation arrangement would make South Africa's fiscal "burden" heavier.[4] The announcement also said that the South Africa Government had composed a task force which would study the issues in the broader context. The report of the group was said to be expected at the annual meeting of SACU in October 1991.[5] At the time, the South Africa government apparently invited the BLNS ministers of finance to discuss broader aspects of regional cooperation.

As far as can be established, the terms of reference of the task force is very open and according to one comment recently the group "is going nowhere". This fits with the more general picture of the regional foreign policy of the present government, apart for tactical moves, appears to be the one of "no decisions". The task force is therefore likely to be a reflection of the time honoured tactic of studying instead of taking decisions. This may of course change if the interim government structure decided upon during CODESA becomes a decision making entity. The preoccupation with internal issues in South Africa may however well mean that SACU issues are put on the "back burner" and that at least two or three years may lapse without any attempts to change SACU.

The balance between the different attitudes to SACU from the Ministry of Finance and the Ministry of Foreign Affairs is likely to be influenced by the increasing recognition of South Africa in Africa, weakening the Foreign Affairs case. The present government's "non-action" stance would however make it unlikely that South Africa would unilaterally dissolve SACU. What would change this would be strong behind the scenes "advice" from the ANC. However tempting it would be for the ANC to start off regional relations with a "clean slate" and be able to blame the painful breakup of SACU of the racist regime, it is difficult to see that the ANC would prefer this course of action unless it opted strongly for bilateralism because it would leave South Africa's closest neighbours in an unfortunate "hanging" position. The greater likelihood is therefore that the SACU issue will be "left as it is" until after democratic transition has taken place. If South Africa budgetary pressures after transition become as strong as expected, it may not take long before the issue is raised by the new government.

PTA

Lesotho and Swaziland[6] are members of the Preferential Trade Area for Eastern and Southern African States (PTA). A main focus is the creation, through successive duty reductions, of a common market for the region by the year 2000. Based on past experience with trade and economic cooperation in Africa, this appears overly optimistic to many observers. PTA however has a number of other forms of cooperation on the agenda.

A special "BLS" protocol to the PTA treaty allows for Lesotho and Swaziland membership for a limited period of time after which they would have to choose between SACU and PTA.

If the new South Africa takes a multilateral approach to regional trade relations instead of a bilateral approach, PTA, involving favourable trade access to a large number of African countries, would obviously be high up on the list of regional institutions to join.

If South Africa joins PTA, the Most Favoured Nation (MFN) character of PTA would however make it difficult to allow SACU to go on, particularly if two members were not even in PTA. A straightforward application of MFN rules would mean that South Africa, at least eventually, should grant the same favourable customs treatment to the other PTA states as is does to the SACU members, which, in turn, the other PTA member would have to reciprocate. Such a bold step would be theoretically possible and even advantageous in the long run, but equally unrealistic as the present PTA objective. As most of the PTA members would fear for South Africa competition, they would be likely to insist that protective measures within the new customs union would have to be arranged. In that case it would be a moot point whether it could be called a SACU or just a (reformulated) PTA including South Africa. South Africa would certainly not be able to give compensation on the scale which it now gives the smaller SACU members.[7]

Variations of this scenario might be more workable: One scenario would be that the present SACU transforms itself to somewhat nearer an economic union, and that the Union would be accepted as a member of the PTA. Another would be that the present PTA allowed South Africa and SACU in under long term transitional arrangements whereby intra-PTA trade barriers were reduced and external barriers unified to reach the stage of a Customs Union. If one were to take the present PTA plans seriously this would perhaps not take so long time. In case South Africa joins the Lome convention this arrangement could mean a boost to the exports for many of the bordering countries.

SADCC

All BLNS countries are members of Southern Africa Development Coordination Conference (SADCC). Since SADCC as an organization so far was not focused on trade, SACU membership has been deemed compatible with SADCC membership. For the same reason post apartheid South African membership in SADCC would probably not effect SACU.

In the apartheid era some non-BLNS members of SADCC did question the economic and political wisdom of SACU membership. On the other hand, according to recent rumours, some of the same countries have made advances toward South Africa about the possibility of membership of SACU.

Non-BLNS SADCC countries' attitudes towards the future of SACU would be more influenced by their membership of PTA than their SADCC membership. Perhaps they, as a subgroup of PTA, would have a more lenient attitude towards the continuation of SACU, since the four BLNS countries form part of the ten country grouping. The interest in joining SACU expressed by some (SADCC, non-SACU) members, opens for a perspective of a SADCC based extension of SACU, which however would be problematic (to say the least) for the PTA, and difficult for South Africa in terms of compensation although not as difficult in the case of the SACU-isation of the entire PTA.

World Bank/IMF

Traditionally the IFI's have had little time for regional and sub-regional cooperation and integration, their concern having been to get domestic policies "right". Some interest has however emerged recently. As the interregional effects of the domestic policies pushed by Bank and Fund are becoming clearer the concern for integration is likely to increase.

A study of post apartheid options for integration has been under way in the Bank for some time now. Rumours are that it has been put on the backburner for at least a while and efforts shifted more to South Africa domestic issues post apartheid. This may indicate that the IFI's will assume a fairly disinterested or neutral stance in the shaping of future regional economic relations.

If they, however, decide to take an active interest, the Bank would be likely to be the lead agency. Its role as a bank would indicate an emphasis on regional solutions where capital injections would be central. Its ideological make-up would mean an emphasis on the strongest possible element of free markets in terms-of-trade, human resources and capital flows. Countries where, by the IFI's perceptions, macro economic policies were likely to be "right" would be favoured as members.

A kind of Marshall plan cum free trade proposal including SACU and perhaps other countries within the SADCC grouping, although hardly all, would seem a possible solution. The Bank/Fund's finan-

cial muscle and their considerable bell-sheep effect on bilateral donors would make their preferred solutions perhaps the most important
external influence in forming sub regional post apartheid integration.

European Community

The deepening crises in Soviet and other "east bloc" economies would
continue the trend towards more EC attention to these economies and
less towards developing countries, excluding perhaps humanitarian
aid to Africa as evidenced by the recent decision to assist considerably in the current drought crisis in the region. A great deal of attention and coordinated policies to influence events would not be expected from EC.

The EC decision as to whether South Africa will be given full ACP
status would affect EC exports from the region as a whole. South
African goods would fully benefit from the EC's GSP scheme. For the
other countries, inputs originating in South Africa are presently not
considered to be of ACP origin for the purpose of GSP preferential
access. ACP membership for South Africa would remove this barrier
which may have been important for some goods produced by SA's
neighbours.

The effects on regional production and trade flows would be several and the balance hard to guess: If South Africa was not granted
ACP status, non-South Africa producers would have an incentive to
look to ACP sources in the region for their inputs. In the case of South
Africa membership, it would be more advantageous for the other
countries of the region to import inputs for their EC exports from
South Africa. On the other hand, South Africa producers who now
export (legally or illegally) through neighbouring countries (sometimes using "tricks" to comply with ACP-content rules) would most
likely prefer to export directly to EC. More analysis and access to data
is needed to find out how this would work out overall.

Improved access for South Africa to other markets for manufactured exports would lessen its dependence on the other SACU countries for its manufactured exports. Whether this would apply to such
an extent that its economic interest in SACU would be appreciably
reduced is also hard to say without further analysis.

African relations

The major economies in Africa are likely to have a common problem
with a democratic and acceptable South Africa: How to secure access
to the South Africa market and benefit from investment and at the

same time be allowed to protect their own industry from what many of them regard as a dangerously strong competition from South African exports. South Africa is likely to benefit from trade relations with major African markets like Nigeria and Kenya. Favourable bilateral arrangements with such countries are likely to be strongly promoted by business interest in South Africa. In so far as such agreements may be built on an MFN basis, SACU may be seen to involve constraints in SA's bilateral negotiations with potentially more important trade partners.

SCENARIOS AND CONCLUSIONS

It is unavoidable that at some point in the post apartheid period the SACU treaty will come up for renegotiation. It has now become commonplace to assume that the budgetary pressures in a democratic South Africa will lead to an increased preoccupation by the new government to increase revenues and cut unnecessary expenditure. If the Agreement is not taken up from the South Africa side, the BLNS are likely to voice their concerns as stated above.

A main question would be to what extent the stronger party in the game could achieve its will with regard to a reduction of compensation payments without going so far that the BLNS would loose interest. It is quite likely that faced even with the total elimination of financial compensation, the BLNS would have some interest in an agreement which e.g. involved the present transport sector arrangement and which gave them a legal basis for enforcing fair competition between the smaller countries and South Africa through e.g the existing anti dumping clauses. As argued above the extent to which SACU could be transformed into a real development oriented integration scheme would be enhanced by more easy diplomatic relations post apartheid.

Would the BLNS choose individual solutions? The difference between them which have been highlighted would make them pull in slightly different directions, but they are so small that an offer from South Africa to continue SACU in one form or another would hardly be neglected by any of them.

The most unlikely outcome of negotiations is a straight renewal of the present SACU. Breakdown of negotiations and dissolution of SACU appears likelier. This could be the result of negotiations where all parties over-focus the compensation mechanism, where views are likely to be diametrically opposite at the outset. The BLNS would be arguing that there is undercompensation, South Africa that it would not be able to "give away" as much as under the present compensation mechanism because of its domestic budgetary situation. The strength of the latter argument will depend much on exactly *how* constrained the South Africa budget situation is and thus on a large number of economic and political factors in South Africa.

The most likely is however that a number of changes will be agreed upon. As these changes would have to tie in with South Africa's probable membership in other organizations, SACU negotiations would probably go on simultaneously with other negotiations which, in a multilateral setting could well be protracted. In the meantime the organization would most likely be left as it is.

How SACU would be changed is pretty impossible to predict. Below, a "minimum" and a "maximum" solution are sketched out. The *minimum* change might be the transformation of SACU to become a true international organization with a secretariat not being part of the administration of any of the partners and/or changes to the compensation mechanism. The trade off along these lines would be greater influence to the BLNS in running SACU against a greater share of the revenue pool to South Africa. If even such changes are considered to constitute the "death" of SACU it is possible to agree with those who argue that SACU "is terminally ill" (Green, 1991).

At the *maximum* end, the two main options could be called "widening" and "deepening" of SACU. The "widening" option would be to draw one or more SADCC countries into SACU. According to Maasdorp, there are strong rumours that Mozambique, Malawi and Zambia have unofficially expressed an interest in joining SACU (Maasdorp, 1992). From the BLNS it may seem advantageous to bring in more countries that would "take their side" in the running of SACU if they any way would have to concede some loss of compensation revenue. Objectively, under a "widening" scenario it would also make more sense to give the smaller countries a greater influence in the fixing of customs duties. Major influence for BLNS alone would amount to a case of the "tail wagging the dog".

What advantages would a widened SACU have for South Africa? Increasing the membership, e.g. with the countries mentioned above would increase the South Africa "domestic market" with some 30 million people, i.e roughly double the present CCA market in terms of population (not in terms of purchasing power). If it is right that the IFI's would be interested in spearheading a kind of Marshall effort for such a grouping of "well behaved" countries the attraction would be substantial through the opportunities for South Africa agriculture, manufacturing and construction. These sectors (as well as others) would post apartheid be very well placed to take advantage of increased capital inflows to the region.

A widening of SACU would obviously not be without repercussions on the other regional groupings. PTA would face a de facto break up and thus probably resist the SACU widening. Whether the enlarged SACU grouping would meet similar objections from SADCC is less certain. On the one hand, the SADCC philosophy has always been that sub groupings would be allowed to have their own agreements within the organization. On the other hand SADCC has not, so far, included trade cooperation. Moreover, the proposals for formalization of SADCC and the new proposed treaty would seem to indicate that trade relations in some way or other would be encompassed by the organization. The main difficulty for South Africa with a widened SACU would most likely be its limited ability to grant financial compensation at anywhere near the level presently granted to the BLNS.

There are a number of measures which might ameliorate the problems caused by a widening. The relations with the other regional institutions could be handled through transitional arrangements, assuming a merger of the two sub-groupings at some future stage. The compensation could be dealt with through a widening of the infant industry clauses in SACU or a limited opportunity for the smaller countries to impose certain tariffs on imports from South Africa, similar to the transfer tax system of the East African community.

A "deepening" of SACU could take the form of including into the agreement (keeping the present membership) free movement of labour and capital, monetary and exchange measures, thus changing it towards or into an economic union. For Botswana, monetary cooperation may be considered as a retrograde step, but the other members are already more or less in a monetary union with South Africa.[8] Presumably, this would not imply the same difficulties vis-à-vis PTA or SADCC which would the widening of SACU, because the union could be allowed into the groupings as one unit. The problems from the BLNS' side would lie more on the general level of economic and political independence, including arrangements for them to have a real say in Union issues.

A main problem for South Africa would be the handling of migrant labour issues where pressures on the new government for descalation of labour migration from neighbouring countries are likely to be considerable. A free labour market would be to the benefit of the BLNS and in particular Lesotho.

In between these extremities there would be a large number of permutations drawn of the elements of the present agreement. Whether the new agreements reached would be a continuation of SACU or a new form of cooperation would hardly be an important issue.

NOTES

1. The argument in Guma (1990) is right only under his own understanding of the expectancy of BLS and the SA that the rate of revenue should be 20. In reality, which the BLS negotiation team foresaw, the future emphasis of the SA fiscal system would increasingly be on non pool taxation (direct taxation and GST/VAT) so that the rate which is largely determined by the SA collections and imports/production of dutiable goods would have a decreasing trend. Therefore, the BLS's acceptance of the revenue distribution mechanism proposed by SA during the 1976 negotiations has prevented BLS revenue rates from sinking below 17 per cent. In other words, most years (as pointed out by McCarthy, 1986) the compensation factor has been far bigger than the built in 42 per cent.
2. For example, Botswana Government has now initiated a thriving local industry making government uniforms etc, where government imports duty free from cheap Far East sources, have uniforms made by the private sector industry through "labour only" contracts so that duties do not have to be paid because government all the time owns the material.
3. Finance Ministries are in all BLNS countries lead ministries for SACU affairs.
4. Since SA's revenue share, according to the SACU compensation formula is residually determined, its share will decline rapidly when duties are reduced, while customs revenues of BLNS will stay at the floor level. If SA e.g. reduces all duties and excises to zero they will according to the present agreement still have to pay the 17 per cent to the BLNS.
5. According to one member of the task force, by the beginning of October 1991 there had only been one meeting in the task force, considerable time ago. It therefore seems wholly unlikely that a report would be tabled in October (Personal communication with a member of the task force)
6. Namibia became a member in January 1993.
7. Cf. the discussion by Ofstad on the same topic, as seen from the PTA perspective in chapter 10.
8. Namibia has declared its intention to launch its own currency but remain inside the CMA, with arrangements probably similar to those of Swaziland. It has thus reneged on its erstwhile plans of introducing an independent currency, like Botswana, at an early stage.

10. Will PTA be Relevant in the Post-Apartheid Era?

Arve Ofstad

THE SETTING: A REALISTIC VIEW ON PTA

The Preferential Trade Area for Eastern and Southern African States (PTA) was formally established in 1984, and has at present 18 member states. Another four have for long been considered potential member states: Namibia (which became a member in January 1993), Botswana, Madagascar and the Seychelles. The big question is of course whether South Africa will become a full member, and under what arrangements. If all these countries do join, the PTA will grow from eighteen to twenty-three countries with a population of approx. 270 million (at present 220 million), and a combined GNP of approx. USD 160 billion (at present approx. USD 70 billion). PTA will then cover practically half of Sub-Saharan Africa.[1] This size and the heterogeneity of its member states have been among the major problems for PTA as an effective organisation from the beginning.

It is important to be realistic about what the PTA has achieved, and what it may possibly achieve under present circumstances. The overall long-term aim of PTA is to "promote cooperation and development in all fields of economic activity (particularly in the fields of trade, customs, industry, transport, communication, agriculture, natural resources, and monetary affairs) with the aim of raising the standards of living of its peoples, of fostering closer relations among its member states, and to contribute to the progress and development of the African continent". (Article 3 of the PTA Treaty)

As we all know, however, large areas of the PTA region are unable to move in any such direction at the moment, while the possibilities for "fostering closer relations" between many of its members can hardly be much more than rhetoric for a long time to come.

Secondly, there are hardly any trade links or even the infrastructural basis for such links between many of the member states of PTA, particularly among those relatively further apart. This is clearly indicated by the intra-PTA trade matrix for 1988 (see Table 10.1). Out of a possible 240 possible (16 x 15) trade links[2], a total of 129 were empty, and another 58 had a value of less than USD 1 million that year.

Table 10.1. *Intra-PTA trade for 1988 by country of origin and country of destination* (Fob value in millions of USD)

Destination of exports

Exporting countries (reporting country)	Burundi	Comores	Djibouti	Ethiopia	Kenya	Lesotho	Malawi	Mauritius	Mozambique	Rwanda	Somalia	Swaziland	Tanzania	Uganda	Zambia	Zimbabwe	Total fob exports
1. Burundi									4.2								4.2
2. Comores							0.4										0.4
3. Djibouti	1.7	2.4								16.0							20.7
4. Ethiopia			18.5											0.4			19.9
5. Kenya	5.1	4.3	4.4	5.4			0.7	3.7	9.4	7.5	34.8		27.5	149.8	5.1	7.8	265.5
6. Lesotho																0.1	0.1
7. Malawi					0.1			0.6	13.7				0.7		8.7	3.7	31.4
8. Mauritius		1.0	0.0		0.4				0.0						0.1	1.3	3.3
9. Mozamb.		0.6			0.3					0.8			1.1			0.6	3.6
10. Rwanda	0.1			0.0	6.1									0.2	0.0		6.5
11. Somalia			0.8	0.0	0.4									0.1			1.4
12. Swaziland				0.3	1.5								0.3		8.3	6.2	15.2
13. Tanzania	1.4				1.8		0.3	3.2	1.5	0.2				2.7	1.3	0.6	12.9
14. Uganda													3.7				5.9
15. Zambia	6.3			0.2	4.2	2.2	5.0						7.3			17.1	42.7
16. Zimbabwe	2.4			5.2	16.0	3.7	22.8		51.2	1.1		2.6	5.0	1.1	40.3		154.0
Total fob imports	20.7	5.3	23.7	13.5	31.6	5.9	29.5	7.6	77.7	25.4		2.6	45.9	154.6	63.9	37.4	587.4

Note: Rwanda exports to Kenya in 1988 is extrapolated using average annual growth rate of Rwanda exports to Kenya for the period of 1980–87.

Source: IMF, *Direction of Trade Statistics Yearbook 1989*, Washington D.C.

Exports from two countries, Kenya and Zimbabwe, accounted for more than 70 per cent of the recorded total intra-regional trade, and the major part of these were exports to the nearest neighbouring countries: from Kenya to Uganda, Rwanda and Tanzania, and from Zimbabwe to Mozambique, Zambia and Malawi. These six links, plus another five were the only trade links with a value above USD 10 million in 1988. Since 1988, Angola and Sudan have joined, but this have added very little to intra-regional trade. It is only Botswana (and eventually, South Africa) of the potential members that will bring along substantial existing and potential trade, and of these Botswana has Zimbabwe as its main trading partner of the present PTA members.

At the same time, there are substantial volumes of unrecorded trade across most borders in the region. The very nature of this trade makes any assessment of the exact volumes and values very difficult, but many observers would argue that this in several cases surpass the official recorded trade. With some notable exceptions, however, most of this is trade across only one border: from one country to its neighbour.

It is therefore hard to escape the conclusion that trade within the PTA region mainly takes place within two "clusters"; one which centres around Kenya, and the other around Zimbabwe.[3] In addition to these two clusters, there is only limited, or unrecorded, trade.

Another important conclusion to be drawn from evidence of present trade, is that intra-regional trade does primarily develop in manufactured goods, and in inputs to manufacturing.[4] It is therefore not surprising, that intra-regional trade mainly takes place to/from the relatively more industrialised countries in the region.

From this follows what may be termed the *paradox* of intra-regional trade in these regions: Intra-regional trade stems mainly from industrialisation. But in order to industrialise, the countries need export earnings to pay for the necessary capital imports, and these initial earnings can only be made from exports outside the region. Therefore, the countries in the region will have to increase their exports outside the region, in order to develop the economic structures enabling them to increase their intra-regional trade. It is therefore not possible to regard intra-regional trade as an alternative to extra-regional trade, at least not in the short run.

Achievements

According to available statistics, recorded intra-PTA-trade decreased in actual value from around USD 600 million in 1980, to a low of USD

Arve Ofstad

Table 10.2. *Global and intra-PTA trade 1980–1988*

Type of indicator	Actual figures (USD billion)		
	1980	1984	1988
1. Total world exports	1,895.5	1,786.6	2,707.5
2. Total world import	1,946.4	1,849.7	2,793.1
3. Total world trade	3,841.9	3,636.3	5,500.6
4. Total PTA exports	6.2	5.3	7.3
5. Total PTA imports	8.9	7.8	11.4
6. Total PTA trade	15.2	13.1	18.8
7. Intra-PTA exports	0.6	0.4	0.6
8. Intra-PTA imports	0.7	0.5	0.7
9. Total intra-PTA trade	1.3	0.9	1.2
	Share		
10. Intra-PTA exports as a % of total PTA exports	10	8	8
11. Intra-PTA imports as a % of total PTA imports	7	6	6
12. Total intra-PTA trade as a % of total PTA trade	8	7	7
13. Total PTA exports as a % of total PTA imports	70	68	64

Source: IMF, *Direction of Trade Statistics Yearbook 1987, 1988 and 1989*, Washington D.C.

400 million in 1985, but then increased to nearly USD 600 million again in 1988 (see Table 10.2). This meant a decrease from around 10 per cent of total exports in 1980/81, to around 8 per cent in 1988. For individual countries this percentage varies, from as much as 20 per cent in the case of Kenya, to less than 2 per cent for countries like Mauritius, Somalia and Uganda.

Most of the efforts of PTA have been directed to trade matters. This is also where the major achievements have been recorded, at least on paper. The main instrument has been the introduction of *preferential tariffs* for intra-regional trade, for goods on a specifically agreed "Common List". The second major instrument is the *PTA Clearing House* whereby only the net balance of each country's intra-regional trade needs to be settled in convertible currencies. In addition, PTA has introduced a *Road Customs Transit Declaration Document* to facilitate the movement of goods across borders, a PTA Programme for

Trade Information *(TINET)*, *PTA Travellers Cheques* (made out in the PTA Unit of Account, UAPTA), promoted PTA Chamber of Commerce meetings, PTA Trade Fairs, and other measures to improve trade contracts and information. A *PTA Trade and Development Bank* was established in 1986 with its headquarters in Bujumbura.

In addition, PTA has commissioned a number of studies covering a wide variety of subjects in accordance with its overall objectives to cover most economic sectors. PTA claims several successes in promoting industrial collaboration, and the setting up of a Metallurgical Technology Centre in Zimbabwe, a Leather Products Institute in Ethiopia, and a fertilizer plant to be located in Uganda. PTA has also promoted a few projects in infrastructure development, including the future establishment of a common PTA Airline (PTA, 1991).

On practically all accounts, however, the achievements are far from what could be expected from stated declarations and decisions. Both the decision-making and the implementation processes for these measures have also been riddled with disagreements and poor follow-up by the member states. The best example is probably the programme for elimination of all tariffs and non-tariff trade barriers for intra-PTA trade by 1994. This programme has met all kinds of problems: First, the list of products to be entered on the "Common List" was very short, and not very relevant. This list has since been expanded. Next, there were very strict rules of origin in order to benefit from the preferential tariffs, including rules on minimum national ownership and management of companies producing eligible goods. Although these rules are in the process of being softened, in the meanwhile, very few products have in reality been eligible for the PTA tariffs, and it is not known (by this author) the value and volume of trade that have actually benefited. Finally, for a number of countries it took several years before they actually published the tariff reductions to be accorded to other PTA countries. As one consequence of all these problems and delays, PTA at its summit in 1987 decided to delay the further reduction of tariffs, in order to obtain first and "original reduction", then a further reduction of 50 per cent of the remaining tariffs by 1996, and thereafter a rapid total elimination by year 2000. It remains to be seen whether this revised schedule will be achieved.

Another case seems to be the PTA Trade and Development Bank, which was formally established in 1986. At that time, long before most member states had provided for their subscription to the Bank's capital stock, the PTA Council of Ministers were equally concerned about the appointment of the Bank's directors and alternative directors (PTA, 1985:13–17). The Bank only became operational in 1989, but there are still no reports of any lending operations.

A possible exception to this dismal picture may be the PTA Clearing House, which has been operated by the Reserve Bank of Zimbabwe since its inception in 1984. The Clearing House was also off to a slow start, however, with few member states really utilising its facilities, and ending up with most of the accounts to be settled in convertible currencies because of lack of balancing trade. Problems were also accounted when Zambia during the first periods treated the Clearing House as if trade could always be covered in local currencies, and when several other countries insisted that certain transactions never-theless had to be paid up in convertible currencies without going through the Clearing House. According to the latest available reports, the Clearing House is now handling more than 70 per cent of total intra-regional trade[5], and approximately half is settled in convertible currencies (Walraet, 1991:40).

According to its Treaty, the PTA has a clear mandate to develop fur-ther into a free trade area and eventually a common market. Decisions are to be taken by consensus, but once agreed, the member states are at least on paper legally bound by these decisions. The examples given above, as well as other reports and observations, give a clear indication, however, that the member states do not feel strongly com-mitted to the decisions taken even by the PTA Authority (summit). In my opinion, it is quite obvious that no country in the region is will-ing to accept PTA as a supra-national organisation, or let any real eco-nomic decision be taken by such a regional body. National govern-ments will only implement those policies to which they have them-selves agreed. This may, of course, include measures such as those mutually agreed at a PTA meeting, based on the assumption that also the other countries will implement the same measures.

It should therefore also be realised that PTA is a relatively weak organisation, with little or no influence on national policies or prior-ities in the region. In addition, the PTA is also becoming increasing-ly dependent on donor funding. According to recent information, donor contributions now provide USD 10 million out of an annual budget of USD 13 million.[6]

Despite the above picture, PTA do have a certain backing and sup-port, and not only at the rhetoric level. The primary supporters seem to be the private business and trading sectors, who probably see PTA as a means of reducing trade barriers and liberalise the economies of the region. This is the case especially for exporters, and perhaps strongest in countries like Kenya and Zimbabwe. However, traders (importers) are also looking for ways of acquiring goods at lower tariff rates, with a possible premium price (profit) when sold at the local markets. Local manufacturers, however, will often be hesitant to open up the borders to competitive imports, even from neighbouring countries. In most PTA countries, the Ministers of Trade (and Industry) will often be supporting PTA and its policies, while Ministries of Finance, or of Development (and Planning) may be more sceptical.

There may therefore be concluded from the above that PTA is primarily beneficial to, and therefore also primarily supported by private industry and commercial interests in Kenya and Zimbabwe, to a much lesser extent to similar interests in at least some of the other member states, and very little beyond that. However, the increasing concerns and activities of PTA in other sectors, such as industrial ventures, regional training programmes, and communication projects are signs that the organisation is realising that its aim of regional cooperation and integration will not be achieved by trade measures alone.

PTA AS AN INSTRUMENT FOR PROMOTING INTRA-REGIONAL TRADE

It is well known that the constraints limiting intra-PTA trade are several, and go far beyond tariffs and non-tariff barriers. These constraints may roughly be grouped in the following broad categories:

Lack of complementarities. This is the overriding problem: that goods produced in the region are not those demanded within the region: The PTA members are still basically producers/exporters of agricultural and other primary products, while they import manufactured consumer goods, capital goods, fuels and industrial inputs. As mentioned above, there is scope for an expansion of intra-regional trade based on the present economic structures, but in the longer run these structures will have to be changed primarily through industrialisation. A related problem, is that certain products in regional demand may be produced, but at such low quality that there is no market outside a very protected national one. I have earlier suggested in the case of SADCC that without major structural changes, it may still be possible to increase the present level of intra-regional trade by at least 40 per cent (Ofstad et al., 1986). If we also consider unregistered trade, it may not be reasonable to expect a potential doubling of the present recorded level. But expansion beyond that, will only be possible through economic restructuring and industrialisation.

Cost and relative prices. For many potential products, the cost of production and pricing policies in many PTA member states have resulted in high and non-competitive prices, as seen by the importers. This has partly been related to inefficient production, but also the stiff and administered pricing policies, and the over-valued currencies of many PTA members. In many countries industrial production was especially heavily protected and could only produce for a well protected national market. However, as a result of the liberalisation, deregulation and devaluations that have taken place in most PTA member states as part of the so-called structural adjustment programmes, this particular type of trade constraints is gradually being reduced. Local production units are being forced into more open international competition.[7]

Transport costs and inadequate transports. As mentioned above, trade has mainly taken place among neighbouring countries where there is a reasonable transport and communication infrastructure. For longer distances the lack of or inadequacy of surface transport facilities such as roads and railways, represents a serious constraint. Exceptions exist for high-value goods that can travel by air, or some cases where sea transport is feasible. Local wars add to the transport problem, and increase costs further. In many cases, transported goods run a high risk of losses through theft or damages. The solution to these problems will only be found in the longer term, when peaceful conditions are re-established, and large-scale investments in infrastructures have been made over several years. In the shorter run, the scope is to develop trade opportunities along existing and improved transport routes, over shorter distances, and perhaps within smaller clusters of countries than the present PTA.

Established interests and trade patterns, including donor policies. Even when products are available, at the right price, and without transport problems, non-regional products may still be preferred. The explanation may then be found in limited information, the transaction costs (perceived or real) for importers to look for alternative suppliers or change supplier, lack of incentives for the potential exporter to exploit new regional markets, or even that established trading patterns carry additional benefits to the involved partners. Some of these constraints may be overcome through information networks, trade fairs, increased business contacts, etc., while other types of well-established business contacts and practices may be difficult to change.

A similar problem exists in relation to donor financing of specific projects, commodity imports, or various forms of tied aid, which are still widespread. Official development assistance (ODA) finances between 50 and 100 per cent of all imports in at least eleven of the eighteen PTA countries. There are a few exceptional cases where donor funds have been earmarked for regional imports. But in most cases deliveries from the donor countries have a real or imagined preference. Since donor financed commodities are often exempted from customs duties and from all non-tariff barriers, their removal also in intra-regional trade will have no direct effect. The negative effects for intra-regional trade from donor tying, can only be overcome by competitive international bidding and treatment of donor-financed imports at par with ordinary imports.

Finance and payments restrictions. The general lack of foreign currency to pay for imports has hampered not only intra-regional trade, but also overall trade. Regional traders do not have the same opportunity, however, to obtain donor financing, or provide export credits. For two countries with import restrictions, it has been difficult to make counter trade efficient. The PTA Clearing House has been an important measure for the reduction of the direct payments problem. It has also indirectly provided short-term credits. On-going liberalisation programmes in member states might reduce the relevance of foreign exchange limitations, and partly make the Clearing House redundant. However, the need for an export credit facility still remains.[8]

Uncertainties. Another common problem for regional traders, is the uncertainties often encountered for either the importer in terms of timeliness and qualities of deliveries, or for the producer in terms of payments, etc. While some of these problems are imagined and related to limited information or well-established trading patterns as described above, there are also real problems involved. These constraints can be overcome by improved quality on both sides, and to some extent by improved credit systems.

Non-tariff barriers. In the PTA region, the main non-tariff barrier has been the system of administered imports and import licences. The existence of rationed foreign exchange, has provided the successful importers with an additional premium (which has only partly been countered by high tariffs and extra-ordinary payments), and thereby less incentive to purchase from the most competitive source. In some cases, however, bilateral trade agreements and countertrade deals have benefited intra-regional trade, under a system of trade licensing. Under the present economic reforms and liberalisation programmes, an increasing number of products may be imported under an Open General Licence (OGL) system. While undermining the system of bilateral agreements, the OGL nevertheless removes the non-tariff barriers, resulting in open import systems.

Tariffs. Tariff rates do play a role in certain cases, particularly where trade has been facilitated by other means. A study covering thirty-nine development countries found that a reciprocal tariff reduction of 20 per cent, resulted on average, in a 5.5 per cent increase in trade in the short run, and a 15 per cent increase in the longer run, after new investments had been made (Linnemann and Verbruggen, 1991). A similar study has not been made for the PTA region, however, so the quantative effects of the initial PTA tariff reductions have not been established. There are now two trends that have opposite effects on the role of tariffs; the general liberalisation taking place resulting in more competitive economic environments may lead to a relatively greater role of tariffs. At the same time many countries are also reducing their overall tariff rates for all imports, and this naturally leads to a reduced relative role for tariffs and tariff preferences.

The relevance of PTA

When we consider the PTA programme and institutions in relation to the above discussion about trade constraints, we see that PTA has primarily attacked the problems of tariffs, the lack of trade information, and that of payments. PTA has only to a limited extent dealt with the problems related to transport, and to poor compatibility (industrial joint ventures and cooperation). At best, it has therefore had a limited positive impact on the intra-regional trade structures.

We have also seen that due to the profound economic reforms being undertaken in most PTA countries, the relative roles of the different trade constraints are changing. In particular, the role of over-valued currencies, payment restrictions, and non-tariff barriers may be reduced. The future role of tariffs may remain of less importance. This may even reduce the need for the Clearing House, and make tariff preferences of even less relevance. To be relevant in the future, PTA will therefore have to reconsider its strategy for economic integration through trade measures, and will have to concentrate more on the means to increase economic compatibility and improve transport and communication in the region, and to influence donor policies.

WILL SOUTH AFRICA'S TRADE BENEFIT FROM PTA MEMBERSHIP?

South Africa's exports (excluding gold) total around USD 13.5 billion (1989), while that of the entire PTA is approx. 10 billion. While intra-PTA trade has been fluctuating around USD 600 annually, South Africa's exports to the PTA region (and thus excluding Botswana) may be around USD 2,600 million, of which approximately 60 per cent are to the neighbouring SACU members.[9] This is four times as much as the present intra-PTA exports! In addition, there is an estimated unrecorded export from South Africa to its nearest neighbours or around USD 300 million annually (Tjønneland, 1992:72). South Africa's imports from the PTA region are more limited, probably around USD 700 million, but are still comparable with the present intra-PTA trade.

The pattern and limitations on South Africa's regional trade, are very similar to what has been described above, and it is also primarily geared towards the nearest countries and others with good communications. South Africa's regional trade is substantially based on South Africa's manufactures. South Africa has the additional advantage, however, of a preferential status in the members of the SACU (Botswana, Lesotho, Swaziland), and in Namibia. On the other hand, it has had a disadvantage in those PTA countries that have applied sanctions against the apartheid regime, and to some extent also in the SADCC region, where several donors have avoided purchases from South Africa.

With the complete lifting of sanctions, only those particular constraints will disappear. This may result in increased exports to countries like Angola, Tanzania and Kenya. But it may not have an immediate impact in countries that have been trading freely all along. There are presently several on-going studies, attempting to foresee the impact on regional trade from the lifting of sanctions and reintegration of South Africa into more normal economic relationships with the whole African continent, and it may therefore be too early to predict the expected quantative changes. Tjønneland cautions that there are a number of severe limitations on future South African trade expansions to Africa and the region, among them the medium to high costs of South Africa's manufacturing industries, and the limited ability to pay in the PTA countries. At the same time, the new situation may provide opportunities for some neighbouring countries to penetrate the South African market with labour-intensive low-cost industrial products (Tjønneland, 1992:73–74).

If South Africa was to join PTA, South Africa's membership of the PTA could only be carried out if specific clauses and conditions are negotiated. One of the most important elements in the PTA Treaty, is the most-favoured-nation (MFN) clause. This clause may not have been strictly implemented, but these exceptions have not had much impact on other member countries, and have therefore been implicitly accepted as a means of promoting intra-regional trade. However, there is a specific exemption for Botswana (if it were to join), Lesotho and Swaziland because of their membership in the SACU. In the case of South Africa, this problem has to be solved, either:

a. South Africa will have to grant all PTA members the same free entry into South Africa for their goods on an MFN-basis, in accordance with the PTA Treaty, or

b. PTA will have to accept a similar exception for South Africa, allowing it to continue its free trade within SACU without automatically granting the same to all other PTA members, or

c. SACU will have to be re-negotiated, and new tariff barriers will have to be erected within SACU, or

d. Negotiation will take place, allowing for a transitional period, partial tariff reductions, or other possible agreed compromise solutions.

Of the above, alternative a) may carry excessively high costs for South Africa if it is to be acceptable, although one should not rule out this possibility completely. The b) alternative will bring very few immediate benefits to the trade regime, if everything just continues as at present. Alternative c) also seems rather unlikely, but should perhaps not be ruled out, as there are also other arguments for dissolving or renegotiating SACU. The most likely outcome may therefore be alternative d), but this is most difficult to predict. There is a possibility that the negotiated agreement will tend towards alternative a), if South Africa by joining PTA would like to be seen to accept some balancing of the benefits from regional integration, in favour of the less developed PTA members.[10]

There is also a more limited trade agreement between Zimbabwe and South Africa, providing duty free entry for most agricultural products and preferential tariffs for manufactured goods with a high local value added component (Ridell, 1992:43). This agreement has been accepted, at least in practice, by PTA, without requiring Zimbabwe to grant the same preferences to all PTA members. However, it is less likely that PTA will accept this agreement if South Africa also joins. The arguments and alternatives are parallel to the above regarding the SACU obligations.

If South Africa joins the PTA, and does provide lower preferential tariffs on a mutual and reciprocal basis in accordance with the PTA agreements, this will therefore not affect its trade with SACU and with Namibia, and probably not with Zimbabwe. It may, however, improve the competitive position of South African exporters in countries like Malawi, Zambia, Mozambique, Tanzania, Angola and Kenya. However, in many of these countries substantial parts of their imports are financed by tied donor funds, which will limit the opportunities for the South Africans. From South Africa's point of view, it would therefore be beneficial, if it was granted preferential status in these countries under the PTA agreement. It should be noted that five of these are also SADCC countries, and of the PTA non-SADCC countries, very few outside of Kenya will be of much interest to South

Africa in the next five to ten years, for the reasons outlined. At the same time, it can be assumed that South Africa may be equally interested in trade agreements and preferential status in some non-PTA countries, such as Zaïre, Nigeria, and other West African countries, which represent an equally interesting market for South Africa.

While South Africa stands to gain from preferential trade agreements, it may therefore be questioned whether PTA is a useful framework for such agreements, as seen from South Africa. We also see that from the point of view of South Africa, preferential tariffs may be of less importance than the general liberalisation of import regimes in many of these potential markets, including the untying of development aid.

Viewed from the importing countries, however, it is not obvious that they will gain from providing South Africa preferential entry. Such policies may result in more expensive imports from South Africa being preferred by the importers, because of the lower tariffs. This will result in both higher outlays in foreign exchange, and lower tariff revenues for the government. It may, in some cases, also result in increased competition for local producers.

This can only be justified, if the country's exporters will gain even more from obtaining preferential treatment on the South African market. Again, since SACU members, Namibia and Zimbabwe already have such preferential access, this will only affect the countries outside of this group. There are few PTA countries today in a position to make use of such opportunities. One could imagine that countries like Malawi, Mozambique (after the war is over), Kenya, and Mauritius will become candidates for increased exports to South Africa in the short and medium term. In the somewhat longer term, Tanzania may also recuperate and also develop a stronger economy in export markets. But at the same time, experiences have shown that those countries that already have free access to the South African market, such as the SACU members, have not been able to use this as an opportunity to industrialise and penetrate into this market. On the contrary, it is often argued (and can also be shown, see e.g. Nordås, 1992) that being a part of a customs union with South Africa, has actually reduced industrialisation in these countries. In order to benefit from South Africa's membership, there may therefore be a need for some sort of non-reciprocal preferential treatment. (There may also be other benefits arising from South African membership in PTA, such as a greater opportunity to attract South African investments, easier movement of manpower, access to training centres, etc. In all of these, there will be pros and cons that cannot be discussed in this chapter, where we are concentrating on trade and trade related issues.)

My conclusion is that South Africa stands to gain more than the present PTA countries, if South Africa were to join PTA and accept mutual and reciprocal tariff preferences. Those countries to be most affected are likely to be the SADCC countries outside of SACU, plus possibly Kenya and Mauritius. The net benefits to Zimbabwe seem particularly uncertain. Since I have argued above that the main interest groups behind PTA are the industrial and trading sectors in Kenya and Zimbabwe, it is not certain that they will accept South African membership in PTA without considerable negotiations.

I have also questioned whether PTA is the best framework for such trade negotiations. It may be more relevant for regional development to strengthen the ties within closer and more coherent regional groupings, such as SADCC including South Africa, but possibly excluding Tanzania. Such an economic grouping could enter into separate agreement with other countries outside of the grouping, such as Kenya and Mauritius (possibly with an East African grouping), or Nigeria and ECOWAS.

PTA MECHANISMS TO PROMOTE A BALANCED REGIONAL DEVELOPMENT

I have argued above that there will be a need for some balancing mechanisms if South Africa is to join PTA, in order for the PTA to benefit from this expansion. But does the PTA Treaty in theory and practice allow for such unbalanced treatment?

At the outset, PTA aims to develop a free trade area, and eventually a common market. As a preferential trade area, non-discrimination and MFN treatment on an equal basis, have also been important elements. Under these conditions, any discrimination of individual members, be they weak or strong, is against the text as well as the spirit of the PTA. Any deviation from this, will therefore have to be treated as exceptions to the rule.

Nevertheless, some such exceptions have been made. The most notable exception relates to the SACU members who are not obliged to follow the agreed tariff reduction schedules. But this exception is not based on the relative weakness of these countries. Another central exception has been made in the definition of the rules of origin for goods to be accorded preferential treatment. One of the requirements has been that a certain minimum proportion of the ownership and management had to comprise nationals of the producing country. This rule, however, was agreed in order to protect national industries vis-a-vis international companies, and not necessarily related to the level of development in the particular country.

The less developed countries as well as crisis-affected newcomers such as Mozambique, have been afforded special derogations both in relation to the requirements in terms of national ownership, and postponement in implementing the tariff reductions. After several years of studies and negotiations also the formula for contributions to the PTA budget was also amended, in order to reduce the burden on the smaller countries (Martin, 1990:168–171). Few other special programmes have been implemented. In the PTA Secretary General's own summary of achievements and problems (PTA, 1991), the question of uneven distribution of benefits was not even mentioned. Though he did allude to the need to design and implement special programmes to assist the PTA Least Developed Countries (LDCs) to industrialise much faster, this priority is not repeated in the new *PTA Trade and Development Strategy*, which was being drafted in 1991 (PTA, 1991b).

One reason why little emphasis has been given to special measures in favour of the less developed countries in the region, may be that most members belong to the group of LDCs as defined by the UN, and most countries are indeed relatively underdeveloped and disadvantaged. It is therefore difficult to design special policies that will in fact cover the majority of the members.

If South Africa joins, the situation will be quite different, however. South Africa is so far ahead of the rest in terms of economic development, that some differentiation will have to be introduced. However, as indicated above, there are examples of such differentiation having been made, dealing with South Africa may require a more total reconsideration of the PTA concept and spirit of non-discrimination. It is difficult in this chapter to foresee or prescribe how this can be done. Nevertheless, a few possible methods could be mentioned:

— South Africa may accept non-reciprocal tariff reductions and other trade preferences, for instance along the line of the GSP system accorded by industrial countries to developing ones, or along the lines of the Lomé agreements,
— A system of compensation for tariff revenue may be developed foregone, for instance along the line of the SACU mechanisms,
— Special incentives may be implemented for South African investments and soft loans to other PTA members, in order to encourage transfer of capital and technology from South Africa to the other PTA members.

Again, one could question whether PTA provides a suitable framework for such negotiations. Since South Africa's interests will be limied in most of the PTA region outside of the SADCC, it may be more feasible to negotiate within a smaller grouping. This will also be less costly for South Africa, and possibly provide more benefits to those countries most directly affected. On the other hand, PTA is a larger unit and will possibly have a stronger bargaining position vis-a-vis South Africa. This last point is uncertain , however, since most of the other PTA countries are of only marginal interest for South Africa.

CONCLUDING REMARKS

If PTA is to become an effective tool for regional cooperation and development, it will have to re-orient its policies, along lines that are already under way. I have also argued that further revisions are necessary, if South Africa is to join as a full ordinary member. Finally, I have questioned whether PTA is the best framework for such renegotiations, and have argued that a smaller and more coherent grouping of countries might be more suitable and efficient.

There are many good reasons, however, why regional cooperation and integration are also useful mechanisms for development in the Southern Africa region. One of these is the world-wide tendency towards regional groupings, and in negotiations on an international and global level, individual countries in the region will be able to improve their bargaining power if they cooperate more closely. One area of negotiation which seems close and most relevant, concerns international donors and their policies and practices. A good starting point might be a joint effort to negotiate un-tying of development aid, at least in order to provide preferences for regional products.

NOTES

1. In addition. Egypt has been present as an observer during PTA meetings.
2. Before Angola and Sudan joined as member states.
3. In more peaceful times, there may also develop a third "cluster" for the countries on the Horn of Africa: Ethiopia, Djibouti and Somalia.
4. This is not to be taken as an absolute condition. Countries in the region also trade in products like maize, sugar, meat, fish etc. Even based on such products alone, there is a potential for increased trade. The potential is far greater for manufactured goods, however.
5. According to one source, it handled USD 550 million in 1990 (PTA, 1991a).

6. Information provided by PTA to Norway in April 1991, according to report from the Norwegian Embassy in Harare, 23 April 1991.
7. Whether the local producers manage to survive under increased competition, is a separate question.
8. The role of the Clearing House is further elaborated by Harvey and Hudson in chapter 5.
9. These are rough calculations, based on Tjønneland (1992:72) and Ofstad et al. (1986:139).
10. This issue is also discussed by Isaksen in chapter 9.

EXTERNAL RESOURCES
ORIENTED PERSPECTIVES

11. Factors Affecting Flows of External Capital to Post-Apartheid Southern Africa

Bertil Odén

The aim of this chapter is to discuss the prospects for external capital flows to Southern Africa in the post-apartheid era. Southern Africa is defined as South Africa plus the ten SADC(C)[1] states. Three categories of external resources will be discussed: Direct investments, long term non-concessional loans and development assistance (ODA as defined by OECD and therefore including credits with a grant element of 25 per cent or more).

The discussion will not be related to calculations of any "resource gaps" for the region. Any such calculation will most probably be futile due to the high degree of uncertainty in any attempted projection. Nor will the arguments related to the possible negative effects of large external capital inflows on domestic resource mobilisation, "dutch disease" effects etc. be discussed in this context, although they are relevant in some of the SADCC countries.

As is always stated, the development in Southern Africa after the fall of apartheid will be closely linked to the development in South Africa. Many scholars, main economic actors and aid agencies are producing regional scenarios based on various assumptions regarding the South African process. They range from annihilation or chaos over regional fragmentation, market led regional integration to regional development integration aimed at reducing the present regional imbalances. See for instance Davies (1990c), Green (1991), Stoneman-Thompson (1991b), Martin (1991) and SADCC (1991a). Studies commissioned by the World Bank and the African Development Bank, ADB, are planned to be ready later this year.

I will not use much space on this issue here, as it is dealt with in other chapters (See those by Davies, Ohlson-Stedman and Tostensen). It is sufficient simply to state that the following discussion is based on a "main-stream scenario" for development in South Africa, including *inter alia* that the on-going process towards a post-apartheid society continues and that an interim government is elected no later than 1994. As a result of these steps, the on-going dismantling of the international sanctions can be expected to continue. Although political and social events may continue to be turbulent, no major set-backs are assumed to occur and furthermore it is foreseen that the violence in the society can be kept under reasonable control by the new government.

A further assumption is that the economic policy of the new government will be some type of mixed economy, which is largely accepted by private capital at the same time as it delivers gradual improvements to the majority of the population, who were previously heavily discriminated by the apartheid system.

Such a scenario may be criticised for being far too optimistic. However, we shall see that it is still not enough to paint a rosy picture for the future capital flows to the region.

As a starting point, some brief facts on the flows of external resources during the 1980s will be provided. This is followed by a discussion of how a number of factors might affect the three categories of external flows. I will deal with these factors at three levels: the global or world system level, the regional and the national level. Finally I will offer some tentative conclusions.

The chapter is mainly empirical; to the extent there is a theoretical basis, it falls within the realistic international political economy (RIPE) context.

THE DEVELOPMENT DURING THE 1980s

Our starting point will be the situation in the 1980s. Due to the apartheid policy in South Africa, which isolated that country from normal international contacts up to the beginning of the 1990s, we have to analyse the links with the rest of the world separately for South Africa and the SADCC countries.

International sanctions against South Africa were significantly strengthened in the mid-1980s. USA, EC, the Nordic countries, and the Commonwealth countries introduced or sharpened legislation regarding trade and investment relations. The decision by the large international banks in August 1985, to no longer renew their outstanding short term loans to South African debtors, was of the utmost economic importance. This led to a declaration of moratorium from the South African government and a total lack of access to long term debt for three years and only very limited access up to the present.

This resulted in a change in the net capital flows to South Africa. Up to 1984, it had been positive, whereas from 1985 it turned negative and forced the government to reintroduce the financial rand and to restrict import to provide the necessary current account surplus.

Table 11.1. *Net capital flows to South Africa 1985–1990*
(Rand million)

	1985	1986	1987	1988	1989	1990	1991
Long-term[1]	−522	−3,162	−1,701	1,173	−1,230	−1,945	−2,706
Short–term[1]	−7,799	−1,910	−1,150	−5,035	−3,115	−929	−3,345
Total[1]	−8,321	−5,072	−2,851	−6,208	−4,345	−2,874	−6,051
Net flow as[2] % of GDP	−6.8	−3.6	−1.7	−3.1	−1.9	−1.1	

[1] South African Reserve Bank
[2] IMF

Direct investment

According to Table 11.2, taken from Stoneman-Thompson (1991b),
foreign direct investment flows changed significantly during the
decade. In 1980–84, the total inflow of foreign direct investments to
South Africa was almost 1 billion USD, while the disinvestment
during 1985–89 was almost 0,5 billion USD. The main sellers were US
companies and to a lesser extent companies from UK and other countries. (IRRC, 1991). During this period a significant outflow of South
African direct investment capital also took place as a number of South
African companies invested in European countries. (AAM, 1988).

Table 11.2. *Foreign direct investment into Southern Africa*
(Total for period, USD million)

Country	1980–84	1985–89
Angola	373.6	−27.5
Botswana	307.1	354.2
Lesotho	19.4	37.5
Malawi	13.2	1.0
Mozambique	6.3	1.7
Swaziland	47.7	192.3
Tanzania	33.9	10.1
Zambia	106.0	128.8
Zimbabwe	−0.2	−20.1
SADCC total	907.0	678.0
South Africa	944.0	−453.0

Source: Stoneman, C., & C. B. Thompson, 1991, *Southern Africa after Apartheid*, Africa
Recovery Briefing Paper No. 4. They refer to UN Centre for Transnational
Corporations, based on IMF, OECD and national government data.

For the SADCC countries as a group, the picture was different and individual countries underwent different developments. As can be seen from Table 11.2, the direct investments in the SADCC countries during 1980–84 were almost as big as those in South Africa, while during 1985–89 a net inflow of direct investments continued in some of the SADCC countries. Most investments during this period took place in Botswana, Swaziland and Zambia. Statistics on direct investments differ between sources, and the figures published in the World Debt Tables (Table 11.3) for the SADCC countries are not exactly the same as those in Table 11.2, but the main trend is similar.

Table 11.3. *Direct investment in the SADCC countries*
(Net, USD million)

Country	1980	1985	1986	1987	1988	1989	1990	1986–90
Angola	0	0	0	0	0	0	0	0
Botswana	112	54	70	114	40	98	148	470
Lesotho	5	5	2	6	21	13	17	59
Malawi	10	1	0	0	0	0	0	0
Mozambique	0	0	0	0	0	0	0	0
Swaziland	27	11	31	48	51	74	45	249
Tanzania	0	0	0	0	0	0	0	0
Zambia	62	52	28	75	93	0	0	196
Zimbabwe	2	3	8	–31	–18	0	0	–41
Total SADCC	218	126	139	212	187	185	210	933

Source: The World Bank, 1992, *World Debt Tables 1991–92.*

Commercial loans

Commercial long term capital was a scarce commodity in the region during the second half of the 1980s. The net long-term capital outflow from South Africa was negative and fluctuated between 1.2 and 3.2 billion Rand per year in the period 1986–1991, which corresponded to between 0.5 and 2.2 per cent of GDP. An excellent review of South African international borrowing has been published by Jonathan Garner and Jonathan Leape at the London School of Economics (Garner & Leape, 1991).

Some of the bigger SADCC countries (Mozambique, Tanzania and Zambia) are in a serious debt crisis, and cannot pay scheduled debt service. They try to pay their debts to the IFIs in order to be eligible for new loans.In addition, they hope to receive new ODA from the bilateral aid agencies. Normally they will only repay other commercial loans if this paves the way for new loans from the same source. However, as can be seen in Table 11.4, non-concessional loans were made available to Mozambique and Zambia. In the case of Zambia, this is probably explained by the fact that the copper mining company, ZCCM, may receive loans due to its economically semi-autonomous position in the Zambian economy.

The main borrowing country in the region during the period was Angola, which took 95 per cent of the total net flow, in spite of the on-going war. The registered non-concessional loans are probably related to the oil exploration, carried out as an enclave economy, separated from the rest of the Angolan economy. Four countries—Malawi, Swaziland, Tanzania and Zimbabwe—registered negative net flows during the period.

The net flow of non-concessional loans to the SADCC countries as a whole amounted to 13 per cent of the total aid inflows during 1986–90. With the exception of Angola, commercial loans have played a minor role for the SADCC countries during the period. However, the net outflows of commercial capital from Malawi, Swaziland, Tanzania and Zimbabwe constituted a further strain on their current accounts.

Table 11.4. *Non-concessional loans to the SADCC countries*

Country	1980	1985	1986	1987	1988	1989	1990	1986–90
Angola		1.168	329	397	382	368	488	1.964
Botswana	12	32	18	50	0	–4	–49	15
Lesotho	3	5	1	18	12	2	2	35
Malawi	66	–21	–32	–16	–11	–7	–29	–95
Mozambique	70	61	74	7	53	10	205	
Swaziland	6	10	1	–15	–11	–12	–30	–67
Tanzania	179	31	3	–12	–19	–18	–23	–69
Zambia	157	109	75	–22	37	26	25	141
Zimbabwe	97	–22	–68	–59	–91	73	81	–64
Total SADCC		1.382	388	415	306	481	475	2.065

Note: The table includes net flows, excl. IMF, USD million. It excludes Namibia.
Source: The World Bank, 1992, *World Debt Tables 1991–92*.

Aid

During the 1980s and particularly the latter half of the decade the
SADCC area has been very "aid intensive". The inflow of aid per capita to the region is around three times the average for the third world.
In spite of the low share of third world population (2 per cent) and
third world GDP (1 per cent), the region receives more than 7 per cent
of total development assistance.

As shown in Table 11.5, the ODA flows to the SADCC countries
have increased significantly from 1986. Over the three-year period
1988–90, the region received around double the amount it received
during 1983–85, in current USD terms. Although changing prices and
exchange rates make exact comparisons difficult, it is obvious that
the aid flow has also increased significantly in real terms. Part of the
increase is explained by the additional aid which is given as support
to on-going structural adjustment programmes. The increased aid
financing of the SADCC transport corridors through Mozambique
and the Tazara and the DSM harbour in Tanzania accounts for another portion of the increase in aid.

The main donors to SADCC and the SADCC countries are Sweden,
EC, IDA, Japan, UK, Germany, Italy, Norway and the Netherlands.
(See Table 11.6 for the main donors to the region and Table 11.7 for
the main donors to the individual SADCC countries). The EC and its
member countries provide almost half of the aid to the region and
the Nordic countries more than 23 per cent. Or expressed differently: The aid from the Nordic countries constitutes a larger inflow than
all commercial capital.

Let us now turn from the 1980s to the 1990s and discuss some of
the factors that will influence the future development.

FACTORS AT THE GLOBAL LEVEL AND THEIR IMPLICATIONS[2]

Southern Africa's share of world trade and the world economy has
been generally reduced during the 1980s, as has the share of the entire Sub-Saharan Africa. Southern Africa plays a marginal role in the
global economy. Together the region exports less than 1 per cent of
global exports and its imports are around 0.9 per cent of global
imports. In both cases, the region as a whole plays a role similar to
Denmark in the world trade.

As has so often been stated, the potential of the region is much
greater. Its population is around 100 million, it is one of the richest
regions in the world with regards to mineral and energy resources.

Table 11.5. *Net disbursements of ODA from all sources to the SADCC countries 1980, 1986–1990.*

Country	1980	1986	1987	1988	1989	1990
Angola	53	131	135	159	146	211
Botswana	106	102	156	151	159	151
Lesotho	94	88	108	108	127	138
Malawi	143	198	280	366	396	450
Mozambique	169	422	651	893	762	923
Namibia	0	(15)	(17)	(23)	(59)	(62)
Swaziland	50	35	45	38	29	54
Tanzania	679	681	882	982	916	1,155
Zambia	318	464	430	478	389	430
Zimbabwe	164	225	294	273	265	336
Total SADCC	1,776	2,346	2,981	3,448	3,189	3,848

Note: USD million at current prices and exchange rates. The total excludes Namibia.
Source: *DAC Development Report 1991* and previous years.

Table 11.6. *Main sources of aid to the SADCC countries in 1990*
ODA net disbursements to all SADCC countries.

Donor	million USD	per cent of total
1. Sweden	432	10.9
2. IDA	356	9.0
3. Germany	327	8.2
4. EC	287	7.2
5. Italy	274	6.9
6. Norway	269	6.8
7. Netherlands	232	5.9
8. UK	213	5.4
9. USA	193	4.9
10. Japan	167	4.2
11. Denmark	160	4.0
12. France	154	3.9
13. Finland	144	3.6
14. Canada	142	3.6
15. African Dev. Fund	111	2.8
(16.) Others	506	12.8
Total	3,967	100.0

Source: OECD, 1992, *Geographical Distribution of Financial Flows to Developing Countries 1987/90*, Paris.

Table 11.7. *Main donors to the individual SADCC countries, 1990*

SADCC country	Total ODA (million USD)	Main donors	% of total
Angola	211.7	1. Sweden	18 %
		2. Italy	18 %
		3. EC	9 %
		4. ADF	8 %
		5. Canada	5 %
Botswana	148.1	1. Sweden	17 %
		2. Norway	15 %
		3. Germany	13 %
		4. USA	10 %
		5. Canada	8 %
Lesotho	137.8	1. France	12 %
		2. Germany	10 %
		3. USA	10 %
		4. ADF	10 %
		5. EC	9 %
Malawi	478.7	1. IDA	20 %
		2. Germany	11 %
		3. UK	11 %
		4. EC	9 %
		5. WFP	9 %
Mozambique	946.1	1. Sweden	14 %
		2. Italy	11 %
		3. EC	9 %
		4. France	8 %
		5. IDA	7 %
Swaziland	55.1	1. USA	25 %
		2. EC	15 %
		3. Italy	10 %
		4. Denmark	9 %
		5. Germany	7 %
Tanzania	1,154.9	1. IDA	16 %
		2. Sweden	13 %
		3. Italy	9 %
		4. Norway	9 %
		5. Netherlands	8 %
Zambia	491.6	1. Germany	16 %
		2. Norway	11 %
		3. Netherlands	9 %
		4. UK	9 %
		5. Japan	8 %
Zimbabwe	343.2	1. Germany	14 %
		2. Sweden	11 %
		3. Japan	8%
		4. Netherlands	7 %
		5. Norway	7 %

Source: OECD, 1992, *Geographical Distribution of Financial Flows to Developing Countries 1987/90*, Paris.

Its agricultural potential under peaceful and economically sound policy conditions is also very high. This means that under ideal circumstances, there should be a substantial external economic interest in the region. However, the real world is much harsher than the ideal and a number of external and regional factors makes it less probable that the outside world will show much interest in the region.

At the global level, one short-term factor is the low economic growth in the OECD countries. A continuation of the low demand for minerals and base metals will reduce the scope for increased exports from Southern Africa. The long term structural changes in the international division of labour due to technological breakthroughs in for instance the electronics, informations technology and bio-engineering as well as resource-saving processing methods in other branches, are however factors of much greater importance than this short term trend. They threaten to further marginalise raw material and especially mineral producers. The implications of this development for a new democratic government in South Africa is less resources for restructuring and dealing with issues related to a more balanced development in the region.

There are both short and long term implication of the disintegration of the Soviet Union and the collapse of the socialist system in Eastern Europe. Some of those implications for Southern Africa are:

— Less political and economic interest in the region, no longer being an area of super-power competition.
— Former Soviet Union and the Eastern European countries are now competitors with the third world, including Southern Africa, for investment, capital and aid from the OECD countries.
— A rapidly growing interest in some of the countries of the former Soviet Union and Eastern Europe in trade and other economic co-operation with South Africa. A restriction on such a development, however, is the precarious foreign exchange situation of those countries.
— The former inflow of aid and loans from the socialist countries to some of the SADCC countries, mainly Mozambique and Angola, is now replaced by demands for repayments.
— The present global ideological hegemony of the market economy and multi-party democracy excludes any alternative economic and political system in Southern Africa for governments interested in inflow of external resources—be it commercial capital or aid resources. The scope for manoeuvre is *within* this paradigm.
— The economic trilateralisation and regionalisation of the world core economy between USA, Germany and Japan and their neigh-

bouring regions might create a degree of competition between commercial actors from those regions in Southern Africa, especially South Africa.

Hence changes at the world system level mainly suggest reduced flows of commercial capital and ODA to Southern Africa, due to the competition from the former Soviet Union, Eastern Europe, the Middle East and South East Asia.

The structural trends due to technological breakthroughs as well as continued low economic growth in the core countries will also reduce the interest in new mineral investments. The only exception to this trend might be the Japan centred economic block. This has been and will probably continue to be the fastest growing of the three core economic regions. During the sanctions period, South Africa increased its economic links with Japan and most of the NICs, especially Taiwan, Hong-Kong and South Korea. Those countries are dependent for their economic growth on further imports of minerals and raw material. The links with South Africa might therefore be further developed and include direct investments. This could give a certain economic pull effect in South Africa as well as possibly in the Southern Africa region.

Eastern Europe and the former Soviet Union are also interested in rapidly increased economic interchange with South Africa. One important restriction on the rate of growth of these links will be the scarcity of foreign exchange. As the trend during the last few years has indicated, the main resource flowing into South Africa is that of skilled labour.

FACTORS AT THE REGIONAL AND NATIONAL LEVEL

Direct investment

One factor is the acceptance of South Africa in the international community, including the gradual dismantling of sanctions. You can still hear the opinion that this will create a large inflow of foreign investments and foreign capital into South Africa. However, there has been a gradual change in this opinion. Most observers now suggest that large scale foreign investment will not take place just simply because of the dismantling of sanctions. This conclusion is built on several arguments. The last seven years have seen a discouraging rate of economic development in the country with an average GDP growth rate of between 1 and 2 per cent negative growth in 1990–1992, increasing unemployment, an inflation rate of around 16 per cent, lower productivity in mining and manufacturing. Violence, social disorder and an uncertain transition period do not improve the enthusiasm of foreign investors. Of even greater importance, however, is the uncertainty of the economic policy of the future government. The ANC leadership has not yet presented a coherent outline and the signals coming from different quarters are not consistent. Before this issue is clarified, it is unlikely that much foreign direct investment will take place.

Another important factor is the behaviour of the South African companies. If they continue to be reluctant to invest in South Africa and are rather seen to disinvest, this will not encourage foreign investors. There is also a practical and a psychological issue involved, which emerges in interviews with the management of US companies that have sold their subsidiaries in South Africa. The market has to be very promising if a company is to return after recently having decided to leave. On top of that some of the agreements are reported to include a clause, according to which the US company guarantees that it will not return and compete with the South African company taking over.

One sign of the reluctance is that so far no British firm has made any major investment since the voluntary restrictions were lifted in early 1990. Japanese and south east Asian companies might turn out as exceptions from this trend. Japanese companies are for instance reported to have invested in office buildings in central Johannesburg.

It should also be noted that it is in the interest of the present white government in South Africa to give the impression that foreign interest is strong, which means that any exploratory discussion and visiting fact-finding delegation will be as heavily exposed as possible in the media. For other motives, the ANC has also an interest in emphasising the interest of foreign companies, although the movement would like to see the companies postponing their actual investments until an interim government is in place in South Africa.

Hence it would seem that for a number of years, the foreign investment from the core countries in South Africa will be limited, and that long term development will depend on the policy carried out by the new government in South Africa.

Meanwhile the reduced isolation of South Africa has increased the scope for South African companies to invest in the neighbouring countries. This interest is especially evident in Mozambique and Angola, although in the latter case, only a few agreements have so far been reported.

It should however be noted that most South African companies are reluctant to finance investments in Mozambique using their own resources and therefore try to mobilize as much capital as possible in Mozambique, or seek other financial means.

The pattern of direct investment in the SADCC region may thus change in the 1990s compared to the 1980s. In the 1980s, the main foreign investment took place in Botswana, Swaziland and Zambia, while in the 1990s, Angola, Mozambique, Zambia and Zimbabwe may be of greater interest for foreign investors, provided the development towards peace continues in the first-mentioned two countries. In all cases, South Africa-based companies will be interested, and especially in Angola they will compete with companies from Portugal, Brazil and USA if present trends continue. In Zambia, Anglo-American Corporation has for example indicated an interest in modernizing copper mining.

The large foreign investments registered for Botswana during the 1980s are mainly related to two big projects, the Jwaneng diamond mine and the Sua Pan soda ash project. In the case of Swaziland an important part of the investments during the second half of the 1980s can be related to actions to avoid the effects of international sanctions against South Africa, e.g. the Coca-Cola removal of its extract factory and the removal of some textile factories from bantustans. To the extent the "sanction-busting" factor has been important, a reduction of investments in Swaziland will take place.

A successful process towards regional integration whether of the market or development category, might increase the interest for foreign investments in the region. The allocation pattern might however be the same as indicated above.

Loans

While the prospects for direct foreign investment do appear to be limited, the situation as regards South African borrowing on the international capital market is different.

South Africa´s gradual re-entry to international capital markets is documented by Garner and Leape (1991). It began in December 1988 with a small private placement on behalf of the government in the Swiss market. 1989 saw three issues in the Swiss market, ranging from 50 to 70 million CHF, and one in the German market. In 1990 there was an increase in the number of issues and the amount raised, seven issues of totally 264 million USD, which was more than twice the 128 million USD raised in 1989, The maturities of the new loans were also increased. Furthermore with this increase, the new loans only corresponded to one fifth of the bonds and syndicated loans that had to be re-paid during the year.

The trend toward increased South African access to long-term loans on the international capital market continued in 1991. In the first nine months of the year, eight bond issues were launched, including the first public bond since the debt crisis in 1985. The total amount was 554 million USD, once again more than doubling the total of the previous year. Nevertheless this was not sufficient to cover all bond repayments due during the year, although the net outflow is significantly reduced. The long term borrowing in the first half of the 1970s was of the order of 2.8 billion USD per annum. According to Garner and Leape a number of foreign capital investors are still reluctant to accept South African bonds, and none of the issues has so far been in the USA. During the first half of 1992 five bond issues, of which one by the South African government, are reported.[3] Their total of around Rand 2 billion is more than total repayment during the period. Due to the increasing violence in South Africa international lenders have been reluctant and no more loans were reported in the period June–November 1992.

The trend since 1989 will, however, in the medium term perspective, most probably be strengthened and South African companies, parastatals and governmental institutions will have increased access to the international capital market. Garner and Leape emphasize that three factors will determine South Africas access to international capital markets in the future:

— The degree of political and economic uncertainty in South Africa.
— The continued legal and political restrictions on new lending. The most important of these is the Gramm Amendment to the US Bretton Woods Agreements Act, which effectively prohibits the extension of an IMF facility to South Africa. This also affects private lending and the Debt Standstill that will have to be renegotiated in 1993.
— Developments in international capital markets. The present trend seems to be an increased investor interest in high-yielding bond issues from weaker international credits, which should favour South Africa.

This new situation will reduce the restriction on increased imports which has been in place since 1985 and a situation with an annual net capital inflow could be re-established. Thereby one—out of several—important obstacles to increased economic growth in South Africa will be removed.

The supply of loans to the SADCC countries will probably continue to be limited and selective, mainly related to specific projects or branches, such as oil production in Angola and possibly in Namibia as well as the few large scale mineral projects that might come on stream. The precarious economic position, including the debt crisis in Mozambique, Tanzania and Zambia, is a serious obstacle.

Further signs of improved regional economic integration might increase the interest of the international capital market to supply loans to the region. On the other hand, none of the SADCC countries, except Botswana and Swaziland, should be advised to increase their commercial lending.

ODA

As was stated in the previous section, some of the changes in the world system will probably reduce the international interest in allocating aid to Southern Africa, the main factor being the competition with other geographical areas, especially Eastern Europe. Another factor will be the reduced interest in the USA as Southern Africa is no longer an arena of global strategic interest. However, regional and national factors will probably be more decisive for the future aid flows.

One important factor is the fall of apartheid in South Africa and the subsequent lifting of its international isolation. This means that development aid to SADCC countries will be assessed outside the framework of an anti-apartheid policy, and therefore those countries will have to compete for aid on the same terms as other countries. Economic policy including implementation of structural adjustment programmes, a demonstrated interest in parliamentary democracy within a multi-party system, and the degree of emergency will be crucial factors in this context.

When it comes to development aid, a post-apartheid South Africa will play three different roles. It will receive a certain amount of aid for its own development. It might also be a modest donor country towards its neighbours. Finally, it will be a market where other donors, bilateral and multilateral, not least the World Bank, will to a significant extent procure goods and services under their respective aid programmes. This will constitute a major boost to the South African exports to the region.

In spite of the comparatively high GDP/capita of South Africa, which is twice as high as for Namibia and Botswana and three times as high as for Zimbabwe, the new government in South Africa can expect an inflow of international development aid, at least in the short and medium term perspective. The legacy of the apartheid system, with the enormous needs for improvement in the social sectors and physical infrastructure for the majority of the population, is a strong argument for significant aid to a post-apartheid South Africa. The main donors will probably be the main supporters of the anti-apartheid opposition such as the Nordic countries, the Netherlands and Canada, but also the EC, USA and the UK. The World Bank has indicated a strong interest in starting cooperation with South Africa, perhaps already under an interim government. The African Development Bank, ADB, is also preparing loans. ODA funds will probably also be used to support companies from the various donor countries in their export competition on the South African market.

Accurate figures on the volume of present ODA funding for anti-apartheid and humanitarian purposes in South Africa are difficult to obtain. A rough estimate is made in Table 11.8. According to this esti-

Table 11.8. *Estimated anti-apartheid and humanitarian aid to South Africa, 1990–1991*

Aid donor	million USD
Australia[a]	7
Canada[a]	11
Commonwealth[a]	2
Denmark[c]	11
ECa) and[b]	80
Finland[c]	3
France[d]	1
Germany (Fed.Rep.)[d]	4
Italy[d]	2
Netherlands[d]	7
Norway[c]	20
Sweden[c]	50
Switzerland[d]	4
UNDP[b]	2
United Kingdom[a]	16
USA[b]	40
Total	260

Sources: a. *Beyond Apartheid. Human Resources in a New South Africa.* Report of a Commonwealth Expert Group, London, 1991.
b. A. W. Marx, *Consultant Report to the UNDP on the Education Sector in South Africa*, New York, 1991.
c. Information from the Nordic aid agencies.
d. A. Whiteside, "Aid to South Africa" in *International Affairs Bulletin*, Vol. 15, No. 2, Johannesburg, 1991.

mate the total amount for 1990–1991 should be around USD 260 million and the indications are that some of the major donors such as EC and USA will increase their aid significantly during the next few years.

If South Africa should receive as much aid per capita (counting the African population only) as the present SADCC countries, that would imply around 800 m USD p.a. Alternatively if we take another comparison, Zimbabwe with one third of the African South African population has received around 250 m USD p.a. Three times that is 750 m USD. The high GDP/cap in South Africa will probably reduce the willingness among some donors and reduce that figure somewhat. On the other hand, the World Bank and the ADB have indicated a willingness to provide significant loans to South Africa.

A rough guess would be that South Africa can count upon commitments up to 1000 million USD per annum, of which more than half will come in the form of loans on IBRD-terms from the international financial institutions. One important prerequisite is that the new government is prepared to follow IMF and World Bank conditions. This will on the other hand reduce the government´s scope for short term actions to restructure the economy and improve the standard of living of the majority of the population, who form the political base for the new government. The choice for the new government will not be easy, especially as good relations to the IMF and the World Bank will also be necessary for the flows of commercial loans and direct investments.

During the 1980s the apartheid regime provided aid to some of the "cooperative" governments in the SADCC region, mainly to Malawi, but also technical assistance to Swaziland and Mozambique. While South African investments in the neighbouring states after apartheid will be dominated by private capital, it is possible that a modest technical assistance programme for neighbouring states will be developed. According to available information, the Development Bank of Southern Africa, DBSA, is interested in expanding their schemes from the bantustans to the SADCC countries as soon as that becomes politically possible. South African institutions, such as the DBSA might approach other donors, suggesting three-part projects/programmes, where a European donor agency finances technical assistance carried out by the South African institution.

This latter suggestion moves us to the third role as regards aid for a post-apartheid South Africa, namely as a market for the procurement of goods and services under DAC countries' aid programmes. This market has been restricted as long as apartheid ruled in South Africa, but will expand quickly as the comparative advantage of procurement in South Africa, due to transport, maintenance and service factors, becomes significant. It will provide South Africa based industrial and construction companies as well as technical, economic and other consultants with new markets. There they will normally compete with companies from the donor country and other companies in the region. Seminars to prepare South African based companies for these new business opportunities are already organised in the country. (See for instance the advertisement in *Star* 23/1 1991).

The aid disbursements to the SADCC countries in 1990 were around USD 3.9 billion of which around 20 per cent was in the form of technical assistance. If South African based companies could obtain 30 per cent of the procurement of goods and services, their exports to the region would increase by something like 1/4—the figure is uncertain, as trade statistics to individual African countries are not officially published. Ultimately the outcome will depend on the competitiveness of the South African companies. I have just pointed at the potential.

ODA to the SADCC Action programme is likely to decline in the post-apartheid era. There are numerous factors that would support such a conclusion. Some of the donors looked upon aid to SADCC as part of their anti-apartheid policy. Some of the other reasons for supporting SADCC might be weaker now as for instance the USA representative at the SADCC Annual Consultative Meeting in Maputo in January 1992 pointed out. So far SADCC has seemed to prepare itself slowly for adjustments to the new situation. Some of the SADCC members seem also to be more interested in improving their bilateral relations with South Africa, rather than using SADCC as an instrument.

The most important factor regarding the future support to SADCC from the donors will be the attitudes of the member governments. Some of the donors have already shown signs of weariness, among them USA, the World Bank and the UK. None of them have been in the frontline regarding the support for SADCC. Nevertheless they are donors with substantial general influence.

Other regional integration schemes based on SACU, PTA or any new concept might attract the interest of donors, provided they are considered to be viable. This interest might be further encouraged if the form of integration is seen as an instrument that can be used to reduce the present heavy regional imbalance, giving also the poorer countries in the region a share.

It should be noted that so far disbursement statistics do not indicate lower aid flows to the SADCC countries, but the contrary. Figures for 1990 are higher than ever. It should however also be noted that this is mainly due to a strong increase in the volume of aid to Mozambique and Tanzania that can be related to the SAPs of those countries, although funding of the transport corridors in Mozambique and Tazara/DSM harbour in Tanzania are also included in the figures. (See Table 11.5) Unfortunately SADCC does not publish annual statistics on pledges and disbursements to the SADCC Action Programme, which makes it difficult to assess the situation.

CONCLUDING REMARKS

Following an assumed "main-stream scenario" for the development in South Africa, the possible effects of the changes at the global level on flows of external capital to the post-apartheid Southern Africa may accordingly be tentatively summarized as follows:

— The disintegration of the Soviet Union and the collapse of the socialist system in Eastern Europe will on the whole reduce the political and economic interest of the OECD countries in Southern Africa. However, two outside regions—Eastern Europe and South East Asia—will probably increase their interest in South Africa. In the first case due to political change in the Eastern European countries and in the second case due to the increased relations during the sanctions era.
— Technological breakthroughs will reduce the global demand for minerals and metals. A short term factor reducing the OECD interest is the low economic growth in the industrialised countries, which reduces the demand for minerals and other raw materials.

The changes in South Africa pave the way for normal international relations with both the industrialised world and with the neighbouring African countries. It also changes the context for regional cooperation in Southern Africa. Some of the trends evident in early 1992 indicate *inter alia* the following developments due to regional and national factors:

— Given the removal of international sanctions, both international and domestic companies will be reluctant to make major new investments in South Africa. The main reasons for this will be the uncertain political situation with a high degree of violence, uncertainty concerning the economic policy of a new, democratically elected government and the long period of slow economic growth.
— A great interest in developing further trade relations with South Africa from all quarters.

— A gradually increasing inflow of loans from the international capi-
  tal markets to private and government borrowers in South Africa.
  This will remove one of the previous restrictions for increased economic growth.
— Significant South African borrowing from IFIs, mainly the World
  Bank and the ADB, provided the new government is prepared to
  follow IMF and the World Bank policy, and a certain inflow of
  ODA, mainly to support social sectors and activities to reduce the
  effects of the apartheid system.
— Selective investments in the SADCC countries by South African
  based companies and farmers. Most of those investments will take
  place in Mozambique and Angola, some of them perhaps also in
  Zimbabwe and Zambia.
— A reduced volume of ODA to the SADCC region, partly due to
  the absence of the "anti-apartheid factor", partly due to competing
  aid arenas, such as Eastern Europe, Middle East and Horn of
  Africa (emergency aid), and partly due to reallocation of ODA
  funds from SADCC to South Africa.
— A continued weak interest for direct investments and loans from
  the OECD countries to the SADCC countries, with the possible
  exception of Angola, provided the peace process continues.

For all of the categories of external capital discussed here, it can be
assumed that successful regional integration will increase the interest in supporting Southern Africa. In the case of direct investment, it
would be mainly due to the potential of a larger market. In the case
of commercial loans, it is the political and economic stability that an
on-going regional integration symbolises which would be important.
ODA will be particularly attracted if the integration scheme is seen
as an instrument for more equitable development in the region. The
motives of the various external actors can thus be assumed to be different. Nevertheless it may be concluded that Southern Africa is more
interesting to the outside world if the steps towards economic integration are seen to take place, rather than that there is an absence of
such such signs.

NOTES

1. At the SADC summit meeting in August 1992 it was decided to change the
   organisation into *Southern African Development Community*, SADC. The organisation will, however, be referred to as SADCC throughout this chapter.
2. These issues are also briefly discussed by Tostensen in chapter 7.
3. Bureau of Foreign Economic Research, University of Stellenbosch.

12. Swedish Aid Priorities for Regional Development in Southern Africa

Jan Cedergren

Development aid to Southern Africa has been very substantial during the last decade. The SADCC approach has been attractive to donors mainly for two reasons: infrastructural projects offered good commercial opportunities, both in terms of hardware and software, and aid through SADCC became for some donors a form of political compensation for continued economic relations with South Africa. The anti-apartheid creed, has been a strong force for substantial aid to the region and traditional economic criteria have often been replaced by political criteria. The introduction of structural adjustment programmes in the region has meant increased aid inputs, but at the same time an unprecedented level of conditionality, adding to the already large aid dependency of many countries in the region. Apartheid gone, or seemingly gone, will certainly change donor priorities, decrease aid volumes to the region and reestablish more traditional criteria for project/program selection. The hitherto negligence of the region to promote local resource mobilization for development will become more apparent. With this strong aid dependency, not only in terms of funding, but also in mentality, it should be of no surprise if South Africa is invited in where donors go out.

THE CHALLENGE

The GDP of all SADCC countries amounts to around USD 28 billion with a total population of around 80 million. Add South Africa and the figure becomes almost USD 108 billion with a market of around 115 million people. Obviously regional integration becomes really meaningful when South Africa is included.

Around half of SADCC countries imports originate in OECD countries and more than 60 per cent of exports go there. About 50 per cent of PTA imports are aid funded out of which about 30 per cent is tied.

Views in this document are only those of the author and do not necessarily reflect official Swedish aid policy.

Intra-PTA trade has stayed around 6 per cent of total trade for many years. Physical and financial infrastructure in the region benefits an OECD orientation rather than intra-regional. Historical links and perceptions of quality also favour that orientation, as well as the aid dependency. Countries in the region are more competitive than complimentary with regard to both raw materials and industrial products. There is too little to trade and more emphasis has to be placed in productive investments in the future. South Africa has substantially increased its trade with Africa during the last few years. Outside the BLNS countries, Zimbabwe is the most important trade partner but also other SADCC countries have increased their trade with South Africa. The trade balance is heavily in favour of South Africa. Bilateral trade offensives from the South African business community, may be very beneficial in the short term, but detrimental to long term regional integration, if the trade balance continues to grow in South Africa's favour. The market led free trade integration concept has thus its drawbacks.

What has the present SADCC region to offer? Mainly an abundance of natural resources. Oil, hydropower, gas, forests, water, minerals and agricultural land. About 75 per cent of the region's exports are primary products. Proper and sustainable management of these resources will require regional cooperation. This drought year is a reminder of possible future conflicts for water in the region, conflicts which can only be resolved on regional level. Environmental issues also often require supra-national action. If the region opts for a balanced regional integration, these resources represent important SADCC assets in negotiations with South Africa.

Development is very much a matter of human resources. There is still a great shortage of skills and experience in the region in many important sectors; engineering, finance, science, management, health etc. In higher education regional concepts are already worked at and the inclusion of South Africa will offer new opportunities. The virtual breakdown of reasonable wage-structures in many countries, has provoked an intra-regional braindrain towards South Africa including the bantustans, Namibia and Botswana, where salaries and working conditions are more favourable. A democratic South Africa may strengthen this trend. The migrant labour problem, specifically acute in Lesotho, will also be affected by the changes in South Africa. Some of these problems require regional solutions. A regional integration including free movement of people in the region is still a distant proposition, but a lot can be done on a regional basis to pave the way.

The basic preconditions for regional integration in Southern Africa are difficult. The macro-economic environment is not favourable.

Fiscal and monetary policies are not harmonized, exchange rates are not stabilized and most currencies not convertible. Hard currency is still used in most intra-regional economic transactions and non-tariff barriers all too common. Many countries are struggling in various stages of SAPs, trying to cope with debt problems, balance of payments deficits and chronicle inflation. Looking at previous integration efforts like the East African Community, EAC, and Economic Community of West African States, ECOWAS, factors contributing to failure in those cases are also prevalent in Southern Africa. One obvious conclusion is that there is a clear need to "put the national houses in order" to facilitate regional action. Although there is not necessarily any contradiction between national and regional development efforts, regional efforts can not replace necessary national action.

The apparent competitive climate between PTA and SADCC and conflicting statements on regional issues show, that member states have not yet seriously addressed the issue of regional integration and even less institutional rationalization. Deeds have yet to follow words. It is also a reflection of member states' lacking capacity to deal with long-term problems and the difficulty of developing a truly regional spirit. Regional integration means giving up some aspects of sovereignty in return for regional benefits, a fact that may be difficult to appreciate for weak, poor and struggling states, especially if the returns are distant and somewhat unclear. In the emerging new situation in Southern Africa there may be scope for more solid action with regard to confidence building, new security structures and demilitarization. Arrangements along the lines of the Conference on Security and Cooperation in Europe, CSCE, have been proposed.

The Southern Africa region needs both growth and equitable development. This will require more than just market forces. Balanced integration means some sort of negotiations between South Africa and the other regional states as perceived in the latest SADCC annual theme document. This in its turn requires quick and bold action by SADCC member states. It assumes a new level of political commitment to regional development. Should SADCC work as a subregional unit to PTA but with the same objectives? Should there be a major review of all existing institutions in order to create something new more adapted to the new realities? Should regional action be more ad hoc along functional lines? These and other questions must soon be answered by regional leaders if they want to have any influence on forthcoming regional developments. Passivity on the SADCC side may favour other actors with more extreme ideas; e.g. a non-racial CONSAS with the power-house in South Africa.

A major issue for regional aid donors will be: How can a positive and constructive South African entry in the region best be achieved and supported? And how can an equitable regional development best be achieved and supported?

THE AID PRIORITIES

Sweden has for a long time been a major donor in Southern Africa on a national and regional level. Bilateral cooperation agreements are in force with all SADCC countries except Malawi and Swaziland. However, these two countries benefit from regional programmes. Substantial humanitarian assistance has also been given to the ANC and various anti-apartheid activities in South Africa. Table 12.1 shows Swedish aid budget allocations to Southern Africa for budget year 1992/93. On top of the volumes shown in the table significant volumes of emergency aid and aid via non-governmental organisations go to countries in the region. Around 40 per cent of the Swedish bilateral aid can be estimated to go to Southern Africa.

A continued strong focus on Southern Africa can be expected in the Swedish aid programme, although types, forms and distribution of aid may change. The anti-apartheid factor will no longer be there and traditional criteria like level of income, economic policies, adjustment performance etc. will be more important when deciding on aid levels and direction.

Table 12.1. *Swedish aid budget allocations for Southern Africa 1992/93*

Recipient	Million SEK
Angola	210
Botswana	90
Lesotho	35
Mozambique	395
Namibia	110
Tanzania	530
Zambia	110
Zimbabwe	220
SADCC projects	140
South Africa, humanitarian aid[1]	250
Total	2,090

[1] Mainly through NGOs and to the ANC.

Continued support should be given to assist poor countries to "put their house in order". This means continued support to SAPs with active participation in dialogues on conditionality and due regard to social dimensions of adjustment. A specific effort should be made, together with other donors, to reconcile the SAPs with regional development and integration ambitions. Support should be given to create and strengthen institutions necessary to promote a positive enabling environment for economic change. Specific attention should be given to factors facilitating regional interaction; trade policies, fiscal and monetary policies, tariff and non-tariff barriers etc. Thereby basic preconditions for regional integration can be improved.

Assuming continued peace in Angola and an early peace accord in Mozambique, there is a special case for substantial aid to resettlement, reconstruction and rehabilitation in these two countries.

South Africa's level of income is far above normal aid criteria. However, as is the case in Namibia, this figure tells only a part of the reality. The living conditions for the majority, are rather similar to those of the people in the poorest countries in the region, and very bad in relation to the conditions of the minority. Enormous tasks await a democratic government in the social sectors; health, education and housing i.a. To sustain democratic development in South Africa and political stability, the new government must be able to respond quickly to at least some of the grievances of the large majority. Two aid priorities seem obvious in this perspective: to support in all ways possible the fragile, emerging democracy and its supporting institutions, and to poverty alleviation through support to programmes in the social sectors directed at the poor segments of the population. It is important to South Africa, to the region and to the world that a new government does not fail. South Africa has also a great need to improve its productive sector; rehabilitate manufacturing industry, improve productivity, create employment and diversify. Whether aid is needed to support private flows still remains to be seen.

SADCC's Programme of Action should get continued support. However, emphasis is shifting from project investments to management, maintenance, training, effective planning and market orientation. Railway authorities must become viable customer-oriented, commercial entities. Ports must increase their productivity to be able to compete. Effective and efficient utilization of existing investments should be a prime objective in the SADCC region. With a changing regional agenda and uncertainty of the institutional future, a greater degree of flexibility is called for with regard to the utilization of Swedish regional aid.

Swedish regional aid funds should be used to promote a balanced regional development in a post-apartheid Southern Africa. This means more support to the weaker partners in the region in a way that does not add to the aid dependency or subsidizes non-viable activities. A more prominent role for trade, production and increased productivity, calls for greater participation by the business community. In countries like Zimbabwe, Botswana and Namibia, all with relatively higher income levels, such participation should be stimulated in the development cooperation. Whether private investors will be attracted to a democratic South Africa remains to be seen. The potential dominance of South African industry may necessitate donor incentives to promote a spread of productive investments to the rest of the region. In this perspective a revitalization of the so called Nordic Initiative and the Norsad Fund is desirable.

A regional criteria in the appraisal of all bilateral aid projects/programmes should always be applied. What is supportive or detrimental to regional integration efforts? Regional benefits can be used as a positive selection criteria.

Preferences can be given to aid procurement in the region of goods and services, which is already the case, but can be further extended and promoted. Local consultants should be used more for regional assignments. With a democratic South Africa in the region, it can be expected to have a strong competitive edge with regard to provision of goods and services in the area. This could certainly benefit the region, but may also provoke calls for further tying from the Swedish business community.

One important obstacle for development in the region is the heavy aid dependency. Future aid must be designed in a way that does not add to this dependency. It is a question of both resources and mentality. Recipients must participate to a larger extent both with financial and personnel resources. There should be a clear plan from the beginning regarding when aid should be phased out. Project analyses should always include recurrent implications of investments projects and grant funds should always be on-lended on commercial terms when the activities are competitive and commercial in nature. The present scramble for South African attention and favours in the region, should hopefully not develop into a new dependency. To achieve positive results of the SAPs and of the integration efforts, a wider participation of various segments of the populations is necessary. Such programmes need to be internalized and accepted on a broad level to be successful. The public need to be better informed and more involved. Aid can support such efforts. The present development of more democratic systems and decision processes in the region should be strongly encouraged and supported. In a time of

Jan Cedergren

unprecedented external influence and conditionality, it is also of utmost importance to reestablish self-confidence and pride. All problems do not always have to be and cannot be solved by outsiders.

Whatever form of regional integration that emerges on the Southern African scene will imply a lot of hurdles along the road. To achieve regional integration is a very long-term proposition, a fact that has to be accepted by all parties. In the meantime a lot of small steps can be taken inside or outside more grand concepts. In a functional concept, for example, trade, transport and higher education seem ripe for more rapid regional action and integration. Suggestions have already been made how this could be achieved. Aid with a regional bias can support such steps. Subregional groups can decide to move ahead on their own and can be supported to do so.

Awaiting the outcome and future policies on the South African scene, regional leaders have been hesitant to make up their minds on regional policy issues. This has left a play-ground for other more active actors. Bilateralism can be gaining ground at the expense of multilateralism. This is not in the long-term interest of the region. Donors should support dialogue, intellectual debate, studies and other actions conducive to multilateral concepts of development in the region.

13. Swedish Trade and Investment Links with Southern Africa

Åke Magnusson

Southern Africa has had, and still has, an important role in Swedish foreign policy as well as in the public debate when it comes to international issues. A good portion of all funds for Swedish bilateral development cooperation is devoted to countries in this part of the world. When it comes to trade and corporate investments, Southern Africa does not, generally speaking, play a role anything near to that. In some specific sectors and for a few individual companies, Southern Africa has however been, and will remain, a relatively important market place in the years to come.

Why has the region of Southern Africa commercially not become of greater interest and concern to Swedish business? How is the present development perceived and evaluated in Swedish business circles? What can and will emerge when it comes to trade and investment links between Sweden and the region of Southern Africa in the foreseeable future?

WHY A STATIC OR DECLINING PRESENCE?

The relative and in cases also the absolute decline in commercial links between Southern Africa and Sweden during the eighties is explained by a combination of several factors. It seems to be at least three elements of relevance at hand.

Cutting economic ties to the Republic of South Africa

Starting in 1978 the Swedish Government embarked step by step on a policy of cutting all economic ties with the Republic of South Africa (and up to 1990 Namibia). The original investment legislation banned every "expansion investment" and was passed by the Parliament under the assumption that Swedish companies could and also should go on operating, the "hibernation assumption"

Gradually, and due to public and political pressure, the investment ban however turned into a real one and in practice implied the withdrawal of Swedish companies. The ban on all trade passed by the Parliament 1987 was the ultimate indication of that policy direction.

Thus, as a result of *unilateral* legislation Swedish corporate presence in the South African market dramatically changed during the 1980s, which is shown in Table 13.1 and 2.

Atlas Copco 1991 still had about 23 per cent of the share capital, but felt forced in 1987 to end the management of the local company, Delfos & Atlas Copco. Consequently the former daughter company was deconsolidated and management ties were cut. However, through international acquisitions, the Group become owner of three other corporations which were also active in South Africa.

The reduction of Swedish controlled business presence in South Africa did not only influence the market share position in that country, but doubtlessly also negatively the position and prospects of trade and investment links with the SADCC region as well.

Table 13.1. *Swedish companies in South Africa*

	1982	1989
Turnover (million Rand)	287	445
Number of employees	3,143	1,740

Source: *Swedish Government reports, Regeringsskrivelse 1990/91:62, Redogörelse för svenska företags verksamhet i Sydafrika och Namibia,* Stockholm.

Table 13.2. *Swedish companies in South Africa*
        Established units

Company	1983	1991
1. Alfa-Laval	x	
2. Atlas Copco	x	(x)
3. Bahco	x	
4. Esselte	x	
5. Secoroc	x	x
6 Johnson & Co.	x	
7. Sandvik	x	x
8. SAS	x	
9. SKF	x	x
10. Skega	x	x
11. Transatlantic	x	

Source: NIR (Näringslivets Internationella Råd), Stockholm.

By tradition and for rational reasons, the market presence in most of the states in the region had been dependent on the fact that there was a firmly established and well developed operation in South Africa. For logistical and similar reasons the establishment in that country was a key to the after all marginal operations that took place in other parts of the region (mainly in Zimbabwe, Zambia, Botswana and Namibia).

When the centre and the periphery in the region were separated, several factors contributed to make business operations harder in the latter:

— Large scale production and trading incentives were sharply reduced if not totally removed.
— Supply of spare parts and components became very difficult.
— All units in the region showed poor results, and at headquarters
  the willingness to grant investment funds subsequently declined.
— At headquarters in Sweden scarce top management time was of
  necessity concentrated on how to survive in South Africa rather
  than how to expand in the SADCC region.

Small economies and poor economic performance

A second and indeed a vital parameter in explaining the decline, or in some cases the lack of increase in economic relations, is the poor economic performance in the region during the 1980s. Civil wars in some of the states and government economic mismanagement in others made the small Botswana the only state recording a positive growth rate of any relevance in the region.

It must also be recalled that not only the growth rate but also the absolute size of the economies of the region are relatively insignificant as seen by a globally operating company. The fact is that the measurable size of the total economies of the nine SADCC countries in 1989 was only marginally bigger than Chile's GNP or less than half of Portugal's. Clearly visible commercial reasons for investments in production and marketing in the region were, with a few important exceptions, not too convincing.

Alternatives

Decision making at global corporate level is in its simplicity to a high degree concerned with growth perspectives for different regions and allocating funds as well as top managerial resources to where the future markets seem to be. In that light Africa, including Southern Africa, does not come out positively.

Compared to other regions, the historical record and the projections for the future clearly indicate that Southern Africa generally speaking is of minor interest, as its predicted economic performance is meagre in comparison to other areas. Whether one likes it or not the relative macro comparisons contribute significantly to influence corporate thinking and strategy.

Table 13.3. *Growth of real GDP per capita, 1965–2000*

Group	Population 1989 (millions)	1965–73	1973–80	1980–89	Projected for 1990s
		(average annual percentage change)			
Industrial countries	773	3.7	2.3	2.3	1.8–2.5
Developing countries	4,053	3.9	2.5	1.6	2.2–2.9
Sub-Saharan Africa	480	2.1	0.4	–1.2	0.3–0.5
East Asia	1,552	5.3	4.9	6.2	4.2–5.3
South Asia	1,131	1.2	1.7	3.0	2.1–2.6
Europe, Middle East and North Africa	433	5.8	1.9	0.4	1.4–1.8
Latin America and the Caribbean	421	3.8	2.5	–0.4	1.3–2.0
Developing countries weighted by population		3.0	2.4	2.9	2.7–3.2

Source: World Bank, *World Development Report 1991*, p. 3, New York, Oxford
    University Press.

SADCC-REGION: COMPENSATING FOR LOST SOUTH AFRICA MARKETS?

An increasingly vital element in official Swedish policy during the last decade as regards Southern Africa has been to try to support the expansion of commercial relations with the SADCC-region and its member countries. In part this could be seen as a serious attempt to compensate Swedish business for diminished or totally lost markets in South Africa.

Two other motives have however probably been more immediate. First, the economic interdependence between South Africa and the Front Line States was seen to weaken the capability of the latter to take a firm anti-apartheid stand and to resist political pressure from

Pretoria. Swedish development cooperation as well as intensified commercial relations with Sweden would strengthen the economic performance of the weak SADCC-states. This would be a necessary, rather than a sufficient condition for a relatively strong anti-apartheid position in the region. The Nordic governments held all similar views in this respect and developed joint programmes and initiatives to meet this objective.

Secondly, the expansion of economic ties between Sweden and the SADCC-region could in the view of a number of Swedish policy makers contribute to an enhancement of the growth of the market economy orientation as a substitute for the obviously mismanaged socialist experiments in nation-building.

No secret was made of the existence of the commercial element in Swedish foreign policy as regards the SADCC-region. On the contrary, it was pronounced as a clear objective in the Nordic/SADCC Initiative and in other contexts as well.

The Swedish Government authorities used, sometimes in an unorthodox fashion, several different instruments to stimulate the growth of economic relations with the SADCC-region. On the aggregate level and with reference to the currently available empirical evidence, it is fairly easy to conclude that these intentions did not materialize.

Swedish/SADCC-region total trade 1980 was SEK 791 million and the corresponding figure for 1991 is SEK 820 million at current

Table 13.4. *Trade between Sweden and the SADCC-region*
       (million SEK)

Country	1980		1991	
	Export to	Import from	Export to	Import from
Angola	297.0	0	67.5	0.3
Botswana	3.3	0	88.5	0.2
Lesotho	0.6	0	10.5	1.9
Malawi	10.4	0.5	13.4	14.8
Mozambique	73.9	2.7	94.2	13.3
Namibia	1.0	3.9	16.7	0.4
Swaziland	6.2	6.5	5.7	28.1
Tanzania	120.3	28.5	173.2	6.5
Zambia	117.3	103.5	102.4	10.7
Zimbabwe	7.1	8.7	111.5	59.7
Total	637.1	154.3	683.6	135.9

Source: Swedish Trade Council.

prices. This is in fact a significant *decrease* in trade relations if inflation effects are taken into account. One must bear in mind, however, that annual fluctuations in trade could be sizeable. Nevertheless the general observation is valid.

In spite of well-intentioned efforts through instruments like IMPOD (government agency for import of Third World products to Sweden) and SUKAB (the counter trade organization), trading relations have not improved. To a large degree, this is explained by the single fact that only a few export and import oriented Swedish companies were established under market conditions in the region.

As regards Swedish investments in the region during the 1980s, the same general pattern applies. On the whole, the level of investments in terms of size and number of established companies remained static. However, while others declined, a number of companies did manage to expand (the best example is the truck manufacturer Scania via a number of joint-ventures).

Starting in the second half of the 1980s a number of commercially important project orders in the infrastructural sector in the SADCC area have been granted to Swedish companies. ASEA/ABB (power generation and transmission), Ericsson (telecom) and Skanska (construction and civil engineering) are three important examples in this respect.

In comparison to a number of individual countries, the record of Swedish business in terms of direct investments is, as mentioned above, not impressive, particularly if bearing in mind the extent of development cooperation.

In *Mozambique* there were 14 Swedish companies in 1991, of which only 3 operated on a purely commercial basis, including Scanmo (agent for Scania) and Frexbo (agent for Volvo). The others were involved in SIDA-supported industry projects or as consultants. Some 29 companies in *Zimbabwe* are in one way or another associated with Sweden. A few of these are Swedish owned subsidiaries that produce locally, while several others are only sales-/service organizations. The bulk of the 29 are, however, Zimbabwean owned companies that act as representatives of Swedish corporations. Approximately 20 per cent of total "Swedish business" in Zimbabwe is directly tied to development/aid cooperation.

There are 10 directly Swedish owned and operated undertakings in *Zambia*. As in the other neighbouring SADCC countries, the picture has on the whole been unchanged since the beginning of the 1980s. Only 2 of these 10 companies can be said to rely heavily on official Swedish development aid financing. In addition there are a handful of Swedish consultant companies whose operations are associated with aid programmes in the country.

WEAK PERFORMANCE

Why has the Swedish Government and its authorities, together with the African countries and the SADCC organization, failed to stimulate increased commercial presence and relations? The general answer to this question has been examined earlier. However, there are also a number of specific explanations for this failure, which might be considered somewhat subjective and merely based on soft, impressionistic evidence.

During the 1980s several new Swedish companies became directly involved in the region as a result of the flow of aid money. These companies mainly provided consultancy services or were similarly directly associated with projects in the field of state financed development cooperation. These companies, which also occasionally included Swedish "Blue Chip" firms, did not establish their presence on normal markets terms. The length of their stay was a direct function of availability of aid money.

On the other hand, companies established on normal commercial terms, such as Sandvik, SKF and Atlas Copco, faced growing obstacles to their day-to-day business operations. Shortage of foreign exchange and a general unfavourable economic climate made life anything but easy for these companies.

There would appear to have been only limited cooperation between private Swedish subsidiaries that were already on the spot and Swedish Government authorities aiming to *expand* business presence. There is an evident absence of joint strategic thinking.

Rather than seeking constructive cooperation, the Swedish Government authorities and the business sector indulged in an extensive political and organisational exercise in creating governmental and semi-governmental institutions and instruments for promoting commercial relations between Sweden and the SADCC-region. Swedfund (SwedeCorp), IMPOD and similar institutions became active in promoting investments and trading links. The intentions were good, the results were harder to measure, subsequently and undoubtedly fairly limited.

On a Nordic basis, the Norsad-fund (a revolving fund aimed at stimulating joint-venture undertakings) was set up in the latter half of the 1980s. It did not actually start its operations until several years later due mainly to a power struggle between the SADCC Secretariat, the then 9 SADCC member states and the five Nordic Governments. Up to now, Norsad has been a failure in spite of all its financial resources. Not a single project has to my knowledge been approved and come into operation. A major obstacle has been the institutional and operational requirements regarding lending. Already at an early stage, the Swedish business community voiced its critical attitude towards the excessively rigid rules laid down for Norsad's operations. Our view was that *in practice* the Norsad would be of a very limited use in stimulating new business on a Nordic/SADCC-basis. It is regrettable that Norsad has up to now never played that constructive role as designed for it by its architects when this Flag Ship on Nordic/SADCC collaboration was launched. (It is my understanding that Norsad and its way of operating at present is under rather intensive review by the governments concerned. The intention is to make the rules less rigid in order to make the fund *practically* functioning.)

SWEDFUND/SWEDECORP: THE EXCEPTION?

It would be unfair and incorrect in this context to disregard the role played by the Swedish government agency Swedfund/SwedeCorp and its activities in the SADCC-region. 12 joint-venture projects were initiated in 5 of the SADCC countries, mainly during the latter part of the 1980s. In 1991 around 5,500 employees were directly involved in these undertakings. The highest concentration in terms of employment was in Mozambique (a company for seed production and distribution).

The basic philosophy of Swedfund/SwedeCorp is to organize commercially sound companies through cooperation between a local firm and a Swedish partner with the agency as a third pillar. This venture has been undoubtedly successful in the sense that both good Swedish

Table 13.5. *Swedfund/Swedecorp in the SADCC region 1991*

Country	Number of projects	Number of employees	Total investment/Swedfund share of total
Botswana	2	85	BWP 3.49m/0.49m
Mozambique	1	4,000	SEK 20m/0.6m
Tanzania	4	820	USD 10.6m/ca 15%
Zambia	1	400	ZMK 8m/2m
Zimbabwe	4	217	ZMD 20m/2.6m
Total	12	5,522	

Source: Swedfund, *Swedfund Annual Report 1991*, Stockholm, and Mr. Henric Thörnberg, SwedeCorp, Stockholm.

partners and local companies have been found. Through share capital and loan capital as well as management participation, the agency is highly involved in the projects.

It is, however, in most cases too early to judge the success of these projects. As in all business, there are obstacles and problems. It looks as if at least some of the joint-ventures are really viable and can look forward to a commercially sound future. Others may for different reasons have a much bleaker future.

CONCLUSION

In my view, it would have been far more rational from a strict goal achievement point of view if the Swedish Government and the private business sector that were already established in one way or another in the region, had tried from the very outset to find ways and means to cooperate extensively while still bearing their different roles in mind.

I realize that traditional and well established principles and other obstacles were and still are in operation, which made such joint efforts hard but far from impossible to bring about. With regards to the future, all of the interested parties, in my view, can learn obvious lessons from the past.

In short there are several reasons why a constructive policy should have been based on cooperation between the already existing Swedish business undertakings, rather than primarily creating new institutions and policy instruments based on government intervention in order to stimulate the creation of new enterprises in the form of Swedish direct investment or joint ventures:

— By definition the existing companies are already physically established on the market. Compared to new investors the "traditional companies" would be able to expand their production and sales volumes, number of employees, etc. with relatively marginal additional resources.

— Based on existing firms, it would have been relatively easy with additional resources and other incentives to extend the network of African subcontractors as a matter of deliberate policy. Given Swedish Government support, companies like SKF would have fairly easily developed its maintenance concept and applied it to the African private and public sector.

— The existing companies have market know-how and are largely regionally market orientated. If these companies had received con-

structive support, they could have contributed more than marginally to improve the low share of intra-regional trade.
— The existing companies could, if they had been in a healthier condition, have been used a a vehicle for transferring positive market knowledge and experiences to "newcomers".
— From a credibility point of view, when it comes to attracting new
investors, it would have been wise for the Swedish and national
African Governments to take steps to make life easier for the existing firms. As part of the pre-study, a serious market oriented
potential Swedish investor would have included talks with existing companies. If the experience of the latter is mainly negative
which is often said to be the case, and the emphasis is on problems
rather than opportunities, the potential investor would certainly
be reluctant.
— A strengthening of the established Swedish companies in individual SADCC countries could in many cases have been a contribution to exports and to the generation of foreign exchange as
most of these companies exist in an international structure or
group that has ample experience of international trade.

FUTURE TRADE AND INVESTMENT LINKS

The intensity and pattern of Swedish trade and investments links to
Southern Africa in the future will be decided by a mix of several factors and considerations. Predominant factors will concern actual,
rather than stated, intentions of economic policy and performance.
Indeed the level of political stability is also of fundamental importance.

Low level of Swedish presence

As shown above, Swedish business and commerce has undoubtedly
a fairly insignificant economic presence in and limited commercial
relations with Southern Africa. The pattern has to a large extent
remained static over the last 15 years and in the particular case of
South Africa, the decline is obvious. Over the years, our international
and local competitors have, on the other hand, strengthened their
market positions and are relatively well equipped in facing the future. Swedish companies have in many important respects been
weakened relative to others.

The conclusion to be drawn is that the platform for the future is in
relatively bad shape. With the exception of firms that basically de-

pend on the large allocations of Swedish aid money, Swedish companies operating in the region have serious problems and obstacles to overcome.

Sectoral concentration

Looking at the region as a whole, a striking feature of Swedish business established in the area its the heavy concentration within the mining equipment sector. Such a pattern could be an asset, but may also rapidly develop into a short-coming if the mining industry runs into structural problems and becomes even more exposed to negative cyclical pressures.

Economic performance

Due to civil strife, external destabilisation and pure mismanagement, the countries in the region are characterised, to varying degrees, by poor economic performance. However, more or less all states concerned have now embarked on restructuring and readjustment policies and programmes. There seems to exist a very healthy re-thinking and an increased devotion to a market economy strategy.

Whether or not this re-orientation will result in increased foreign investments and expanded trade links remains, however, to be seen. We simply do not yet know if these changed policies will yield results which can be measured in actual growth. The confidence of international investors is at the end of the day a function of recorded performance rather than declared intentions.

Political pluralism and stability

Swedish as well as other potential investors are watching carefully the political developments in the region. The final political settlement, which will hopefully be reached in South Africa, plays of course a key role in this context. Political developments in other countries in the region are however of similar importance. Will the new Government in Zambia be able to manage the country in a more efficient way? Will elections in Angola produce a stable and convincing government? Is it probable that Zimbabwe will succeed in finding a way to reconcile a market economy orientation with high social ambitions? These and similar questions are put and the search for answers is on. Underlying all of them is a concern for future political stability. The investor regards political stability as a necessary but not in itself a sufficient condition for an acceptable supportive environment.

Regional cooperation

A further dimension of importance when considering Swedish investment and trade links is what will happen in terms of regional cooperation. For several established and potentially interested Swedish
companies the regional factor is of vital importance. With the exception of South Africa, the pure market size of any individual country
is not impressive. We realize that SADCC, PTA and SACU as well as
individual governments are all considering the question of the regional framework. We understand that it is a complex political process in which the key role of South Africa for good reasons has not
yet been defined. What we know for sure is that a functioning regional market will be a real incentive for new investors and an undoubt-
ed stimulus for established firms in the region.

Relative performance

The flow of Swedish investments and trade to Southern Africa will
be dependent on how the region and its countries perform in comparison to other nations. Given the scarcity of funds and management
resources, the corporate strategists will scrutinize carefully all of the
possible options. If developments in Eastern Europe, from a business
point of view seem to be as promising, it may tend to reduce Swedish
commercial interest in Southern Africa. If developments in EC/EU
and USA generate, as we think they will, conditions for real renewed
growth, there are good grounds at the end of the day that they will
influence the willingness to take risks in Southern Africa.

The role of South Africa

A vital factor in corporate planning and performance is the actual
and perceived future position of market competitors. When discussing Southern Africa, the future role of South Africa is crucial. From
a Swedish business point of view, we have to realize that South
African industry and commerce has developed regionally into a real
competitor in many important fields. Given that political stability and
sound macro economic policies are high on the agenda of the day,
South Africa and its industry and commerce seem to have several
comparative advantages to offer:
— Geographically and infrastructurally South Africa has obviously
   an advantage to be exploited even more than today. This is not to
   say that for instance South African ports will be without competition, but as in the past, Beira and other ports in the region will
   find it hard to compete with South Africa.

— South African business and commerce know the business culture and the "right channels" in the region far better than for instance Swedish managers. South African industry and commerce has in a significant way used the last 10–15 years to expand its network of business contacts and de facto partners in the region.

— South African industry has expanded its direct ownership of production and service capacity in several states in the region. For instance, in the mining sector, Swedish companies like Atlas Copco and Sandvik is faced with a serious South African "in-house-trading" in Zambia and Zimbabwe.

— South Africa's emerging manufacturing industry is "production wise" said to be of medium quality and has problems selling to Europe and USA. Maybe the products are from both a technological and cost point of view ideal for "African needs". Could this factor in part explain the success of South African trade penetration into the region during the last years?

My firm impression is that there is a genuine business interest in the Swedish corporate world for Southern Africa. Both emotional and objective factors point in that direction. However, real obstacles are present. Most of these can only be sorted out by the governments and citizens concerned. Further, one must not forget that Sweden in business terms has a weak platform relative to others in the region. It will be an important task therefore to find efficient and principally acceptable ways and means for cooperation between the Swedish government and the business community. It would be somewhat of a "historical failure" if the substantial solidarity with Southern Africa, shown for more than 20 years from Swedish side, could not find the new forms needed, including commercial ones, to transform that solidarity into an effective partnership when finally the nations of the region start to build modern and democratic societies.

Concluding remarks

Bertil Odén

To write about Southern Africa after apartheid implies that you believe the apartheid system will fall in South Africa, although the detailed features of the new system are still hazy. Hence an implicit assumption underlying the analyses by the authors in this book is that the process towards democratization in South Africa does not come to a definite halt. The authors probably share the opinion that this process will be difficult and pass through several set-backs, as those experienced in the shade of Boipatong and Bisho in mid 1992, when this book was edited. This also means that the time perspective is uncertain. The escalation of violence in South Africa, and the involvement of security forces generals and leading white politicians in this violence, is the strongest threat to the future of the region.

Instead of trying to agree on a common resolution or plan of action, the seminar sought to analyse the possible future of the region from the four selected perspectives of regional integration theory, issue-orientation, existing regional organisations and external capital. Some issues, however, tended to come into focus, irrespective of which of the four perspectives was the starting point of the discussion. This signals their relevance for future regional development. Among those issues, the following selection can be made. These issues may also serve as suggestions for further research and activities:

1. The advantages of less ambitious regional cooperation schemes are obvious, in the present situation with their great regional imbalances and the national question unresolved in a number of countries, including South Africa itself. This means, for instance, that far-reaching financial and monetary harmonization will come as a result of gradual integration in other areas, rather than as an instrument for creating such integration.
2. It also means that regional cooperation along specific functions emerges as a realistic method of further strengthening regionalisation, rather than ambitious regional integration schemes. With a general liberalisation going on in the countries forming the region, there is expanded scope for other players than the states, especially strong South African companies, parastatals and institutions. This again emphasizes the risk of polarisation as well as the important role of the states when it comes to monitoring and creating supportive and compensatory institutions and systems in the region.

3. There is a certain confusion concerning the role of the various existing regional organisations, both within the organisations themselves and among external players. South African initiatives will in many cases be decisive, including the remaining capacity and political will of the post-apartheid South African government to handle regional issues, taking into consideration the overwhelming domestic tasks ahead of it.

4. The trend towards converging mandates of the regional organisations will increase the internal and external pressure for rationalisation. The greater the ambitions to integrate, the more important the restructuring of the organisations. The creation of SADC in 1992 will require concrete measures to resolve this complicated issue.

5. Development aid will continue to play an important role in the region although the total volume might diminish due to competition from other geographical areas such as the former Soviet Union, Eastern Europe and Middle East. The allocation of aid will change as the "apartheid premium" will be replaced by "normal" aid criteria and conditions. In the short term perspective, the reduction of aid to the SADC countries might be compensated for by increased aid to South Africa.

6. The prospects for large private capital flows into the region are unfavourable due to the uncertainty of future economic policy and the modest prospects for economic growth in South Africa and the rest of the region.

7. Security aspects, including analysis of possible new conflicts in the post-apartheid era, must be combined with economic and political analysis. The risks of a "polarization scenario" are also evident in this field.

8. The whole issue of regional polarisation is critical, although it seems as if the strong players are not the most concerned. An important task is therefore to show that if this issue is ignored, regional development may not be sustainable. Finally,

9. A prerequisite for a balanced regional scenario is significant cooperation between internal and external forces. Concern is growing among outsiders that the main actors, such as the governments in the individual Southern African states, seem to be prepared to improve their short term bilateral links with South Africa instead of working for a more sustainable regional scenario where improvements can be distributed to all. The aggregate effect of such a "business as usual" scenario might well be a weaker region in the end.

The issues above are "region specific". It might be pertinent to end
this text by reminding the reader that any regionalization in Southern
Africa will take place in the context of a rapidly changing international political economy, which will continue to affect regional development as well as that of individual countries in the region. Some of
these global issues have been briefly referred to in the previous chapters, such as:

— Marginalisation due to lower political, commercial and aid interest in core countries.
— The formation of three trade blocks in the core countries might
  result in increased competition, with risks of spill-over effects into
  stronger protectionism.
— Increased trade competition from South Eastern and East Asia in
  the field of manufactured goods.
— Technical development in the core countries reducing and changing the demand for minerals and metals.
— No superpower competition in the region in the post-cold war era.
  This would increase the arena for action for the regional countries
  themselves. The extent to which they can develop this potential is
  crucial for the long term development of the region.

A post-apartheid economic integration in this global setting might
have two, not necessarily conflicting aims. One is defensive; to improve the capacity of the individual countries to meet the marginalisation of the changing global economy and reduce the dependence
on the core countries in the North. This may be viewed as a necessary adjustment to given global circumstances rather than as a preferred first choice strategy of "de-linking". The second aim is offensi-
ve, namely to use regional integration to strengthen the economic
potential of the region, and thereby its individual countries, and use
this increased strength to integrate with the North from an improved
position in the international division of labour.

Bibliography

Abrahamsson, H., 1989, "Transport structures and dependence relations in Southern Africa: The need for a reorientation of Nordic aid", in Odén, Bertil & Haroub Othman (eds.), *Regional Cooperation in Southern Africa. A Post-Apartheid Perspective*, The Scandinavian Institute of African Studies, Seminar Proceedings No. 22, Uppsala.

Africa Business, 1980, "Central Africa's transport tangle", October.

ANC, Department of Economic Policy, 1990, *Discussion Document on Economic Policy*, Johannesburg.

ANC, Department of Economic Policy, 1991, *Discussion Document: Economic Policy*, Centre for Development Studies, University of Western Cape.

Anglin, Douglas G., 1983, "Economic liberation and regional cooperation in Southern Africa: SADCC and PTA", *International Organization*, 37(4).

AAM (Anti-Apartheid Movement), 1988, *The South African Disconnection*, London.

Arndt, Heinz W. & Ross Garnaut, 1979, "ASEAN and the industrialization of East Asia", *Journal of Common Market Studies*, Vol. 17.

Arrow, Kenneth J., 1950, "A difficulty in the concept of social welfare", *Journal of Political Economy*, Vol. 58.

Axline, Andrew, 1977, "Underdevelopment, dependence and integration: The politics of regionalism in the Third World", in P. Ghosh (ed.) (1984), *Economic Integration and the Third World*, Connecticut, Greenwood Press.

Balassa, Bela, 1961, *The Theory of Economic Integration*, London, George Allen & Unwin.

Balassa, Bela & Ardy Stoutjesdijk, 1975, "Economic integration among developing countries", *Journal of Common Market Studies*, Vol. 14.

Balassa, Bela, 1988, "Economic integration", in John Eatwell, et al. (eds.), *The New Palgrave. A Dictionary of Economics*, Vol. 2, E to J, London, Macmillan.

Blomqvist, Hans C. & Christian Lindholm, 1992, "The economic integration in Central America—Doomed to fail?", *Ibero Americana*, Vol. 22.

Blomqvist, Hans C. & Mats Lundahl, 1992, *Ekonomisk utveckling*, Stockholm, SNS Förlag.

Blomqvist, Hans C., 1992, *Economic Interdependence in Asia-Pacific—Some Preliminary Results*, Working paper No. 237, Swedish School of Economics and Business Administration, Helsinki.

Bulmer-Thomas, Victor, 1982, "The Central American Common Market", in Ali M. El-Agraa, (ed.), *International Economic Integration*, London, Macmillan.

Bulmer-Thomas, Victor, 1987, *Studies in the Economics of Central America*, London and Basingstoke, Macmillan.

Burdette, Marcia M., 1988, *Zambia Between Two Worlds*, Boulder, Colorado, Westview Press.

Buszynski, Leszek, 1987, "ASEAN, A changing regional role", *Asia Survey* 17(7).

Buzan, Barry, et al., 1990, *The European Security Order Recast. Scenarios for the Post Cold War Era*, London, Pinter Publishers.

Buzan, Barry, 1991, *People States and Fear*, 2nd. ed., Hemel Hempstead, Harvester Wheatsheaf.

Chacholiades, Miltiades, 1981, *Principles of International Economics*, New York, McGraw-Hill.

Chitala, Derric, 1987, "The political economy of SADCC and imperialism's response", in S. Amin et al. (eds.), *SADCC: Prospects for Disengagement and Development in Southern Africa*, New Jersey, Zed Books.

Chr. Michelsen Institute/SADCC, 1986, *Intra-Regional Trade Study, SADCC*.

Chr. Michelsen Institute, 1990, *The Nordic/SADCC Initiative: A Nordic Review*, Report No. 8, Bergen.

Cline, William R., 1978, "Benefits and costs of economic integration in Central America", in William R. Cline & Enrique Delgado (eds.), *Economic Integration in Central America*, Washington D.C., The Brookings Institution.

Colman, David & Frederick Nixson, 1986, *Economics of Change in Less Developed Countries*, 2nd ed. Oxford, Philip Allan.

Commonwealth Secretariat, 1991, *Namibia, Indicative Industrial Plan*, CFTC Industrial Development Unit.

Cooper, C.A. & B.F. Massell, 1965, "Toward a General Theory of Customs Unions for Developing Countries", *Journal of Political Economy*, 73(5).

Corden, W. Max, 1972, "Economies of Scale and Customs Union Theory", *Journal of Political Economy*, Vol. 80.

Curry, Robert L. Jr., 1991, "Regional Economic Cooperation in Southern Africa and Southeast Asia", *ASEAN Economic Bulletin*, Vol. 8.

Danida, 1989, *Annual Report on Project Cooperation Between SADCC and Denmark*, Copenhagen.

Davies, Robert, 1990a, "Key issues in reconstructing South–Southern African economic relations after apartheid", *Southern African Perspectives*, No. 2, November, CSAS, University of Western Cape.

Davies, Robert, 1990b, "A statistical profile of all SADCC countries in the 1980s", *Southern African Perspectives*, No. 3, December, CSAS, University of Western Cape.

Davies, Robert, 1990c, "Post-apartheid scenarios for the Southern African region", *Transformation*, No.11.

Deutsch, K. & S. Burrell, 1957, *Political Community and the North Atlantic Area*, Princeton, N.J., Princeton University Press.

Development Bank of Southern Africa, 1990/91, *Annual Report*.

Eckert, J.B., 1991, "Regional economic impact of a South African solution", *Development Southern Africa*, Vol. 8, No.2.

The Economist, 1991, "The business of the American hemisphere", August 24.

Economist Intelligence Unit, 1991/92, *Country Report: Namibia, Botswana, Lesotho, Swaziland*.

Economist Intelligence Unit, 1991/92, *Country Report: Angola*.

Edlin, John, 1983, "SADCC key to Southern Africa's economic independence", *Africa Report*, 28(3).

El-Agraa, Ali M. & Anthony J. Jones, 1981, *The Theory of Customs Unions*, Oxford, Philip Allan.

"The end of SADCC?", 1991, Cover story in *Southern African Economist* April/May.

Etzioni, A., 1965, *Political Unification*, New York.

Financial Mail, 1986, 15 August, Johannesburg.

Financial Mail, 1990, November, Johannesburg.

Frey, Bruno S., 1984, *International Political Economics*, Oxford and Cambridge, MA, Basil Blackwell.

Friedrich, Carl, 1968, *Trends of Federalism in Theory and Practice*, New York, Praeger.

Fuentes, Juan Alberto, 1989, "Central American economic integration: Renewed prospects in the midst of crisis", in George Irvin & Stuart Holland (eds.), *Central America. The Future of Economic Integration*, Boulder, Westview Press.

Garner, John and Jonathan Leape, 1991. *South Africa's Borrowings on International Capital Markets: Recent Developments in Historical Perspective*. Research Paper No. 5, Centre for the Study of the South African Economy and International Finance, London School of Economics.

GATT, 1990, *International Trade 89–90*, Vol. II, Geneva.

Gelb, Stephen (ed.), 1991, *South Africa's Economic Crisis*, Cape Town, David Phillip.

Government of Botswana, 1991, *Statistical Bulletin*.

Government of Swaziland, 1985, *Annual Statistical Bulletin*.

Green, H. G., 1991, *How to Add 10 and One, Some Reflections on Attaining Creative Economic Interaction Between Southern Africa and the "New" South Africa*. Paper for Africa Leadership Forum Conference, Windhoek, Namibia.

Guelke, Adrian, 1974, "Africa as a market for South African goods", in *Journal of Modern African Studies*, Vol. 12, No. 1.

Guillaumont, P. et al.,1988, "Participating in African monetary unions: An alternative evaluation", *World Development*, 16:5.

Guma, X. P., 1990, "The Revised South African Customs Union Agreement: An Appraisal", in *The South African Journal of Economics*, March.

Gustafsson, G., 1983, "Symbolic and pseudo policies as responses to diffusion of power", *Policy Sciences*, (15).

Haarløv, Jens, 1988, *Regional Cooperation in Southern Africa: Central Elements of the SADCC Venture*, CDR Research Report No. 14, Centre for Development Research, Copenhagen.

Haas, Ernst, 1958, *The Uniting of Europe*, London, Stevens & Sons Limited.

Haas, Ernst, 1971, "The study of regional integration: Reflections on the joy and anguish of pretheorizing", in Lindberg et al. (eds.), *Regional Integration: Theory and Research*, Cambridge, Harvard University Press.

Haas, Ernst, 1975, "The obsolescence of regional integration theory", *Research Series* (25), Berkeley, Institute of International Studies, University of California.

Hanlon, Joseph, 1986, *Beggar Your Neighbours: Apartheid Power in Southern Africa*, London, Catholic Institute of International Relations /James Currey.

Hanlon, Joseph, 1989, *SADCC in the 1990s: Development on the Frontline*, Special Report No. 1158, London, Economist Intelligence Unit.

Harvey, Charles, 1983, "Analysis of project finance in developing countries", Heinemann, reprinted Gower 1986.

Harvey, Charles, 1985, "The use of monetary policy in Botswana, in good times and bad", *IDS Discussion Paper* 204.

Harvey, Charles, 1991, "On the perverse effects of financial reform in Anglophone Africa", *South African Journal of Economics*, 59:3.

Harvey, Charles, 1992, "Botswana: Is the economic miracle over?", *IDS Discussion Paper*, 298.

Hazlewood, Arthur, (ed.), 1967, *African Integration and Disintegration*, London, Oxford University Press.

Hazlewood, Arthur, 1985, "The end of the East African Community: What are the lessons for regional integration schemes?", in R. Onwuka & A. Sesay *The Future of Regionalism in Africa*, London, MacMillan.

Hogendorn, James, 1987, *Economic Development*, New York, Harper & Row.

Hunt, Diana, 1989, *Economic Theories of Development: An Analysis of Competing Paradigms*, New York, Harvester Wheatsheaf.

Huntington, Samuel, 1968, *Political Order in Changing Societies*, New Haven, Yale University Press.

Hyden, Goran, 1983, *No Shortcuts to Progress: African Development Management in Perspective*, Los Angeles, University of California Press.

IMF, 1991, "South Africa: Selected background issues", mimeo, Washington D.C.

IMF, various issues, *Direction of Trade Statistics*, Washington, D.C.

IMF, 1990, *International Financial Statistics (IFS) Yearbook*.

IMF, various years, *Direction of Trade Statistics Yearbook*.

IRRC (Investor Responsibility Research Centre), 1990, *International Business in South Africa 1990*, Washington D.C.

IRRC (Investor Responsibility Research Centre), 1991, *US Business in South Africa, 1991*, Washington D.C.

Isaksen, Jan & Bertil Odén, 1989, "Majoritetsstyrt Sydafrika och fritt Namibia. Konsekvenser för biståndet till södra Afrika", mimeo, Nordiska Afrika-institutet, Uppsala.

Jaster, Robert, 1982, "Security Regimes", *International Organization*, Vol. 36, No. 2.

Johnson, Harry G., 1965, "An economic theory of protectionism, tariff bargaining, and the formation of customs unions", *Journal of Political Economy*, 73(5).

Johnson, Harry, 1967, *Economic Policies Toward Less Developed Countries*, Washington D.C., The Brookings Institution.

Johnson, Omotunde E.G., 1991, "Economic integration in Africa: Enhancing prospects for success", *Journal of Modern African Studies*, 29(1).

Jourdan, Paul, 1989, *Problems and Prospects of the Mining Sector of the SADCC*, Report No 98, Institute of Mining Research, University of Zimbabwe.

Jourdan, Paul, 1990, "The minerals economies of the SADCC: Namibia", *Raw Materials Report*, 7.1.

Jourdan, Paul, 1991, "Mining in Southern Africa". Paper to SAPES Conference on SADCC and Southern Africa in the 1990s, Gaborone, 8–11 October.

Jourdan, Paul, 1991b, "Possibilities for a Resource-Based Industrialisation Strategy", mimeo, December.

Kahn, Brian, 1991, "South African exchange-rate policy, 1979–81", mimeo, LSE Centre for the Study of the South African Economy and International Finance.

Kaplan, David, 1987, "Beyond the indicators: A perspective on the South African economy", *South African Review* 4, Johannesburg, Ravan Press.

Kumar, Umesh, 1991, "Economic dominance and dependence: The case of the Southern African Customs Union" in Oliver Saasa (ed.), *Joining the Future: Economic Integration and Cooperation in Africa*, Nairobi, ATCS Press/Africa Centre for Technology Studies.

Landsberg, Martin, 1979, "Export-led industrialization in the Third World: Manufacturing imperialism", *Review of Radical Political Economics*, 11(4).

Langhammer, Rolf J., 1989, "Trade in manufactures between Asian Pacific rim countries", *ASEAN Economic Bulletin*, Vol. 6.

Langhammer, Rolf J. & Ulrich Hiemen, 1990, *Regional Integration among Developing Countries: Opportunities, Obstacles and Options*, Tübingen, J.C.B. Mohr.

Langhammer, Rolf J., 1991, "ASEAN economic co-operation. A stock-taking from a political economy point of view", *ASEAN Economic Bulletin*, Vol. 8.

Leistner, Erich & Pieter Esterhuysen (eds.), 1988, *South Africa in Southern Africa: Economic Interaction*, Africa Institute of South Africa.

Leistner, E., 1991a, "Zambia in post-apartheid Southern Africa: Prospects for enhanced production and trade", IAS Seminar paper, September, Lusaka.

Leistner, E., 1991b, *The role of South Africa in Africa*, Department of Foreign Affairs of South Africa, Pretoria.

Lesotho Bureau of Statistics, 1988, *Statistical Yearbook*.

Lewis, R. Stephen Jr., 1990, *The Economics of Apartheid*, New York, Council on Foreign Relations Press.

Lewis, S. & J. Sharpley, 1988, "Botswana's industrialisation", mimeo.

Lewis, Stephen R. Jr., 1990, "The economics of apartheid", *Council of Foreign Relations*.

Lewis, W. Arthur, 1980, "The slowing down of the engine of growth", *American Economic Review*, Vol. 70.

Leys, Roger & Arne Tostensen, 1982, "Regional cooperation in Southern Africa: The SADCC", *Review of African Political Economy* (23).

Libby, R. T., 1991, *The Politics of Economic Power in Southern Africa: From Conflict to Cooperation*, London, Pinter.

Lipsey, Richard G., 1957, "The theory of customs unions. Trade diversion and welfare", *Economica*, Vol. 24.

Lipsey, Richard G., 1960, "The theory of customs unions: A general survey", *Economic Journal*, Vol. 70.

Livi, G., 1992, Speech at a seminar on Post-Apartheid Regional Cooperation: International Support for Transforming Southern Africa, 27–29 April, Gaborone.

Lundahl, Mats, 1990, "Export-led growth as a determinant of social development in Costa Rica", *Scandinavian Journal of Social Medicine,* Supplement 46.

Lundahl, Mats & Lennart Petersson, 1991, *The Dependent Economy. Lesotho and the Southern African Customs Union,* Boulder, Westview Press.

Maasdorp, Gavin, 1990, "The role of the South African economy, SACU, CMA and other regional groupings". Paper presented to the Conference on Rethinking Strategies for Mozambique and Southern Africa, ISRI, Maputo, May.

Maasdorp, Gavin, 1991a, "Into a second Century: Whither Customs Unions in Southern Africa?" (Mimeo, being revised for publication).

Maasdorp, Gavin, 1991b, "Regional Economic Groupings: Cooperation or Integration?", mimeo, University of Natal.

Maasdorp, Gavin & Alan Whiteside, 1991, "South Africa: The Economy and Closer Regional Co-operation". Paper presented at a symposium on regional economic integration and national development, 5–8 May, Harare.

Maasdorp, Gavin, & Alan Whiteside (eds.), 1992, *Towards a Post-Apartheid Future: Political and Economic Relations in Southern Africa,* London, Macmillan.

Maasdorp, Gavin, forthcoming 1992, *Regional Economic Groupings: Cooperation or Integration?,* London Research Institute for the Study of Conflict and Terrorism.

Mandaza, Ibbo, 1987, "Perspectives on Economic Cooperation and Autonomous Development in Southern Africa", in S. Amin et al. (eds.), *SADCC: Prospects for Disengagement and Development in Southern Africa,* New Jersey, Zed Books.

Mandaza, Ibbo, 1991, "Southern Africa in the 1990s: Resolving the South African (National) Question", *Southern Africa Political and Economic Monthly,* Vol. 4, No. 8.

Mandaza, Ibbo & Arne Tostensen, *Towards a Southern African Community?,* Gaborone, Heinemann.

Mandela, Nelson, 1991, "Statement at the SADCC Annual Conference, delivered on behalf of the Liberation Movements: Windhoek, Namibia, January 31, 1991", mimeo.

March, James G. & Johan P. Olsen, 1989, *Rediscovering Institutions: The Organizational Basis of Politics,* New York, Free Press.

Martin, Guy, 1989, "The Preferential Trade Area (PTA) for Eastern and Southern Africa: Achievements, problems and prospects", *Africa Spectrum,* 89(2).

Martin, Guy, 1990, "The Preferential Trade Area (PTA) for Eastern and Southern Africa: Achievements, problems and prospects", in Anyang' Nyong'o, *Regional Integration in Africa,* Kenya, Academy Science Publishers.

Martin, William G., 1991, "The futures of Southern Africa: What prospects after majority rule?", *Review of African Political Economy* No. 50.

Mbeki, Thabo, 1991, "South Africa's international relations—today and tomorrow", *South Africa International,* Vol. 21, No. 4.

McCarthy, C. L., 1985, *Southern African Customs Union—Report Prepared for Central Economic Advisory Service* (unpublished).

McFarland Jr., Earl A., 1983, "The benefits to the RSA of her exports to the BLS countries", in M. A. Oommen, et al., (eds.), *Botswana's Economy since Independence*, New Delhi, Tata McGraw-Hill.

McFarland, E., 1981, *The Benefits to South Africa in Terms of Import Substitution and Employment Growth of BLS Membership in SACU*, Ministry of Finance and Development Planning, Gaborone.

Meade, James, 1955, *The Theory of Customs Unions*, Amsterdam, North Holland.

Meier, Gerald M. (ed.), 1989, *Leading Issues in Economic Development*, 5th ed., New York & Oxford, Oxford University Press.

Mhlongo, T., 1991, "Southern Africa in cross roads: Regional economic cooperation and integration in Southern Africa in a post-apartheid era—integration or cooperation ?", mimeo, Centre for Southern African Studies, University of York.

Mikesell, R.F., 1963, "The theory of common markets as applied to regional arrangements among developing countries", in R. Harrod & D. Hague, *International Trade Theory in a Developing World*, London, MacMillan.

Mills, G. & S. Baynham, 1990, "Changing the guard: South African foreign policy in the 1990s", *Africa Insight*, Vol. 20, No. 3.

Mitrany, David, 1966, "A Working Peace System", Chicago, Quardrangle Books.

Mistry, P.S., 1992, "Issue paper on study of economic integration in Southern Africa" (ADB Project), January, mimeo, Oxford.

Mkandawire, Thandika, 1985, "Dependence and economic cooperation: The case of SADCC", *Zimbabwe Journal of Economics*, 1(2).

Mmusi, P.S. (Chairman of the SADCC Council of Ministers), 1991, *Statement at the 1991 SADCC Annual Consultative Conference*, Windhoek, January 31.

Mozambique National Planning Commission, 1990, *Informacao Estatistica*.

Mutharika, Bingu Wa, 1981, "A case study of regionalism in Africa", in D. Nicol (ed.), *Regionalism and the New International Economic Order*, New York, Pergamon Press.

Myrdal, Gunnar, 1957, *Economic Theory and Underdeveloped Regions*, New York.

Mytelka, Lynn Krieger, 1973, "The salience of gains in Third-World integrative systems", *World Politics* (25).

Mytelka, Lynn Krieger, 1979, *Regional Development in a Global Economy: The Multinational Corporation, Technology, and Andean Integration*, London, Yale University Press.

Nafziger, E. Wayne, 1990, *The Economics of Developing Countries*, Englewood Cliffs, Prentice-Hall.

Naya, Seiji & Michael G. Plummer, 1991, "ASEAN economic co-operation in the new international economic environment", *ASEAN Economic Bulletin*, Vol. 7.

Ndlela, Daniel B., 1987, "The manufacturing sector in the East and Southern African subregion, with emphasis on the SADCC", in S. Amin et al. (eds.), *SADCC: Prospects for Disengagement and Development in Southern Africa*, New Jersey, Zed Books.

Ngonga, B., 1992, "Transport sector yawning", *Financial Mail* (Zambia), March 31–April 6.

Ngwenya, S.N. et al., 1991, "Review of SADCC's transport and communi-cations strategies programmes and policies, 1980–1990", SAPES Commis-sioned project, mimeo.

Nordås, Hildegunn, 1992, *Southern African Customs Union (SACU): Costs and Benefits to Botswana from SACU Membership.* (Forthcoming as Chr. Michelsen Institute Report)

Novicki, Margaret A., 1990, "A decade of regional cooperation. Interview with Simba Makoni, Executive Secretary, SADCC", *Africa Report*, July–August.

Nye, J.S., 1971, "Comparing common markets: A revised neo-functionalist model", in Lindberg et al. (eds.), *Regional Integration: Theory and Research*, Cambridge, Harvard University Press.

OAU, 1991, *The Lagos Plan of Action of 1980 and the Treaty establishing the African Economic Community*, signed by OAU Heads of State or Government, June.

Odén, Bertil & Haroub Othman (eds.), 1989, *Regional Cooperation in Southern Africa. A Post-Apartheid Perspective*, The Scandinavian Institute of African Studies, Seminar Proceedings No. 22, Uppsala.

Odén, Bertil, 1988, *Sydafrika i Södra Afrika*, Nordiska Afrikainstitutet/SIDA, Uppsala.

Odén, Bertil, 1992, "Will Southern Africa get any aid in the post-apartheid era?", in *Beyond Apartheid, Discussion Paper on a Democratic Development in South Africa*, Centre for Development Research, Copenhagen.

OECD, 1988, *Implementing the SADCC Programme of Action*, Paris.

OECD, 1991, *External Debt Statistics*, Paris.

OECD, 1992, *Geographical Distribution of Financial Flows to Developing Countries 1987/90*, Paris.

OECD, various years, *DAC Development Report*, Paris.

Ofstad, Arve et al., 1986, *SADCC Intra-Regional Trade Study*, Gaborone, Southern African Development Coordination Conference.

Ohlson, Thomas & Stephen J. Stedman, 1992, "Trick or treat? The end of bipo-larity and conflict resolution in Southern Africa", *Southern African Perspectives*, No. 11, CSAS, University of Western Cape.

Ohlson, Thomas & Stephen J. Stedman, forthcoming 1993, *The New Is Not Yet Born. Conflict and Conflict Resolution in Southern Africa*, Washington, D.C., Brookings.

Ojo, Olatunde et al., 1985, *African International Relations*, London, Long-man.

Okolo, Julius & Nkiru, 1991, "Intra-ECOWAS monetary union problems and prospects", *Scandinavian Journal of Development Alternatives*, 10(1&2).

Olaniyan, Omotayo, 1989/90, "Reflective Notes on Regionalism in Africa", *Quarterly Journal of Administration*, October–January.

Olson, Mancur, 1965, *The Logic of Collective Action. Public Goods and the Theory of Groups*, Cambridge, MA and London, Harvard University Press.

Olson, Mancur & Richard Zeckhauser, 1966, "An economic theory of allian-ces", *Review of Economics and Statistics*, Vol. 48.

Orantes, Isaac Cohen, 1981, "The concept of integration", *Cepal Review* (15).

Packenham, Robert, 1973, *Liberal America and the Third World*, Princeton, Princeton University Press.

Panild, Troels Norup, 1989, "Det indre marked og integrationsteori" (Danish), *Politica*, 21(4).

Pomfret, Richard, 1986, "The trade-diverting bias of preferential trading arrangements", *Journal of Common Market Studies*, 25(2).

Potholm, Christian P. & Richard A. Fredland (eds.), 1980, *Integration and Disintegration in East Africa*, Washington D.C., University Press of America.

PTA, 1985, *Report of the Sixth Meeting of the Council of Ministers*, July, (PTA/CM/VI/5)

PTA, 1991a, *Achievements, Problems and Prospects*, Speaking notes for the PTA Secretary General on visit to Norway, October 1991.

PTA, 1991b, *Draft PTA Trade and Development Strategy*, Lusaka.

PTA, 1991c, *Synopsis of PTA Programme Activities January–December 1991*, Lusaka.

Ravenhill, John, (ed.), 1979, "Regional integration and development in Africa: Lessons from the East African Community", *Journal of Commonwealth & Comparative Politics*, 17(3).

Ravenhill, John, 1980, "The theory and practice of regional integration in East Africa", in Christian P. Potholm & Richard A. Fredland (eds.), *Integration and Disintegration in East Africa*, Washington D.C., University Press of America.

Ravenhill, John, 1985, "The future of regionalism in Africa" in R. Onwuka & A. Sesay (eds.), *The Future of Regionalism in Africa*, London, MacMillan.

Republic of South Africa, 1985, *Commission of Inquiry into the Monetary System and Monetary Policy in South Africa*, Final Report.

Republic of South Africa, various years, *Foreign Trade Statistics*, Pretoria, Government Printer.

Ridell, Roger, 1992, *Zimbabwe to 1996. At the Heart of a Growing Region*, The Economist Intelligence Unit, Special Report, No. M 205, London.

Robson, Peter, 1968, *Economic Integration in Africa*, London, George Allen and Unwin Ltd.

Saasa, O.S., 1987, "Western response to development cooperation in Southern Africa", Seminar paper, April, Harare.

Saasa, O.S., 1988, "Politico-economic commitment to the expansion of intra-regional trade: The case of SADCC and PTA", Conference Paper, July, Lusaka.

Saasa, O.S., 1989a, "SADCC transport and communications systems and the South African destabilisation policies: An overview", Conference paper, February, Harare.

Saasa, O.S., 1989b, "International support for SADCC", in K. Kiljunen, (ed.), *Mini-NIEO: The Potential of Regional North–South Cooperation*, Helsinki, IDS/University Press.

Saasa, O.S. (ed.), 1991a, *Joining the Future: Economic Integration and Cooperation in Africa*, Nairobi, Acts Press.

Saasa, O.S., 1991b, "The South African factor in the SADCC transport and communications systems", G. Nieuwkerk & G. Staden (eds.), *Southern Africa at the Crossroads: Prospects for the Political Economy of the Region*, SAIIA special studies series, Johannesburg.

SADCC Challenges for the 1990s, 1991. Papers from a conference organised by The Centre for Third World Studies, State University of Ghent.

SADCC, 1981, *Transport and Communications Progress and Status*, Blantyre.

SADCC, 1986, *Macro Economic Survey*, Gaborone.

SADCC, 1987, *SADCC Annual Report, July 1986–August 1987*, Gaborone.

SADCC/OECD, 1988a, *Implementing the SADCC Programme of Action*, SADCC, Paris/Gaborone.

SADCC, 1988b, *Transport and Communications*, January, Arusha.

SADCC, 1989a, *Issues in Financial Strategy*, SADCC Transport Corridors Workshop, December, Maputo.

SADCC, 1989b, *SADCC Regional Economic Survey 1988*, Gaborone.

SADCC, 1990a, *SADCC Export Development and Promotion Strategy*, Draft report, Dar es Salaam.

SADCC, 1990b, *Transport and Communications*, Lusaka.

SADCC, 1990c, *SADCC: The Second Decade—Enterprise, Skills and Productivity*, Gaborone.

SADCC, 1991a, *Annual Progress Report, July 1989–June 1990*.

SADCC, 1991b, "SADCC: Towards economic integration", mimeo, Gaborone.

SADCC, 1992a, *SADCC: Towards Economic Integration.* Theme Document presented at SADCC Annual Consultative Conference, January, Maputo.

SADCC, 1992b, *Transport and Communications*, SADCC, Maputo, January.

SADCC, 1992c, *SADCC Annual Report, July 1990–June 1991*, SADCC, Maputo.

SADCC, 1992d, "Formalisation of SADCC: A report of the Team of Advisors", mimeo, draft "Declaration towards the Southern African Development Community" and draft "Treaty of the Southern African Development Community".

SADCC/OECD, 1988a, *Implementing the SADCC Programme of Action*, SADCC, Paris/Gaborone.

Sandbrook, Richard, 1990, "Taming the African Leviathan", *World Policy Journal*, Vol. 7, No. 4.

SATCC, 1988, *A Scenario Model for Goods Transport Demand in the SADCC Region: The Main Results*, SATCC, Maputo, September.

SATCC, 1989, *Preparation of a Regional Transport Operations Plan*, Draft final report, Vol. 1, August.

SATCC, 1992, "Agenda items of meeting of the working group on transport and communication", SADCC Annual Consultative Conference, Maputo, January.

Senhadji, Abdel & Michael Walton, 1991, "South Africa: Macro-economic issues for the transition", mimeo, October.

South African Institute of Race Relations, 1990, *Race Relations Survey 1989–90*, Johannesburg.

South African Reserve Bank, various issues, *Quarterly Bulletin*.

South Scan, 1991, Vol. 6, No. 27.

The Star, 1992, 28 January.

Stoneman, Colin & Carol B. Thompson, 1991a, "Free South Africa's role in the region", Conference Paper, State University, Ghent.

Stoneman, Colin & Carol B. Thompson, 1991b, *Southern Africa after Apartheid*.

Economic Repercussions of a Free South Africa, Africa Recovery, Briefing Paper No. 4, UN Department of Public Information, New York.

Swedfund, *Swedfund Annual Report 1991*, Stockholm.

Swedish Government reports, Regeringsskrivelse 1990/91:62, Redogörelse för svenska företags verksamhet i Sydafrika och Namibia, Stockholm.

Thomas, Clive Y., 1974, *Dependence and Transformation: The Economics of the Transition to Socialism*, New York, Monthly Review Press.

Tironi, Ernesto, 1977, "Estrategias de desarrollo e integración: divergencias en el caso andino", *Estudios CIEPLAN 7*.

Tjønneland, Elling Njål, 1992, *Southern Africa after Apartheid: Challenges, Prospects and Implications for Development Aid*, Chr. Michelsen Institute, Bergen.

Tostensen, Arne, 1982, *Dependence and Collective Self-Reliance in Southern Africa: The Case of SADCC*, Research Report No. 62, The Scandinavian Institute of African Studies, Uppsala.

Tostensen, Arne, 1991a, "Challenges for SADCC in the 1990s", Conference paper, State University, Ghent.

Tostensen, Arne, 1991b, "Post-apartheid perspectives on the South African region", Seminar paper, Oslo.

Transformation, 1990, No. 12.

Tussie, Diana, 1982, "Latin American Integration: From LAFTA to LAIA", *Journal of World Trade Law*, 16(5).

UN, 1991, *Final Review and Appraisal of the Implementation of the United Nations Programme of Action on African Economic Recovery and Development 1986–1990*, August, New York.

Vaitsos, Constantine, 1978, "Crisis in regional economic cooperation (integration) among developing countries: A survey", *World Development*, Vol. 6.

Vale, Peter, 1982, "Prospects for transplanting European models of regional integration to Southern Africa", *The South African Journal of Political Science*, 9(2).

Vale, Peter, 1989, "Integration and disintegration in Southern Africa", *Reality: A Journal of Liberal and Radical Opinion*, May.

Vale, Peter, 1990, "Starting over: Some early questions on a post-apartheid foreign policy", Working paper No. 1, Centre for Southern African Studies, the University of Western Cape.

van Nieuwkerk, Anthoni & Gary van Staden, 1991, *Southern Africa at the Crossroads. Prospects for the Political Economy of the Region*, The South Africa Institute of International Affairs, Johannesburg.

Vargas-Hidalgo, Rafael, 1979, "The crisis of the Andean Pact: Lessons for integration among developing countries", *Journal of Common Market Studies*, 27(3).

Vieira, Sergio et al., 1992, *How Fast the Wind? Southern Africa, 1975–2000*, Africa World Press, Trenton, New Jersey, USA.

Viner, Jacob, 1950, *The Customs Union Issue*, Carnegie Endowment for International Peace, New York.

Wagner, Norbert, 1989, "The market economics of Southeast Asia. Market forces on the rise?", *Southeast Asian Affairs 1989*, Vol. 16.

Wallensteen, Peter, 1988, "Understanding conflict resolution: A framework", in Peter Wallensteen (ed.), 1988, *Peace Research: Achievements and Challenges*, Boulder, Colorado, Westview Press.

Walraet, Anne, 1991, *Regional cooperation in Southern Africa: SADCC versus PTA*, Centre for Third World Studies, Ghent.

Whiteside, Alan W., 1987, "Industrialization in Southern Africa: Policies and results", *Analysen*, No. 132, Friedrich Ebert Stiftung, Bonn.

Whiteside, Alan, 1991, "Labour migration in Southern Africa to the year 2000 and beyond". Paper prepared for presentation and discussion in Scandinavia and the UK, mimeo.

Willmore, Larry, 1976, "Trade creation, trade diversion and effective protection in the Central American Common Market", *Journal of Development Studies*, Vol. 12.

Willmore, Larry, 1989, "Export promotion and import substitution in Central American industry", *CEPAL Review*, Vol. 38.

Wong, John, 1985, "ASEAN's experience in regional economic cooperation", *Asian Development Review*, Vol. 3.

World Bank, 1988, *World Development Report 1988*, New York, Oxford University Press.

World Bank, 1989a, *Sub-Saharan Africa: From Crisis to Sustainable Growth*, Washington D.C.

World Bank, 1989b, *World Development Report 1989*, New York, Oxford University Press.

World Bank, 1990a, "Mozambique Country Economic Memorandum", Vol. III, Statistical Appendix Table 10 a. 1, March 14, Washington D.C.

World Bank, 1990b, *World Development Report 1990*, New York, Oxford University Press.

World Bank, 1991, *World Development Report 1991*, New York, Oxford University Press.

World Bank, 1992, *World Debt Tables 1991–92*, New York, Oxford University Press.

Zehender, Wolfgang, 1983, *Cooperation versus Integration: The Prospects of the SADCC*, German Development Institute, Berlin.

Østergaard, Tom, 1989a, *SADCC Beyond Transportation. The Challenge of Industrial Cooperation*, Centre for Development Research Publications, No. 8, Copenhagen/Uppsala.

Østergaard, Tom, 1989b, "Industrial development in Southern Africa and the role of SADCC", CDR Working paper, 89.4, Centre for Development Research, Copenhagen.

Østergaard, Tom, 1989c, "Aiming beyond conventional development assistance: An analysis of Nordic Aid to the SADCC Region", in B. Odén & H. Othman (eds.), *Regional Cooperation in Southern Africa: A Post-Apartheid Perspective*, The Scandinavian Institute of African Studies, Uppsala.

Østergaard, Tom, 1990, "SADCC's brave new strategy", in the *SADCC-NGO Newsletter*, October, International Coalition for Development Action, Brussels.

Østergaard, Tom, 1991a, "Industrial policy in Zimbabwe: The role of the national bourgeoisie". Paper presented at workshop on African bourgeoisies, 12–13 April, Queen's University, Canada.

Østergaard, Tom, 1991b, "Regional integration in Southern Africa", extract from unpublished PhD-thesis at the University of Copenhagen, mimeo.

List of contributors

Hans C. Blomqvist, Professor, Swedish School of Economics and Business Administration, Helsinki, Finland

Jan Cedergren, DCO/Embassy of Sweden, Gaborone, Botswana. Former deputy Director General, SIDA.

Robert Davies, Director, Centre for Southern African Studies, University of Western Cape, Republic of South Africa

Charles Harvey, Professor, Institute of Development Studies, University of Sussex, England

Derek Hudson, Phaleng consultancies Ltd, Gaborone, Botswana

Jan Isaksen, Chr. Michelsen Institute, Bergen, Norway

Christian Lindholm, Swedish School of Economics and Business Administration, Helsinki, Finland

Mats Lundahl, Professor, Department of International Economics and Geography, Stockholm School of Economics, Sweden

Åke Magnusson, The International Council of Swedish Industry, Stockholm, Sweden

E. M. Maphanyane, SADCC Secretariat, Gaborone, Botswana

Bertil Odén, Southern Africa Programme, Nordiska Afrikainstitutet (The Scandinavian Institute of African Studies), Uppsala, Sweden

Arve Ofstad, Chr. Michelsen Institute, Bergen, Norway

Due to a technical mistake in the printing process two names in the List of Contributors have been omitted. This is the correct List of Contributors.

List of contributors

Hans C. Blomqvist, Professor, Swedish School of Economics and Business Administration, Helsinki, Finland

Jan Cedergren, DCO/Embassy of Sweden, Gaborone, Botswana. Former deputy Director General, SIDA.

Robert Davies, Director, Centre for Southern African Studies, University of Western Cape, Republic of South Africa

Charles Harvey, Professor, Institute of Development Studies, University of Sussex, England

Derek Hudson, Phaleng consultancies Ltd, Gaborone, Botswana

Jan Isaksen, Chr. Michelsen Institute, Bergen, Norway

Christian Lindholm, Swedish School of Economics and Business Administration, Helsinki, Finland

Mats Lundahl, Professor, Department of International Economics and Geography, Stockholm School of Economics, Sweden

Åke Magnusson, The International Council of Swedish Industry, Stockholm, Sweden

E. M. Maphanyane, SADCC Secretariat, Gaborone, Botswana

Bertil Odén, Southern Africa Programme, Nordiska Afrikainstitutet (The Scandinavian Institute of African Studies), Uppsala, Sweden

Arve Ofstad, Chr. Michelsen Institute, Bergen, Norway

Thomas Ohlson, Department of Peace and Conflict Research Uppsala University, Sweden

Oliver Saasa, Director, Institute for African Studies, University of Zambia, Lusaka

Sven Schauman, Swedish School of Economics and Business Administration, Helsinki, Finland

Stephen J. Stedman, Paul H. Nitze School of Advanced International Studies, Johns Hopkins University, Washington D.C., USA

Arne Tostensen, Director, Chr. Michelsen Institute, Bergen, Norway

Tom Østergaard, Division South Group, Foreign Ministry, Copenhagen, Denmark. Former researcher at the Center for Development Research, Copenhagen.

Sven Schauman, Swedish School of Economics and Business Administration, Helsinki, Finland

Stephen J. Stedman, Paul H. Nitze School of Advanced International Studies, Johns Hopkins University, Washington D.C., USA

Arne Tostensen, Director, Chr. Michelsen Institute, Bergen, Norway

Tom Østergaard, Division South Group, Foreign Ministry, Copenhagen, Denmark. Former researcher at the Center for Development Research, Copenhagen.

Seminar Proceedings
from the Scandinavian Institute of African Studies

1. *Soviet Bloc, China and Africa.* Eds. Sven Hamrell and C.G. Widstrand. 173 pp. Uppsala 1964. (Out-of-print)
2. *Development and Adult Education in Africa.* Ed. C.G. Widstrand. 97 pp. Uppsala 1965. (Out-of-print)
3. *Refugee Problems in Africa.* Ed. Sven Hamrell. 123 pp. Uppsala 1967. SEK 30,-
4. *The Writer in Modern Africa.* Ed. Per Wästberg. 123 pp. Uppsala 1968. SEK 30,-
5. *African Boundary Problems.* Ed. C.G. Widstrand. 202 pp. Uppsala 1969. SEK 30,-
6. *Cooperatives and Rural Development in East Africa.* Ed. C.G. Widstrand. 271 pp. Uppsala 1970. (Out-of-print)
7. *Reporting Africa.* Ed. Olav Stokke. 223 pp. Uppsala 1971. SEK 30,-
8. *African Cooperatives and Efficiency.* Ed. C.G. Widstrand. 239 pp. Uppsala 1972. SEK 60,-
9. *Land-locked Countries of Africa.* Ed. Zdenek Cervenka. 368 pp. Uppsala 1973. SEK 80,-
10. *Multinational Firms in Africa.* Ed. C.G. Widstrand. With an introduction by Samir Amin. 425 pp. Uppsala 1975. (Out-of-print)
11. *African Refugees and the Law.* Eds. Göran Melander and Peter Nobel. 98 pp. Uppsala 1978. SEK 50,-
12. *Problems of Socialist Orientation in Africa.* Ed. Mai Palmberg. 243 pp. Uppsala 1978 (Out-of-print)
13. *Canada, Scandinavia and Southern Africa.* Eds. D. Anglin, T. Shaw and C.G. Widstrand. 190 pp. Uppsala 1978. SEK 70,-
14. *South-South Relations in a Changing World Order.* Ed. Jerker Carlsson. 166 pp. Uppsala 1982. SEK 90,-
15. *Recession in Africa.* Ed. Jerker Carlsson. 203 pp. Uppsala 1983. SEK 95,-
16. *Land Management and Survival.* Ed. Anders Hjort. 148 pp. Uppsala 1985. SEK 100,-
17. *Religion, Development and African Identity.* Ed. Kirsten Holst Petersen. 164 pp. Uppsala 1987. SEK 110,-
18. *The IMF and the World Bank in Africa: Conditionality, Impact and Alternatives.* Ed. Kjell J. Havnevik. 179 pp. Uppsala 1987. SEK 110,-
19. *Refugees and Development in Africa.* Ed. Peter Nobel. 120 pp. Uppsala 1987. SEK 110,-

20. *Criticism and Ideology. Second African Writers' Conference—Stockholm 1986.* Ed. Kirsten Holst Petersen. 221 pp. Uppsala 1988. SEK 150,-

21. *Cooperatives Revisited.* Ed. Hans Hedlund. 223 pp. Uppsala 1988. SEK 170,-

22. *Regional Cooperation in Southern Africa. A Post–Apartheid Perspective.* Eds. Bertil Odén and Haroub Othman. 243 pp. Uppsala 1989. SEK 170,-

23. *Small Town Africa. Studies in Rural–Urban Interaction.* Ed. Jonathan Baker. 268 pp. Uppsala 1990. SEK 170,-

24. *Religion and Politics in Southern Africa.* Eds. Carl Fredrik Hallencreutz and Mai Palmberg. 219 pp. Uppsala 1991. SEK 170.-

25. *When the Grass is Gone. Development Intervention in African Arid Lands.* Ed. P.T.W. Baxter. 215 pp. Uppsala 1991. SEK 170,-

26. *Authoritarianism, Democracy and Adjustment. The Politics of Economic Reform in Africa.* Eds. Peter Gibbon, Yusuf Bangura and Arve Ofstad. 236 pp. Uppsala 1992. SEK 230,- (hard cover), SEK 145,- (soft cover)

27. *The Rural–Urban Interface in Africa. Expansion and Adaptation.* Eds. Jonathan Baker and Poul Ove Pedersen. 320 pp. Uppsala 1992. SEK 280,-

28. *Southern Africa after Apartheid. Regional Integration and External Resources.* Ed. Bertil Odén. 279 pp. Uppsala 1993. SEK 200,-

The Valhalla Exchange

Harry Patterson

G.K.HALL&CO.

 Boston, Massachusetts

1977

Library of Congress Cataloging in Publication Data

Patterson, Henry.
  The Valhalla exchange.

  Large print ed.
  1. Sight-saving books. I. Title.
[PZ4.P3194Vo14] [PR6066.A87] 823'.9'14
ISBN 0-8161-6496-7 77-9599

Published in Large Print by arrangement
with Stein and Day, Incorporated

Set in Compugraphic 18 pt English Times

British Commonwealth rights granted courtesy of
Hutchinson Publishing Group Limited.

*For my mother and father, who helped
more than a little with this one*

Whether Martin Bormann survived the holocaust that was Berlin at the end of the Second World War may be arguable, but it is a matter of record that Russian radar reported a light aircraft leaving the vicinity of the Tiergarten in Berlin on the morning of April 30, the very day on which Adolf Hitler committed suicide. As for the remainder of this story, only the more astonishing parts are true — the rest is fiction.

One

On the Day of the Dead in Bolivia, children take food and presents to the cemetery to leave on the graves of the departed. An interesting blend of the pagan and Christian traditions, and highly appropriate the way things turned out. But even the most superstitious of Bolivian peasants would hardly expect the dead to get up and walk on such an occasion. I did.

La Huerta was a mining town of five or six thousand people, lost in the peaks of the high Andes. The back of beyond. There was no direct passenger flight from Peru, so I'd flown in from Lima in an old DC-3 that was doing some kind of cargo run to an American mining company.

It was raining hard when I arrived, but by some dispensation or other there was a cab standing outside the small terminal building. The driver was a cheerful Indian with a heavy moustache. He wore a yellow oilskin coat and a straw hat and seemed surprised and gratified at the sight of a customer.

"The hotel, *señor?*" he asked as he seized my valise.

"The Excelsior," I said.

"But that is the hotel, *señor.*" His teeth gleamed in the lamplight. "The only one."

The interior of the cab stank, the roof leaked, and as we started down the hill to the lights of the town, I felt unaccountably depressed. Why the hell was I here, doing the same thing I'd done so many times before? Chasing my tail for a story that probably didn't exist in the first place. And La Huerta itself didn't help as we turned into a maze of narrow streets, each one with the usual open sewer running down the center, decaying, flat-roofed houses crowding in, poverty and squalor on every side.

We emerged into a central plaza a few minutes later. There was a large and rather interesting baroque fountain in the center — some relic of colonial days, water gushing forth from the mouths and nostrils of a score of nymphs and dryads. The fact that it was working at all seemed a small miracle. The hotel was on the far side. As I got out I noticed a number of people sheltering under a colonnade to my right. Some of them were in carnival costume, and there was the smell of smoke on the damp air.

"What's all that?" I asked.

"All Saints' Day, *señor*. A time of festival."

"They don't look as if they're enjoying themselves too much."

"The rain." He shrugged. "It makes it difficult for the fireworks. But then this is a solemn occasion with us. Soon they will go in the procession to the cemetery to greet their loved ones. The Day of the Dead, we call it. You have heard of this, *señor?*"

"They have the same thing in Mexico."

I paid him off, went up the steps, and entered the hotel. Like everything else in La Huerta, it had seen better days, but now its pink stucco walls were peeling and there were damp patches on the ceiling. The desk clerk put down his newspaper hurriedly, as

3

amazed as the cabdriver had been at the prospect of custom.

"I'd like a room."

"But of course, *señor*. For how long?"

"One night. I'm flying back to Peru in the morning."

I passed my papers across so that he could go through the usual rigmarole the government insists on where foreigners are concerned.

As he filled in the register he said, "You have business here, *señor?* With the mining company, perhaps?"

I opened my wallet and extracted an American ten-dollar bill, which I placed carefully on the counter beside the register. He stopped writing, the eyes dark, watchful.

"It was reported in one of the Lima newspapers that a man died here Monday. Dropped dead in the plaza, right outside your front door. It rated a mention because the police found fifty thousand dollars in cash in his suitcase and passports in three different names."

"Ah, yes, *Señor* Bauer. You are a friend of his, *señor?*"

4

"No, but I might know him if I see him."

"He is with the local undertaker. In such cases they keep the body for a week while relatives are sought."

"So I was informed."

"Lieutenant Gómez is chief of police in charge of the affair, and police headquarters are on the other side of the plaza."

"I never find the police too helpful in these affairs." I laid another ten-dollar bill beside the first. "I'm a journalist. There could be a story in this for me. It's as simple as that."

"Ah, I see now. A newspaperman." His eyes lightened. "How may I help you?"

"Bauer — what can you tell me about him?"

"Very little, *señor*. He arrived last week from Sucre. Said he expected a friend to join him."

"And did anyone?"

"Not that I know of."

"What did he look like? Describe him."

"Sixty-five, maybe older. Yes, he could have been older, but it's difficult to say. He was one of those men who give

5

an impression of vitality at all times. A bull of a man."

"Why do you say that?"

"Powerfully built. Not tall, you understand me, but with broad shoulders." He stretched his arms. "A thick, powerful neck."

"A fat man?"

"No, I don't remember him that way. More the power of the man, an impression of strength. He spoke good Spanish, with a German accent."

"You can recognize it?"

"Oh, yes, *señor*. Many German engineers come here."

"Can I see the entry in the register?"

He turned it around to show me. It was on the line above mine. There were the details from his passport entered by the clerk, and beside it Bauer's signature — a trifle spidery, but firm — and the date beside it, using a crossed seven, continental style.

I nodded and pushed the two bills across. "Thank you."

"*Señor*." He snapped up the twenty dollars and tucked it into his breast

6

pocket. "I'll show you your room."

I glanced at my watch. It was just after eleven. "Too late to visit the undertaker now."

"Oh, no, *señor*, there is a porter on duty all night. It is the custom here for the dead to be in waiting for three days, during which time they are watched over both night and day in case. . . ." Here, he hesitated.

"Of a mistake?" I suggested.

"Exactly, *señor*." He smiled sadly. "Death is a very final affair, so one wants to be sure. Take the first street on the left. You will find the undertaker's at the far end. You can't miss it. There's a blue light above the door. The watchman's name is Hugo. Tell him Rafael Mareno sent you."

"My thanks," I said formally.

"At your orders, *señor*. And if you would care to eat on your return, something could be managed. I am on duty all night."

He picked up his newspaper, and I retraced my steps across the hall and went outside. The procession had formed up and started across the square as I paused at the top of the steps. It was much as I

7

had seen in Mexico. There were a couple of characters in front, blazing torches in hand, dressed to represent the lords of death and hell. Next came the children, clutching guttering candles, some already extinguished in the heavy rain, the adults following on behind with baskets of bread and fruit. Someone started to play a flute, low and plaintive, and a finger drum joined in. Otherwise, they moved in complete silence.

We seemed to be going the same way, and I joined on at the tail of the procession, turning up the collar of my trenchcoat against the heavy rain. The undertaker's was plain enough, the subdued blue light above the door as Mareno had indicated. I paused, watching the procession continue, the sound of that flute and drum strangely haunting, and only when they had turned into another alley and moved out of sight did I pull the bell chain.

There was silence for quite some time, only the rain. I was about to reach for the chain again when I became aware of a movement inside, dragging footsteps

8

approaching. A grille opened at eye level, a face peered out, pale in the darkness.

"Hugo?"

"What is it you want, *señor?*" The voice was the merest whisper.

"I would like to see the body of *Señor* Ricardo Bauer."

"Perhaps in the morning, *señor.*"

"Rafael Mareno sent me."

There was a pause, then the grille was closed. There was the sound of bolts being withdrawn; the door creaked open. He stood there, an oil lamp in one hand, very old, very frail, almost as if one of his own charges had decided to get up and walk. I slipped inside; he closed the door.

"You will follow me, please?"

He led the way along a short passage and opened an oaken door, and I could smell death instantly, the cloying sweetness of it heavy on the cold air. I hesitated, then followed him through.

The room into which I entered was a place of shadows, a single oil lamp suspended from a chain in the center supplying the only light. It was a waiting mortuary of a type I had seen a couple of

9

times before in Palermo and Vienna, although the Viennese version had been considerably more elaborate. There were perhaps a dozen coffins on the other side of the room, but first he led me up some steps to a small platform on which stood a desk and chair.

I gazed down into the shadows in fascination. Each coffin was open, a corpse clearly visible inside, the stiff fingers firmly entwined in one end of a string that went up over a pulley arrangement and across to the desk, where the other end was fastened to an old-fashioned bell that hung from a wall bracket.

He put down his lamp. I said, "Has anyone ever rung that thing?"

"The bell?" I saw now that he was very old, eighty at least, the face desiccated, the eyes moist. "Once, *señor,* ten years ago. A young girl. But she died again three days later. Her father refused to acknowledge the fact. He kept her with him for a month. Finally the police had to intervene."

"I can see how they would have to."

He opened a ledger and dipped a pen in

an inkwell. "Your relationship to *Señor* Bauer, *señor?* I must enter it in the official record."

I took out my wallet and produced another of those ten-dollar bills. "Nothing so formal, my friend. I'm just a newspaperman passing through. I heard the story and thought I might recognize him."

He hesitated, then laid down the pen. "As you say, *señor.*" He picked up the lamp. "This way."

It was the end coffin in the back row, and I received something of a shock as the old man raised his lamp to reveal red lips, a gleam of teeth, full, rounded cheeks. And then I realized, of course, that the undertaker had been going to work on him. It was as if a wax tailor's dummy had been laid out for my inspection, a totally unreal face heavy with makeup, resembling no photo that I had ever seen. But how could he hope to, thirty years later? A big, big difference between forty-five and seventy-five.

When the bell jangled I almost jumped out of my skin, and then realized it had sounded from outside. Hugo said, "You

11

will excuse me, *señor*. There is someone at the door."

He shuffled off, leaving me there beside Bauer's coffin. If there had been rings, they'd taken them off, and the powerful fingers were intertwined on his chest, the string between them. They'd dressed him in a neat blue suit, white collar, dark tie. It really was rather remarkable.

I became aware of the voices outside in the corridor, one unmistakably American. "You speak English? No?"

Then the same voice continuing in bad Spanish. "I must see the body of the man Bauer. I've come a long way, and my time is limited."

Hugo tried to protest, "*Señor* — it is late," but he was obviously brushed aside.

"Where is the body? In here?"

For some reason, some sixth sense operating if you like, I moved back into the darkness of the corner. A moment later I was glad that I had.

He stepped into the room and paused, white hair gleaming in the lamplight, rain glistening on his military raincoat, shoulders firm, the figure still militarily

12

erect, only the whiteness of the hair and the clipped moustache hinting at his seventy-five years.

I don't think I've ever been so totally astonished, for I was looking at a legend in his own time, General Hamilton Canning, Congressional Medal of Honor, DSC, Silver Star, Médaille Militaire, the Philippines, D-Day, Korea, even Vietnam in the early days. A piece of walking history, one of the most respected of living Americans.

He had a harsh, distinctive voice, not unpleasant, but it carried with it the authority of a man who'd been used to getting his own way for most of his life.

"Which one?"

Hugo limped past him, lamp held high, and I crouched back in the corner. "Here, *señor.*"

Canning's face seemed calm enough, but in the eyes I saw the turbulence, a blazing intensity, and also a kind of hope as he stood at the end of the coffin and looked down at the waxen face. And then hope died, the light went out in the eyes — something. The shoulders sagged, and for the first time he looked his age.

He turned wearily and nodded to Hugo. "I won't trouble you any further."

"This is not the person you were seeking, *señor?*"

Canning shook his head. "No, my friend, I don't think so. Good night to you."

He seemed to take a deep breath, all the old vigor returning, and strode from the room. I came out of the shadows quickly.

"Señor." Hugo started to speak.

I motioned him to silence and moved to the entrance. As Canning opened the door, I saw the cab from the airstrip outside, the driver waiting in the rain.

The general said, "You can take me to the hotel now," and closed the door behind him.

Hugo tugged at my sleeve. *"Señor,* what passes here?"

"Exactly what I was wondering, Hugo," I said softly, and I went along the passage quickly and let myself out.

The cab was parked outside the hotel. As I approached, a man in a leather flying jacket and peaked cap hurried down the steps and got in. The cab drove away through the rain. I watched it go for a moment, unable to see if Canning was inside.

Rafael wasn't behind the desk, but as I paused, shaking the rain from my coat, a door on my left opened and he emerged.

He smiled. "Were you successful, *señor?*"

"Not really," I said. "Did I see the cab driving away just now?"

"Ah, yes, that was the pilot of Mr. Smith, an American gentleman who has just checked in. He was on his way to La Paz in his private airplane, but they had to put down here because of the weather."

"I see. Mr. Smith, you say?"

"That is correct, *señor*. I've just given him a drink in the bar. Could I perhaps get you something?"

"Well, now," I said. "A large brandy might be a sensible idea, considering the state I'm in."

I followed him, unbuttoning my trenchcoat. It was a pleasant enough room, rough stone walls, a well-stocked bar at one side. Canning was seated in an armchair

15

in front of a blazing log fire, a glass in one hand. He looked up sharply.

"Company, *señor,*" Rafael said cheerfully. "A fellow guest. *Señor* O'Hagan — *Señor* Smith. I'll just get your brandy now," he added and moved away.

"Not a night for even an old tomcat to be out," I said, throwing my coat over a chair. "As my old grannie used to say."

He smiled up at me, the famous Canning charm well in evidence, and stuck out his hand. "English, Mr. O'Hagan?"

"By way of Ulster," I said. "But we won't get into that, General."

The smile stayed firmly in place — only the eyes changed, cold, hard — and the hand tightened on mine with a grip of surprising strength, considering his age.

It was Rafael who broke the spell, arriving with my brandy on a tray. "Can I get you another one, *señor?*" he asked.

Canning smiled, all charm again. "Later, my friend. Later."

"*Señores.*"

Rafael departed. Canning leaned back, watching me, then swallowed a little Scotch. He didn't waste time trying to tell me how mistaken I was, but said simply, "We've met before, presumably?"

"About fifteen minutes ago, up the street at the mortuary," I said. "I was standing in the shadows, I should explain, so I had you at something of a disadvantage. Oh, I've seen you before at press conferences over the years, that sort of thing, but then one couldn't really specialize in writing about politics and military affairs without knowing Hamilton Canning."

"O'Hagan," he said. "The one who writes for the *Times?*"

"I'm afraid so, General."

"You've a good mind, son, but remind me to put you straight on China. You've been way out of line in that area lately."

"You're the expert." I took out a cigarette. "What about Bauer, General?"

"What about him?" He leaned back, legs sprawled, all negligent ease.

I laughed. "All right, let's try it another way. You ask *me* why a reasonably well-known correspondent for *The Times* of London takes the trouble to haul himself all the way from Lima to a pesthole like this just to look at the body of a man called

17

Ricardo Bauer who dropped dead in the street here on Monday."

"All right, son," he said lazily. "You tell me. I'm all ears."

"Ricardo Bauer," I said, "as more than one expert will tell you, is one of the aliases used by Martin Bormann in Brazil, Argentina, Chile, and Paraguay on many occasions during the past thirty years."

"Martin Bormann?" he said.

"Oh, come off it, General. *Reichsleiter* Martin Bormann, head of the Nazi Party Chancellery and secretary to the *Führer*. The one member of Hitler's top table unaccounted for since the war."

"Bormann's dead," he said softly. "He was killed attempting to break out of Berlin. Blown up crossing the Weidendammer Bridge on the night of May 1, 1945."

"Early hours of May second, General," I said. "Let's get it right. Bormann left the bunker at one-thirty A.M. It was Erich Kempka, Hitler's chauffeur, who saw him come under artillery fire on that bridge. Unfortunately for that story, the Hitler Youth leader, Artur Axmann, crossed the Spree River on a railway bridge as part of a group led by Bormann, and that was considerably later."

He nodded. "But Axmann asserted also that he'd seen Bormann and Hitler's doctor, Stumpfegger, lying dead near Lehrter Station."

"And no one else to confirm the story," I said. "Very convenient."

He put down his glass, took out a pipe, and started to fill it from a leather pouch. "So you believe he's alive. Wouldn't you say that's kind of crazy?"

"It would certainly put me in pretty mixed company," I said. "Starting with Stalin and lesser mortals like Jacob Glas, Bormann's chauffeur, who saw him in Munich after the war. Then there was Eichmann — when the Israelis picked him up in 1960, he told them Bormann was alive. Now why would he do that if it wasn't true?"

"A neat point. Go on."

"Simon Wiesenthal, the Nazi-hunter, always insisted he was alive, maintained he had regular reports on him. Farago said he actually interviewed him. Since 1964, the West German authorities have had a hundred thousand marks on his head, and he was found guilty of war crimes at Nuremberg and sentenced to death *in absentia.*" I leaned forward. "What more do you want, General? Would you like to hear the one about the Spaniard who maintains he traveled to Argentina from Spain with Bormann in a U-boat in 1945?"

He smiled, leaning over to put another log on the fire. "Yes, I interviewed him soon after he came out with that story. But if Bormann's been alive all these years, what's he been doing?"

"The *Kameradenwerk,*" I said. " 'Action for comrades.' The organization they set up to take care of the movement after the war, with hundreds of millions in gold salted away to pay for it."

"Possible." He nodded, staring into the fire. "Possible."

"One thing is sure," I said. "That isn't him lying up there at the mortuary. At least you don't think so."

He glanced up at me. "Why do you say that?"

"I saw your face."

He nodded. "No, it wasn't Bormann."

"How did you know about him? Bauer, I mean. Events in La Huerta hardly make front-page news in *The New York Times*."

"I employ an agent in Brazil who has a list of certain names. Any mention of any of them anywhere in South America and he informs me. I flew straight down."

"Now that I find truly remarkable."

"What do you want to know, son? What he looked like? Will that do? Five feet six inches, bull neck, prominent cheekbones, broad, rather brutal face. You could lose him in any crowd because he looked so damned ordinary. Just another working stiff off the waterfront or whatever. He was virtually unknown to the German public and press. Honors, medals meant nothing to him. Power was all." It was as if he were talking to himself as he sat there staring into the fire. "He was the most powerful man in Germany, and nobody appreciated it until after the war."

"A butcher," I said, "who condoned the Final Solution and the deaths of millions of Jews."

"Who also sent war orphans to his wife

in Bavaria to look after," Canning said. "You know what Göring said at Nuremberg when they asked him if he knew where Bormann was? He said, 'I hope he's frying in hell, but I don't know.'"

He heaved himself out of the chair, went behind the bar, and reached for a bottle of Scotch. "Can I get you another?"

"Why not?" I got up and sat on one of the bar stools. "Brandy."

As he poured some into my glass he said, "I was once a prisoner of war, did you know that?"

"That's a reasonably well-known fact, General," I said. "You were captured in Korea. The Chinese had you for two years in Manchuria. Isn't that why Nixon hauled you out of retirement the other year to go to Peking with him?"

"No, I mean way, way back. I was a prisoner once before. Toward the end of the Second World War, the Germans had me. At Schloss Arlberg in Bavaria. A special setup for prominent prisoners."

And I genuinely hadn't known, although it was so far back it was hardly surprising — and then his really enduring fame had been gained in Korea, after all.

I said, "I didn't know that, General."

He dropped ice into his glass, and poured a very large measure of whisky. "Yes, I was there right to the bitter end. In the area erroneously known as the Alpine Redoubt. One of Dr. Goebbels's smarter pieces of propaganda. He actually had the Allies believing there was such a place. It meant the troops were very cautious about probing into that area at first, which made it a safe resting place for big Nazis on the run from Berlin in those last few days."

"Hitler could have gone, but didn't."

"That's right."

"And Bormann?"

"What do you mean?"

"The one thing that's never made any sense to me," I said. "He was a brilliant man. Too clever by half to leave his chances of survival to a mad scramble at the final end of things. If he'd really wanted to escape, he'd have gone to Berchtesgaden when he had the chance, instead of staying in the bunker till the end. He'd have had a plan."

"Oh, but he did, son." Canning nodded slowly. "You can bet your sweet life on that."

"And how would you know, General?" I asked softly.

And at that he exploded, came apart at the seams.

"Because I saw him, damn you," he cried harshly. "Because I stood as close to him as I am to you, traded shots with him, had my hands on his throat, do you understand?" He paused, hands held out, looking at them in a kind of wonder. "And lost him," he whispered.

He leaned on the bar, head down. There was a long, long moment in which I couldn't think of a thing to say, but waited, my stomach hollow with excitement. When he finally raised his head, he was calm again.

"You know what's so strange, O'Hagan? So bloody incredible? I kept it to myself all these years. Never mentioned it to a soul until now."

Two

It began, if it may be said to have begun anywhere, on the morning of Wednesday, April 25, 1945, a few miles north of Innsbruck.

When Jack Howard emerged from the truck at the rear of the column just after first light, it was bitterly cold, a powdering of dry snow on the ground, for the valley in which they had halted for the night was high in the Bavarian Alps, although he couldn't see much of the mountains because of the heavy clinging mist which had settled among the trees. It reminded him too much of the Ardennes for comfort. He stamped his feet to induce a little warmth, and lit a cigarette.

Sergeant Hoover had started a wood fire, and the men — only five of them now — crouched beside it. Anderson,

25

O'Grady, Garland, and Finebaum — who'd once played clarinet for Glenn Miller and never let anyone forget it. Just now he was on his face trying to blow fresh life into the flames. He was the first to notice Howard.

"Hey, the captain's up, and he don't look too good."

"Why don't you try a mirror?" Garland inquired. "You think you look like a daisy or something?"

"Stinkweed — that's the only flower he ever resembled," O'Grady said.

"That's it, hotshot," Finebaum told him. "You're out. From here on in, you find your own beans." He turned to Hoover. "I ask you, Sarge. I appeal to your better nature. Is that the best these mothers can offer after all I've done for them?"

"That's a truly lousy act, Finebaum, did I ever tell you that?" Hoover poured coffee into an aluminum cup. "You're going to need plenty of practice, boy, if you're ever going to get back into vaudeville."

"Well, I'll tell you," Finebaum said.

"I've had kind of a special problem lately. I ran out of audience. Most of them died on me."

Hoover took the coffee across to the truck and gave it to Howard without a word. Somewhere thunder rumbled on the horizon.

"Eighty-eights?" the captain said.

Hoover nodded. "Don't they ever give up? It don't make any kind of sense to me. Every time we turn on the radio, they tell us this war's as good as finished."

"Maybe they forgot to tell the Germans."

"That makes sense. Any chance of submitting it through channels?"

Howard shook his head. "It wouldn't do any good, Harry. Those Krauts don't intend to give in until they get you. That's what it's all about."

Hoover grunted. "Those mothers better be quick, or they're going to miss out, that's all I can say. You want to eat now? We still got plenty of K-rations, and Finebaum traded some smokes last night for half a dozen cans of beans from some of those Limey tank guys up the column."

"The coffee's just fine, Harry," Howard said. "Maybe later."

The sergeant moved back to the fire, and Howard paced up and down beside the truck, stamping his feet and clutching the hot cup tightly in mittened fingers. He was twenty-three years of age, young to be a captain in the Rangers, but that was a circumstance of war. He wore a crumpled mackinaw coat, wool-knit muffler at his throat, and a knitted cap. There were times when he could have passed for nineteen, but this was not one of them, not with the four-day growth of dark beard on his chin, the sunken eyes.

But once he had been nineteen, an Ohio farmer's son with some pretensions to being a poet and the desire to write for a living which had sent him to Columbia to study journalism. That was a long time ago — before the Flood. Before the further circumstance of war which had brought him to his present situation in charge of the reconnaissance element for a column of the British Seventh Armored Division, probing into Bavaria toward Berchtesgaden.

Hoover squatted beside the fire. Finebaum passed him a plate of beans. "The captain not eating?"

"Not right now."

"Jesus," Finebaum said. "What kind of a way is that to carry on?"

"Respect, Finebaum." Hoover prodded him with his knife. "Just a little more respect when you speak about him."

"Sure, I respect him," Finebaum said. "I respect him like crazy, and I know how you and he went in at Salerno together, and how those Krauts jumped you outside Anzio with those machine guns zeroed in and took out three-quarters of the battalion, and how our gracious captain saved the rest. So he's God's gift to the army — so he should eat occasionally. He ain't swallowed more than couple of mouthfuls since Sunday."

"Sunday he lost nine men," Hoover said. "Maybe you're forgetting."

"Those guys are dead — so they're dead, right? He don't keep his strength up, he might lose a few more, including me. I mean, look at him! He's got so skinny, that stinking coat he wears is two sizes too big for him. He looks like some fresh kid in his first year at college."

"I know," Hoover said. "The kind they give the Silver Star with Oak Leaf Cluster to."

The others laughed, and Finebaum managed to look injured. "Okay, okay. I've come this far. I just figure it would look kind of silly to die now."

"Everybody dies," Hoover said. "Sooner or later. Even you."

"Okay — but not here. Not now. I mean, after surviving D-Day, Omaha, Saint-Lô, the Ardennes, and a few interesting stop-offs in between, it would look kind of stupid to buy it here, playing wet nurse to a bunch of Limeys."

"We've been on the same side for nearly four years now," Hoover said. "Or hadn't you noticed?"

"How can I help it with guys going around dressed like that?" Finebaum nodded to where the commanding officer of the column, a lieutenant colonel named Denning, was approaching, his adjutant at his side. They were Highlanders and wore rather dashing Glengarry bonnets.

" 'Morning, Howard," Denning said as he got close. "Damn cold night. Winter's hung on late up here this year."

"I guess so, Colonel."

"Let's have a look at the map, Miller." The adjutant spread it against the side of the truck, and the colonel ran a finger along the center. "Here's Innsbruck, and here we are. Another five miles to the head of this valley and we hit a junction with the main road to Salzburg. We could have trouble there, wouldn't you say so?"

"Very possibly, Colonel."

"Good. We'll move out in thirty minutes. I suggest you take the lead and send your other jeep on ahead to scout out the land."

"As you say, sir."

Denning and the adjutant moved away, and Howard turned to Hoover and the rest of the men, who had all edged in close enough to hear. "You got that, Harry?"

"I think so, sir."

"Good. You take Finebaum and O'Grady. Garland and Anderson stay with me. Report in over your radio every five minutes without fail. Now get moving."

As they swung into action, Finebaum said plaintively, "Holy Mary, Mother of God, I'm only a Jewish boy, but pray for us sinners in the hour of our need."

On the radio, the news was good. The Russians had finally encircled Berlin and had made contact with American troops on the Elbe River seventy-five miles south of the capital, cutting Germany in half.

"The only way in and out of Berlin now is by air, sir," Anderson said to Howard. "They can't keep going any longer — they've got to give in. It's the only logical thing to do."

"Oh, I don't know," Howard said. "I'd say that if your name was Hitler or Goebbels or Himmler and the only prospect offered was a short trial and a long rope, you might think it worthwhile to go down taking as many of the other side with you as you possibly could."

Anderson, who had the wheel, looked worried, as well he might, for, unlike Garland, he was married, with two children, a girl of five and a boy aged six.

He gripped the wheel so tightly that the knuckles on his hands turned white.

You shouldn't have joined, old buddy, Howard thought. You should have found an easier way. Plenty did.

Strange how callous he had become where the suffering of others was concerned, but that was the war. It had left him indifferent where death was concerned, even to its uglier aspects. The time when a body had an emotional effect was long since gone. He had seen too many of them. The fact of death was all that mattered.

The radio crackled into life. Hoover's voice sounded clearly. "Sugar Nan Two to Sugar Nan One. Are you receiving me?"

"Strength nine," Howard said. "Where are you, Harry?"

"We've reached the road junction, sir. Not a Kraut in sight. What do we do now?"

Howard checked his watch. "Stay there. We'll be with you in twenty minutes. Over and out."

He replaced the handmike and turned to Garland. "Strange — I would have expected something from them up there. A good place to put up a fight. Still . . ."

There was a sudden roaring in his ears, and a great wind seemed to pick him up and carry him away. The world moved in and out and then somehow he was lying in a ditch, Garland beside him, minus his helmet and most of the top of his skull. The jeep, or what was left of it, was on its side, the Cromwell tank behind blazing furiously, its ammunition exploding like a fireworks display. One of the crew scrambled out of the turret, his uniform on fire, and fell to the ground.

There was no reality to it at all — none. And then Howard realized why. He couldn't hear a damn thing. Something to do with the explosion, probably. Things seemed to be happening in slow motion, as if under water — no noise, not even the whisper of a sound. There was blood on his hands, but he got his field glasses up to his eyes and traversed the trees on the hillside on the other side of the road. Almost immediately a Tiger tank jumped into view, a young man with a pale face in the black uniform of a *Sturmbannführer* of SS panzer troops standing in the gun turret, quite exposed. As Howard watched helplessly, he saw the microphone raised. The lips moved, and then the Tiger's 88 belched flame and smoke.

The man whom Howard had seen in the turret of the lead Tiger was SS Major Karl Ritter, of the Third Company, 502nd SS Heavy Tank Battalion, and what was to take place during the ensuing five minutes was probably the single most devastating Tiger action of the Second World War.

Ritter was a Tiger ace, with 120 claimed victories on the Russian Front, a man who had learned his business the hard way and knew exactly what he was doing. With only two operational Tigers on the hillside with him, he was hopelessly outnumbered — a fact which a reconnaissance on foot had indicated to him that morning — and it was obvious that Denning would expect trouble at the junction with the Salzburg road. Therefore, an earlier attack had seemed essential — indeed, there was no alternative.

It succeeded magnificently, for on the

particular stretch of forest track he had chosen there was no room for any vehicle to reverse or change direction. The first shell from his Tiger's 88 narrowly missed direct contact with the lead jeep, turning it over and putting Howard and his men into the ditch. The second shell, seconds later, brewed up the leading Cromwell tank. Ritter was already transmitting orders to his gunner, Sergeant Major Erich Hoffer. The 88 traversed again, and a moment later scored a direct hit on a Bren-gun carrier bringing up the rear.

The entire column was now at a standstill, hopelessly trapped, unable to move forward or back. Ritter made a hand signal, the other two Tigers moved out of the woods on either side, and the carnage began.

In the five minutes which followed, their three 88s and six machine guns left thirty armored vehicles ablaze, including eight Cromwell tanks.

The front reconnaissance jeep was out of sight among the trees at the junction with the road to Salzburg. O'Grady was sitting behind the wheel, Hoover beside him lighting a cigarette. Finebaum was a few yards away, directly above the road, squatting against a tree, his M1 across his knees, eating beans from a can with a knife.

O'Grady was eighteen and a replacement of only a few weeks' standing. He said, "He's disgusting, you know that, Sarge? He not only acts like a pig, he eats like one. And the way he goes on, never stopping talking, making out everything's some kind of bad joke."

"Maybe it is as far as he's concerned," Hoover said. "When we landed at Omaha, there were a hundred and twenty-three guys in the outfit. Now there are six, including you, and you don't count worth a shit. And don't ever let Finebaum fool you. He's got a pocketful of medals somewhere, just for the dead men he's left around."

There was the sudden dull thunder of heavy gunfire down in the valley below, the rattle of a machine gun.

Finebaum hurried toward the jeep, rifle in hand. "Hey, Harry, that don't sound too good to me. What do you make of it?"

"I think maybe somebody just made a bad mistake." Hoover slapped O'Grady on the shoulder. "Okay, kid, let's get the hell out of here."

Finebaum scrambled into the rear and positioned himself behind the Browning heavy machine gun as O'Grady reversed quickly and started back down the track to the valley road. The sound of firing was continuous now, interspersed with one heavy explosion after another, and then they rounded a bend and found a Tiger tank moving up the road toward them.

Finebaum's hands tightened on the handles of the machine gun, but they were too close for any positive action and there was nowhere to run, the pine trees pressing in on either side of the road at that point.

O'Grady screamed, at the last moment releasing the wheel and flinging up his arms as if to protect himself, and then they were close enough for Finebaum to see the death's-head badge on the cap of the SS major in the turret of the Tiger.

A moment later the collision took place, and he was thrown headfirst into the brush. The Tiger moved on relentlessly, crushing the jeep beneath it, and disappeared around the bend in the road.

Howard had lost consciousness for a while and came back to life to the sound of repeated explosions from the ammunition in another burning Cromwell. It was a scene from hell — smoke everywhere, the cries of the dying, the stench of burning flesh. He could see Colonel Denning lying in the middle of the road on his back a few yards away, revolver still clutched firmly in one hand, and, beyond him, a Bren-gun carrier was tilted on its side against a tree, bodies spilling out, tumbled one on top of another.

He tried to get to his feet, started to fall, and was caught as he went down. Hoover said, "Easy, sir. I've got you."

Howard turned in a daze and found Finebaum there, also. "You all right, Harry?"

"We lost O'Grady. Ran head-on into a Tiger up the road. Where are you hit?"

"Nothing serious. Most of the blood's Garland's. He and Anderson bought it."

Finebaum stood holding his M1 ready. "Hey, this must have been a real turkey shoot."

"I just met Death," Howard said dully. "A nice-looking guy in a black uniform, with a silver skull-and-crossbones in his cap."

"Is that so?" Finebaum said. "I think maybe we had a brush with the same guy." He stuck a cigarette in his mouth and shook his head. "This is bad. Bad. I mean to say, the way I had it figured, this stinking war was over, and here some bastards are still trying to get me."

The 502nd SS Heavy Tank Battalion, or what was left of it, had temporary headquarters in the village of Lindorf, just off the main Salzburg road, and the battalion commander, *Standartenführer* Max Jager, had set up his command post in the local inn.

Karl Ritter had been lucky enough to get possession of one of the first-floor bedrooms and was sleeping, for the first time in thirty-six hours, the sleep of total exhaustion. He lay on top of the bed in full uniform, having been too tired even to remove his boots.

At three o'clock in the afternoon he came awake to a hand on his shoulder and found Hoffer bending over him. Ritter sat up instantly. "Yes, what is it?"

"The colonel wants you, sir. They say it's urgent."

"More work for the undertakers." Ritter ran his hands over his fair hair and stood up. "So — did you manage to snatch a little sleep, Erich?"

Hoffer, a thin, wiry young man of twenty-seven, wore a black Panzer sidecap and one-piece overalls camouflaged to look like autumn foliage. He was an innkeeper's son from the Harz Mountains, had been with Ritter for four years, and was totally devoted to him.

"A couple of hours."

Ritter pulled on his service cap and adjusted the angle to his liking. "You're a terrible liar — you know that, don't you, Erich? There's oil on your hands. You've been at those engines again."

41

"Somebody has to," Hoffer said. "No more spares."

"Not even for the SS." Ritter smiled sardonically. "Things must really be in a mess. Look, see if you can rustle up a little coffee and something to eat. And a glass of schnapps wouldn't come amiss. I shouldn't imagine this will take long."

He went downstairs quickly and was directed by an orderly to a room at the back of the inn where he found Colonel Jager and two of the other company commanders examining a map which lay open on the table.

Jager turned and came forward, hand outstretched. "My dear Karl, I can't tell you how delighted I am. A great, great honor, not only for you, but for the entire battalion."

Ritter looked bewildered. "I'm afraid I don't understand."

"But of course. How could you?" Jager picked up a signal flimsy. "I naturally passed full details of this morning's astonishing exploit straight to Division. It appears they radioed Berlin. I've just received this. Special orders, Karl, for you

42

and *Sturmscharführer* Hoffer. As you can see, you're to leave at once."

Hoffer had indeed managed to obtain a little coffee — the real stuff, too — and some cold meat and black bread. He was just arranging it on the small night table in the bedroom when the door opened and Ritter entered.

Hoffer knew something was up at once, for he had never seen the major look so pale, a remarkable fact when one considered that he usually had no color at all.

Ritter tossed his service cap onto the bed and adjusted the Knight's Cross with Oak Leaves that hung at the neck of his black tunic. "Is that coffee I smell, Erich? Real coffee? Who did you have to kill? Schnapps, too?"

"Steinhager, Major." Hoffer picked up the stone bottle. "Best I could do."

"Well, then, you'd better find a couple of glasses, hadn't you? They tell me we've got something to celebrate."

"Celebrate, sir?"

"Yes, Erich. How would you like

43

a trip to Berlin?''

''Berlin, Major?'' Hoffer looked bewildered. ''But Berlin is surrounded. It was on the radio.''

''Still possible to fly to Templehof or Gatow if you're important enough, and we are, Erich. Come on, man, fill the glasses.''

And suddenly Ritter was angry, the face paler than ever, the hand shaking as he held out a glass to the sergeant major.

''Important, sir? Us?''

''My dear Erich, you've just been awarded the Knight's Cross — long overdue, I might add. And I am to receive the Swords, but now comes the best part. From the *Führer* himself, Erich. Isn't it rich? Germany on the brink of total disaster, and he can find a plane to fly us in specially — with *Luftwaffe* fighter escort, if you please.'' He laughed wildly. ''The poor sod must think we've just won the war for him or something.''

Three

On the morning of April 26, two JU-52s loaded with tank ammunition managed to land in the center of Berlin, in the vicinity of the Siegessäule, on a runway hastily constructed from a road in that area.

Karl Ritter and Erich Hoffer were the only two passengers, and they clambered out of the hatch into a scene of indescribable confusion, followed by their pilot, a young Luftwaffe captain named Rösch.

There was considerable panic among the soldiers who immediately started to unload the ammunition. Hardly surprising, for Russian heavy artillery was pounding the city hard, and every so often a shell whistled overhead to explode among the ruined buildings to the rear of them. The air was filled with sulfur smoke and dust, and a heavy pall blanketed everything.

Rösch, Ritter, and Hoffer ran to the shelter of a nearby wall and crouched. The young pilot offered them cigarettes. "Welcome to the City of the Dead," he said. "Dante's new Inferno."

"You've done this before?" Ritter asked.

"No, this is a new development. We can still get into Templehof and Gatow by air, but it's impossible to get from there to here on the ground. The Ivans have infiltrated all over the place." He smiled sardonically. "Still, we'll throw them back — given time, needless to say. After all, there's an army of veterans to call on. *Volkssturm* units, average age sixty. And a few thousand Hitler Youth at the other end, mostly around fourteen. Nothing much in between, except the *Führer,* whom God preserve, naturally. He should be worth a few divisions, wouldn't you say?"

An uncomfortable conversation which was cut short by the sudden arrival of a field car with an SS military police driver and sergeant. The sergeant's uniform was immaculate; the *Feldgendarmerie* gorget around his neck sparkled.

"*Sturmbannführer* Ritter?"

"That's right."

The sergeant's heels clicked together; his arm flashed briefly in a perfect party salute. "General Fegelein's compliments. We're here to escort you to the *Führer*'s headquarters."

"We'll be with you in a minute." The sergeant trotted away, and Ritter turned to Rösch. "A strange game we play."

"Here at the end of things, you mean?" Rösch smiled. "At least I'm getting out. My orders are to turn around as soon as possible and take wounded with me from the Charité Hospital, but you, my friend — you, I fear, will find it rather more difficult to leave Berlin."

"My grandmother was a good Catholic. She taught me to believe in miracles." Ritter held out his hand. "Good luck."

"And to you." Rösch ducked instinctively as another of the heavy 17.5 shells screamed overhead. "You'll need it."

The field car turned out of the Wilhelmplatz and into Vosstrasse, and the bulk of the Reich Chancellery rose before them. It was a sorry sight, battered and defaced by the bombardment, and every so often another shell at random screamed in to further the work of destruction. The streets were deserted, piled high with rubble, so that the driver had to pick his way with care.

"Good God," Hoffer said. "No one could function in such a shambles. It's impossible."

"Underneath," the police sergeant told him. "Thirty meters of concrete between those Russian shells and the *Führer*'s bunker. Nothing can reach him down there."

Nothing? Ritter thought. Can it truly be possible this clown realizes what he is saying, or is he as touched by madness as his masters?

The car ramp was wrecked, but there was still room to take the field car inside. As they stopped, an SS sentry moved out of the gloom. The sergeant waved him away and turned to Ritter. "If you will follow me, please. First we must report to Major General Mohnke.''

Ritter removed his leather military greatcoat and handed it to Hoffer. Underneath, the black panzer uniform was immaculate, the decorations gleamed. He adjusted his gloves. The sergeant was considerably impressed and drew himself stiffly to attention as if aware that this was a game they shared and eager to play his part.

"If the *Sturmbannführer* is ready?"

Ritter nodded, the sergeant moved off briskly, and they followed him down through a dark passage with concrete walls that sweated moisture in the dim light. Soldiers crouched in every available inch of space, many of them sleeping — mainly SS, from the look of things. Some glanced up with weary, lackluster eyes that showed no surprise, even at Ritter's bandbox appearance.

When they talked, their voices were low and subdued, and the main sound seemed to be the monotonous hum of the dynamos and the whirring of the electric fans in the ventilation system. Occasionally there was the faintest of tremors as the earth shook high above them, and the air was musty and unpleasant, tainted with sulfur.

Major General Mohnke's office was as uninviting as everything else Ritter had seen on his way down through the labyrinth of passageways. Small and Spartan, with the usual concrete walls, too small even for the desk and chair and half a dozen officers it contained when they arrived. Mohnke was an SS *Brigadeführer* who was now commander of the Adolf Hitler Volunteer Corps, a force of two thousand supposedly handpicked men who were to form the final ring of defense around the Chancellery.

He paused in full flight as the immaculate Ritter entered the room. Everyone turned; the sergeant saluted and placed Ritter's orders on the desk. Mohnke looked at them briefly, his eyes lit up, and he leaned across the table, hand outstretched.

"My dear Ritter, what a pleasure to meet you." He reached for the telephone and said to the others, *"Sturmbannführer* Ritter, gentlemen, hero of that incredible exploit near Innsbruck that I was telling you about."

Most of them made appropriate noises, one or two shook hands, others reached out to touch him as if for good luck. It was a slightly unnerving experience, and he was glad when Mohnke replaced the receiver and said, "General Fegelein tells me the *Führer* wishes to see you without delay." His arm swung up dramatically in a full party salute. "Your comrades of the SS are proud of you, *Sturmbannführer.* Your victory is ours."

"Am I mad, or are they, Erich?" Ritter whispered as they followed the sergeant ever deeper into the bunker.

"For God's sake, Major." Hoffer put a hand briefly on his arm. "If someone overheards that kind of remark . . ."

"All right, I'll be good," Ritter said soothingly. "Lead on, Erich. I can't wait to see what happens in the next act."

They descended now to the lower levels of the *Führerbunker* itself. A section which, although Ritter did not know it then, housed most of the *Führer*'s personal staff, as well as Goebbels and his family, Bormann, and Dr. Ludwig Stumpfegger, the *Führer*'s personal physician. General Fegelein had a room adjacent to Bormann's.

It was similar to Mohnke's — small, with damp concrete walls, and furnished with a desk, a couple of chairs, and a filing cabinet. The desk was covered with military maps which the general was studying closely when the sergeant opened the door and stood to one side.

Fegelein looked up, his face serious, but when he saw Ritter he laughed excitedly and rushed around the desk to greet him. "My dear Ritter, what an honor — for all of us. The *Führer* can hardly wait, I assure you."

Such enthusiasm was a little too much, considering that Ritter had never clapped eyes on the man before. A onetime commander of SS cavalry — he knew that — awarded the Knight's Cross, so he was no coward, but the handshake lacked firmness and there was sweat on the brow, particularly along the thinning hairline. This was a badly frightened man, a breed with which Ritter had become only too familiar over the past few months.

"An exaggeration, I'm sure, General."

"And you, too, *Sturmscharführer.*" Fegelein did not take Hoffer's hand, but nodded briefly. "A magnificent performance."

"Indeed," Ritter said dryly. "His was, after all, the finger on the trigger."

"Of course, my dear Ritter, we all acknowledge that fact. On the other hand . . ."

Before he could take the conversation any further, the door opened and a broad, rather squat man entered the room. He wore a nondescript uniform. His only decoration was the Order of Blood, a much-coveted Nazi medal specially struck for those who had served prison sentences for political crimes under the old Weimar Republic. He carried a sheaf of papers in one hand.

"Ah, Martin," Fegelein said. "Was it important? I have the *Führer's* orders to escort this gentleman to him the instant he arrives. *Sturmbannführer* Ritter, hero of Wednesday's incredible exploit on the Innsbruck road. You of course know *Reichsleiter* Bormann, Major.''

But Ritter did not, because — as he was for most Germans — Martin Bormann was only a name to him, a face that was occasionally to be found in a group photo of party dignitaries, with nothing memorable about it. Not Goebbels or a Himmler — once seen, never forgotten.

And yet here he was, the most powerful man in Germany, particularly now that Himmler had run off. *Reichsleiter* Martin Bormann, head of the Nazi Party Chancellery and secretary to the *Führer*.

''A great pleasure, Major.'' His handshake was firm, with a hint of even greater strength there if necessary.

He had a harsh, yet strangely soft, voice, a broad, brutal face with Slavic cheekbones, a prominent nose. The impression was of a big man, although Ritter found he had to look down at him.

''Reichsleiter.''

''And this is your gunner, Hoffer.'' Bormann turned to the sergeant major.

"Quite a marksman, but then I sometimes think you Harz Mountain men cut your teeth on a shotgun barrel."

It was the first sign from anyone that Hoffer was more than a cipher — an acknowledgment of his existence as a human being — and could not fail to impress Ritter, however reluctantly.

Bormann opened the door and turned to Fegelein. "My business can wait. I'll see you downstairs, anyway. I, too, have business with the *Führer.*"

He went out, and Fegelein turned to the two men — Ritter magnificent in the black uniform, Hoffer somehow complementing the show with his one-piece camouflage suit, sleeves rolled up to the elbow. It couldn't be better. Just the sort of fillip the *Führer* needed.

Bormann's sleeping quarters were in the Chancellery bunker, but his office, close to Fegelein's, was strategically situated so that he was able to keep the closest of contact with Hitler. One door opened into the telephone exchange and general communications center, the other to

Goebbels's personal office. Nothing, therefore, could go into the *Führer* or out again without the *Reichleiter*'s knowledge, which was exactly as he had arranged the situation.

When he entered his office directly after leaving Fegelein, he found SS Colonel Willi Rattenhuber, whose services he had utilized as an additional aide to Zander since March 30, leaning over a map on the desk.

"Any further word on Himmler?" Bormann asked.

"Not as yet, *Reichsleiter.*"

"The bastard is up to something — you may depend on it — and so is Fegelein. Watch him, Willi — watch him closely."

"Yes, *Reichsleiter.*"

"And there's something else I want you to do, Willi. There's a *Sturmbannführer* named Ritter, of the 502nd SS Heavy Tank Battalion, on his way down now to receive the Swords from the *Führer.* When you get a moment, I want his records — everything you can find on him."

"*Reichsleiter.*"

"That's what I like about you, Willi,

you never ask questions." Bormann clapped him on the arm. "And now we'll go down to the garden bunker, and I'll show him to you. I think you'll approve. In fact, I have a happy feeling that he may serve my purpose very well indeed."

In the garden bunker was the *Führer's* study, a bedroom, two living rooms, and a bathroom. Close by was the map room used for all high-level conferences. The hall outside served as an anteroom, and it was there that Ritter and Hoffer waited.

Bormann paused at the bottom of the steps and held Rattenhuber back in the shadows. "He looks good, Willi, don't you agree? Quite magnificent in that pretty uniform, with the medals gleaming, the pale face, the blond hair. Uncle Heini would have been proud of him — all that's fairest in the Aryan race. Not like us at all, Willi. He will undoubtedly prove a shot in the arm for the *Führer*. And notice the slight, sardonic smile on his mouth. I tell you there's hope for this boy, Willi. A young man of parts."

Rattenhuber said hastily, "The *Führer*

comes now, *Reichsleiter."*

Ritter, standing at the end of a line of half a dozen young boys in the uniform of the Hitler Youth, felt curiously detached. It was rather like one of those dreams in which everything has an appearance of reality, yet events are past belief. The children on his right hand, for instance. Twelve or thirteen, here to be decorated for bravery. The boy next to him had a bandage around his forehead, under the heavy man's helmet. Blood seeped through steadily, and occasionally the child shifted his feet as if to prevent himself from falling.

"Shoulders back," Ritter said softly. "Not long now." And then the door opened. Hitler moved out, flanked by Fegelein, Jodl, Keitel, and Krebs, the new chief of the General Staff.

Ritter had seen the *Führer* on several occasions in his life. Speaking at Nuremberg rallies, Paris in 1940, on a visit to the Eastern Front in 1942. His recollection of Hitler had been of an inspired leader of men, a man of magical rhetoric whose spell could not fail to touch anyone within hearing.

But the man who shuffled into the anteroom now might have been a totally different person. This was a sick old man, shoulders hunched under the uniform jacket that seemed a size too large, pale, hollow-cheeked, no sparkle in the lackluster eyes; and when he turned to take the first Iron Cross Second Class, from the box Jodl held, his hand trembled.

He worked his way along the line, muttering a word or two of some sort of encouragement here and there, patting an occasional cheek, and then reached Ritter and Hoffer.

Fegelein said, *"Sturmbannführer* Karl Ritter and *Sturmscharführer* Erich Hoffer of the Five Hundred and Second SS Heavy Tank Battalion."* He started to read the citation, "Shortly after dawn on the morning of Wednesday, April twenty-fifth —" but the *Führer* cut him off with a chopping motion of one hand.

There was fire in the dark eyes, a sudden energy as he snapped his fingers impatiently for Jodl to pass the decoration. Ritter stared impassively ahead, aware of the hands touching him lightly, and then, for the briefest of moments, they tightened on his arm.

He looked directly into the eyes, aware of the power, the burning intensity, there again if only for a moment, the hoarse voice saying, "Your *Führer* thanks you, on behalf of the German people."

Hitler turned. "Are you aware of this officer's achievement, gentlemen? Assisted by only two other tanks, he wiped out an entire British column of the Seventh Armored Division. Thirty armored vehicles left blazing. Can you hear that and still tell me that we cannot win this war? If one man can do so much, what could fifty like him accomplish?"

They all shifted uncomfortably. Krebs said, "But of course, my *Führer*. Under your inspired leadership, anything is possible."

"Goebbels must have written that line for him," Bormann whispered to Rattenhuber. "You know, Willi, I'm enjoying this — and look at our proud young *Sturmbannführer*. He looks like

Death himself with that pale face and black uniform, come to remind us all of what waits outside these walls. Have you ever read 'Masque of the Red Death,' by the American writer Poe?"

"No, I can't say that I have, *Reichsleiter*."

"You should, Willi. An interesting parable of the impossibility of locking out reality for long."

An orderly clattered down the steps, brushed past Bormann and Rattenhuber, and hesitated on seeing what was taking place. Krebs, who obviously recognized the man, moved to one side and snapped his fingers. The orderly passed him a signal flimsy, which Krebs quickly scanned.

Hitler moved forward eagerly. "Is it news of Wenck?" he demanded.

He was still convinced that the Twelfth Army, under General Wenck, was going to break through to the relief of Berlin at any moment.

Krebs hesitated, and the *Führer* said, "Read it, man! Read it!"

Krebs swallowed hard, then said, "No

possibility of Wenck and the Ninth Army joining. Await further instruction."

The *Führer* exploded with rage. "The same story as Sunday. I gave the Eleventh Panzer Army, and all available personnel in his area, to SS General Steiner, with orders to attack. And what happened?"

The fact that the army in question had existed on paper only, a figment of someone's imagination, was not the point, for no one would have had the courage to tell him.

"So even my SS let me down — betray me in my hour of need. Well, it won't do, gentlemen." He was almost hysterical now. "I have a way of dealing with traitors. Remember the July plot? Remember the films I ordered you to watch of the executions?"

He turned, stumbled back into the map room, followed by Jodl, Keitel, and Krebs. The door closed. Fegelein, moving as a man in a dream, signaled to one of the SS orderlies, who took the children away.

There was silence, then Ritter said, "What now, General?"

Fegelein started. "What did you say?"

"What do we do now?"

"Oh, go to the canteen. Food will be provided. Have a drink. Relax." He forced a smile and clapped Ritter on the shoulder. "Take it easy for a while, Major. I'll send for you soon. Fresh fields to conquer, I promise."

He nodded to an orderly, who led the way. Ritter and Hoffer followed him up the steps. Bormann and Rattenhuber were no longer there.

At the top, Ritter said softly, "What do you think of that, then, Erich? Little children and old men led by a raving madman. So now we start paying the bill, I think — all of us."

When he reached his office, Fegelein closed the door, went behind his desk, and sat down. He opened a cupboard, took out a bottle of brandy, removed the cork, and swallowed deeply. He had been a frightened man for some time, but this latest display had finished him off.

He was exactly the same as dozens of other men who had risen to power in the

Nazi party. A man of no background and little education. A onetime groom and jockey who had risen through the ranks of the SS and, after being appointed Himmler's aide at *Führer* headquarters, had consolidated his position by marrying Eva Braun's sister Gretl.

But now even Himmler had cleared off, had refused every attempt aimed at returning him to the death trap which Berlin had become. It occurred to Fegelein that perhaps the time had come for some definite action on his own part. He took another quick pull on the brandy bottle, got up, took down his cap from behind the door, and went out.

It was seven o'clock that evening, and Ritter and Hoffer were sitting together in the canteen, talking softly, a bottle of Moselle between them, when a sudden hubbub broke out. There were cries outside in the corridor, laughter, and then the door burst open and two young officers ran in.

Ritter grabbed at one of them as he went by, "Hey, what's all the excitement?"

"*Luftwaffe* General Ritter von Greim has just arrived from Munich with the air ace, Hannah Reitsch. They landed at Gatow and came on in a Fieseler Storch."

"The general himself flew," the other young officer said. "When he was hit, Reitsch took over the controls and landed the aircraft in the street near the *Brandenburger Tor*. What a woman!"

They moved away. Another voice said, "A day for heroes, it would seem."

Ritter looked up and found Bormann standing there. *"Reichsleiter."* He started to rise.

Bormann pushed him down. "Yes, a remarkable business. What they omitted to tell you was that they were escorted by fifty fighter planes from Munich. Apparently over forty were shot down. On the other hand, it was essential General von Greim get here. You see, the *Führer* intends to promote him to commander-in-chief of the *Luftwaffe,* with the rank of *Feldmarschall,* Göring having finally proved a broken reed. Naturally he wished to tell General von Greim of this himself. Signal flimsies are so impersonal, don't you think?''

He moved away. Hoffer said in a kind of awe, ''Over forty planes — forty, and for what?''

''To tell him in person what he could have told him over the telephone,'' Ritter said. ''A remarkable man, our *Führer*, Erich.''

''For God's sake, Major.'' Hoffer put out a hand, for the first time real anger showing through. ''Keep talking like that and they might take you out and hang you. Me, too. Is that what you want?''

When Bormann went into his office, Rattenhuber was waiting for him.

''Did you find General Fegelein?'' the *Reichsleiter* inquired.

''He left the bunker five hours ago.'' Rattenhuber checked his notes. ''According to my information he is at present at his home in Charlottenburg — wearing civilian clothes, I might add.''

Bormann nodded calmly. ''How very interesting.''

''Do we inform the *Führer?*''

''I don't think so, Willi. Give a man

66

enough rope — you know the old saying. I'll ask where Fegelein is in the *Führer's* hearing later on tonight. Allow him to make this very unpleasant discovery for himself. Now, Willi, we have something far more important to discuss. The question of the prominent prisoners in our hands. You have the files I asked for?"

"Certainly, *Reichsleiter.*" Rattenhuber placed several manila folders on the desk. "There is a problem here. The *Führer* has very pronounced ideas on what should happen to them. It seems that he was visited by *Obergruppenführer* Berger, head of the Prisoner-of-War Administration. Berger tried to discuss the fate of several important British, French, and American prisoners, as well as of Schuschnigg, the Austrian chancellor, and Halder and Schacht. It seems the *Führer* told him to shoot them all."

"Conspicuous consumption, I would have thought, Willi. In other words, a great waste." Bormann tapped the files. "But it's these ladies and gentlemen who interest me. The prisoners at Arlberg."

"I'm afraid several have already been

moved since my visit, on your instructions, two months ago. Orders of the *Reichsführer,*" Rattenhuber told him.

"Yes, for once Uncle Heini moved a little faster than I had expected," Bormann said dryly. "What are we left with?"

"Just five. Three men, two women."

"Good," Bormann said. "A nice round number. We'll start with the ladies first, shall we? Refresh my memory."

"Madame Claire de Beauville, *Reichsleiter*. Age, thirty. Nationality, French. Her father made a great deal of money in canned foods. She married Etienne de Beauville. A fine old family. They were thought to be typical socialites flirting with their new masters. In fact, her husband was working with French Resistance units in Paris. He was picked up in June last year on information received and taken to *Sicherheitsdienst* headquarters on the Avénue Foch in Paris. He was shot trying to escape."

"The French," Bormann said. "So romantic."

"The wife was thought to be involved.

There was a radio at the house. She insisted she knew nothing about it, but Security was convinced she could well have been working as a 'pianist.' "

He looked up, bewildered, and Bormann smiled. "Typical English schoolboy humor. This is apparently the British Special Operations Executive term for a radio operator."

"Oh, I see." Rattenhuber returned to the file. "Through marriage, she is related to most of the great French families."

"Which is why she is at Arlberg. So — who's next?"

"Madame Claudine Chevalier."

"The concert pianist?"

"That's right, *Reichsleiter.*"

"She must be seventy, at least."

"Seventy-five."

"A national institution. In 1940 she made a trip to Berlin to give a concert at the *Führer*'s special request. It made her very unpopular in Paris at the time."

"A very clever front to mask her real activities, *Reichsleiter.* She was one of a group of influential people who organized an escape line which succeeded in spiriting several well-known Jews from Paris to Vichy.''

''So — an astute old lady with nerve and courage. Does that dispose of the French?''

''No, *Reichsleiter*. There is Paul Gaillard to consider.''

''Ah, the onetime cabinet minister.''

''That is so, *Reichsleiter*. Aged sixty. At one time a physician and surgeon. He has, of course, an international reputation as an author. Dabbled in politics a little before the war. Minister for internal affairs in the Vichy government, who turned out to be signing releases of known political offenders. He was also suspected of being in touch with de Gaulle. Member of the French Academy.''

''Anything else?''

''Something of a romantic, according to the Security report. Joined the French Army as a private in 1915, as some sort of public gesture against the government of the day. It seems he thought they were making a botch of the war. Flirted with communism in the twenties, but a visit to Russia in 1927 cured him of that disease.''

''What about his weaknesses?''

"Weaknesses, *Reichsleiter?*"

"Come now, Willi, we all have them. Some men like women, others play cards all night — or drink, perhaps. What about Gaillard?"

"None, *Reichsleiter,* and the Security report is really most thorough. There is one extraordinary thing about him, however."

"What's that?"

"He's had a great love of skiing all his life. In 1924, when they held the first Winter Olympics at Chamonix, he took a gold medal. A remarkable achievement. You see, he was, at the time, thirty-nine years of age, *Reichsleiter.*"

"Interesting," Bormann said softly. "Now that really does say something about his character. What about the Englishman?"

"I'm not too certain that's an accurate description, *Reichsleiter.* Justin Fitzgerald Birr, fifteenth earl of Dundrum, an Irish title, and Ireland is the place of his birth. He is also tenth Baron Felversham. The title is, of course, English, and an estate goes with it in Yorkshire."

"The English and the Irish really can't

make up their minds about each other, can they, Willi? As soon as there's a war, thousands of Irishmen seem to join the British Army with alacrity. Very confusing."

"Exactly, *Reichsleiter*. Lord Dundrum, which is how people address him, had an uncle who was a major of infantry in the First World War. An excellent record — decorated and so on — then, in 1919, he went home, joined the IRA, and became commander of a flying column during their fight for independence. It apparently caused a considerable scandal."

"And the earl? What of his war record?"

"Aged thirty. DSO and Military Cross. At the beginning of the war he was a lieutenant in the Irish Guards. Two years later, a lieutenant colonel in the Special Air Service. In its brief existence his unit destroyed one hundred and thirteen aircraft on the ground behind Rommel's lines. He was captured in Sicily. Made five attempts to escape, including two from Colditz. It was then they decided that his special circumstances merited his transfer to Arlberg as a *prominenti*."

"Which explains the last and most important point concerning the good earl of Dundrum."

"Exactly, *Reichsleiter*. It would seem the gentleman is, through his mother, second cousin to King George."

"Which certainly makes him prominent, Willi. Very prominent, indeed. And now — the best saved till last. What about our American friend?"

"Brigadier General Hamilton Canning, aged forty-five."

"The same as me," Bormann said.

"Almost exactly. You, *Reichsleiter,* I believe, were born on the seventeenth of June. General Canning on the twenty-seventh of July. He would seem typical of a certain kind of American — a man in a perpetual hurry to get somewhere."

"I know his record," Bormann said. "But go through it again for me."

"Very well, *Reichsleiter*. In 1917 he joined the French Foreign Legion as a private. Transferred to the American Army the following year, with the rank of second lieutenant. Between the wars he didn't fit in too well. A troublemaker who was much disliked at the Pentagon."

"In other words, he was too clever for them, read too many books, spoke too many languages," Bormann said. "Just like the High Command we know and love, Willi. But carry on."

"He was a military attaché in Berlin for three years — 1934 to 1937. Apparently became very friendly with Rommel."

"That damn traitor." Bormann's usually equable poise deserted him. "He would."

"He saw action on a limited scale in Shanghai against the Japanese in 1939, but he was still only a major by 1940. He was then commanding a small force in the Philippines. Fought a brilliant defensive action against the Japanese in Mindanao. He was given up for dead, but turned up in a Moro junk at Darwin in Australia. The magazines made something of a hero of him, so they had to promote him then. He spent almost a year in the hospital. Then they sent him to England. Some sort of headquarters job, but he managed to get into Combined Operations."

"And then?"

"Dropped into the Dordogne just after D-Day with British SAS units and Rangers to work with French partisans. Surrounded on a plateau in the Auvergne Mountains by SS paratroopers in July last year. Jumped from a train taking him to Germany, and broke a leg. Tried to escape from the hospital. They tried him at Colditz for awhile, but that didn't work."

"And then Arlberg."

"It was decided, I believe, by the *Reichsführer* himself, that he was an obvious candidate to be a *prominenti.*"

"And who do we have in charge of things at Schloss Arlberg, Willi?"

"*Oberstleutnant* Max Hesser, of the Panzer Grenadiers. Gained his Knight's Cross at Leningrad, where he lost his left arm. A professional soldier of the old school."

"I know, Willi, don't tell me. Held together by guts and piano wire. And who does he have with him now?"

"Only twenty men, *Reichsleiter.* Anyone capable of frontline action has been taken from him in the past few weeks.

Oberleutnant Schenck, now his second-in-command, is fifty-five, a reservist. *Sturmscharführer* Schneider is a good man. Iron Cross Second and First Class, but he has a silver plate in his head. The rest are reservists, mostly in their fifties or cripples.''

He closed the last file. Bormann leaned back in his chair, fingertips together. It was quiet now, except for the faintest rumblings far above them as the Russian artillery continued to pound Berlin.

''Listen to that,'' Bormann said. ''Closer by the hour. Do you ever wonder what comes after?''

''*Reichsleiter?*'' Rattenhuber looked faintly alarmed.

''One has plans, of course, but sometimes things go wrong, Willi. Some unexpected snag that turns the whole thing on its head. In such an eventuality one needs what I believe the Americans term an 'ace-in-the-hole.' ''

''The *prominenti, Reichsleiter?* But are they important enough?''

''Who knows, Willi? Excellent bargaining counters in an emergency, no

76

more than that. Madame Chevalier and Gaillard are almost national institutions, and Madame de Beauville's connections embrace some of the most influential families in France. The English love a lord at the best of times — doubly so when he's related to the king himself."

"And Canning?"

"The Americans are notoriously sentimental about their heroes."

He sat staring into space for a moment.

"So, what do we do with them?" Rattenhuber said. "What does the *Reichsleiter* have in mind?"

"Oh, I'll think of something, Willi," Bormann smiled. "I think you may depend on it."

Four

And at Schloss Arlberg, on the Inn River, 450 miles south of Berlin and 55 miles northwest of Innsbruck, Lieutenant Colonel Justin Birr, fifteenth earl of Dundrum, leaned out the narrow window at the top of the north tower and peered down into the darkness of the garden, 80 feet below.

He could feel the plaited rope stir beneath his hands, and behind him in the gloom Paul Gaillard said, "Is he there?"

"No, not yet." A moment later the rope slackened, there was a sudden flash of light below, then darkness again. "That's it," Birr said. "Now me, if I can get through this damned window. Hamilton certainly can pick them."

He stood on a stool, turned to support himself on Gaillard's shoulders, and eased his legs into space. He stayed there for a moment, hands on the rope. "Sure you won't change your mind, Paul?"

"My dear Justin, I wouldn't get halfway down before my arms gave out."

"All right," Birr said. "You know what to do. When I get down — or perhaps I should say *if* I do — we'll flash you a signal. You haul the rope up, stick it in that cubbyhole under the floorboards, then get the hell out of there."

"You may rely on me."

"I know. Give my regards to the ladies."

"Bon chance, my friend."

Birr let himself slide and was suddenly alone in the darkness, swaying slightly in the wind, his hands slipping from knot to knot. Homemade rope and eighty feet to the garden. I must be mad, he thought.

It was raining slightly, not a single star to be seen anywhere, and already his arms were beginning to ache. He let himself slide faster, his feet banging against the wall, scratching his knuckles, at one point twirling around madly in circles. Quite suddenly, the rope parted.

My God, that's it! he thought, clamping his jaws together in the moment of death to stop himself from crying out, then hit the ground after falling no more than ten feet, and rolled over in the wet grass, winded.

There was a hand at his elbow, helping him to his feet. "You all right?" Canning said.

"I think so." Birr flexed his arms. "A damn close thing, Hamilton, but then it usually is when you're around."

"We aim to please." Canning shined his flashlight upward briefly. "Okay, let's get moving. The entrance to the sewer I told you about is in the lily pond on the lower terrace."

They moved down through the darkness cautiously, negotiated a flight of steps, and skirted the fountain at the bottom. The ornamental lily pond was on the other side of a short stretch of lawn. There was a wall at the rear of it, water gushing from the mouth of a bronze lion's head, rattling into the pool below. Birr had seen it often enough during exercise. "Okay, here we go."

Canning sat down and lowered himself into the water, knee-deep. He waded forward. Birr followed him and found the American crouched beside the lion's head in the darkness.

"You can feel the grille here, half under the water," Canning whispered. "If we can get that off, we're straight into the main drainage system. One tunnel after the other, all the way down to the river."

"And if not?" Birr inquired.

"Short rations again and a stone cell, but that, as they say, is problematical. Right now we've got about ten minutes before Schneider and that damned Alsatian of his come by on garden patrol."

He produced a short length of steel bar from his pocket, inserted it on one side of the bronze grille, and levered. There was an audible crack, the metal, corroded by the years, snapping instantly. He pulled hard, and the entire grille came away in his hands.

"You see how it is, Justin. All you have to do is live right. After you."

Birr crouched down on his hands and

knees in the water, switching on his flashlight, and crawled through into a narrow brick tunnel. Canning moved in behind him, pulling the grille back into place.

"Don't you think you're getting a little old for the Boy Scouts, Hamilton?" Birr whispered over his shoulder.

"Shut up and get moving," Canning told him. "If we can reach the river and find a boat by midnight, we'll have six or seven hours to play with before they find out we're gone."

Birr moved on, crawling on his hands and knees through a couple of feet of water, the flashlight in his teeth. He emerged, after a few yards, into a tunnel that was a good five feet in diameter, so that he could actually walk if he crouched a little.

The water was only about a foot deep here, for the tunnel sloped downward steeply, and the smell was not unpleasant — like old leaves and autumn on the river in a punt.

"Keep going," Canning said. "From what I found out from that gardener, we emerge into the main sewer pretty quickly. From there, it's a straight run down to the Inn.''

"I can smell it already," Birr told him.

A few minutes later the tunnel did indeed empty into the main sewer in a miniature waterfall. Birr pointed his flashlight at the brown, foam-flecked waters which rushed by several feet below.

"My God, just smell it, Hamilton. This really is beyond a joke."

"Oh, get in there, for Christ's sake." Canning gave him a shove, and Birr dropped down, losing his balance, and disappeared beneath the surface. He was on his feet in an instant and stood there cursing, still clutching his flashlight. "It's liquid shit, Hamilton. Liquid shit."

"You can have a wash when we get to the river," Canning said as he lowered himself down to join him. "Now let's make time."

He started down the tunnel, flashlight extended before him, and Birr followed for perhaps sixty or seventy yards, and then the tunnel petered out in a blank wall.

"That's it, then," Birr said. "And a bloody good job, too, as far as I'm concerned. We'll have to go back."

"Not on your sweet life. The water's got to go somewhere." Canning slipped his flashlight into his pocket, took a deep breath, and crouched. He surfaced at once. "As I thought. The tunnel continues on a lower level. I'm going through."

Birr said, "And what if it's twenty or thirty yards long, you idiot — or longer? You'll not have time to turn and come back. You'll drown."

"So, I'll take that chance, Justin." Canning was tying one end of the rope about his waist now. "I want out — you understand? I've no intention of sitting on my ass up there in the castle waiting for the *Reichsführer's* hired assassins to come and finish me off." He held out the other end of the rope. "Fasten that around your waist if you want to come, too. If I get through, I'll give it a pull."

"And if not?"

"Winter roses on my grave. Scarlet ones like those Claire cultivated in the conservatory." He grinned once, took a deep breath, and disappeared beneath the surface of the water.

Justin Birr waited. The flashlight gave only minimal illumination, barely sufficient to pick out the slime on the ancient stone walls or the occasional rat that swam past in the dark water. The stench was frightful — really most unpleasant — and by now the cold had cut through to his very bones, or so it seemed.

He was aware of a sudden tug and hesitated, wondering for a moment whether it was simply his imagination. There was another tug, more insistent this time. "All right, damn you," he said and extinguished the flashlight and put it into his breast pocket. His hands felt under the water for the edge of the arched roof. He took a deep breath and went down.

His feet banged against the stonework, but he kicked desperately, aware of the rope tugging at his waist, and then, just when he was convinced he couldn't keep going any longer, he saw a faint light ahead and surfaced, gasping for breath.

Canning, crouching out of the water at

the side of a larger tunnel, reached down to pull him up. "Easy does it."

"Really, Hamilton, this particular small jaunt of yours is getting out of hand. I smell like a lavatory gone wrong, and I'm frozen into the bargain."

Canning ignored him. "Listen — I can hear the river. Can't be far now."

He set off at a fast pace, slipping and sliding on the slope of the tunnel, and Birr got to his feet wearily and went after him. And then Canning was laughing excitedly and running, splashing knee-deep in the brown water.

"I can see it. We're there."

"Indeed you are, gentlemen. Indeed you are."

A brilliant spot was turned on, flooding the tunnel with light. Birr hesitated, then went forward and dropped on his hands and knees beside Canning, who crouched at the large circular grille which blocked the end of the tunnel. Schneider knelt on one knee on the other side, several armed men behind him.

"We've been waiting for you, gentlemen. Magda was growing impatient."

His Alsatian bitch whined eagerly, pushing her muzzle between the bars. Canning tugged at her ears. "You wouldn't hurt me, you silly old bitch, would you?"

"All right, Sergeant Major," Justin Birr said. "We'll come quietly."

Oberstleutnant Max Hesser leaned back in his chair, got out his cigarette case, and opened it one-handed with a skill born of long practice. *Oberleutnant* Schenck waited at the other side of the desk. He was dressed for duty, a pistol at his belt.

"Extraordinary," the colonel said. "What on earth will Canning be up to next?"

"God knows, *Herr Oberst.*"

"And the note you received telling you that the escape attempt was to take place. You say it was unsigned?"

"As you may see for yourself, *Herr Oberst.*"

He passed a slip of paper across, and Hesser examined it. " 'Canning and Birr escaping through the main sewer tonight.' Crudely done in pencil and block capitals

but perfect German.'' He sighed. ''So —
there is a traitor in the camp. One of their
friends betrays them.''

''Not necessarily, *Herr Oberst,* if I
might make a suggestion.''

''But of course, man. Carry on.''

''The general's knowledge of the sewer
and drainage system must have been
gained from somewhere. One of the
soldiers or a servant, perhaps.''

''Ah, I see your point,'' Hesser said.
''Someone who took a bribe, then slipped
you that anonymous note to make sure the
escape attempt would prove abortive.'' He
shook his head. ''I don't like it, Schenck.
It leaves a bad taste.'' He sighed.
''Anyway, I suppose I'd better have them
in.''

Schenck withdrew, and Hesser stood up
and moved to the liquor cabinet. He was a
handsome man in spite of the deep scar
which bisected his forehead, curving into
the right eye which was now glass, and the
uniform was trim and well-fitting, the
empty left sleeve tucked into the belt.

He was pouring himself a brandy when
the door opened behind him. He turned as

Schenck ushered Canning and Birr into the room, Schneider behind them.

"Good God in heaven," Hesser said.

They presented a sorry sight indeed — barefoot, covered with filth, water dripping onto the carpet. Hesser hurriedly filled two more glasses.

"From the looks of you, I'd say you needed it."

Canning and Birr slopped forward. "Very civil of you," Birr said.

Canning grinned and raised his glass. *"Prosit."*

"And now to business." Hesser went back to his desk and sat down. "This nonsense, gentlemen. It must stop."

"It is the duty of an officer to make every attempt to achieve his liberty and rejoin his unit," Canning said. "You know that."

"Yes. Under other circumstances I would agree with you, but not now. Not on April 26, 1945. Gentlemen, after five and a half years, the war draws to a close. It's almost over — any day now. All we have to do is wait."

"What for — an SS execution squad?"

Canning said. "We know what the *Führer* told Berger when he asked about the *prominenti*. He said, Shoot them. Shoot all of them. Last I heard, Himmler agreed with him."

"You are in my charge, gentlemen. I have tried to make this plain many times before."

"Great," Canning said. "And what happens if they drive up to the front door with a directive from the *Führer*. Will you pull up the drawbridge, or order us to be shot? You took the soldier's oath, didn't you, just like everyone else in the German armed forces?"

Hesser stared up at him, very white, the great scar glowing angrily. Birr said gently, "He does have a point, Colonel."

Hesser said, "I could put you gentlemen on short rations and confine you to your cells, but I won't. Under the circumstances and considering the point in time at which we all stand, I shall have you returned to the prisoners' section and your friends. I hope you will respond in kind to this gesture."

Schenck placed a hand on Canning's

arm, and the general pulled himself free. "For God's sake, Max." He leaned across the desk, voice urgent. "There's only one way out for you. Send Schenck here in search of an Allied unit while there's still time. Someone you can surrender to legally, saving your own honor and our skins."

Hesser stared at him for a long moment, then said, "Have the general and Lord Dundrum returned to their quarters now, Schenck."

"*Herr Oberst.*" Schenck clicked his heels and turned to the two men. "General?"

"Oh, go to hell," Canning told him, turned, and walked out.

Birr paused. For a moment it was as if he intended to say something. Instead, he shrugged and followed. Schenck and Schneider went after them. Hesser went back to the cabinet and poured himself another drink. As he was replacing the bottle, there was a knock on the door and Schenck came back in.

"Would you care for one?" Hesser asked.

"No, thank you, *Herr Oberst*. My stomach takes kindly only to beer these days."

He waited patiently. Hesser walked across to the fire. "You think he's right, don't you?" Schenck hesitated, and Hesser said, "Come on, man. Speak your mind."

"Very well, *Herr Oberst*. Yes, I must say I do. Let's get it over and done with, that's my attitude. If we don't, then I greatly fear that something terrible may take place here, the results of which may drag us all down."

"You know something?" Hesser kicked a log that had rolled forward back into place in a shower of sparks. "I'm inclined to agree with you."

Canning and Birr — followed by Schneider, two soldiers with Schmeissers, and Magda — crossed the main hall and mounted the staircase, so wide that a company of soldiers could have marched up, line abreast.

"I was once shown around the MGM studios by Clark Gable," Birr said. "This place often reminds me of Stage Six. Did I ever tell you that?"

"Frequently," Canning told him.

They crossed the smaller, upper landing and paused at an iron-bound oak door, outside of which stood an armed sentry. Schneider produced a key about a foot long, inserted it in the massive lock, and turned. He pushed open the door and stood back.

"Gentlemen." As they moved in, he added, "Oh, by the way, the upper section of the north tower is out of bounds, and in the future there will be two guards in the water garden at all times."

"That's really very considerate of you," Birr said. "Don't you agree, General?"

"You can play that vaudeville act all night, but I've had it," Canning said and started up the dark stone stairway.

Birr followed him, and the door clanged shut behind them. They were now in the north tower, the central keep of the castle, that portion to which, in the old days, the defenders had always retreated in the last resort. It was completely isolated from the rest of Schloss Arlberg, the lowest window fifty feet from the ground and heavily barred. It made a relatively secure prisoners' section under most circumstances and meant that Hesser was able to allow the inmates a certain freedom, at least within the confines of the walls.

Madame Chevalier was playing the piano — they could hear her clearly — a Bach prelude, crisp and ice-cold, all technique, no heart. The kind of thing she liked to play to combat the arthritis in her fingers. Canning opened the door of the dining hall.

It was a magnificent room, with a high, arched ceiling festooned with battle standards from other times, and a magnificent selection of fifteenth- and sixteenth-century armor on the walls. The fireplace was of baronial proportions. Gaillard and Claire de Beauville sat beside the log fire, smoking and talking quietly. Madame Chevalier was at the Bechstein.

At the sight of Canning and Birr, she stopped playing, gave a howl of laughter, and started the "Dead March from Saul."

"Very, very humorous," Canning told her. "I'm splitting my sides laughing."

Claire and Paul Gaillard stood up. "But what happened?" Gaillard said. "The first I knew that there was anything amiss was when men arrived to lock the upper tower door. I'd just come down after securing the rope."

"They were waiting for us, that's what happened," Birr said. "Dear old Schneider, and Magda panting eagerly over Hamilton as usual. He's become the great love of her life."

"But how could they have known?" Claire demanded.

"That's what I'd like to know," Canning said.

"I should have thought it obvious." Birr crossed to the sideboard and helped himself to a brandy. "That gardener, Schmidt. The one you got the information about the drainage system from. Maybe a hundred cigarettes weren't enough."

"The bastard," Canning said. "I'll kill him."

"But after you've had a bath, Hamilton — please." Claire waved a hand delicately in front of her nose. "You really do smell a little high."

"Camembert — out of season," said Gaillard.

There was general laughter. Canning said grimly, "The crackling of thorns under a pot, isn't that what the Good Book says? I hope you're still laughing, all of you, when the *Reichsführer*'s thugs march you out to the nearest wall." He walked out angrily during the silence that followed.

Birr emptied his glass. "Strange, but I can't think of a single funny thing to say, so, if you'll excuse me. . . ."

After he'd gone, Gaillard said, "He's right, of course. It isn't good. Now if Hamilton or Lord Dundrum had got away and reached American or British troops, they could have brought help."

"Nonsense, this whole business." Claire sat down again. "Hesser would never stand by and see us treated like that. It isn't in his nature."

"I'm afraid Colonel Hesser would have very little to do with it," Gaillard said. "He's a soldier, and soldiers have a terrible habit of doing what they're told, my dear."

There was a knock at the door, it opened, and Hesser came in. He smiled, his slight half-bow extending to the three of them, then turned to Madame Chevalier.

"Chess?"

"Why not?" She was playing a Schubert nocturne now, full of passion and meaning. "But first settle an argument for us, Max. Paul here believes that if the SS come to shoot us, you'll let them. Claire doesn't believe you could stand by and do nothing. What do you think?"

"I have the strangest of feelings that I will beat you in seven moves tonight."

"A soldier's answer, I see. Ah, well."

She stood up, came around the piano, and moved to the chess table. Hesser sat opposite her. She made the first move. Claire picked up a book and started to read. Gaillard sat staring into the fire, smoking his pipe. It was very quiet.

After a while the door opened and Canning came in wearing a brown battledress blouse and cream slacks. Claire de Beauville said, "That's better,

Hamilton. Actually you really look rather handsome tonight. Crawling through sewers must be good for you."

Hesser said, without looking up, "Ah, General, I was hoping you'd put in an appearance."

"I'd have thought we'd seen enough of each other for one night," Canning told him.

"Perhaps, but the point you were making earlier — I think your argument may have some merit. Perhaps we could discuss it in the morning. Let's say directly after breakfast?"

"Now you're damn well talking," Canning said.

Hesser ignored him, leaned forward, moved a bishop. "Checkmate, I think."

Madame Chevalier examined the board and sighed. "Seven moves, you told me. You've done it in five."

Max Hesser smiled. "My dear Madame, one must always try to be ahead of the game. The first rule of good soldiering."

And in Berlin, just after midnight, Bormann still sat in his office, for the

Führer himself worked through the night these days, seldom going to bed before seven A.M., and Bormann liked to remain close. Close enough to keep others away.

There was a knock at the door and Rattenhuber entered, a sealed envelope in his hand. "For you, *Reichsleiter.*"

"Who from, Willi?"

"I don't know, *Reichsleiter.* I found it on my desk, marked 'priority seven.' "

Which was a code reference for communications of the most secret sort, intended for Bormann's eyes alone.

Bormann opened the envelope, then looked up, no expression in his eyes. "Willi, the Fieseler Storch in which *Feldmarschall* von Greim and Hannah Reitsch flew into Berlin has been destroyed. Get on the phone to Gatow at once. Tell them they must send another plane by morning, one capable of flying directly out of the city."

"Very well, *Reichsleiter.*"

Bormann held up the envelope. "Know what's in here, Willi? Some very interesting news. It would appear that our beloved *Reichsführer,* dear Uncle Heini, has offered to surrender to the British and Americans."

"My God," Rattenhuber exclaimed.

"But what will the *Führer* say, Willi? That's the most interesting thing." Bormann pushed back his chair and stood up. "Let's go and find out, shall we?"

Five

From his window, Hesser could see out across the courtyard and outer walls to the road winding steeply down the valley to the river below. Beyond the trees was the tiny village of Arlberg, looking rather like something out of a fairy tale by the Brothers Grimm, the pine trees on the lower slopes of the mountain behind it green against the snow. In fact it was snowing again now, only slightly, but for a moment it seemed to make the world a cleaner, more shining place. Some throwback to childhood, probably.

The door opened behind him, and Schenck entered. Hesser said, "Snowing again. It's hanging on this year."

"True, *Herr Oberst,*" Schenck said. "When I passed through the village early this morning, I noticed the woodcutters' children from the outlying districts skiing to school."

Hesser moved to the liquor cabinet and poured himself a brandy. Schenck tried to stay suitably impassive, and Hesser said, "I know, the road to ruin, but it's bad this morning. Worse than usual, and this helps a damn sight more than those pills."

He could feel his left arm in every detail within the empty sleeve, every wire inside his broken body, and the glass eye was sheer torture.

"What does it matter, anyway? The same roads all lead to hell in the end. But never mind that now. Did you try Berlin again this morning?"

"Yes, *Herr Oberst,* but we're just not succeeding in getting through."

"And the radio?"

"*Kaput, Herr Oberst.* Stern found a couple of valves gone."

"Can't he replace them?"

"When he opened the box of spares, they had all suffered damage in transit, from the look of things."

"Are you trying to tell me we've no kind of communication at all with anyone?"

"For the moment I am afraid that is true, *Herr Oberst*, but with luck we should still get through to Berlin if we keep trying, and Stern is out in a field car now, touring the district to see if he can find the spares he needs."

"Very well. Is there anything else?"

"General Canning and Colonel Birr are here."

"All right, show them in. And Schenck," he added as the old lieutenant moved to the door.

"Herr Oberst."

"You stay, too."

Canning wore a sidecap and olive-drab officer's trenchcoat. Birr was in a reversible camouflage-and-white winter uniform parka with a hood of a type issued generally in the German Army on the Eastern Front.

Hesser said, "Ready for exercise, I see, gentlemen."

"Never mind that," Canning said brusquely. "What have you decided?"

Hesser raised a hand defensively. "You go too fast, General. There is a great deal to consider here."

103

"For Christ's sake," Canning said. "Here we go again. Are you going to do something positive, or aren't you?"

"We've been trying to get through to Prisoner-of-War Administration headquarters in Berlin since last night, without success."

"Berlin?" Canning said. "You must be joking. The Russians are walking all over it."

"Not quite," Hesser said evenly. "The *Führer,* you may be dismayed to know, still lives, and there are considerable German forces in the capital."

"Four hundred and fifty miles away," Canning said urgently. "This is here, Max. What are *you* going to do *here,* that's what I want to know."

"Or to put it another way," Birr said, "have you thought any more about sending Lieutenant Schenck to look for a British or American unit, perhaps in company with one of us?"

"No." Hesser slammed his good hand against the desk. "That I will not permit. That would be going too far. I am a German officer, gentlemen, you must not

104

forget that. I serve my country the best way I can.''

''So what the hell is that supposed to mean?'' Canning demanded.

Hesser frowned, thinking for a moment, then nodded. ''For today, I will still keep trying to reach Berlin. I must know what their definite orders are in this matter.'' Canning started to protest, but Hesser cut him short. ''No, this is the way I intend to handle things. You must make up your mind to it. First — to use a phrase you are fond of — we try channels.''

''And then?'' Birr asked.

''If we are no further forward by this time tomorrow, I shall consider sending *Oberleutnant* Schenck out into the wide world to see what he can find. Always supposing he is willing to take his chances.'' He turned to Schenck. ''I will not make this an order, you understand?''

Schenck smiled bleakly. ''I shall be happy to do as the *Herr Oberst* sees fit.''

''Why waste another day?'' Canning began, but Hesser simply stood up.

''That is all I have to say, gentlemen. Good morning.'' He nodded to Schenck.

"You will take the general and Colonel Birr to exercise now."

It was cold in the water garden, snow flying every which way in the wind. The guards on each gate wore parkas, and Schneider trailed along with Magda behind Canning and Birr. Canning turned at one point and snapped his fingers. The Alsatian strained at her lead and whined.

"Oh, let her go, man," he snapped at Schneider in German.

Schneider slipped her chain reluctantly, and the bitch ran to Canning and licked his hand. He knelt and fondled her ears and said to Birr, "Well, what do you think?"

"More than I'd hoped for. Hesser's a Prussian, remember. A professional soldier of the old school, God and the Fatherland branded on his backbone. You're asking him to throw in his hand. Not only to string up the white flag, but to go running around, trying to attract somebody's attention with it. That's expecting a hell of a lot. I'd settle for what you've got if I were you."

106

"Yes, maybe you're right." Canning stood up as Paul Gaillard and Madame Chevalier appeared from the lower water garden, walking briskly. She wore a German military greatcoat and a head scarf, and Gaillard had on a black beret and overcoat.

"How did you get on?" the Frenchman demanded as they approached.

"Oh, you tell them, Justin," Canning said. "I've had enough for one day."

He moved away, Magda at his knee, went down the steps past the lily pond, and entered the conservatory. Schneider followed but stayed on the porch.

It was warm and humid in there, plants everywhere, palms and vines heavy with grapes. He followed the black-and-white mosaic of the path and came to the center fountain, where he found Claire de Beauville tending the scarlet winter roses that were her special pride.

Canning paused for a moment, watching her. She was really beautiful, the dark hair pulled back to the nape of the neck, exposing the oval triangle of the face. The high cheekbones, the wide,

107

quiet eyes, the generous mouth. He was conscious of the old familiar stirring and the slight feeling of anger that went with it.

Orphaned at an early age and supported by an uncle in the shipping business in Shanghai whom he never saw, he had spent most of his youth at boarding schools of one kind or another before he finally entered West Point. From that moment he had given his all to the army, sacrificed everything to the demands of military life with single-minded devotion. He had never felt the need for wife or family. There had been women, of course, but only in the most basic way. Now everything had changed. For the first time in his life another human being could touch him, and that was not a concept that fitted comfortably into his scheme of things.

Claire turned, gardening fork in one hand, and smiled. "There you are. What happened?"

"Oh, we have to wait another twenty-four hours. Max wants to make one last attempt to get in touch with Prisoner-of-

War Administration headquarters in Berlin. The correct Junker officer, right to the bitter end."

"And you, Hamilton, what do you want?"

"To be free now," he said, his voice suddenly urgent. "It's been too long, Claire, don't you see?"

"And you've missed too much, isn't that it?" He frowned, and she carried on. "The war, Hamilton. Your precious war. Bugles faintly on the wind, the smoke of battle. Meat and drink to you, what your soul craves. And who knows, if you were free now, there might still be the chance to get involved. Have one last, glorious fling."

"That's a hell of a thing to say."

"But true. And what can I offer as a substitute? Only winter roses."

She smiled slightly. He caught her then, pulling her into his arms, his mouth fastening hungrily on hers.

Ritter, seated at the piano in the canteen, was playing a Chopin etude, a particular favorite of his. It was a piece which comforted him, in spite of the fact that this present instrument was distinctly out of tune. It reminded him of other days. Of his father and mother and the small country estate in Prussia where he had been raised.

The Russians were shelling constantly now, the sound of the explosions audible even at that depth, the concrete walls trembling. There was that pervasive smell of sulfur, dust everywhere.

A drunken SS lieutenant lurched against the piano, slopping beer over the keys. "We've had enough of that rubbish. What about something rousing? Something to lift the heart. A chorus of 'Horst Wessel,' perhaps?"

Ritter stopped playing and looked up at him. "You're speaking to me, I presume?" His voice was very quiet, yet infinitely dangerous, the white face burning, the eyes dark.

The lieutenant took in the Knight's Cross, the Oak Leaves, the Swords, the insignia of rank, and tried to draw himself together. "I'm sorry, *Sturmbannführer.* My mistake."

"So it would appear. Go away."

The lieutenant moved off to join a noisy, jostling throng as drunk as himself. A young nurse in service uniform was passing by. One of them pulled her across his knee. Another slipped a hand up her skirt. She laughed and reached up to kiss a third hungrily.

Ritter, totally disgusted, helped himself to a bottle of Steinhager at the bar, filled a glass, and sat at an empty table. After a while, Hoffer entered. He looked around the canteen, then came across quickly, his face pale with excitement.

"I saw a hell of a thing a little while ago, Major."

"And what would that be?"

"General Fegelein being marched along the corridor by two of the escort guard, minus his epaulettes and insignia. He looked frightened to death."

"The fortunes of war, Erich. Get yourself a glass."

"Good God, Major, a general of the SS. A Knight's Cross holder."

"And like all of us in the end, clay of the most common variety, my friend —

111

or at least his feet were.''

''We shouldn't have come here to this place.'' Hoffer glanced about him, his face working. ''We're never going to get out. We're going to die here like rats, and in bad company.''

''I don't think so.''

There was an immediate expression of hope on Hoffer's face. ''You've heard something?''

''No, but all my instincts tell me that I shall. Now get yourself a glass and bring that chessboard over here.''

Bormann and Rattenhuber, watching from a doorway at the rear of the room, had observed the entire scene. Rattenhuber said, ''His mother was a really big aristocrat. One of those families that go all the way back to Frederick.''

''Look at him,'' Bormann said. ''Did you see the way he handled that drunken swine? And I'll tell you something, Willi. A hundred marks says he hasn't raised his arm and said *Heil Hitler* for at least two years. I know his kind. They salute like a British Guards officer — a finger to the peak of the cap. And the men, Willi. Shall I tell you what they think, even the men of the SS? Would you imagine they'd still follow old peasants like you and me?"

"They follow." Rattenhuber hesitated. "They follow their officers, *Reichsleiter*. They have discipline, the *Waffen*-SS. The finest in the world."

"But Ritter, Willi. A man like him they'll follow into the jaws of hell, and you know why? Because men like him don't give a damn. They're what they are. Themselves alone."

"And what would that be, *Reichsleiter?*"

"In his case, a very gentle perfect knight. You see, Willi? All that reading I do — even English literature. They think me Bormann the boor, Goebbels and company, but I know more than they do — about everything. Don't you agree?"

"But of course, *Reichsleiter.*"

"And Ritter — fine Aryan stock, like one of those idealized paintings the *Führer* loves so much. A standard impossible for the rest of us to attain. Forget the nasty things, Willi. The rapes, the burnings, the camps, the executions. Just think of the

113

ideal. The finest soldier you've ever known. Decent, honorable, chivalrous, and totally without fear. What every soldier in the *Waffen*-SS would like to imagine himself to be, that's what Ritter *is*."

"And you think these Finnish barbarians we discussed earlier would concur?"

"The Knight's Cross, Willi, with Oak Leaves *and* Swords? What do you think?"

Rattenhuber nodded. "I think that perhaps the *Reichsleiter* would like me to bring him to the office now."

"Later, Willi. Now I must go to the *Führer*. The news of Himmler's defection and Fegelein's cowardice has considerably angered him. He needs me. You speak to Ritter, Willi, when he's had a drink or two. Judge if it's changed him. I'll see him later. After midnight."

The shelling increased in intensity, the thunder overhead continuous now, so that the walls shook constantly and, in the canteen, behavior deteriorated considerably. The place was crowded with a noisy, jostling throng, here and there a drunk lying under the table.

When Rattenhuber returned a couple of hours later, Ritter and Hoffer were still at the table at the rear of the room, playing chess.

Rattenhuber said, "May I join you?"

Ritter glanced up. "Why not?"

Rattenhuber winced as a particularly thunderous explosion shook the entire room. "I didn't like the sound of that. Do you think we're safe here, Major?"

Ritter looked at Hoffer. "Erich?"

Hoffer shrugged. "Seventeen-point-five caliber is the heaviest they've got. Nothing that could get down this far."

"A comforting thought." Rattenhuber offered them both cigarettes.

Ritter said, "Hoffer saw a strange sight some hours ago. General Fegelein being led along the corridor under escort, minus epaulettes and insignia."

"Yes, very sad. A disgrace to all of us," Rattenhuber said. "He cleared off yesterday. When the *Führer* found he was missing, he sent a detachment out looking for him. The fool was actually at his own house in Charlottenburg in civilian clothes and with a woman. They took him outside and shot him half an hour ago."

Ritter showed no emotion whatsoever. "If what you say is so, then there could be no other penalty."

"No, we can't just leave the war by taking off our uniform and putting on a raincoat, not at this stage," Rattenhuber said. "Not any of us." He lit another cigarette. "By the way, Major, the *Reichsleiter* would like to see you a little later on. I'd be obliged if you'd hold yourself in readiness."

"Naturally," Ritter said. "I'm at the *Reichsleiter*'s orders." The slight, sardonic smile that touched his mouth had an edge of contempt to it. "Was there anything else?"

Rattenhuber felt in some curious way as if he were being dismissed. "No," he said hurriedly. "I'll look for you here."

An SS orderly entered the room, gazed around quickly, then bore down on them. He clicked his heels and offered a message to Rattenhuber. Rattenhuber read it, his face broke into a delighted smile, and he waved the orderly away.

"Excellent news. The Fieseler Storch in which *Feldmarschall* von Greim and Hannah Reitsch flew into Berlin on the twenty-sixth was destroyed this morning by artillery fire."

"So the *Feldmarschall* is also a permanent guest here?" Ritter said. "Bad luck."

"No, he got away this evening in a replacement plane, an Arado trainer piloted by Hannah Reitsch after she'd made two unsuccessful attempts. They took off near the *Brandenburger Tor.*" He stood up. "You must excuse me. The *Reichsleiter* has been waiting for such news, and the *Führer,* also." He went out.

Hoffer said, "But what does he want you for?"

"I expect I'll find that out when he sees me," Ritter said. He nodded at the chessboard. "And now, if you don't mind, it's your move."

Just before midnight, Walter Wagner, a city councilor and minor official of the propaganda ministry, was hustled into the bunker under armed guard. Totally bewildered and still not quite believing what was happening to him, at approximately one o'clock in the morning he married Adolf Hitler and Eva Braun. The only other two people present were the witnesses, Martin Bormann and Joseph Goebbels, Reich minister for propaganda.

A wedding breakfast was served immediately afterward, at which champagne was available in copious quantities. At approximately two o'clock, the *Führer* went into an adjoining room to dictate his will and final political testament to one of his two secretaries, Frau Junge. Bormann, who had been waiting for an appropriate moment, seized his chance and left, also.

Rattenhuber was waiting for him in the corridor. "And now we've got that out of the way, I'll see Ritter," the *Reichsleiter* said. "Bring him to me, Willi."

When Rattenhuber ushered Ritter into the office, there was a particularly intense bombardment taking place. The

Reichsleiter looked up as smoke and dust drifted from the ventilator. "If that hadn't been happening for some days now, I'd be alarmed."

"Not pleasant," Ritter said.

"No place to be at the moment — Berlin — if it can be avoided."

Rattenhuber took up his position beside the door. There was a long silence during which Bormann gazed up at the young SS officer calmly. Finally he said, "You would like to leave Berlin, *Sturmbannführer?*"

Ritter actually smiled. "I think you may say that I would dearly love to, *Reichsleiter,* but I would not have thought it a possibility now."

"Oh, all things are possible to men who are willing to dare anything. I had formed the opinion that you were of that breed. Am I right?"

"If you say so."

"Good, we must see if we can accommodate you, then. This man of yours — Hoffer. He is to be trusted?"

"With my life — yes," Ritter said. "I would not depend too much on his loyalty to any political idea, however — not at this stage."

"In other words, a man of sound sense and judgment. I like that." Bormann turned to the map which lay before him. "You know this area here, northwest of Innsbruck, on the Inn River?"

"I know where it is," Ritter said. "Let's put it that way. My unit was in that general area when I left. Perhaps fifty miles away."

"Not now," Bormann said. "What was left of them was wiped out by tanks of the American Sixth Army a hundred miles or more from there yesterday morning."

For a moment his voice seemed to fade for Ritter as he thought of the regiment, old comrades, Colonel Jager. He came back to reality to hear Bormann saying, "I'm sorry — a bad shock for you."

"No matter," Ritter said. "An old and tired story, repeated many times. Please continue."

"Very well. This entire area — the triangle between Innsbruck, Salzburg, and Klagenfurt — is still in our hands, but the situation is very fluid. The enemy are probing in with great care because they believe the stories they've heard of an Alpine Fortress where we can hold out for years. Once they appreciate the truth of the situation, they'll be through to Berchtesgaden like a hot knife into butter.''

"And this could happen at any time?''

"Undoubtedly. So, to accomplish what I seek, we must move fast.''

"And what would that be, *Reichsleiter?*''

Bormann picked up a pencil and drew a circle around Arlberg. "Here at Schloss Arlberg, on the Inn, you will find five important prisoners. What we call *prominenti*. One of them is the American general, Canning. Who the others are needn't concern you at the moment. It's enough to know that they are all people held in special regard by their individual nations. You can read the files later.''

"A moment,'' Ritter said. "You speak as if you expect me to go there in person. As if it is an accomplished fact. But this would first mean leaving Berlin.''

"Naturally.''

"But how can this be?''

"You may have heard that the Fieseler Storch in which *Feldmarschall* von Greim and Hannah Reitsch flew into Berlin was destroyed yesterday."

"Yes, I know that. They flew out last night in a replacement, an Arado training plane." And then, with a sudden flash of insight, Ritter saw it all. "Ah, I see now. The Fieseler Storch . . ."

". . . is in a garage at the back of an automobile showroom just off the main avenue near the *Brandenburger Tor*. I'll give you the address before you leave. You will fly out tonight, or probably just after midnight tomorrow, the best time to evade the Russian antiaircraft. About ten miles from Arlberg, here at Arnheim, there's an airstrip. Used for mountain rescue operations before the war. No one there now. You should arrive by breakfast time."

"Then what?"

"You'll find transport. It's all arranged. Even my enemies admit I'm an organizer." Bormann smiled. "You will proceed from there to Arlberg, where you will take charge of the five prisoners I

122

have mentioned and bring them back to Arnheim with you. They'll be picked up from there by transport plane later in the day. Any questions?"

"Several. The purpose of this operation?"

"The prisoners, you mean?" Bormann waved a hand. "Put out of your mind any wild rumors you may have heard about the execution of prominent persons. I abhor waste, Major, believe me. These people will be useful bargaining counters when we reach the situation of having to sit down and discuss peace terms with our enemies."

"Hostages might be a better word."

"If you like."

"All right," Ritter said, "but what about the situation at the castle? Who's in charge?"

"Soldiers of the *Wehrmacht,* but only just. A Colonel Hesser — a good man, but crippled, and nineteen or twenty old men. Reservists. Nothing to worry about."

"And I'll have a piece of paper, I suppose, ordering him to hand them over?"

"Signed by the *Führer* himself."

"What if he refuses, not that I'm trying to be difficult, you understand. It's just that after six years of service I've got accustomed to the fact that in war anything can happen, especially when one expects the opposite. I like to take care of all eventualities."

"And so you shall." Bormann indicated the map again, tapping with his pencil. "At this very moment, no more than ten miles west of Arnheim you'll find an SS unit, or what's left of it. Thirty or forty men, according to my information."

"These days, as the *Reichsleiter* knows, the term 'SS' can cover a multitude of sins. Are they German?"

"No, but firstrate troops. Finns, who were with Wiking Division in Russia, operating mainly as ski troops."

"Mercenaries?" Ritter said.

"Soldiers of the *Waffen*-SS whose contract does not expire until nine A.M. on the first of May. You will hold them to their contract and bend them to your purpose until you have secured your prisoners. Do you understand me?"

"I believe so."

"Good." Bormann handed him a small folder. "Everything you need is in there, including the address of the garage where you'll find the Stork. The pilot's name is Berger. He's SS, too, so you see it's all being kept in the family. Oh, and there's just one other rather important thing."

"What's that, *Reichsleiter?*"

"Someone will be going along with you, as my personal representative, just to see that everything goes all right. A Herr Strasser. I hope I can rely on you to offer him every courtesy."

Ritter stood looking down at the folder which he gripped tightly in both hands. "Is there something worrying you, Major?" Martin Bormann asked gently.

"The prisoners," Ritter said and looked up. "I want your assurance, your personal word on your honor, that no harm will come to them. That the situation will be exactly as you have stated."

"My dear Ritter." Bormann came around the desk and put a hand on his shoulder. "Anything else would simply be stupid, and I'm not that, believe me."

Ritter nodded slowly. "As you say, *Reichsleiter.*"

"Good," Bormann said. "Excellent. I'd get some sleep now if I were you. Rattenhuber here will see that you and Hoffer get a pass that will get you out of here sometime tomorrow afternoon. I may not see you again before you go, although I'll try. If not, good luck."

He held out his hand. Ritter hesitated, then took it briefly. Rattenhuber held the door open for him. As he closed it, Bormann went around the desk. When he turned, there was a strange expression on his face.

"My honor, Willi. He asked me to swear on my honor. Did you ever hear of such a thing, with almost everyone else I know doubting its very existence for the past twenty years or more?"

Hoffer was waiting in the canteen and leaned over excitedly as Ritter sat down. "What was it all about?"

"I'm not sure, Erich," Ritter said. "You see, there was what he told me and what he left out. Still, for what

126

it's worth . . ."

He leaned forward, his hands on the folder, and started to talk.

Six

At Schloss Arlberg it was still snowing when Schenck knocked at the door and entered Hesser's office. The colonel was standing at the window, looking out across the valley. He turned and walked to the desk.

"So, the situation is still the same?"

"I'm afraid so, *Herr Oberst*. We are still unable to get through to Berlin."

"And the radio?"

"Stern has visited every village in these parts, without success. There are certain to be radios in the area, of course, that may well use the right type of valve, but as the *Herr Oberst* knows, their possession in this district has been declared illegal for more than a year now. Those individuals guilty of breaking the law are unlikely to admit to the fact at this stage."

"Understandable in the circumstances." Hesser sat down. "The time for a definite decision has come."

"So it would appear, *Herr Oberst.*"

Hesser sat for a moment, plucking at his empty sleeve. "As I said yesterday, I will not make an order of this business. I would be failing in my duty if I didn't point out that it could be extremely hazardous. In the fluid state of the front line in this area, any enemy unit you run into may be inclined to shoot first and ask questions afterward. You understand this?"

"Perfectly."

"And you're still willing to take a chance?"

"*Herr Oberst,*" Schenck said, "I'm an old man by military standards, perhaps too old for this sort of game. I last saw action on the Western Front in 1918, but it would be quite out of the question for you to go, sir, and certainly improper to send one of other ranks on such a mission. As I am the only other available officer, it would seem to me that we have little choice in the matter."

"Who would you take with you?"

"Schmidt, I think. He's my own age, but an excellent driver. We'll take one of the field cars."

"Very well," Hesser said. "It would seem, as you say, that there is no other choice. Please bring General Canning and Colonel Birr, and I'll inform them of my decision."

"They are outside now, *Herr Oberst.*"

Schenck moved to the door, and Hesser said, "Schenck?"

"Herr Oberst."

"I appreciate this. You're a brave man."

"No, *Herr Oberst,* anything but that. A very frightened man." Schenck smiled. "But I do have a wife and two daughters I'm more than anxious to see again. What I do now, I'm doing for them. The best thing for all of us, believe me."

"Yes, perhaps you're right."

Schenck went out and returned a few moments later with Canning and Birr. The general came forward eagerly. "Well, have you come to a decision?"

Hesser nodded. *"Oberleutnant* Schenck

will be leaving" — here he glanced at his watch — "at noon, precisely. He'll take a field car and one driver with him, and he will search for an Allied unit somewhere in the general direction of Innsbruck. You agree, Schenck?"

"Whatever you say, *Herr Oberst.*"

"Thank God you've come to your senses," Canning said. "Can we go now and tell the others?"

"I don't see why not."

Canning and Birr turned to the door, and Hesser stood up. "One thing before you go."

"What's that?" Canning turned impatiently.

"*Oberleutnant* Schenck and *Korporal* Schmidt will be running a considerable personal risk in this business. I hope you appreciate that."

Canning frowned, and it was Birr who held out his hand to Schenck. "We certainly do, and I for one would like to thank you now on behalf of all of us."

"I will do my best, *Herr Oberst*" — Schenck smiled briefly — "to stay alive for all our sakes."

Paul Gaillard and Claire were sitting at the window in the dining hall when Canning and Birr entered; Madame Chevalier was at her daily practice at the piano. She stopped playing at once.

Gaillard stood up. "What happened?"

"We go," Canning said excitedly. "Or at least Schenck does. He leaves at noon." He stood in front of the fire, hands behind his back. "Do you folks realize that with any kind of luck he could be back here in a matter of hours? That by this evening we could be free?"

Birr lit a cigarette. "On the other hand, if he runs into the wrong sort of trigger-happy bunch, he could also be dead by then. Have you considered that?"

"Nonsense," Canning said. "Schenck spent four years on the Western Front in the First World War. Wounded three times. He's too old a bird to get knocked off now."

"But if he does, Hamilton." Claire walked to the fire and sat down. "What do we do?"

"Then it may be necessary for us to

take more positive action ourselves.'' Canning crossed to the door and opened it. He turned. ''I know one thing. If anybody tries to take me out of here, SS or whoever, they're going to have to do it the hard way.''

He went out, closing the door behind him.

When Rattenhuber went into Bormann's office, the *Reichsleiter* was writing at his desk. ''I'll only be a moment, Willi. I missed my diary entry last night. I was with the *Führer* for hours.'' After a while he put down his pen and closed the book. ''So, Willi, and how are things going out there? How's morale?''

Rattenhuber looked uncomfortable. ''Morale, *Reichsleiter*?''

''Come on, man. No need to beat about the bush at this stage of the game.''

''Very well, *Reichsleiter*. If you must know, it's a total disgrace. I've never seen so many drunks in uniform in all my life. The canteen is full of them. And the women aren't behaving any better. Everything seems to be going to pieces.''

133

"What do you expect, Willi? You know why the Russian artillery has stopped? Because they were killing their own people as their tanks and infantry pushed toward Wilhelmplatz. According to the latest reports, they've come to a halt no more than sixteen hundred feet from the Chancellery. There's heavy fighting in Belle-Allianceplatz and in the Potsdamerstrasse, though I understand our troops are holding their own near Bismarckstrasse."

"But what about Wenck's army?"

"Still maintaining its link with Reimann's corps, but that's no use to us, Willi. We're finished."

Rattenhuber looked shocked. "Finished, *Reichsleiter?*"

"Oh, for quite some time now, didn't you know? When Steiner's counterattack failed to materialize on the twenty-second, the *Führer* announced that the war was lost. That he intended to die in Berlin. Did you know that at his wedding breakfast he actually talked of suicide?"

"My God!" Rattenhuber said in horror.

"Perhaps the greatest service he could

render the German people."

He seemed to be waiting for some kind of comment. Rattenhuber licked dry lips nervously. *"Reichsleiter?"*

"An interesting thought. To die for the cause, if you are the right person, can sometimes be more important than to live." He smiled gently, contriving to look even more sinister than usual. "But for lesser mortals, such excesses are not always necessary. You, for instance, Willi."

"Me, *Reichsleiter?* I don't understand."

"Your destiny is to live, Willi. To put it simply, you are to leave this evening."

Rattenhuber stared at him in astonishment. "Leave Berlin, you mean?"

"Together with the *Führer*'s army adjutant, Johannmeier, Lorenz from the propaganda ministry, and Zander. His task is to take a copy of the *Führer*'s political testament and will to Admiral Dönitz. I suggested sending you as well, and the *Führer* agreed."

"I — I am honored," Rattenhuber stammered.

"I'm sure you are, Willi," Bormann

said dryly. "But whether you reach Dönitz or not is problematical and of no particular consequence. There are other tasks for you now of more importance."

Rattenhuber's face was pale. "The *Kameradenwerk?* It begins?"

"Of course, Willi. Did I not always say it would? In my end is my beginning. I read that once somewhere. Highly appropriate."

There was a tremendous explosion somewhere close by, the walls of the bunker shook, a cloud of dust filtered in through the ventilator.

Bormann glanced up, showing absolutely no sign of fear. "There goes the Ivan artillery again. You know, in some ways it reminds me of the Twilight of the Gods. All the forces of evil are in league against them, and then suddenly a new citadel arises, more beautiful than ever, and Baldur lives again." He turned, his face grave. "It will be so for us, Willi, for Germany. This I promise you."

And Rattenhuber, in spite of the noise of the shells landing without cease thirty yards above his head, the sulfurous stench, the dust which threatened to choke him, straightened his shoulders.

"I, too, believe, *Reichsleiter*. Have never ceased to believe in the destiny of the German people."

"Good, Willi. Excellent." Bormann took a letter from his desk and shook the dust from it. "This is the reason it is so important you get out of Berlin, and that clown Dönitz has nothing to do with it."

At Schloss Arlberg, in the main courtyard, Schenck was preparing to leave. He stood beside the field car, the collar of his greatcoat turned up against the snow, and waited as Corporal Schmidt made a final check on the engine.

"Everything all right?" Schenck asked.

"As far as I can see, *Herr Leutnant.*"

"Good man."

As he turned, Hesser, Canning, and Birr came down the steps of the main entrance and moved across the courtyard.

"All set, Schenck?" Hesser demanded.

"Yes, *Herr Oberst.*"

"Good. General Canning has something for you."

Canning held out an envelope. "This is a letter I've written, explaining the situation here. Hand it to the first British or American officer you come to. I think it should do the trick."

"My thanks, General." Schenck put the envelope in his pocket, then unfastened the service belt that carried the holstered Walther automatic pistol at his waist. He held it out to Hesser. "Under the circumstances, I shan't be needing this." He reached inside the field car and picked up Corporal Schmidt's Schmeisser from the rear seat. "Or this."

Hesser hesitated, then took them. "Perhaps the wiser course."

"I think so, sir." Schenck nodded to Schmidt, who started the engine. The *Oberleutnant* drew himself together and delivered a punctilious military salute. *"Herr Oberst,* gentlemen."

They all saluted in return; he climbed into the passenger seat and nodded. Schmidt drove away, out of the main entrance across the drawbridge, and they disappeared around the first bend in the road.

As the sound of the engine faded, Birr said, "You know, I've just thought of something."

"What's that?" Canning asked.

"That if Schenck runs into a German unit, and they find that letter on him, it isn't going to do him a great deal of good."

"I know," Canning said harshly. "I thought of that when I was writing the damn thing, but at this stage of the game he must just take his chances — like the rest of us," he added and turned and walked back across the courtyard.

At approximately four o'clock in the afternoon, Rattenhuber conducted Ritter and Hoffer to the bunker exit leading onto Hermann-Göringstrasse. They each had a small field pack loaded with provisions for the journey and wore camouflaged ponchos and steel helmets. They were armed with Schmeisser machine pistols, and in true SS fashion carried two stick grenades in the top of each boot.

The artillery barrage was still as relentless as ever, and there was the sound of heavy fighting up near Potsdamerplatz.

Rattenhuber put a hand on Ritter's shoulder. "What can I say, except good luck and God go with you."

God? Ritter thought. Is He on my side, too? He smiled ironically, tapped Hoffer on the shoulder, and moved out. There was a burst of machine-gun fire, and Rattenhuber watched them flatten themselves on the ground. A moment later they were up and running and safely into the ruined buildings opposite.

Bormann moved out of the shadows behind him. "So, they are on their way, Willi."

"Yes, *Reichsleiter.*"

Bormann glanced at his watch. "I can afford to be away from the bunker for perhaps three hours at the most. In any case, you, too, must be back by then to make your own departure on schedule. We must move fast."

"Yes, *Reichsleiter.*"

Rattenhuber hurried away into the darkness of the vehicle ramp. A moment later there was the sound of an engine starting, and he drove out of the shadows at the wheel of a field car. There was an MG34 machine gun in the back, and Bormann mounted it on the windshield swivel and got in. Rattenhuber put on a steel helmet and offered the *Reichsleiter* another.

Bormann shook his head. "If there's a bullet for me, that won't save me. I haven't worn one since my field artillery days in 1918. Now, let's get moving. We haven't got time to waste."

Rattenhuber accelerated away, driving very fast, and they turned out of Hermann-Göringstrasse and moved in the general direction of Potsdamerplatz.

Once past the Tiergarten, Ritter and Hoffer moved fast through the blocks of apartment houses. A continuous mortar barrage fell around them, and after a while a squadron of Russian fighter-bombers came in low over the rooftops, spraying everything in sight with cannon fire.

They dodged into a doorway beside a sandbagged gun emplacement from which Hitler Youth fired light machine guns ineffectually into the sky.

"My God," Hoffer said in disgust. "Children playing soldiers, and for all the good they're doing, they might as well be firing Christmas toys."

"But willing to die, Erich," Ritter said. "They still believe."

He was examining the rough map which Rattenhuber had given him. Hoffer tugged at his sleeve. "And us, Major. What about us? What in hell are we doing here? What's the point?"

"Survival, Erich," Ritter said. "A game we've been playing for quite some time now, you and I. We might as well see it through. Who knows? It could prove interesting."

"That's all it's ever been to you, isn't it?" Hoffer said. "Some kind of black joke. That's why you can only smile with that curl to your lips."

"And it will still be there when you fold my hands on my chest, Erich," Ritter told him. "I promise you. Now let's get moving. We've about a quarter of a mile to go."

They moved from street to street, from

one mortar crater to the next, through the charnel house that was Berlin, passing on the way groups of terrified civilians, mostly women and children, and the soldiers of the *Volkssturm,* mainly tired old men, most of them already walking corpses.

Finally, they reached the East - West Avenue, saw the Victory Column in the distance. There were few people here now, and for some reason the bombardment seemed to have faded and the avenue was strangely quiet and deserted.

"Over here," Ritter said and darted toward the side street opposite. The showrooms on the corner were shattered, plateglass windows gaping. The sign above the main entrance said "Burgdorf Autos."

Ritter led the way along the pavement and paused outside the garage doors at the rear. They were closed. "This is it," he said. There was a judas gate to one side. He turned to Hoffer and grinned lightly. "I'll lead, you cover."

Hoffer cocked the Schmeisser and flattened himself against the wall. Ritter tried the handle of the gate gingerly. It opened to his touch. He paused, then shoved the door open and went in fast, going down hard. There was a burst of machine-gun fire, a pause, then Hoffer fired an answering burst around the door.

In the silence, as the echoes died, Ritter called, "Friends. We're looking for *Obersturmführer* Heini Berger."

It was very quiet, the garage a place of shadows in the evening light. A voice called softly, "Identify yourselves."

"Valhalla Exchange," Ritter called.

He could see the Fieseler Storch now, over to one side, and then a boot scraped and a young, dark-haired SS officer in camouflage uniform moved out of the shadows. His old-style field cap was tilted at a rakish angle and he carried an American Thompson submachine gun in one hand.

"Nice to see you," he said. "For a moment there, I thought you might be a bunch of Ivans smelling out foxes."

Ritter nodded toward the Thompson, which carried a round, hundred-drum magazine. "They'd have been in for a nasty surprise."

Berger grinned lazily. "Yes, a little item I picked up in the Ardennes. I always did like to overdo things." He put a cigarette in his mouth and flicked a lighter made from a Russian rifle bullet.

"What about Herr Strasser?" Ritter said, looking around.

"Oh, he isn't due for a while yet." Berger sat down on a packing case, putting the Thompson on the floor. "No rush — we're not due out of here until midnight."

"I see." Ritter sat down beside him, and Hoffer wandered over to the Stork. "This man Strasser — you know him?"

Berger hesitated perceptibly. "Don't you?"

"Never met him in my life before."

"Neither have I. I'm just the bloody bus driver on this show."

Ritter nodded toward the Stork. "We're not going to make the Bavarian Alps in one hop in that."

"No, we're scheduled to put down halfway, at an airstrip in the Thuringian Forest, west of Plauen. Always supposing it's still in our hands."

"And if it isn't?"

"An interesting thought."

"You think we'll make it? Out of Berlin, I mean?"

"I don't see why not. Hannah Reitsch made it with Greim, didn't she?"

"Not in total darkness, which it will be when we take off."

"Yes, I was aware of that fact," Berger said. "On the other hand, it does mean that the Russians won't be expecting us. They aren't likely to have any fighters up. No need now they've taken Templehof and Gatow. With any kind of luck, we could be away before they know what's happening."

"But you would still have to take off along the avenue in the dark," Ritter said, "and the Victory Column. . . ."

"I know. Very large and very solid. Still, I expect I'll manage to think of something." There were a couple of old sacks on the floor, and he lay down on them, cradling the Thompson in his arms. "I think I'll get a little shut-eye. Something tells me I'm going to need it. If you wouldn't mind watching the front door and give me a push when Strasser comes . . ."

He pulled the peak of his service cap over his eyes. Ritter smiled slightly and turned to Hoffer, who looked bewildered. "What's going on, Major? What's he playing at?"

"He's sleeping, Erich. Very sensible under the circumstances. Now do you want to take the first watch, or shall I?"

It was toward evening when *Oberleutnant* Schenck and *Korporal* Schmidt drove into the village of Graz, on the road to Innsbruck. It was completely deserted, not a soul in sight. They had traveled a distance of approximately forty miles since leaving Arlberg, had lost nearly three hours on the way due to a fault in the field car's fuel system. It had taken Schmidt that length of time to diagnose what was wrong and put it right.

They hadn't seen a single soldier, of either side, and there had also been a total absence of refugees on the road. But that made sense. Typical peasants, these mountain people. They would stick with their land, whatever happened. No running away for them. Nowhere to go.

A curtain moved at a ground-floor window of a house opposite. Schenck got out of the field car, crossed the street, and knocked at the door. There was no response, so he kicked impatiently. "Come on, for God's sake!" he called. "I'm Austrian like you. I'm not here to cause trouble."

After a while, the bolts were drawn and the door opened. An old, white-haired man with a bristling white moustache stood there, a young woman cowering behind him, holding a baby.

"Herr Leutnant," he said, civilly enough.

"Where is everybody?"

"They stay inside."

"Waiting for the Americans to come?"

"Or the British or the French." He managed a smile. "As long as it isn't the Russians."

"Are there any German units left in this area?"

"No — there were some panzers, but they pulled out two days ago."

148

"And the other side? Have you seen anything of them?" The old man hesitated, and Schenck said, "Come on. It's important."

"This morning I visited my son's farm, just to see if everything was all right. He's away in the army, and his wife here is staying with me. It's three miles down the road from here. There were English troops camped in the meadow and using the farm buildings, so I came away."

"What kind of troops? Tanks? Infantry?"

The old man shook his head. "They'd put up a great many tents — large tents — and there were ambulances coming in and out all the time. All their vehicles carried the red cross."

"Good." Schenck felt a surge of excitement. "I won't bother you any more."

He hurried back to the field car and climbed in. "Three miles down the road, Schmidt. A British Army field hospital, from the sound of it."

It's going to work, he thought. It's going to be all right. It couldn't be better.

Schmidt accelerated out of the square, bouncing over the cobbles between the old medieval houses that leaned out, almost touching each other, so that there was room for only one vehicle along the narrow street.

They came around a corner and entered another, smaller square and found a British Army field ambulance bearing down on them. Schmidt spun the wheel desperately, skidded on the light powdering of snow. For a single frozen moment in time, Schenck was aware of the sergeant in the leather jerkin, the young private in a tin hat sitting beside him, and then they collided with the ambulance's front offside wheel and bounced to one side, mounting the low parapet of the fountain in the center of the square and turning over.

Schmidt had been thrown clear and started to get up. Schenck, who was still inside the field car, saw the young private in the tin hat jump out of the ambulance, a Sten gun in his hand. He fired a short burst that drove Schmidt back across the parapet, into the fountain.

Schenck managed to get to his feet and waved his arms. "No!" he shouted. "No!"

The boy fired again, the bullets ricocheting from the cobbles. Schenck felt a violent blow in his right shoulder and arm and was thrown back against the field car.

He was aware of voices — raised voices. The sergeant was swinging the boy around and wrenching the Sten gun away from him. A moment later, he was kneeling over Schenck.

Schenck's mouth worked desperately as he felt himself slipping away. He managed to get the letter from his pocket, held it up in one bloodstained hand. "Your commanding officer — take me to him," he said hoarsely in English. "A matter of life and death." And then he fainted.

Major Roger Mullholland of the 173rd Field Hospital had been operating since eight o'clock that morning. A long day by any standards, and a succession of cases any one of which would have been a candidate for major surgery under the finest hospital conditions. All he had were tents and field equipment. He did his best, as did the men under his command, as he'd been doing his best for weeks now, but it wasn't enough.

He turned from his last case, which had necessitated the amputation of a young field gunner's legs below the knees, and found Schenck laid out on the next operating table, still in his army greatcoat.

"Who the hell is this?"

His sergeant major, a burly Glaswegian named Grant, said, "Some Jerry officer driving through Graz in a field car. They collided with one of the ambulances. There was a shoot-out, sir."

"How bad is he?"

"Two rounds in the shoulder. Another in the upper arm. He asked to be taken to the CO. Kept brandishing this in his hand."

He held up the bloodstained letter. Mullholland said, "All right, get him ready. Come one, come all."

He opened the envelope, took out the letter, and started to read. A moment later he said, "Dear God Almighty, as if I didn't have enough to take care of."

Seven

At a stage in the war when it had become apparent to him that Germany was almost certain to lose, Adolf Eichmann, head of the Jewish Office of the Gestapo, had ordered a shelter to be constructed, according to the most stringent specifications, under his headquarters at 116 Kurfürstenstrasse. It had its own generating plant and ventilating system and was self-sufficient in every respect.

The entire project was carried out under conditions of total secrecy, but in the Third Reich nothing was secret from Martin Bormann for long. On making the happy discovery, and needing a discreet establishment for purposes of his own, he had announced his intention of moving in, and Eichmann, too terrified to argue, agreed, putting up with the inconvenience of the arrangement until March, when he'd decided to make a run for it.

When Bormann and Rattenhuber arrived, the place seemed deserted. The front door hung crazily on its hinges, the windows gaped, and the roof had been extensively damaged by shelling. Rattenhuber drove along the alley at one side, wheels crunching over broken glass, and pulled into the courtyard at the rear of the building.

For the moment, the artillery bombardment had faded, and most of the shooting that was taking place was some little way off. Bormann got out and walked down a sloping concrete ramp to a couple of gray-painted, steel doors. He hammered with the toe of his boot. A grille was opened. The man who peered through had SS decals on his steel helmet. Bormann didn't say a word. The grille slammed shut, and a moment later the doors opened electronically.

Rattenhuber drove down the ramp, pausing for Bormann to get back in, and they entered a dark tunnel, passing two SS guards, and finally came to a halt in a brightly lit concrete garage.

There were two more SS guards and a young, hard-faced *Hauptsturmführer*. Like his men, he wore a sleeveband on his left arm that carried the legend "RFSS." *Reichsführer der SS*. The cuff-title of Himmler's personal staff, a device of Bormann's to deter the curious.

"So, Schultz, how goes it?" Bormann asked.

"No problems, *Reichsleiter*." Schultz delivered a perfect party salute. "Are you going up?"

"Yes, I think so."

Schultz led the way toward a steel elevator and pressed the button. He stood back. "At your orders, *Reichsleiter*."

Bormann and Rattenhuber moved inside, the colonel pressed the button to ascend, and the doors closed. He carried his Schmeisser, and there was a stick grenade tucked into his belt.

"Not long now, Willi," Bormann said. "The culmination of many months of hard work. You were surprised, I think, when I brought you into this affair?"

"No — an honor, *Reichsleiter,* I assure

you," Rattenhuber said. "A great honor to be asked to assist with such a task."

"No more than you deserve, Willi. Zander was not to be trusted. I needed someone of intelligence and discretion. Someone I could trust. This business is of primary importance, Willi, I think you know that. Essential if the *Kameradenwerk* is to succeed."

"You may rely on me, *Reichsleiter,*" Rattenhuber said emotionally. "To the death."

Bormann placed an arm about his shoulders. "I know I can, Willi. I know I can." The elevator stopped; the door opened. A young man in thick-lensed glasses and a white doctor's coat stood waiting. "Good evening, *Reichsleiter,*" he said politely.

"Ah, Scheel, Professor Wiedler is expecting me, I trust?"

"Of course, *Reichsleiter.* This way."

The only sound was the hum of the generators as they walked along the carpeted corridor. Scheel opened the door at the end and ushered them through into a working laboratory furnished mainly with electronic equipment. The man who sat in front of a massive recording machine in headphones was attired, like Scheel, in a white coat. He had an intelligent, anxious face and wore gold-rimmed, half-moon reading spectacles. He glanced around, took off the glasses, and got up hastily.

"My dear Professor." Bormann shook hands affably. "How goes it?"

"Excellently, *Reichsleiter*. I think I may say it couldn't have gone any better."

Fritz Wiedler was a doctor of medicine of the universities of Heidelberg and Cambridge. A fervent supporter of National Socialism from its earliest days, a Nobel prizewinner for his researches in cell structure, and one of the youngest professors the University of Berlin had ever known, he had a reputation as one of the greatest plastic surgeons in Europe.

He was a supreme example of a certain kind of scientist, a man totally dedicated to the pursuit of his profession, with a fervor that could only be described as criminal. For Wiedler, the end totally justified the means, and when his Nazi masters had come to power, he had prospered mightily.

He had worked with Rascher on low-pressure research for the *Luftwaffe,* using live prisoners as guinea pigs. Then he had tried spare-parts surgery, using the limbs of prisoners where necessary, at Gebhardt's sanatorium near Ravensbruck, where Himmler often went in search of cures for his chronic stomach complaint.

But it was as a member of the SS Institute for the Research and Study of Heredity that he really came into his own, working with Mengele at Auschwitz on the study of twins, first alive and later dead, all for the greater glory of science and the Third Reich.

And then Bormann had recruited him. Had offered him the chance of the ultimate experiment. In a sense, to create life itself. A challenge that no scientist worth his salt could possibly have turned down.

"Where are the rest of the staff?" Bormann asked.

"Having their evening meal."

"Five nurses — three females, two

male, am I right?"

"That is correct, *Reichsleiter*. Is there anything wrong?"

"Not at all," Bormann said tranquilly. "It's just that in these difficult times people tend to panic and make a run for it. I just wanted to make sure none of your people had."

Wiedler looked shocked. "None of them would think of such a thing, *Reichsleiter,* and besides, they'd never get past the guards."

"True," Bormann said. "So it goes well, you say. Are we ready yet?"

"I think so, *Reichsleiter*. You must judge for yourself."

"Let's get on with it, then."

Wiedler took a bunch of keys from his pocket, selected one, and moved to a door at the other end of the laboratory. Bormann, Rattenhuber, and Scheel followed. Wiedler inserted the key in the lock; the door swung open.

Music was playing, Schubert's Seventh Symphony, slow, majestic, the sound of it filling the room. Wiedler led the way in. They followed.

A man in flannel slacks and brown shirt was sitting at a table under a harsh white light, reading a book, his back toward them.

Wiedler said, "Good evening, Herr Strasser."

The man called Strasser pushed back his chair, got to his feet, and turned, and Martin Bormann gazed upon the mirror image of himself.

Rattenhuber's startled gasp had something of horror in it. "My God!" he whispered.

"Yes, Willi, now you know," Bormann said and held out his hand. "Strasser, how are you?"

"Never better, *Reichsleiter*."

The voice was identical, and Bormann shook his head slowly. "Not that I can tell with certainty. I mean, who knows how he speaks, exactly, but it seems all right to me."

"All right," Scheel said indignantly. *"Reichsleiter*, it's perfect, I assure you. Three months we've worked, day and night, using the very latest in recording devices, using tape instead of wire. Here, we'll demonstrate. When I switch on the microphone, say something, *Reichsleiter*. Anything you like."

Bormann hesitated, then said, "My name is Martin Bormann. I was born on June the seventeenth, in Halberstadt, in Lower Saxony."

Scheel ran the tape back, then played it. The reproduction was excellent. Then he nodded to Strasser. "Now you."

"My name is Martin Bormann," Strasser said. "I was born on June the seventeenth, in Halberstadt, in Lower Saxony."

"There, you see?" Scheel said triumphantly.

"Yes, I must agree." Bormann tilted Strasser's chin. "I might as well be looking into the mirror."

"Not quite, *Reichsleiter,*" Wiedler said. "If you stand side by side, a close examination does indicate certain features as not being quite the same, but that doesn't matter. The important thing is that no one will be able to tell you apart. And there are scars — not many, it's true — but I've arranged it so they appear to be creases in the skin, the natural product of age."

"I can't see them," Bormann said.

"Yes, I don't think I've ever worked better with a knife, though I do say it myself."

Bormann nodded. "Excellent. And now I would have a word with Herr Strasser alone."

"Certainly, *Reichsleiter,*" Wiedler said.

He and Scheel moved out, and Bormann pulled Rattenhuber back. "The question of the staff, Willi. You know what to do."

"Of course, *Reichsleiter.*"

He went out, and Bormann closed the door and turned to face himself. "So Strasser, the day is finally here."

"So it would appear, *Reichsleiter.* The *Kameradenwerk* — it begins?"

"It begins, my friend," said Martin Bormann, and he started to unbutton his tunic.

Wiedler and the other man waited patiently in the laboratory. It was perhaps twenty minutes later that the door opened

163

and Bormann and Strasser appeared. The *Reichsleiter* was in uniform. Strasser wore a slouch hat and a black leather coat.

"And now, *Reichsleiter,*" Professor Wiedler began.

"It remains only to say good-bye," Martin Bormann said.

He nodded to Rattenhuber, who was standing by the door. The colonel's Schmeisser bucked in his hands, a stream of bullets knocking Wiedler and Scheel back against the wall. Rattenhuber emptied the magazine and replaced it with a fresh one.

He turned to Bormann, face pale. "The staff?" Bormann inquired.

"I locked them in."

Bormann nodded approvingly. "Good — finish it."

Rattenhuber went outside. A moment later, there was the rattle of the Schmeisser sounding continuously above a chorus of screams. The Russian artillary had started again; the building shook violently far above their heads.

Rattenhuber came back in, walking slowly. "It is done, *Reichsleiter.*"

Bormann nodded. "Good — finish off here now, and we'll go downstairs."

He walked out into the corridor, followed by Strasser. Rattenhuber took the stick grenade from his belt and tossed it in through the door of the laboratory. As the reverberations died away, there was the angry crackling of flames as chemicals ignited.

Smoke drifted out into the corridor as Bormann and Strasser reached the elevator and Rattenhuber ran toward them. "No need to panic," Bormann said. "Plenty of time."

The elevator doors opened. They stepped inside and started down.

When the doors opened at the bottom, Schultz was waiting, a Walther in his hand, his two SS guards behind him, Schmeissers ready.

"No need to worry," Bormann said. "Everything's under control."

"As you say, *Reichsleiter,*" Schultz said, and then he looked at Strasser and his mouth opened in amazement.

"We are leaving now, Schultz, all of

us," Bormann said gently. "Bring in the rest of your men."

Schultz turned, walked a few paces, and whistled, fingers in teeth. A moment later, the two guards from the garage door ran down the ramp.

"If you'd line them up, I'd just like to say a word about the situation we're going to find outside," Bormann said.

"Reichsleiter." Schultz barked orders at his men, they lined up, and he stood in front of them.

"You have done good work. Excellent work." Behind Bormann, Rattenhuber was climbing into the field car behind the MG34. "But now, my friends, the time has come to part."

In the final moment, Schultz realized what was happening. His mouth opened in a soundless cry, but by then Rattenhuber was working the machine gun, driving Schultz and his men back in a mad dance of death across the concrete.

When he finally stopped, a couple of them were still twitching. "Finish it," Bormann ordered.

Rattenhuber picked up his Schmeisser,

166

walked across to the guards, and fired a short burst into the skull of one who still moved. He moved back hastily as blood and brains sprayed his boots, and in the same moment became aware of a harsh metallic click as the MG34 was cocked again.

He swung around to find Strasser standing in the field car behind the machine gun. "To the death, Willi, isn't that what you said?"

His fingers squeezed, the face beneath the brim of the slouch hat totally lacking in any kind of emotion. It was the last thing Willi Rattenhuber saw before he died.

Strasser stopped firing and jumped down. "It's time I was away. I'll take Schultz's Mercedes."

"And me?"

"I suggest you wait here till eleven o'clock. Start back to the bunker then. You should arrive around midnight, allowing for the state of the streets."

"Dangerous times," Bormann said. "An artillery shell, a piece of shrapnel, a stray bullet, not to mention the possibility of running into a Russian patrol."

"Like the *Führer,* I walk with the certainty of a sleepwalker," Strasser said. "I wear invisible armor, believing completely that nothing will happen to me — to either of us. A great deal depends on us, my friend. The future of many people."

"I know."

Strasser smiled. "I must go now."

He crossed to the open Mercedes touring car and climbed behind the wheel. As he started the engine, Bormann picked up a Schmeisser and hurried across to him. "Take this."

"No, thanks, I won't need it," Strasser said, and he drove away up into the darkness of the ramp.

Ritter was squatting on the ground, his back against the wall, Schmeisser across his knees. His eyes were closed, but he wasn't really asleep and heard the sound of the approaching vehicle as soon as Hoffer, who was on guard.

"Major!" Hoffer called.

"I know," Ritter said.

He stood beside the sergeant major, listening, and Berger joined them. "It isn't a tank, anyway."

"No, some sort of car," Ritter said.

It braked to a halt outside, and steps approached.

The three men waited quietly in the darkness; there was a pause, a slight, eerie creaking, and then the judas gate opened. Ritter and Berger pointed their flashlights at the same moment and picked Strasser out of the darkness.

"Herr Strasser," Berger said cheerfully. "We were just getting ready to go into blazing action. Why can't you whistle a few bars of *'Deutschland Über Alles'* or something?"

"If you could get the doors open, I have a Mercedes outside that would probably be better under cover. We don't want to attract any unwelcome attention."

Hoffer said, "My God, it's the. . . ."

Strasser turned toward them. He looked directly at Ritter and said calmly, "Strasser — the name is Heinrich Strasser. I'm here to act on behalf of the head of the Party Chancellery in the matter you already know of. You were expecting me, Major?"

"Oh, yes," Ritter said. "You were expected." He turned to Hoffer as Berger opened the garage doors. "Bring in Herr Strasser's car for him, Erich."

Strasser put an arm around Berger's shoulders. "Have we got any chance of getting away with this thing?"

"I don't see why not," Berger told him. "To try such a thing at all at this stage is something they won't even be considering. At least that's what I'm counting on."

They moved toward the Stork, talking in low tones. Hoffer drove the Mercedes into the garage, and Ritter closed the doors again.

The sergeant major whispered, "But that man isn't Herr Strasser. It's the *Reichsleiter* himself. What's going on here?"

"I know, Erich, and Berger said they hadn't met, when it's obvious they know each other very well indeed."

"So Berger knows who he really is?"

"And who would that be, Erich?" Ritter put a cigarette in his mouth.

170

"Martin Bormann or Heinrich Strasser —
what's in a name, and if he prefers one to
the other, who are we to argue?"

"Major Ritter," Strasser called. "One
moment, if you don't mind." They
crossed to the plane, and Strasser looked
at his watch. "Nine o'clock now. Captain
Berger thinks we should leave around
midnight."

"So I understand," Ritter said. "What
about takeoff? I mean, it will be pitch-
dark — unless they send bombers over
and start a few more fires, that is."

"When we go, we go very fast," Berger
said. "I've got a case of parachute flares
in the Stork. I'll start the engine, and the
moment I'm ready to go, I'd like you to
fire the first one. After the first hundred
yards, another. We might even need a
third, I'm not sure. You'll be able to fire
the pistol quite easily through the side
window."

"During the actual takeoff period, then,
we will be considerably exposed," Strasser
said.

"For two or three minutes only. Of
course, once we're airborne, the darker

the better, but unless you want to end up on top of the Victory Column. . . ." He shrugged.

"Anything but that, Captain," Strasser said. "It should, however, prove an exhilarating few minutes."

Ritter went and sat on a packing case near the door. He put a cigarette in his mouth and felt for a match. Strasser walked across and produced a lighter.

"Thank you," Ritter said.

"Is there anything you would like me to explain?"

"I don't think so," Ritter said. "The *Reichsleiter*'s orders were quite explicit."

"Good, then I think I'll get a little rest. Something tells me I'm going to need my strength before the night is out."

He moved away, and Hoffer, who had been hovering nearby, came and squatted beside Ritter, his back against the wall. "Well, what did he have to say?"

"What did you expect?" Ritter asked.

"Didn't he offer you some sort of explanation?"

"He asked me if there was anything I'd like him to explain. I said there wasn't.

172

Is that what you meant?''

"Yes, Major." Hoffer's voice sounded totally resigned now. "That was exactly what I meant."

At eleven-thirty the Russian bombardment started again, spasmodically at first, but within fifteen minutes it was in full voice.

Berger stood by the doors, checking his watch in the glow of his flashlight. At five minutes to midnight precisely, he said, "All right, let's have those doors open and take her out."

The night sky was very dark, occasionally illuminated by brilliant flashes as shells exploded, although they seemed to be concentrating on the area farther to the east. The four men took the Stork out, two on each wing, and turned her around in the side street. There was just enough room, the wall on either side only inches away from the wing tips.

The sounds of battle increased in the middle distance, and Berger, who pushed beside Ritter, said, "Just think, hundreds of thousands of people trapped in this holocaust tonight face certain death, and yet, if the engine starts and the propeller turns, we, by some special dispensation, will live.''

''Perhaps — perhaps not.''

''You've no faith, my friend.''

''Ask me again when we're passing over the Victory Column.''

They turned the Stork into the East - West Avenue, the wheels crunching over broken glass.

''What about your wind direction, Berger?'' Strasser asked. ''These things should always be pointing the right way, am I right?''

''As far as I can judge, there's a crosswind,'' Berger said. ''North to south, not that it makes much difference. We don't, after all, have a great deal of choice.''

The avenue was very dark and quiet, the Russian artillery devoting itself exclusively to the district around Potsdamerplatz. Berger said, ''Right. Everybody in, except Major Ritter.''

Ritter said, ''What do you want me to do?''

Berger handed him a flare gun and

cartridge. "Walk up the avenue about fifty yards and wait. The moment you hear the engine start, fire the pistol, then turn and run back as fast as you can."

"All right," Ritter said. "I think I can handle that."

Hoffer pulled at his sleeve. "Let me, Major."

"Don't be stupid," Ritter said coldly.

He walked away into the darkness, suddenly angry — with himself as well as Hoffer. The sergeant major meant well, he knew that, but there were times. . . . Perhaps they'd been together for too long.

He was counting out the paces under his breath as he walked, and now he paused and rammed the cartridge home. It was quiet, except for the dull rumble of the guns, and when the engine of the Fieseler Storch roared into life, the noise was shattering. Ritter raised the pistol and fired a couple of seconds later. The flare started to descend on its parachute, bathing the avenue in a cold, white glare for a few moments only.

There were two Russian tanks and half a company of infantry sixty or seventy yards up the street. Ritter saw the white faces, heard the voices raised excitedly, and turned and ran like hell toward the Stork.

They picked him up on the move — Strasser holding the door open while Hoffer reached out to grab him by the scruff of the neck — and already the Russians were firing.

Ritter fell into the cabin on his hands and knees, and Berger yelled excitedly, "More light. I'm going to need more light."

Ritter fumbled in the box for another flare. The Stork was roaring down the avenue now, its tail lifting, but already one of the tanks had started to move. Berger had to swerve violently at the last moment, his starboard wing tip just missing the tank's turret, and for a moment seemed to lose control.

But a second later he was back on course again. Ritter put his hand out of the window and discharged the flare. In its sudden glare, the Victory Column seemed terrifyingly close, but Berger held on grimly. She yawed to starboard in the crosswind, and he applied a little rudder correction.

And then, quite suddenly, they were airborne, lifting off the avenue in a hail of rifle bullets, the Victory Column rushing to meet them.

"We'll hit! We'll hit!" Hoffer cried, but Berger held on grimly, refusing to sacrifice power for height, and only at the very last moment did he pull the stick back into his stomach, taking the Stork clear of the top of the Victory Column by fifteen or twenty feet.

"Dear God, we made it. How truly amazing," Strasser said.

"Surely you never doubted me, *Reichsleiter?*" Berger laughed — unaware in the excitement of the moment of his slip of the tongue — stamped on the right rudder, and turned away across what was left of the rooftops of Berlin.

It was at roughly the same moment that the SS guard on duty at the exit of the bunker leading onto Hermann-Göringstrasse heard a vehicle approach. A field car turned into the entrance of the ramp and braked to a halt. The driver, a shadowy figure in the gloom, got out and came forward.

"Identify yourself!" the sentry demanded.

Martin Bormann moved into the circle of lamplight. The sentry drew himself together. "I'm sorry, *Reichsleiter*. I didn't realize it was you."

"A bad night out there."

"Yes, *Reichsleiter*."

"But it will get better, my friend, very soon now, for all of us. You must believe that." Bormann patted him on the shoulder and moved down the ramp into the darkness.

Eight

There was no immediate easing of tension in the Stork, for as they flew across Berlin, the Russian artillery bombardment seemed to chase them all the way. There were numerous fires in many parts of the city, and the darkness crackled with electricity on the edge of things as one shell after another found its target.

"Something to remember — eh, Major?" Strasser said, looking down at the holocaust. "The Twilight of the Gods."

"All we need is a score by Wagner," Ritter said, "to thoroughly enjoy ourselves. We have been well trained, we Germans, to appreciate the finer things."

"Oh, it would be worse," Strasser pointed out. "We could be down there."

The Stork rocked violently, and something rattled against the fuselage.

"Antiaircraft fire," Berger cried. "I'm going down."

He threw the Stork into a sudden, violent corkscrew that seemed to last forever, the whine of the engine rising to fever pitch, but finally — and only when the fires below seemed very close indeed — he pulled back the stick and leveled out.

Hoffer turned his head away and was violently sick. Strasser said, with a slight edge of contempt to his voice, "He has no stomach for it, I think, your sergeant major."

"So what?" Ritter said. "They tell me Grand Admiral Dönitz is sick every time he puts to sea, but he's still Germany's greatest sailor."

Gradually, the flames — the darting points of light on the ground — faded into the night. Berger shouted above the roar of the engine, "I'll tell you something now we're out of it. I never thought we'd make it. Not for a moment."

"You did well," Strasser said. "A brilliant piece of flying."

It was Ritter, suddenly irritated, who said, "We're not out of the woods yet."

180

"Nonsense," Berger shouted. "A milk run from now on."

And he was right, for conditions could not have been more in their favor. They flew on through the night at five hundred feet in darkness and heavy rain, Berger sitting there at the controls, a slight, fixed smile on his mouth, obviously thoroughly enjoying himself.

Hoffer fell asleep. Strasser, who was sitting next to Berger, made notes in his diary in the light from the control panel. Ritter smoked a cigarette and watched him, wondering what was going on behind the eyes in that calm, expressionless face — but that was a pointless exercise. Just as much a waste of time as asking himself what the hell he was doing here.

It was like a chess game. You made a move in answer to one. A totally open-ended situation. No means of knowing what the end would be until it was reached. And in the final analysis, did it really matter? He leaned back in his seat and closed his eyes.

He came awake instantly in response to a hand on his shoulder. Strasser said, "We're close to Plauen now. Berger's trying to raise the airstrip."

Ritter glanced at his watch and saw, with a slight shock of surprise, that it was three o'clock. He turned to Hoffer. "How are you?"

"Better, Major, much better, now that there's nothing left to come up. I never could stand flying — any kind of flying. Remember that transport plane which brought us out of Stalingrad?"

Berger was talking, using his throat mike. "Red Fox, this is Valhalla. Do you read me?" There was only the confused crackling of the static. He tried again, adjusting one of the dials. "Red Fox, this is Valhalla." A moment later, a voice broke through the static. "Valhalla, this is Red Fox. I read you strength five."

"I am coming in now for refueling as arranged," Berger said. "What is your situation?"

"Heavy rain, slight ground mist, visibility about a hundred and fifty yards. We'll put the landing lights on for you."

"All the comforts of home," Berger said. "My thanks." A moment later, two parallel lines of light flared in the darkness to starboard. "I can see you now," he called. "I'm coming in."

He turned into the wind and started his descent. Ritter said, "Do we stay here for any length of time?"

"For as long as it takes to fill the tanks," Strasser said. "We've still got a long way to go."

They drifted down through the rain and mist into the light, there was the sudden squeal of the tires biting as Berger applied the brakes, they slowed, the tail going down.

And then Berger gave a cry of dismay, for the trucks that raced out of the darkness on either side, converging on them, had red stars emblazoned on their sides.

"Get out of here!" Strasser cried.

Berger increased engine revs. The soldiers in the trucks were already firing. A bullet shattered one of the side windows. Ritter shoved the barrel of a Schmeisser through and let off a long burst. And then they were really moving again, racing toward the end of the runway, the trucks trying to keep up with them, and losing. Berger pulled back the stick; they climbed up into the darkness.

He leveled off at three thousand feet. Strasser said, "Now what?"

For the first time, his composure seemed to have deserted him, and he actually looked worried. For some reason, Ritter found the spectacle strangely comforting.

"The only thing I'm certain of at the moment is that I've got fuel for forty minutes, and that includes the reserve tank," Berger said. And, in the crisis, it was Ritter he turned to. "Have a look at the *Luftwaffe* area map, the one on top. See what there is close to our line fifty miles south of here."

Ritter spread the map across his knees and switched on his flashlight. "There's a place called Plodin marked with a red ring. Perhaps forty miles. According to the key, that means reserve feeder station. What's that?"

"Part of the backup system for nightfighters. The sort of place they can put down if they run into trouble. A

184

hangar and a single runway, usually grass. Probably a private air club before the war. I'll see if I can raise them."

"You raised somebody last time," Strasser said. "They answered in excellent German, and look what happened."

"What do you want me to do?" Berger demanded. "I can't see what we're getting into unless I go down because you won't get even a touch of gray in the sky before four o'clock. I'll be out of fuel twenty minutes before then by my reckoning. You may have read that in such situations people often jump for it. Unfortunately, we only have one parachute, and I'm sitting on it."

"All right, I get the point," Strasser said. "Do as you think fit."

He sat there, his jaw working, fists tightly clenched. He's thrown, Ritter thought — and badly — because, for once, he isn't in charge. He has no control. He isn't playing the game — the game's playing him.

Berger was using plain language. "This is Fieseler Storch AK40, calling Plodin. I am dangerously short of fuel and urgently

185

require assistance. Come in, please."

There was an immediate response. A voice said urgently, "Suggest you try elsewhere. We've been completely cut off by Russian troops since seven o'clock last night."

"I'm afraid I have no choice in the matter," Berger told him. "My estimated time of arrival is oh-three-forty. Five minutes after that, if I'm still airborne, I'll be gliding."

There was silence, only the static, and then the voice said, "Very well, we'll do what we can."

"Right, gentlemen, here we go again," Berger said, and he started to descend.

Two aircraft were burning at the side of the runway as they went in. "Expensive landing lights," Berger said, "but I'm grateful, nevertheless."

There were a couple of hangars, a small control tower, a complex of huts a hundred yards or so away, some trucks parked beside them. There was no sound of conflict, no shooting, only the two planes burning at the side of the runway

186

as they touched down, an old Dornier-17 and a JU-88S nightfighter.

As Berger taxied toward the control tower, half a dozen ground crew ran forward, two of them carrying wheel blocks, and the door opened and an officer stood there framed in the light.

He was an *Oberleutnant,* his *Luftwaffe Fliegerblüse* open at the neck. He was twenty-three or -four, badly in need of a shave, and looked tired.

Berger held out his hand. "Heini Berger. Not too worried about the blackout, I see?"

"What would be the point," the *Oberleutnant* said, "with those two blazing like the candles on a Christmas tree? Our water main was fractured in the initial bombardment, so we've no firefighting facilities. My name's Fraenkel, by the way."

"You are in command here?" Strasser asked.

"Yes, the commanding officer, *Hauptsturmführer* Hagen, was killed last night. Russian tanks shelled us at eleven o'clock and raked the buildings with

187

machine-gun fire."

"No infantry attack?" Ritter asked.

Fraenkel took in the uniform, the Knight's Cross with Oak Leaves and Swords, and straightened his shoulders. "No, they stayed out there in the dark, *Sturmbannführer*. Shelled us again approximately an hour ago. That's when the planes got it."

Ritter walked forward into the shadows. There were bodies here and there, and on the far side of the runway another Junkers tilted forward on its nose, tail up, an enormous ragged furrow in the ground indicating where it had belly-landed.

He turned and came back to the others. "How many men have you left?"

"Half a dozen," Fraenkel said. "The aircrews of those planes all got away before we were hit. And then there are some of your people. Arrived last night just before the Russians. They're down at the huts now. You can just see their trucks — four of them."

"My people?" Ritter said. "You mean by this SS, I presume. Which unit?"

"Einsatzgruppen, Sturmbannführer."

Ritter's face was very pale. He reached out and grabbed Fraenkel by the front of his *Fliegerblüse*. "You will not mention scum like that in the same breath with the *Waffen*-SS, you hear me?"

Einsatzgruppen, action groups or special commandos, had been formed by Himmler prior to the invasion of Russia. They were, in effect, extermination squads, recruited from the jails of Germany, officered by SD and Gestapo officers. Occasionally soldiers of the *Waffen*-SS convicted of some criminal offense were transferred to them as punishment. The phrase "scum of the earth" summed them up perfectly.

It was Strasser who moved forward to pull Ritter away. "Easy, Major, easy does it. What are they doing now, down there?"

"Drinking," Fraenkel said. "And they have some women with them."

"Women?"

"Girls — from the camps. Jewish, I think."

There was a nasty silence. Berger said, nodding toward the blazing wrecks, "Why didn't they fly those out while the going was good?''

''They landed here because they were low on fuel in the first place, and we didn't have any. Used our last a fortnight ago.''

''No fuel,'' Strasser cut in. ''But you must have something, surely, and the Stork doesn't need much — isn't that right, Berger?''

''If it were only ten gallons you wanted, I still couldn't oblige,'' Fraenkel said.

Berger looked toward the Junkers on the far side of the hanger, the one that had crash-landed. ''What about that? Nothing in the tanks?''

''We siphoned the fuel out of her a couple of weeks ago.'' Fraenkel hesitated. ''There might be a few gallons left, but not enough to get you anywhere.''

There was a sudden burst of laughter and singing from the huts. Ritter said to Berger, ''Am I right in assuming that a workhorse like the Fieseler Storch doesn't necessarily need high-octane aviation gasoline to be able to fly?''

''No. She'll function on stuff a lot more

crude than that. With reduced performance, of course.''

Ritter nodded toward the huts. ''Four trucks down there. I should think their tanks between them would hold forty or fifty gallons. Would that do?''

''I don't see why not,'' Berger said. ''Especially if we can siphon a few gallons out of the Junkers to mix with it.''

Ritter said to Fraenkel, ''All right?''

The *Oberleutnant* nodded. ''As far as I'm concerned. But the gentlemen of the *Einsatzgruppen* may have other ideas.''

Strasser said, ''We are on a special mission of vital importance to the Reich. My orders are signed by the *Führer* himself.''

''Sorry, *mein Herr,*'' Fraenkel said, ''but strange things are happening in Germany today. There are actually people around for whom that kind of talk doesn't cut much ice. I suspect that's particularly true of these characters.''

''Then we must change their minds for them,'' Ritter said. ''How many are there?''

''Thirty or so.''

"Good. Put a couple of your men to the task of siphoning the Junkers. Send the rest to the trucks. I'll deal with these" — here he hesitated — "these gentlemen of the *Einsatzgruppen.*" He turned to Strasser. "You agree?"

Strasser smiled slightly. "My dear Ritter, I wouldn't miss it for anything."

There was no one at the trucks, no guard at the steps leading up to the door of the mess hall, as Ritter marched briskly across the compound, Strasser a pace behind his left shoulder.

"I must be mad," Strasser said.

"Oh, I don't know. Like we used to say about those chairborne bastards at headquarters, it does a man good to get up off his backside occasionally and go up to the front to see what it's like for the ordinary troops. A little action and passion for you, *Reichsleiter.*"

He paused at the bottom of the steps to adjust his gloves. Strasser said, "Why do you call me that, Major?"

"You mean I'm mistaken?"

"To the best of my knowledge,

Reichsleiter Martin Bormann is at present in his office in the *Führerbunker,* in Berlin. Even in this day and age, it would take a rather large miracle for a man to be in two places at once."

"Simple enough if there were two of him."

"Which would raise the problem of who is real and who is only the image in the mirror," Strasser said. "A neat point, but relevant, I think you'll agree."

"True," Ritter said. "And perhaps, in the final analysis, an academic point only." He smiled ironically. "Shall we go in now?"

He opened the door and stepped into the light. At first he and Strasser went completely unnoticed, which was hardly surprising, for the men who crowded the tables before them were mostly drunk. There were perhaps a dozen girls huddled in a corner at the far end of the room, hair unkempt, clothes tattered, faces grimy with dirt. In fact, the faces were the most interesting feature about them, the eyes dull, totally without hope, with the look of trapped animals waiting for the butcher's knife.

There was a burly *Hauptsturmführer* seated at one end of the longest table. He was a brute of a man, with slanting eyes and high, Slavic cheekbones. He had a small, dark-haired girl on his knee, an arm around her neck, holding her tight, while his other hand was busy under her skirt. She couldn't have been more than sixteen. She saw Ritter first, her eyes widening in amazement, and the *Hauptsturmführer,* becoming aware of her stillness, turned to see what she was looking at.

Ritter stood, hands on hips, legs slightly apart, and it was as if a chill wind had swept into the room, Death himself come to join them. The *Hauptsturmführer* took in that magnificent black uniform, the decorations, the dark eyes under the peak of the service cap, the silver death's-head gleaming.

"You are in charge here, I presume?" Ritter inquired softly.

The captain shoved the girl off his knee and stood up. The room had gone absolutely quiet. "That's right," he said. "Grushetsky."

"Ukrainian?" Ritter said, his distaste plain. "I thought so."

Grushetsky turned red with anger. "And who the hell might you be?"

"Your superior officer," Ritter told him calmly. "You're aware that there are Russians out there in the dark who might have a more than passing interest in getting their hands on you, and yet you don't even post a guard."

"No need," Grushetsky said. "They won't come in before dawn, I know how they work. We'll be driving out of here long before then. In the meantime . . ." He put an arm around the girl and pulled her close.

"Sorry," Ritter said, "but you won't be driving anywhere, I'm afraid. We need your gasoline for our aircraft."

"You what?" Grushetsky cried.

"Show him your orders," Ritter said casually to Strasser. He glanced at the girl again, ignoring Grushetsky, then walked to the end of the room and looked at the others.

Strasser said, "I'll read it to you. From the leader and chancellor of the State.

Most secret. You recognize the name at the bottom of the page, I trust. Adolf Hitler.''

''Yes, well, he's in Berlin, and this is here,'' Grushetsky said. ''And you'll take the gasoline from those tanks over my dead body.''

''That can be arranged.'' Ritter raised his right arm casually and clicked his fingers. A window was smashed as a Schmeisser poked through, Berger's smiling face behind it. The door crashed open, and Hoffer came in, holding another Schmeisser.

''You see,'' Ritter said to the girl, whom Grushetsky had released now. ''It is still possible for the best to happen in this worst of all possible worlds. What's your name?''

''Bernstein,'' she said. ''Clara Bernstein.''

He recognized her accent instantly. ''French?''

''That's what it says on my birth certificate, but to you bastards I'm just another dirty Jew.''

In a strange way, it was as if they were

alone. "What do you want me to do, say I'm sorry?" Ritter asked her in French. "Would that help?"

"Not in the slightest."

"Positive action then, Clara Bernstein. You and your friends go now. Out there in the darkness beyond the perimeter wire there are Russian soldiers. I suggest you turn toward them, hands high in the air, yelling like hell. I think you will find they will take you in."

"Here, what the hell is going on here?" Grushetsky demanded in his bad German.

Ritter rounded on him. "Shut your mouth, damn you. Feet together when you speak to me, you understand? Attention, all of you."

And they responded, all of them, even those far gone in drink trying to draw themselves together. The girl called to the others in German. They hesitated. She cried, "All right, stay and die here if you want, but I'm getting out."

She ran outside, and the rest of the girls broke instantly and went after her. Their voices could be heard clearly as they ran across the runway to the perimeter wire.

Ritter paced up and down between the tables. "You believe yourselves to be soldiers of the German Reich — a natural assumption in view of the uniforms you wear — but you are mistaken. Now, let me tell you what you are, in simple terms, so that you can understand."

Grushetsky gave a roar of rage and pulled out his Luger, and Strasser, who'd been waiting for something like this to happen for the past few moments, fired twice through the pocket of his leather coat, shattering the Ukrainian's spine, killing him instantly, driving him across one of the tables.

Several men cried out and reached for weapons, and Berger and Hoffer both fired at the same moment, dropping four men between them.

Ritter said to Hoffer, "All right, collect their weapons and hold them here until we're ready to go."

One of the *Einsatzgruppen* took an involuntary step forward. "But *Sturmbannführer*. Without weapons we shall be totally unable to defend ourselves, and the Russians . . ."

"Can have you," Ritter said, and he walked outside, followed by Strasser.

Fraenkel walked to meet them. "It's worked quite well. We've managed to get about fifteen gallons of aviation fuel out of the Junkers. Mixed with gasoline from the trucks, it means we can give you full tanks."

"How long," Strasser asked, "before we're ready to go?"

"Five or ten minutes."

Ritter offered the young *Luftwaffe* lieutenant a cigarette. "I'm sorry we can't take you with us, you and your men. We leave you in a bad situation."

"The moment you've gone, I'm going to go out there and ask for terms," Fraenkel said. "I can't see much point in any other course of action, not at this stage."

"Perhaps you're right," Ritter said. "And I'd keep those bastards back there in the mess hall under lock and key until the Russians get here if I were you. It might help."

A sergeant hurried toward them and saluted. "The Stork's all ready to go now, *Herr Leutnant.*"

There was some movement in the darkness beyond the perimeter, the sound of an engine starting up. Ritter turned and shouted, "Berger! Erich! Let's get out of here. It looks as if the Russians are starting to move in."

He ran back toward the hangar, followed by Strasser. As they scrambled up into the cabin of the Stork, Hoffer and Berger arrived. Berger didn't even bother to strap himself in. He got the door closed and started the engines instantly, so that the Stork was moving down the runway and turning into the wind in a matter of seconds.

The flames from the burning planes had died down, and the field was almost totally dark now. "If you believe in prayer, now's the time," Berger cried, and he pushed up the engine revs and took the Stork forward.

They plunged headlong into darkness, and Ritter leaned back in the seat and closed his eyes, totally unafraid, consumed only by curiosity to know what it would be like. Is this it? he asked himself. Could this possibly be the final moment after all these years? And then the Stork lifted as Berger pulled back the stick, and they climbed up into the darkness.

Ritter turned to find Strasser examining the bullet holes in his coat. "My thanks, but I hardly expected to see the day when you would lay yourself on the line to defend the rights of Jews."

"What happens to those girls back there is a matter of complete indifference to me," Strasser told him. "You, on the other hand, are an essential part of this operation, which could well fail without you. That was the only reason I shot that Slavic ape back there."

"I should be thankful for small mercies, it would seem."

"No more empty gestures, my dear Ritter, I beg you."

"Empty?"

"A fair description. I should imagine the Russians will rape those girls with an enthusiasm at least equal to that of Grushetsky and his motley crew, or had you really imagined it would be different?"

Dawn was a gradual affair from about four-thirty as they flew onward through heavy clouds — at first merely an impression of light, no more than that. Strasser and Hoffer both slept, but Berger seemed as cheerful and relaxed as ever, whistling softly through his teeth.

"You love it," Ritter said. "Flying, I mean."

"More than any woman." Berger grinned. "Which is saying a lot. For a long time I worried about what I would do when it was all over — the war, I mean. No more flying, not for the defeated."

"But now you don't?"

It was a statement as much as a question, and caught Berger off guard. "Plenty of places to go, when you think about it. Places where there's always work for a good pilot. South America, for instance. The *Reichs* —" He pulled himself up quickly. "Herr Strasser already has a pipeline organized that should ensure that some of us will live to fight another day."

"A charming prospect," Ritter said. "I congratulate you."

When he leaned back, he realized that Strasser was awake and watching through half-open eyes. He smiled and leaned forward, a hand on Berger's shoulder.

"He likes to talk, my young friend here. A conversationalist by nature. A good thing he's such a brilliant pilot."

Strasser was smiling genially, but his fingers were hooked into the shoulder so tightly that Berger winced with pain. "I'll take her up now," he shouted. "Try to get above this shit and see what's what. We should be nearly there."

He pulled back the stick and started to climb, but the heavy clouds showed no signs of diminishing. Finally he leveled out. "No good. I'll have to try it the other way. Nothing else for it. Hang on and we'll see what the state of things is downstairs."

He pushed the stick forward, taking the Stork into a shallow dive. The clouds became darker, more menacing, boiling around them, hail rattling against the fuselage, and Berger had to hang onto the stick with all his strength. They were at four thousand and still descending, Berger hanging on grimly, and Hoffer gave an involuntary cry of fear. And then, at three thousand feet, they emerged into the light of day and found themselves, as Berger leveled out, drifting along the course of a wide valley, pine trees very green against the snow, the peaks of the Bavarian Alps rising on either side of them.

"Somebody on board must live right," Berger said. "Now have a look at the *Luftwaffe* area map and see if you can find Arnheim, Major."

It was no more than a feeder station, had never been any more than that. There were a single runway, two hangars. No control tower, simply a couple of single-story concrete huts with tin roofs.

Snow was falling gently, but there was no wind to speak of, and the Fieseler Storch came in from the north like a gray ghost, her engine barely a murmur. Her wheels touched, and there were two puffs of white as snow spurted beneath them.

Strasser said, "Straight up to the

hangars. I want her under cover."

"All right." Berger nodded.

When they were close enough, Strasser, Ritter, and Hoffer all got out and opened the hangar doors. Berger taxied inside and cut the engine. He laughed out loud as he jumped to the ground.

"So, we made it. The Victory Column to Arnheim in five and a half hours." He helped Ritter pull the doors closed. "Smell that mountain air."

Hoffer had gone through the connecting door into the next hangar, and now he returned. "There's a field car in there, Major," he told Ritter. "A basket in the back."

"Good," Strasser said. "I've been expecting that."

He led the way in, and the others followed. The basket was of the picnic type. There was also a small leather suitcase with it. Strasser placed it on the hood of the car and opened it. Inside, there was a radio transmitter and receiver of a kind Ritter had never seen before.

"Excellent," Strasser said. "The best in the world at the present time. Came to us courtesy of an agent of the British Special Operations Executive." He checked his watch. "Five-thirty — am I right?"

"So it would appear," Ritter said.

"Good." Strasser rubbed his hands briskly. "There's a nip in this mountain air. We'll have something to eat, a hot drink, and then . . ."

"Something to eat?" Berger said.

"But of course. What do you think is in this basket?"

Berger unstrapped it and raised the lid. Inside there were three loaves of black bread, sausages, butter, boiled eggs, two large thermos flasks, and a bottle of schnapps. Berger unscrewed the cap of one of the flasks and removed the cork. He inhaled deeply, an expression of delight appearing on his face.

"Coffee — hot coffee." He poured a little into the cup and tasted it. "And it's real," he announced. "A miracle."

"See how good I am to you?" Strasser said.

"You certainly have a flair for organization," Ritter told him.

"It's been said before." Strasser

glanced at his watch.

"And then," Ritter said, "after we've eaten? You were saying?"

Strasser smiled. "I'm expecting another aircraft at seven o'clock. A very reliable man, so he should get here right on time." He opened the small judas gate set in the main door and stepped outside, turning his face up to the snow. "What air. It makes things feel clean again."

Hoffer passed Ritter a cup of coffee and a piece of black bread. "But I don't understand, Major. This other plane he's expecting. Who is it? Why won't he tell us?"

"Probably the *Führer* himself, Erich." Ritter smiled. "After the events of the past couple of days, nothing would surprise me."

It was at precisely five minutes to seven when Berger, lounging against the hood of the field car, smoking a cigarette, straightened. "There's a plane coming now — I hear it."

Ritter opened the judas and stepped outside. Snow was still falling softly, the flakes brushing against his face when he looked up. The sound was still some distance away, but real enough.

He went back inside. "He's right."

Strasser had the suitcase open, the microphone in his hand. He adjusted the dials and said, in English, to everyone's surprise, "Valhalla Exchange. Valhalla Exchange. Plain language. Do you receive me?"

An American voice answered with startling clarity. "Valhalla Exchange. Odin here. Am I cleared for landing?"

"All clear. Closing down now."

He stowed away the microphone and closed the case. Ritter said, "Are we permitted to know what that was all about?"

"Later," Strasser said impatiently. "For the moment, let's get these doors open. I want him under cover and out of sight the moment he's landed."

Ritter shrugged and nodded to Hoffer and, with Berger's assistance, they got the doors open. The sound of the plane, whatever it was, was very close now, and they all moved outside and waited.

And then, suddenly, she was there, coming in out of the grayness at the north end of the runway, twin-engined, camouflaged, and entirely familiar to at least one man there — Berger — who cried, "God in heaven, that's an American Dakota."

"So it would appear," Strasser said.

"Is nothing impossible to you, then?" Ritter asked.

"My dear Ritter, if I'd needed it, I could have had a Flying Fortress or an RAF Lancaster."

The Dakota landed, snow rising in a cloud around her as she rolled forward, turning in toward them as Strasser waved his arms, and then she was close enough for them to see the pilot in the cockpit, the American Army Air Corps insignia plain against the green-and-brown camouflage.

The plane taxied into the hangar; for a moment, the din was colossal, and then, suddenly, the engines were cut. "Right. Get these doors closed," Strasser ordered.

As they turned from the task, the hatch

was opened and the pilot appeared. He had a dark, saturnine face and appeared to be in his early thirties. He was wearing a sidecap with an SS death's-head badge, and a flying jacket. He removed the jacket and caused something of a sensation.

He wore a beautifully tailored uniform of field gray. Under the eagles on his left sleeve was a Stars and Stripes shield, and the cuff-title on his left wrist carried the legend "George Washington Legion" in Gothic lettering. His decorations included the Iron Cross, Second and First Class, and he wore the Winter War ribbon. When he spoke, his German was excellent, but with a definite American accent.

"So, you made it?" he said to Strasser. "Amazing, but then I should have learned to believe you by now."

"Good to see you." Strasser shook hands, then turned to the others. "Gentlemen, allow me to introduce *Hauptsturmführer* Earl Jackson. This is Heini Berger, who got us out of Berlin in the Stork."

"Captain." Berger shook hands. "It gave me something of a shock when I saw you dropping down out of the sky, I can tell you."

"And *Sturmbannführer* Karl Ritter."

Jackson held out his hand, but Ritter ignored him and turned to Strasser. "And now we talk, I think."

"My dear Ritter," Strasser began.

"Now!" Ritter said sharply, and he opened the connecting door and went into the next hangar.

"All right," Strasser said. "What is it now?"

"This American — Jackson — who is he? I want to know."

"Come now, Ritter, the *Waffen*-SS has recruited men from almost every nation possible, you know that. Everything from Frenchmen to Turks. There's even an English contingent — the *Britisches Freikorps*. There have been, admittedly, only a handful of Americans in the George Washington Legion. Exprisoners of war, recruited by prospects of unlimited liquor and women. Jackson is a different specimen, believe me. He flew for the Finns against the Russians in their first war, stayed on in their air force, and got

211

caught up in their second bout with the Russians when they joined our side. When the Finns sued for peace last year, he transferred to us.''

''A traitor is a traitor, however you wrap it up.''

''A point of view, but not objective enough, my friend. All I see is a superb pilot, a brave and resourceful man with a highly specialized background which makes him peculiarly suitable for my purposes. May I also add that, as his own people would most certainly hang him if ever they succeeded in getting their hands on him, he has no choice other than to serve my cause. It is his only chance to live. Now, have you anything else to say?''

''I think you've made your point,'' Ritter said.

Strasser opened the door and led the way back into the other hangar. He made no reference to what had happened, simply took a map from his pocket and unfolded it across the hood of the field car. They all crowded around.

''Here is Arnheim. Arlberg is eight or

nine miles south of here. Ten miles to the west, there's a farm on the edge of the forest. That's where the Finns are.''

"Do we all go?" Ritter asked.

"No, *Hauptsturmführer* Berger can stay with the planes.''

"And me?" Jackson said.

"No, you might well be useful in other ways. You come with us.'' The American didn't look too pleased, but there was obviously nothing he could do about it. Strasser added, ''And from now on, as what might be termed the military part of the operation starts, *Sturmbannführer* Ritter will be in sole command.''

"You mean I have a totally free hand?" Ritter said.

"Well, a little advice now and then never hurt anyone, did it?'' Strasser smiled. "Still, no point in crossing bridges until we come to them, Major. Let's get these Finnish barbarians sorted out first.''

Nine

At the field hospital, Mullholland had had a hard night. Eleven wounded from a skirmish near Innsbruck had been brought in at ten o'clock. He and his team had worked steadily through the night on cases of varying seriousness.

His final patient, a young lieutenant, had two machine-gun bullets in the left lung. Mullholland had used every trick in his now considerable repertoire for more than two hours. The boy had died at seven A.M. after suffering a massive hemorrhage.

When Mullholland went outside, it was snowing gently. He lit a cigarette and stood there, breathing in the clean air, and Sergeant Major Grant approached with a cup of tea.

"A rotten night, sir."

"I could have done without it. The bloody war is as good as over, or so they tell us, and here we are, still up to our armpits in blood and destruction. If I sound depressed, it's because I've just lost a patient. A bad way to start the day." He sipped some of the tea. "How's our German friend?"

"Not too bad, sir. He's been asking for you."

"All right, Sergeant Major," Mullholland said wearily. "Let's see what he wants."

Grant led the way down the line of hospital tents and turned into No. 3. Schenck was in the end bed. He lay there, his heavily bandaged arm on top of the blankets. Mullholland unhooked the chart from the foot of the bed to check on his condition, and Schenck's eyes fluttered open.

"Good morning, *Herr Oberst.*"

"And how are you today?"

"Alive, it would seem, for which I am grateful. I thought that perhaps the arm . . ."

"No, it's fine, or it will be. You

speak excellent English.''

''I worked for ten years in the City of London — not far from St. Paul's — for an export agency.''

''I see.''

There was a pause, then Schenck said, ''Have you had a chance to consider General Canning's letter?''

Mullholland sat on the edge of the bed, suddenly very tired. ''I'm in something of a difficulty here. This isn't a combat unit. We're medical people. I've been thinking that perhaps the best thing I can do is get onto brigade headquarters and see if they can manage anything.''

''Are they nearby?''

''Last I heard, about twenty miles west of here, but the situation, of course, is very fluid.''

Schenck tried to push himself up. ''Forgive me, *Herr Oberst,* but time is of the essence in this matter. I must stress that, to our certain knowledge, orders from Berlin have gone out, authorizing the execution of all *prominenti*. If the SS reach Arlberg first, then General Canning, your own Colonel Birr, and the rest are

216

certain to die. Colonel Hesser wishes to avoid the situation at all costs and is willing to formally surrender his command immediately.''

''But the area between here and Arlberg is in a very confused state — no one knows that better than you yourself. It would require a fighting unit to get through. They could run into trouble.''

''A small patrol, that's all I ask. A couple of jeeps, perhaps. An officer and a few men. If I go with them to show the best route, we could be there in four hours, with any kind of luck at all. They could return at once with the prisoners. General Canning and the others could be here by this evening.''

''And just as much chance that they might run into units of your forces on the way back. They could be taking a hell of a chance, especially the ladies.''

''So, what do you suggest, *Herr Oberst?* That they wait for the SS?''

Mullholland sighed wearily. ''No, you're right, of course. Give me half an hour. I'll see what I can work out.''

He went straight to his command tent

and sat behind the desk. "It's a mess, isn't it, but he's right. We've got to do something."

"I've been thinking, sir," Grant said. "What about the three Americans? Captain Howard, the Ranger officer, and his men?"

Mullholland paused in the act of taking a bottle of Scotch from his drawer. "The survivors of that mess on the Salzburg road last week? By God, you might have something there. What shape is Howard in?"

"It took about fifty stiches to sew him up, sir, if you remember. Shrapnel wounds, but he was on his feet when I last saw him yesterday, and his sergeant and the other bloke weren't wounded."

"See if you can dig him up, and bring him to me."

Grant went out. Mullholland looked at the whisky bottle for a long moment, then he sighed, replaced the cork, and put the bottle back into the drawer, closing it firmly. He lit a cigarette and started on some paperwork. A few moments later, Grant entered.

"Captain Howard, sir."

Mullholland looked up. "Fine, Sergeant Major. Show him in, and see if you can rustle up some tea."

Grant went out, and Howard ducked under the flap a moment later. He wasn't wearing a helmet, and a red, angry-looking scar bisected his forehead, stopping short of the left eye, the stitches still clearly visible. His left hand was heavily bandaged. He was very pale, the eyes sunken, an expression of ineffable weariness on his face.

My God, Mullholland thought, this boy's had about all he can take, and no mistake. He smiled. "Come in, Captain, sit down. With any luck, we might get some tea in a few minutes. Cigarette?"

"Thank you, sir."

Mullholland gave him a light. "How are you feeling?"

"Fine."

Which was as fair a lie as Mullholland had heard in many a day, but he carried on. "I've got a problem I thought you might be able to help me with."

Howard showed no emotion at

all. "I see, sir."

"We carted a German officer in here yesterday with a couple of bullets in him. The unfortunate thing was that he'd been looking for an Allied unit anyway. Had a letter on him from an American general called Canning. Have you heard of him?"

"Hamilton Canning?"

"That's him. He's being held prisoner, along with four other *prominenti,* as the Germans call them." He pushed the blood-stained letter across the table. "But you'll find all the details there."

Howard picked up the letter, read it with lackluster eyes. Grant came in with two mugs of tea and placed them on the desk. Mullholland motioned him to stay.

After a while, the American looked up. "They seem to be in a mess, these people. What do you want me to do about it?"

"I'd like you to go and get them. Accept this Colonel Hesser's surrender formally, then return with the prisoners as soon as possible. The German officer who brought this letter, Lieutenant Schenck, is willing to return with you to show you the way. He was quite badly wounded, but I think we can fix him up well enough to stand the trip.''

"You want me to go?" Howard said.

"And those two men of yours. I've been thinking about it. We could give you an ambulance. Plenty of room then for the others for the return trip."

"Have you any idea what it's like out there, sir, between here and Arlberg?"

"I can guess," Mullholland said evenly.

"And you want me to go with two men and a crippled German?" Howard's voice was flat, unemotional. "Is this an order?"

"No, I've no authority to order you to do anything, Captain, as I think you know. The blunt truth is that I just haven't got anyone else available. This is a medical unit, and as you've seen for yourself, we're up to our eyes in it."

Howard stared down at the letter for a long moment, then he nodded slowly. "I'll put it to Sergeant Hoover and Private Finebaum if that's all right with you, sir. I think, under the circumstances, they should have some choice in the matter."

"Fine," Mullholland said. "But don't take too long about making your decision, please." And he used the phrase Schenck had used to him. "Time really is of the essence in this one."

Howard went out, and Mullholland looked up at Grant. "What do you think?"

"I don't know, sir. He looks as if he's had it to me."

"Haven't we all, Sergeant Major?" Mullholland said wearily.

Finebaum and Hoover shared a pup tent at the end of the rows on the other side of the vehicle area. Hoover was busily writing a letter, while Finebaum crouched in the entrance, heating beans in a mess tin on a portable stove.

"Beans and yet more beans. Don't these Limeys eat anything else?"

"Maybe you'd prefer K-rations," Hoover said.

"Oh, I've got plans for that stuff, Harry," Finebaum said. "After the war, I'm going to buy a whole load of that crap — war surplus, you understand? Then I'm going to take it around to my old grannie, who runs a strictly kosher house. So kosher that even the cat's got religion."

"You mean you're going to feed K-rations to the cat?"

"That's it."

"And break that old woman's heart? I mean, what did she ever do to you?"

"I'll tell you what she did. The day after the Japs bombed Pearl Harbor, she called me in and said, 'Mannie, you know what you've got to do.' Then she opened the front door, pointed me in the general direction of the recruiting office, and shoved."

He spooned beans onto a tin plate and handed it to Hoover. The sergeant said, "You talk too much, but I know how you feel. I'm bored to hell with this place, too."

"When are we going to get out of here?" Finebaum demanded. "I mean, I respect and love our noble captain — nobody more so — but how much longer do we stand around and wait for him to find his goddamned soul?"

"You cut that out," Hoover said. "He's had about all he can take."

223

"In this game there's only two ways to be — alive or dead. Now I've seen a lot of good men go under in the year I've served with you and him. But they're dead, and I'm not. I don't rejoice in it, but it's a fact of life, and I ain't going to sit and cry over them, either."

Hoover put down his plate. "Why, you son of a bitch, I've just made a discovery. You're not doing it because you're here or a patriot or something. You're doing it because you like it. Because it gives you kicks like you've never had before."

"Screw you!"

"What are you after — another battle star? You want to be right up there in the line with those other heroes?"

"What do you want me to do, go back to sewing on fly-buttons in an East Side cellar for thirty bucks a week when I can't get work blowing clarinet? No, thank you. Before I got back to that, I'd rather pull the pin on one of my own grenades. I'll tell you something, Harry." His voice was low, urgent. "I live more in a single day than I did in a year before the war. When my time comes, I hope I take it right between the eyes about one minute before they sign the peace treaty, and if you and the noble captain don't like it, baby, then you can do the other thing."

He got up and, turning, found Howard listening. They stood there, neither Hoover nor Finebaum knowing what the hell to say. It was Howard who spoke first. "Tell me, Finebaum — Garland, Anderson, O'Grady, all those other guys in the outfit, all the way across Europe since D-Day — don't you ever think about them at all? Doesn't the fact of their death have any meaning for you?"

"Those guys are dead — so they're dead. Right, Captain? I mean, maybe some part of my brain is missing or something, but I don't see it any other way."

"And you don't think they accomplished anything?"

"You mean the nobility of war, sir? The strength of our purpose and all that crap? I'm afraid I don't buy that, either. The way I figure it, every day for the past ten thousand years, someone somewhere in the world has been beating hell out of someone else. I think it's in the nature of the species."

"You know something, Finebaum? I'm beginning to think you might have read a book or two."

"Could be, Captain. That just could be."

"All right," Howard said. "You want a little action — I've got a pretty large helping for you. Ever heard of General Hamilton Canning?"

He quickly outlined the situation. When he was finished, Finebaum said, "That's the craziest thing I ever heard of. That's Indian territory out there."

"Forty or fifty miles of it between here and Arlberg."

"And they want *us* to go? Three guys in an ambulance with some Kraut stretcher case?" He started to laugh. "You know? I like it, Captain. Yes, I definitely like it."

"Okay. So you go and tell Sergeant Major Grant we're going. Tell him I'll go along in five minutes to speak to this German lieutenant, Schenck. And move it. If we're going, we've got to go now."

Finebaum went off on the double, and Howard squatted down and helped himself to coffee from the stove. Hoover said, "You sure you're doing the right thing? You don't look too good."

"You want to know something, Harry?" Howard said. "I'm tired right through to my backbone. More tired than I've ever been in my life, and yet I can't sleep. I can't feel. I don't seem to be able to react." He shrugged. "Maybe I need to smell a little gunpowder. Maybe I've gotten like Finebaum and need it." He stuck a cigarette between his lips. "I know one thing. Right now, I'd rather be out there taking my chances than squatting on my backside here, waiting for the war to finish."

The Finns were encamped on a farm just off the main road, about ten miles west of Arnheim. There were thirty-eight of them under the command of a *Hauptsturmführer* named Erik Sorsa.

The Fifth SS Panzer Division Wiking was the first, and without a doubt the best, foreign division of the *Waffen*-SS, composed mainly of Dutch, Flemings, Danes, and Norwegians. The Finns had joined in 1941, providing the ski-troop expertise so essential in the Russian campaign.

The losses on the Eastern Front by January 1945 had been so colossal that it was decided to raise a new regiment, a joint German-Finnish affair. The project had foundered when the few dozen Finnish survivors, with Sorsa as their senior officer, had made it clear that they would not renew their contracts with the German government after May 1. So, from divisional headquarters in Klagenfurt had come the order which had sent them to the farm at Oberfeld to await further instructions, which was what they had been doing for precisely three weeks now.

Sorsa was a handsome, fair-haired young man of twenty-seven. His mountain cap was identical in cut to that of the army, the edelweiss on the left-hand side, the usual SS death's-head at the front. His cuff-title read *"Finnisches Freiwilligen Bataillon der Waffen*-SS" in two lines, and his armshield was black with a white lion. He wore two Iron Crosses, the wound badge in silver, and the Winter War ribbon.

He stood at the door of the farm, smoking a cigarette, watching half a dozen of his men skiing down through the trees on the hillside above, led by the unit's senior sergeant major, Matti Gestrin. Gestrin soared over the wall by the barn, jumping superbly, and they followed him, one by one, with rhythmic precision — tough, competent-looking men in reversible winter uniforms, white on one side, autumn-pattern camouflage on the other.

"Did you see anything?" Sorsa inquired.

"Were we supposed to?" Gestrin grinned. "I thought we were just out for the exercise. Still no word from headquarters?"

"No, I think they've forgotten about us."

Gestrin, in the act of lighting a cigarette, stopped smiling, looking over Sorsa's shoulder. "From the looks of things, I'd say they've just found us again."

The field car came down the track through the snow, Hoffer at the wheel, Ritter beside him wearing a camouflaged parka

with the hood up over his cap. Strasser
and Jackson were in the back seat. Hoffer
drove into the farmyard and braked to a
halt. Sorsa and Gestrin stayed where they
were by the front door, but the rest of the
Finns moved forward perceptibly, one or
two unslinging their Mauser infantry
rifles. Sorsa said something quietly to
them in Finnish.

"What did he say?" Strasser asked
Jackson.

"He said, 'Easy, children. Nothing I
can't handle.' "

Another dozen or fifteen Finns came out
of the barn, mostly in shirtsleeves and all
carrying weapons of one sort or another.
There was total silence as everyone waited,
just the snow falling perfectly straight,
and then, with a sudden whispering rush,
another white-clad skier lifted over the
wall to land perfectly, skidding to a
halt a yard or two from Sorsa. Another,
and yet another, followed.

It was poetry in motion, total
perfection, and there was a slight fixed
smile on Sorsa's face that seemed to say:
That's what we are. What about you?

Jackson murmured, "The greatest skiers in the world, these boys. They knocked hell out of the Russians in the first Winter War. And they're great throat-cutters — maybe I should have warned you."

"Wait here," Ritter said tonelessly. "All of you."

He got out of the field car and walked across the yard to Sorsa. For a moment, he confronted the tall Finn, who could see only the death's-head on his cap, then said, "Not bad, not bad at all."

"You think so?" Sorsa said.

"A fair jump, certainly."

"You could do better?"

"Perhaps."

There were several pairs of skis leaning against the wall. Ritter helped himself, kneeling to adjust the bindings to fit his heavy panzer boots.

Hoffer appeared at his side and knelt down. "Allow me, *Sturmbannführer.*"

Sorsa took in the sergeant major's black panzer uniform, the Knight's Cross. There was a sudden change of expression in his eyes, and he turned and glanced briefly at Gastrin.

Ritter stamped his feet and took the sticks Hoffer offered him. He smiled. "A long time, Erich, eh?"

He pushed forward, past the field car, out of the gate, and started up the steep slope through the pine trees. Nobody said a word. Everyone waited. He felt curiously calm and peaceful as he followed the zigzag of the farm trail, totally absorbed, thoroughly enjoying the whole thing.

When he turned, he was perhaps a hundred feet above the yard, the trail the Finns had made clear before him. Every face was turned, looking up, and he suddenly felt immensely happy, laughter bubbling up inside him.

He threw back his head, howled like a wolf — the old Harz woodcutters' signal — and launched himself forward, away from the track of the Finns, taking the steepest slope down, zigzagging through the pine trees, in a series of stem turns that were breathtaking in their audacity. And then he lifted, soaring effortlessly over the wall, the field car, drifting broadside for a second only, then turning on his left stick, landing in a spray of snow at a dead halt in a perfectly executed stem christiania, no more than a yard from Sorsa.

There was a shout of approval from the Finns. Ritter stood there, Hoffer kneeling to unfasten his bindings for him, then he threw back his hood, unbuttoned the parka, and took it off.

"He should have been on the stage, that one," Strasser whispered to Jackson.

Ritter tightened his gloves and spoke without looking at Sorsa. "My name is Ritter, *Sturmbannführer,* Five Hundred and Second SS Heavy Tank Battalion, and I am here to assume command of this unit, under special orders from the *Führer* himself in Berlin."

Sorsa looked him over, the Winter War ribbon, the Iron Cross, First and Second Class, the silver badge which meant at least three wounds, the Knight's Cross with Oak Leaves and Swords, the dark eyes, the pale Devil's face.

"Death himself come among us," Matti Gestrin said.

"You will speak German, please, in my

presence," Ritter said calmly. "I take it your men are capable of that, *Hauptsturmführer,* considering that they have been in the service of the Reich for some four years now?"

Sorsa said, "Most of them, but never mind that now. What's this nonsense about orders from Berlin? I know nothing of this."

"Herr Strasser?" Ritter called. "You will please show this gentleman our orders?"

"With pleasure, Major."

Strasser came forward, taking them from his pocket, and Ritter walked a few paces away, ignoring the Finns' stares, took out a silver case and selected a cigarette with care. Hoffer jumped to his side to offer him a light.

"Thank you, *Sturmscharführer.*"

It was a nicely calculated piece of theater, a scene they had played many times before, usually with maximum effect.

Sorsa was examining the order Strasser had passed to him. From the leader and chancellor of the State. Most secret. And he was there himself, mentioned by name, everything exactly as Ritter had said. Most explicit. And, most amazing thing of all, the signature at the foot of the paper. *Adolf Hitler.*

He handed the paper back, and Strasser replaced it in his wallet. "Well?" Ritter said, without looking around. "You are satisfied?"

"There is a situation here," Sorsa said awkwardly. "My comrades and I are contract soldiers."

"Mercenaries," Ritter said. "I'm well aware of the fact. So?"

"My men have voted to go home to Helsinki. We have not renewed our contract."

"Why should you," Ritter said loud enough for all to hear, "when your original one is still in force until nine o'clock tomorrow morning — or would you deny that fact?"

"No, what you say is true."

"Then it would appear that you and your men are still soldiers of the *Waffen*-SS, and under the *Führer* directive just shown to you by Herr Strasser here, I now assume command of this unit."

There was a long, long moment while everyone waited for Sorsa's answer. "Yes, *Sturmbannführer*." There was a further pause, and he raised his voice a little. "Until nine o'clock tomorrow morning, we are still soldiers of the *Waffen*-SS. We have taken the blood money, sworn the oath, and we Finns do not go back on our word."

"Good." Ritter turned to Gestrin. "You will please bring the company to attention, Sergeant Major. I wish to address them."

There was a flurry of movement as Gestrin barked orders, and finally the Finns were drawn up in two lines — thirty-five of them, Ritter noted. They stood there, waiting in the falling snow as he paced up and down. Finally, he stopped and faced them, hands on his hips.

"I know you men. You were at Leningrad, Kurland, Stalingrad. So was I. You fought in the Ardennes. So did I. We've a lot in common, so I'll speak plainly. Captain Sorsa here says that you're *Waffen*-SS only until tomorrow morning. That you want to go home to Helsinki. Well, I've news for you. The Russians are in Berlin, they're with the American Army on the Elbe, cutting Germany in half. You're not going anywhere because there's nowhere to go, and if the Ivans get their hands on you, all you'll get is a bullet — and that's if you're lucky.''

The wind increased in force, driving snow down through the trees in a miniature blizzard.

"And I'm in the same boat because the Russians overran my parents' place a month ago. So all we've got is each other and the regiment, but even if it's only till nine o'clock tomorrow morning, you're still soldiers of the *Waffen*-SS, the toughest, most efficient fighting men the world has ever seen, and from now on, you'll start acting that way again. If I ask you a question, you answer *'Jawohl, Sturmbannführer.'* If I give you an order, you get those heels together and shout *'Zu Befehl, Sturmbannführer.'* Do you understand me?'' There was silence. He

237

raised his voice. "Do you understand me?"

"*Jawohl, Sturmbannführer,*" they chorused.

"Good." He turned to Sorsa. "Let's go inside, and I'll explain the situation to you."

The door opened directly into a large, stone-flagged kitchen. There were a wooden table, a few chairs, a wood fire burning on the hearth, and a profusion of military equipment of various kinds, including several *Panzerfausts* — one-man antitank weapons which had been produced in quantity during the last few months of the war.

They all gathered around the table — Sorsa, Strasser, Jackson, Hoffer. Ritter unfolded a map of the area. "How many vehicles do you have?"

"One field car, three troop-carrying half-tracks."

"And weapons?"

"A heavy machine gun in each half-track, otherwise only light infantry weapons and grenades. Oh, and a few *Panzerfausts,* as you can see."

Strasser said, "Aren't you overreacting just a little, Major? After all, if things go as smoothly as they should, this could simply be a matter of driving into the Schloss and driving out again half an hour later."

"I stopped believing in miracles some considerable time ago." Ritter tapped his finger on the map and said to Sorsa, "Schloss Arlberg. That's our objective. Herr Strasser here will now tell you what it's all about, and you can brief the men. We leave in half an hour."

Ten

It was just after ten o'clock, and Colonel Hesser was working at his desk when there was a knock at the door and Schneider entered.

Hesser glanced up eagerly. "Any news of Schenck?"

"I'm afraid not, sir."

Hesser threw down his pen. "He should have been back by now. It doesn't look good."

"I know, sir."

"Anyway, what did you want?"

"Herr Meyer is here, sir, from the village. There's been some sort of accident. His son, I believe. He wants to know if Herr Gaillard can go down to the village with him. He's the only doctor for miles around at the moment."

"Show him in."

Johann Meyer was mayor of Arlberg and owner of the village inn, the Golden Eagle. He was a tall, robust-looking man with iron-gray hair and beard, a well-known guide in the Bavarian Alps. Just now he was considerably agitated.

"What's the trouble, Meyer?" Colonel Hesser asked.

"It's my boy, Arnie, *Herr Oberst,*" Meyer said. "Trying the quick way down the mountain again — tried jumping a tree and ended up taking a bad fall. I think he may have broken his leg. I was wondering whether the *Herr Doktor . . .*"

"Yes, of course." Hesser nodded to Schneider. "Find Gaillard fast as you can and take him and Herr Meyer back to the village in a field car."

"Shall I stay with him, *Herr Oberst?*"

"No, I need you here. Take one of the men with you and leave him there. Anyone will do. Oh, and tell Gaillard that I naturally assume that under the circumstances he gives his word not to try to escape."

Gaillard was, in fact, at that very moment

engaged in an animated discussion about their situation with Canning and Birr.

"We can't go on like this, it's crazy," Canning said. "Schenck should have been back last night. Something's gone wrong."

"Probably lying dead in a ditch somewhere," Birr said. "I did tell you, remember?"

"Okay, so what do we do?"

"Well," Gaillard said. "The garrison of this establishment is composed mainly of old men or cripples, as no one knows better than I. I've been treating them all for months now. On the other hand, they still outnumber the three of us by about seven to one, and they are armed to the teeth."

"But we can't just sit here and wait for it to happen," Canning said.

Claire, sitting by the fire with Madame Chevalier, said, "Has it ever occurred to you, Hamilton, that you just might be making a mountain out of a molehill here? An American or British unit could roll up to that gate at any time, and all our troubles would be over."

"And pigs might also fly."

"You know what your trouble is?" she told him. "You want it this way. Drama, intrigue — up to your ears in the most dangerous game of all again."

"Now you listen to me," he began, thoroughly angry, and then the door opened and Schneider entered.

He clicked his heels. "Excuse me, Herr General, but Dr. Gaillard is wanted urgently in the village. Herr Meyer's son has had a skiing accident."

"I'll come at once," Gaillard said. "Just give me a moment to get my bag."

He hurried out, followed by Schneider. Birr said, "Always work for the healers, eh? Nice to think there are people like Gaillard around to put us together again when we fall down."

"Philosophy now?" Canning said. "May God preserve me."

"Oh, he will, Hamilton. He will," Birr said. "I've got a feeling the Almighty has something very special lined up for you."

As Claire and Madame Chevalier started to laugh, Canning said, "I wonder whether you'll still be smiling when the SS drive into that courtyard down there,'' and he stalked angrily from the room.

Arnie Meyer was only twelve years old, and small for his age. Just now his face was twisted in agony, the sweat springing to his forehead, trickling down from the fair hair. He had no mother, and his father stood anxiously at one side of the bed and watched Gaillard cut the trouser leg open with a pair of scissors.

He ran his fingers around the angry swelling below the right knee, and in spite of his gentleness the boy cried out sharply.

''Is it broken, *Herr Doktor?*'' Meyer asked.

''Without a doubt. You have splints, of course, with your mountain rescue equipment?''

''Yes, I'll get them.''

''In the meantime, I'll give him a morphine injection. I'll have to set the leg, and that would be too painful for him to bear. Oh, and that private Schneider left — Voss, I think his name is. Send him in here. He can assist me.''

The mayor went out, and Gaillard

broke open a morphine ampul. "Were you coming down the north track again?"

"Yes, *Herr Doktor.*"

"How many times have I warned you? Out of the sun among the trees when it's below freezing, conditions are too fast for you. Your father says you tried to jump a tree, but that isn't true, is it?" Here, he gave the boy the injection.

Arnie winced. "No, *Herr Doktor,*" he said faintly. "I came out of the track onto the slope and tried to do a stem christie like I've seen you do, only everything went wrong."

"As well it might, you idiot," Gaillard told him. "Frozen ground — hardly any snow. What were you trying to do, commit suicide?"

There was a knock at the door, and Private Voss came in, a small, middle-aged man with steel spectacles. He was a clerk from Hamburg whose bad eyes had kept him out of the war until the previous July.

"You wanted me, *Herr Doktor?*"

"I'll need your assistance in a short while to set the boy's leg. Have you ever done anything like this before?"

"No." Voss looked faintly alarmed.

"Don't worry. You'll soon learn."

Meyer came back a moment later with mountain rescue splints and several rolls of bandage.

"If I had hospital facilities, I'd put this leg in a pot," Gaillard said. "It is absolutely essential that, once it's set, it remain immobile, especially so in the case of a boy of this age. It will be your responsibility to see that he behaves himself."

"He will, I promise you, *Herr Doktor.*"

"Good. Now let's see how brave you can be, Arnie."

But Arnie, in spite of the morphine, fainted dead away at the first touch. Which was all to the good, of course, for Gaillard was really able to get to work then, setting the bone with an audible crack that turned Voss's face pale. The little private hauled on the foot as instructed and held a splint on the other side from Meyer as Gaillard skillfully wound the bandages.

When he was finished, the Frenchman

stepped back and smiled at Meyer. "And now, my friend, you can serve me a very large brandy. Nothing less than Armagnac will be accepted."

"Do we return to the castle now, *Herr Doktor?*" Voss asked.

"No, my friend. We adjourn to the bar with the mayor here, who will no doubt consider your efforts no less worthy of his hospitality. We will wait there until my patient recovers consciousness, however long it takes — possibly all day — so be prepared."

They started downstairs and at the same moment heard a motor vehicle draw up outside. Meyer went to the window on the landing halfway down, then turned. "There's a military ambulance outside, *Herr Doktor,* and it isn't German, from the looks of it."

Gaillard joined him at the window in time to see Jack Howard jump down from the passenger seat and stand looking up at the Golden Eagle, a Thompson gun under one arm.

Gaillard got the window open. "In here," he called in English. "A pleasure to see you." Howard looked up, hesitated, then advanced to the door. Gaillard turned to Voss. "A great day, my friend, perhaps the most important in your life, because from this moment, for you, the war is over."

The journey in the ambulance from the field hospital had been a total anticlimax. They had driven through a countryside covered with snow, from which the population seemed to have vanished — a strange, lost land of deserted villages and shuttered farms. Most important of all, except for a few abandoned vehicles at various places, they had seen no sign of the enemy.

"But where the hell is everybody?" Hoover demanded at one point.

"With their heads under the bed, waiting for the ax to fall," Finebaum told him.

"The Alpine Fortress," Hoover said. "What a load of crap. One good armored column could go from one end of this country to the other in a day, as far as I can see, and nobody to stop them." He turned to Howard. "What do you think, sir?"

"I think it's all very mysterious," Howard said, "and that's good because if my map reading is correct, we're coming down into Arlberg now."

They came around the corner, saw the village at the bottom of the hill, the spires of the castle peeping above the wooded crest on the other side of the valley.

"And there she is," Finebaum said. "Schloss Arlberg. Sounds like a tailor I used to know in New York."

They drove down the deserted street, turned into the cobbled square, and halted in front of the Golden Eagle.

"Even here," Hoover said, "not a soul in sight. It gives me the creeps."

Howard reached for his Thompson gun and got out of the ambulance's cab. He stood there looking up at the building, and then a window was thrown open and a voice called excitedly in English with a French accent, "In here!"

Gaillard embraced the American enthusiastically. "My friend, I don't think

I've ever been more pleased to see anyone in my life. My name is Paul Gaillard. I am a prisoner with several others here at Schloss Arlberg."

"I know," Howard said. "That's why we're here. I'm Jack Howard, by the way."

"Ah, then Schenck got through?"

"Yes, but he stopped a couple of bullets on the way. He's outside now in the ambulance."

"Then I'd better take a look at him. I was once a doctor by profession. My training has been useful of late."

Just then, Voss appeared hesitantly at the bottom of the stairs. Finebaum called a warning from the doorway. "Watch it, Captain."

As he raised his M1, Gaillard hastily got in the way. "No need for that. Although poor Voss here is technically supposed to be guarding me, he has, to my certain knowledge, never fired a shot in anger in his life." Finebaum lowered his rifle, and Gaillard said to Howard, "There will be no need for shooting by anyone, believe me. Colonel Hesser has already said that he will surrender to the first Allied troops who appear. Didn't Schenck make this clear?"

"It's been a long, hard war, Doctor," Finebaum said. "We only got this far by never taking a Kraut on trust."

"Like perspective, I suppose it's all a question of your point of view," Gaillard said. "It has been my experience that they are as good, bad, or indifferent as the rest of us. Still, I'd better have a look at Schenck now. Voss, please bring my bag."

At the door he paused, looking at the ambulance, then glanced along the street. "There are no others? No one else is coming?"

"You were lucky to get us," Howard told him.

He opened the rear door of the ambulance, and Gaillard climbed inside. Schenck lay there, the heavily bandaged arm outside the blankets, the eyes closed. He opened them slowly and, on finding Gaillard, managed a smile.

"So, *Herr Doktor,* here we are again."

"You did well." Gaillard felt his pulse. "What about Schmidt?"

"Dead."

"He was a good man. I'm sorry. You have a slight fever. Is there much pain?"

"For the past hour it has been hell."

"I'll give you something for that, then you can sleep."

He opened the bag which Voss had brought, found a morphine ampul, and gave Schenck an injection. Then he climbed out of the ambulance again.

"Will he be okay?" Howard asked.

"I think so."

They went back into the inn and found Hoover and Finebaum at one end of the bar, Voss at the other, looking worried. Meyer had the Armagnac out and several glasses.

"Excellent," Gaillard said. "Herr Meyer, here, who is mayor of Arlberg as well as a most excellent innkeeper, was about to treat me to a shot — as I believe you Americans call it — of his best brandy. Perhaps you gentlemen will join me."

Meyer filled the glasses hurriedly. Finebaum grabbed for his, and Hoover said, "Not yet, you dummy. This is a special occasion. It calls for a toast."

Howard turned to Gaillard. "I'd say it was your prerogative, Doctor."

"Very well," Gaillard said. "I could drink to you, my friends, but I think the circumstances demand something more appropriate. Something for all of us. For you and me, but also for Schenck and Voss and Meyer here, all those who have suffered the disabilities of this terrible war. I give you love and life and happiness, commodities which have been in short supply for some considerable time now."

"I'll drink to that," Finebaum said and emptied the glass at a swallow.

"We'd better get on up to the castle now," Howard said.

"Where you will find them awaiting your arrival with a considerable degree of impatience — General Canning in particular," Gaillard told him. "I'll hang on here for the moment. I have a patient upstairs."

"Okay, Doctor," Howard said. "But I'd better warn you. My orders are to pick you people up. turn straight around, and get the hell out. I'd say you've got an hour — that's all.''

They moved outside. Finebaum said, ''What about the Kraut? We take him along?''

''Voss stays with me,'' Gaillard said firmly. ''I'll very probably need him.''

''Anything you say, Doctor.'' Howard shoved Finebaum up into the cab of the ambulance. ''Finebaum's survived on the idea the only good one is a dead one for so long, it's become a way of life.''

''So what does that make me, some kind of animal? It means I'm alive, doesn't it?'' Finebaum leaned down to Gaillard as Hoover started the engine. ''You look like a philosopher, Doc. Here's some philosophy for you. A funny thing about war. It gets easier as you go along.''

The ambulance drove away across the square. Meyer, who was standing on the porch, said in German, ''What did he say — the small one — *Herr Doktor?*''

''He said a terrible thing, my friend.'' Gaillard smiled sadly. ''But true, unfortunately. And now, I think, we'll take another look at that boy of yours.''

Hesser was seated at his desk, writing a letter to his wife, when the door was flung open unceremoniously and Schneider rushed in. He had the Alsatian with him, and his excitement had even infected the dog, which circled him, whining, so that the leash got entangled in his legs.

"What is it, man?" Hesser demanded. "What's wrong with you?"

"They're coming, *Herr Oberst*. A British vehicle has just started up the hill."

"Only one? You are certain?"

"They've just phoned through from the guardhouse, *Herr Oberst*. An ambulance, apparently."

"Strange," Hesser said. "However, we must prepare to receive them with all speed. Turn out the garrison and notify General Canning and the others. I'll be down myself, directly."

Schneider went out, and Hesser sat there, hands flat on the table, a slight frown on his face. Now that the moment had come he felt curiously deflated, but then that was only to be expected. The

255

end of something, after all, and what did he have to show for it? One arm, one eye. But there was still Gerda — and the children — and it was over now. Soon he could go home. When he got up and reached for his cap and belt, he was actually smiling.

As the ambulance came out of the last bend and Schloss Arlberg loomed above them, Finebaum leaned out of the cab and looked up at the pointed roofs of the towers in awe.

"Hey, I seen this place before. The moat, the drawbridge — everything. *The Prisoner of Zenda.* Roland Colman swam across, and some dame helped him in through the window."

"That was Hollywood — this is for real, man," Hoover said. "This place was built to stand a siege. Those walls must be ten feet thick."

"They're hospitable enough, that's for sure," Howard said. "They've left the gate open for us. Straight in, Harry, nice and slow, and let's see what we've got here."

Hoover dropped into bottom gear, and they trundled across the drawbridge. The iron-bound gates stood open, and they moved on through the darkness of the entrance tunnel and emerged into the great inner courtyard.

The garrison was drawn up in a single line, all eighteen of them, Colonel Hesser at the front. General Canning, Colonel Birr, Claire, and Madame Chevalier stood together at the top of the steps leading up to the main entrance.

The ambulance rolled to a halt, and Howard got out. Hesser called his men to attention and saluted politely. "My name is Hesser — *Oberstleutnant,* Forty-second Panzer Grenadiers, at present in command of this establishment. And you, sir?"

"Captain John H. Howard, Second Ranger Battalion, United States Army."

Hesser turned and called, "General Canning? Colonel Birr? Will you join me, please?"

They came down the steps and crossed the yard. It was snowing quite hard now. Howard saluted, and Canning held out his hand. "We're certainly pleased to see you, son, believe me."

"Our pleasure, General."

Hesser said, "Then, in the presence of these officers as witnesses, I formally surrender this establishment, Captain Howard." He saluted, turned, and said to Schneider, "Have the men lay down their arms."

There was a flurry of movement. Within a matter of seconds, the men were back in line, their rifles standing in three triangular stacks before them.

Hesser saluted again. "Very well, Captain," he said. "What are your orders?"

Sorsa headed the German column in one of the armored half-tracks, Ritter and Hoffer, Strasser and Jackson next in line in their field car, the rest of the Finns trailing behind.

Just after noon they emerged from a side road to join the road from Innsbruck to Arlberg, along which the ambulance had passed a short time before. As they reached the crest of the hill above the village, Sorsa signaled a halt. Ritter,

Strasser, and Jackson got out of the field car and went to join him.

"What is it?" Ritter demanded.

"Something's passed along this road very recently. Heavy vehicle. See the tire marks? It stopped here before starting down to the village."

There was fresh oil on the snow. Ritter looked down the hill. "So this is Arlberg."

"Quiet little place, isn't it?" Jackson said. "They're certainly staying out of the way down there."

Ritter held out his hand for Sorsa's field glasses and trained them on the turrets of Schloss Arlberg peeping above the crest of the far ridge. He handed them back to Strasser. "Nothing worth seeing. The vehicle which has preceded us could be anything, but under the circumstances, I think we should press on."

"I agree," Strasser said and for the first time seemed less calm than usual, filled with a kind of nervous excitement. "Let's get there as fast as possible and get things sewn up. We've come too far for anything to be allowed to go wrong now."

They got back into the vehicles, Sorsa waved the column on, and they started down the hill.

It was Meyer who saw them first, when they were halfway down — sheer luck that he'd gone to the landing window to close it. He took one look, then hurried to the bedroom where Gaillard was checking on the boy, who was still unconscious.

"There's an SS column coming down the hill," Meyer said. "Three half-tracks, two field cars. About forty men in all."

Voss's face turned deathly pale. Gaillard said, "You're certain?"

Meyer opened a cupboard and took out an old brass telescope. "See for yourself."

They all went out onto the landing, and Meyer leveled the telescope on the lead half-track. Immediately the divisional signs on the vehicle leaped into view — the SS runes, the death's-head painted in white. He moved on to the field car, picking out Ritter first, then Strasser.

He frowned, and Meyer said, "What is it, *Herr Doktor?*"

"Nothing," Gaillard said. "There's a

civilian with them I thought I knew for a moment, but I must be wrong. They're mountain troops — judging by their uniforms and the skis they carry in the half-tracks.''

He closed the telescope and handed it to Meyer. Voss plucked at his sleeve. ''What are we going to do, *Herr Doktor?* Those devils are capable of anything.''

''No need to panic,'' Gaillard said. ''Keep calm, above all things.'' He turned to Meyer. ''They'll be here within the next two or three minutes. Go out and meet them.''

''And what about the Americans? Look, the tracks of the ambulance are plain in the snow. What if they ask me who made them?''

''Play it by ear. Whatever happens, don't tell them Voss and I are here. We'll keep out of sight for the time being. We can always clear off the back way if we have to, but I want to see how the situation develops here first, and besides, Arnie is going to need me when he wakes up.''

''As you say.'' Meyer took a deep

breath and started downstairs as the first vehicle braked to a halt outside. Gaillard and Voss, peering around the edge of the curtain, saw Ritter, Strasser, and Jackson get out of the field car.

"Strange," Gaillard said. "One of the SS officers has a Stars and Stripes shield sewn on his left sleeve below the eagle. What on earth does that mean?"

"I don't know, *Herr Doktor,*" Voss whispered. "Where the SS are concerned, I've always kept well out of the way. Who's the one in the leather coat speaking to Meyer now? Gestapo, perhaps?"

"I don't know," Gaillard said. "I still have that irritating feeling we've met somewhere before." He eased the window open in time to hear Sorsa shout an order to Matti Gestrin in the rear half-track. "My God," Gaillard whispered, "they're Finns."

He peered down at them, suddenly fearful. Hard, tough, competent-looking men, armed to the teeth, and there was only one road up to the castle, one road down. He turned and grabbed Voss by the shirt front.

"Right, my friend. Your chance to be a hero for the first time in your miserable life. Out the back door, through the trees, take the woodcutters' trail up to the castle, and run till your heart bursts. Tell Hesser the SS are coming. Now get moving!" And he shoved Voss violently along the landing toward the back stairs.

As he turned to the window again, Ritter was saying to Meyer, "From these tracks a vehicle would seem to have passed this way during the past half hour. A heavy vehicle. What was it?"

A direct question — and in the circumstances, there was only one answer Meyer could give. "It was an ambulance, *Sturmbannführer.*"

"A German ambulance?" Strasser asked.

"No, *mein Herr*. A British Army ambulance. There were three American soldiers in the cab. One was an officer — a captain, I think."

"And they took that street out of the square?" Ritter nodded. "Which leads to . . ."

"Schloss Arlberg."

"And is there any other way up or down?"

"Only on foot."

"One more question. How many men in the garrison at Schloss Arlberg now?"

Meyer hesitated, but he was a simple man with his son to consider, and Ritter's pale face, the dark eyes under the silver death's-head were too much.

"Eighteen, *Sturmbannführer*. Nineteen, with the commandant."

Ritter turned to the others. "What you might call a damn close thing."

"No problem, surely," Strasser said.

"Let's go and see, shall we?" Ritter replied calmly, and he turned back to the field car.

Meyer waited on the step until the last half-track in the column had disappeared up the narrow street before going back inside. Gaillard was at the bottom of the stairs.

"Well?" the Frenchman demanded.

"What could I do? I had to tell them." Meyer shivered. "But now what, *Herr Doktor?* I mean, what can they do up there in the castle? Colonel Hesser has no

264

option but to turn your friends over to the SS now."

But before Gaillard could reply, Arnie called out feverishly from the bedroom, and Gaillard turned and hurried upstairs.

In the courtyard, the *prominenti* were making ready to leave. Schenck had been left on board the ambulance, and three German soldiers were loading the prisoners' personal belongings. Claire and Madame Chevalier waited on the porch while Hesser, Birr, and Canning stood at the bottom of the steps smoking cigarettes. Beyond the ambulance, the rest of the tiny garrison still stood in line before their stacked rifles.

It was Magda, Schneider's Alsatian, who first showed signs of agitation, whining and straining at her leash and then breaking into furious barking.

Canning frowned. "What is it, old girl? What's wrong with you?"

There was the hollow booming of feet thundering across the drawbridge, and Voss staggered out of the tunnel.

"Herr Oberst!" he called weakly,

lurching from side to side like a drunken man. "The SS are coming! The SS are coming!"

Hesser reached out his one good arm to steady him as Voss almost fell down, chest heaving, sweat pouring down his face.

"What are you telling me, man?"

"SS, *Herr Oberst*. On their way up from the village. It's true. Finnish mountain troops in charge of a *Sturmbannführer* in panzer uniform."

Canning caught him by the arm and pulled him around. "How many?"

"Forty or so altogether. Three half-tracks and two field cars."

"What kind of armaments did they carry?"

"There was a heavy machine gun with each vehicle, *Herr General,* I noticed that. The rest was just the usual hand stuff. Schmeissers, rifles, and so on."

Finebaum said to Hoover, "They keep telling me the war's over, but here we are, the three of us, with nineteen Kraut prisoners on our hands and forty of those SS bastards coming around the bend fast."

Howard turned to Canning. "It's an impossible situation, sir, and even if we tried to make a run for it, we'd just run slap into them. There's only one road in and out of here."

Canning turned to face Hesser, trying to think of the right words, but strangely enough it was Madame Chevalier who played a hand now.

"Well, Max," she called. "What's it to be? Checkmate? Or have you still got enough juice left in you to act like a man?" She moved forward, leaning on Claire's shoulder. "Not for us, Max, not even for yourself. For Gerda, for your children."

Max Hesser stared up at her wildly for a moment, then he turned to the garrison. "Grab your rifles, quick as you can. Schneider — take two men, get to the guardroom on the double, and shut the gates."

There was a sudden flurry of activity. He turned to Canning, drew himself up, and saluted formally. "General Canning, as you are the senior Allied officer here, I place myself and my men at your command. What are your orders, sir?"

Canning's nostrils flared, his eyes sparkled, tension erupting from deep inside him in a harsh laugh. "By God, that's more like it. All right, for the time being, deploy your men on the walls above the guardroom, and let's see what these bastards want." He clapped his hands together and shouted furiously. "Come on, come on, come on! Let's get this show on the road."

Eleven

The column, Sorsa still leading the way in the front half-track, was no more than fifty yards from the castle entrance when the gates clanged shut. Sorsa immediately signaled a halt.

Ritter stood up in the field car and called, "Line of assault. Quickly, now."

The Finns moved into action instantly. The other two half-tracks took up position on either side of Sorsa; the machine-gun crews made themselves ready for action; the rest of the men jumped to the ground and fanned out.

There was silence for a moment after the engines were cut. Ritter raised his field glasses and looked to where there was movement on the wall.

"What is it? What's happening?" Strasser demanded.

"Interesting," Ritter said softly. "I see American helmets up there, together with German ones. Perhaps the Third World War has started?"

On the wall, Canning, Birr, Hesser, and Howard grouped together in the shelter of the west guardroom turret and peered out.

"Now what?" Birr said. He carried a Schmeisser in one hand, and Canning a Walther pistol.

"We'll stir things up a bit, just to show them we mean business." Canning moved to where Schneider crouched beside the machine-gun crew, who had positioned their weapons to point out through an embrasure beside one of the castle's eighteenth-century cannon. "I want you to fire a long burst into the ground about ten yards in front of the lead half-track," he said in German.

Schneider turned in alarm and looked to Hesser. *"Herr Oberst,* what do I do?"

"As General Canning commands," Hesser said. "We are under his orders now."

Schneider patted the lead gunner on the shoulder. He was another reservist, a man

270

named Strang, who, like most of them, had never in his life fired a shot in anger. He hesitated, sweat on his face, and Finebaum unslung his M1, pushed him out of the way, and grabbed for the handles.

"Maybe you got qualms, uncle, but not me."

He squeezed off a long burst, swinging the barrel so that snow and gravel spurted in a darting line right across the front of the half-tracks.

Ritter turned, arms flung wide. "No return fire. It's a warning only."

Hoover whispered to Howard, "Did you see that? Those guys didn't even move."

Finebaum got up and turned. "They're hot stuff, Harry, believe me. I tell you, this thing could get very interesting."

Ritter jumped down from the field car, and Sorsa moved to meet him. "Do we go in?"

"No, first we talk. They'll want to talk, I think." He turned to Strasser. "You agree?"

"Yes, I think so. Hesser will already be beginning to have second thoughts. Let's give him a chance to change his mind.''

"Good,'' Ritter said and called to Hoffer. "Over here, Erich. We'll go for a little walk, you and I.''

"Zu Befehl, Sturmbannführer," Hoffer replied crisply.

"I, too, could do with some exercise, I think," Strasser said. "If you've no objection, Major Ritter?''

"As you like.''

Strasser turned to Jackson. "You stay back out of the way. Borrow a parka and get the hood up. I don't want them to see you, you understand?''

Jackson frowned, but did as he was told, moving back to one of the half-tracks.

Sorsa said, "What if they open fire?''

"Then you'll have to take command, won't you?'' Ritter said and started forward.

Their feet crunched in the snow. Ritter took out his case, selected a cigarette, and offered one to Strasser.

"No, thank you. I never use them. You are surprised, I think, that I felt the need for exercise?''

"Perhaps. On the other hand, I could say that it shows confidence in my judgment."

"Or a belief in my own destiny — have you considered that?"

"A point of view, I suppose. If it's of any comfort, good luck to you."

On the wall, Canning said, "By God, he's a cool one, the devil in black out there. Obviously in need of conversation."

"What do we do, General?" Hesser asked.

"Why, accommodate him, of course. You, me, and Captain Howard here. Not you, Justin. You stay up here in command, just in case some trigger-happy jerk in one of the half-tracks decides to open up." He smiled savagely, giving every appearance of thoroughly enjoying himself. "All right, gentlemen. Let's see what they have to say."

Ritter, Strasser, and Hoffer paused at their side of the drawbridge and waited. After a while, the small judas door in the main gate opened, and Canning stepped out, followed by Hesser and Howard. As they came forward, Ritter and his party moved also, and they met in the middle of the drawbridge.

Ritter saluted and said in excellent English, *"Sturmbannführer* Karl Ritter, Five Hundred and Second SS Heavy Tank Battalion, at present in command of this unit, and this is Herr Strasser."

"Of the Prisoner-of-War Administration in Berlin," Strasser put in.

"And I am Brigadier General Hamilton Canning of the Army of the United States, Captain Howard here, Second Rangers. *Oberstleutnant* Hesser, you may know."

It was all very polite, very formal, except for Jack Howard, whose face had turned deathly pale and who clutched the Thompson gun in his hands till the knuckles turned white. There was life in his eyes again for the first time in days, for he had recognized Ritter instantly.

"What can we do for you?" Canning said.

"Oberstleutnant Hesser." Strasser produced the Hitler directive and unfolded it. "I have here an order from my department in Berlin, signed, as you will

see, by the *Führer* himself, ordering you to place the five prisoners remaining at Schloss Arlberg in my care."

He held out the letter. Max Hesser waved it away. "Too late, gentlemen. I surrendered my command to Captain Howard on his arrival not more than thirty minutes ago. General Canning is in command here now."

There was silence for a while. The snow falling harder than ever, a sudden, small wind churning it into a miniature blizzard that danced around them.

Strasser said, "This is a totally illegal act, Colonel Hesser. To my certain knowledge there has been no general surrender, no discussion of peace terms — cannot be while the *Führer* still lives to direct the struggle of the German people from his headquarters in Berlin."

"There has been a surrender here," Hesser said, "according to the rules of war. I have done nothing dishonorable."

"A surrender to three members of the American Army?" Strasser said. "You tell me there is nothing dishonorable in this?"

"You will speak to me, if you please,"

Canning said. "As this gentleman has made plain, I command here now as senior Allied officer present."

"No, General, I think not," Ritter said calmly. "Our business is with the officer in command of Schloss Arlberg, and to us he must still be *Oberstleutnant* Max Hesser, until relieved of that duty by the High Command of the German Army." He turned to Hesser. "You took an oath, Colonel Hesser, as did we all, I think. An oath as a German soldier to your *Führer* and the State."

"To a madman," Hesser said, "who has brought Germany to her knees."

"But also to the State, to your country," Ritter said. "You and I are soldiers, Hesser, like General Canning here and Captain Howard. No difference. We play the game on our side, they on theirs. We can't hope to change the rules in the middle, to suit our personal convenience. Not any of us. Is that not so, General?"

It was Howard who answered him. "Is that how you see it? A game? Nothing more?"

"Perhaps," Ritter said. "The greatest game of all, where the stakes are a country and its people, and if a man can't stand by his own, he is less than nothing."

He turned back to Hesser, waiting. Hesser said, "It is my information that a direct order has gone to the SS from the *Führer* himself, authorizing the execution of all prominent prisoners. I consider this order monstrous. A direct violation of the Geneva Convention and a crime against humanity. I will not be a party to it, and neither will the men of this garrison."

Strasser said, "This is, of course, total nonsense. A tissue of lies. As the representative for this area of the Prisoner-of-War Administration, I can give you my word on this absolutely."

"Then why do you want us?" Canning asked. "Tell me that."

"All prominent prisoners are being brought together in one center, for their own protection."

"As hostages against the evil day?"

"A sensible precaution only, *Herr General,* I assure you."

"Who for — you or us?"

There was another brief silence. The snow danced around them. Hesser said slowly, "I stand by what I have done. General Canning is in command here now."

"Which just about wraps it up," Canning said. "I can't see that we have anything further to discuss. If you'll take the advice of an old hand, Major, I'd say you and your men had better get the hell out of here while you still can. Let's go, gentlemen."

He turned and walked briskly back toward the gate, Hesser at his side. Howard stayed there, holding the Thompson gun across his chest. Hoffer never took his eyes off him, his hand close to the butt of the holstered Walther at his belt. Ritter ignored him as he lit a cigarette calmly and examined the gate, the walls above.

"It would seem they mean business," Strasser said.

Ritter nodded. "So it would appear." He turned on his heel.

Howard said, "Major Karl Ritter, of the Five Hundred and Second SS Heavy

Tank Battalion, you said?"

Ritter turned slowly. "That is correct."

"We've met before."

"Have we?"

"Last Wednesday morning. That little affair on the way to Innsbruck, when you took out an entire British armored column. I was one of the survivors, along with my two friends up there on the wall."

"Congratulations," Ritter said calmly. "Your luck is good."

"You can tell your man there to take his hand off the butt of that Walther. I'm not going to kill you — yet. I mean, that wouldn't be playing this game of yours according to the rules — now would it?"

"Your choice, my friend."

"You'll be coming in?" Howard said. "Or you'll try to?"

"Yes, I think so."

"I'll be looking for you."

Canning called from the gate. "Captain Howard." Howard turned and ran back through the snow.

"He means it, that one," Strasser said. "For the past five minutes I've had a finger on the trigger, imagining I might have to put another hole through the pocket of my coat. I wonder if he knew.''

"Oh, yes," Ritter said, "he knew." And he turned and led the way back to the half-tracks.

"What in hell kept you?" Canning demanded as Howard slipped inside and the gate closed. "Go on — up on the wall — and tell Colonel Birr I'll join you in a couple of minutes."

Howard mounted the stone steps, and Canning turned to Hesser. "As I recall, you raised the drawbridge six or seven months back?"

"That's right, *Herr General*. To see if it was working."

"Then let's see if the damn thing still does."

Hesser nodded to Schneider, who immediately opened the door at the foot of the tower on the left-hand side of the gate and led the way in. He switched on the light, disclosing a massive steel drum ten feet across, chains wrapped around it, lifting up into the gloom. There were great spoked wheels on either side.

"Let's get it done." Canning moved to one of the wheels, Schneider ran to the other, and together they started to turn.

Howard crouched beside the cannon, peering out through the embrasure, watching Ritter and his two companions walk back toward the Finns. Hoover and Finebaum dropped down beside him.

"What was going on out there, Captain?" the sergeant asked. "Between you and the Kraut officer?"

"It was him," Howard said. "The guy who took the column out Wednesday. His name's Ritter — Karl Ritter."

"The guy in the Tiger who flattened the jeep?" Finebaum demanded. "Are you saying that's him out there?" He raised the M1 and leaned across the cannon. "Jesus, maybe I can still get him."

Howard pulled him down. "Not now," he said. "And anyway, he's mine."

"Attack now!" Strasser said. "The only way. Use the front half-track as a battering ram. Straight in while they're still wondering what our next move will be.''

''There are twenty armed men on that wall. At least one heavy machine gun mounted beside the old cannon between the turrets. I had a good look at that while I was lighting my cigarette. Rate of fire not far short of a thousand rounds a minute. You served in the First World War, did you not, Herr Strasser? I should have thought you might have remembered what happens to those who attempt frontal attacks on heavy machine guns skillfully positioned.''

''And in any case, the argument now becomes a wholly academic one.'' Sorsa pointed, and Strasser and Ritter turned in time to see the end of the drawbridge lift above the moat.

They watched as it continued its steady progress and finally came to a halt. Strasser said, ''So, a situation which can only be described as medieval. Impossible for us to get in . . .''

''And equally impossible for them to get out,'' Ritter said. ''Which is, after all, the important thing. There is one thing which worries me, however."

"What's that?" Strasser asked.

"The question of radio communication with the outside world. A distress call at random might well be picked up by some Allied unit or other in the vicinity."

"No danger of that," Strasser said. "They've had problems in the communications room at Schloss Arlberg for several days now. Believe me, Major, there is no way in which they can communicate with the outside world."

"Another example of your flair for organization, I presume," Ritter said. "Anyway, that problem being solved, we will now leave, I think."

"You mean that literally, or do you have a plan?"

"The fact of our going may comfort the general and his friends, however temporarily. The question of planning must wait until I've handled the immediate situation." He nodded to Sorsa. "Move out and stop the column around the first bend out of sight of the castle."

"Zu Befehl, Sturmbannführer."

From the walls, Canning and the others watched them go. "What do you think Hamilton?" Birr asked.

"I'm not sure," Canning said. "Strasser, the guy who said he was from the Prisoner-of-War Administration, intrigues me. I'm sure I've seen the bastard before somewhere."

"And the other one — Ritter?"

"The kind who never lets go. Did you see his medals, for Christ's sake?"

"He has quite a reputation, this man," Hesser said. "Something of a legend. A great tank destroyer on the Eastern Front. They made much of him in the magazines last year."

"And Strasser — you've never seen him before?"

"No, never."

Canning nodded. "Right. This is what we do. I want two lookouts in the top of the north tower, linked to here by field telephone. From up there they should be able to see outside the walls for the entire circuit. Any kind of movement must be reported instantly. I want the rest of the garrison split into three fire parties of six or seven each, ready to rush to any point on the wall as directed by the lookouts." He turned to Howard. "You take charge of that operation with Hoover. Finebaum can accompany me as my runner."

"I'm with you, General," Finebaum said. "We'll make a hell of a team, believe me — no disrespect intended, General."

"Which remains to be seen." Canning turned to Hesser. "And now I want to see the armory. Everything you've got here."

Beyond the first bend in the road, the column had halted. Ritter said to Sorsa, "I'm returning to the village now. I'll take Sergeant Major Gestrin and four men with me. They can use the other field car. You stay here with the half-tracks. I want fifteen or twenty men on skis circling those walls without pause. Keep to the woods, but make sure they can be seen. Field-telephone communication at all times."

"And then what?" Sorsa asked.

"I'll let you know," Ritter said.

Paul Gaillard and Meyer were at the landing window as the two field cars drove into the square and pulled up outside the Golden Eagle. Gestrin and his men carried their skis in their car and had a field radio.

Gaillard said, "Better go down and find out what they want. I'll hide in the closet in the dressing room if I hear anyone coming."

Meyer went downstairs as the front door opened, and Ritter led the way into the bar. Strasser and Jackson followed, then Hoffer carrying Strasser's suitcase containing the radio.

Strasser said to Meyer, "You have a room I can use privately?"

Meyer, with little choice in the matter, said, "Through here, *mein Herr*. My office."

"Excellent." Strasser turned to Jackson. "Tell me. The American pilot's uniform — they managed to procure one for you?"

"It's in the Dakota," Jackson told him.

"Good. I want you to run up there now in one of the field cars and get it. Take a

286

couple of Gestrin's men with you. And I want you back here as soon as possible." Jackson hesitated, a look of puzzlement on his face, and Strasser said, "No questions — just do it."

Jackson turned and went out. Strasser picked up his case. "And now," he said to Ritter, "if you will excuse me, I have a little communicating to do," and he nodded to Meyer and followed him out.

Hoffer went behind the bar. "A drink, *Sturmbannführer?*"

"Why not?" Ritter said. "Brandy, I think," and then he gave a small exclamation and crossed the room quickly.

On the opposite wall hung a large, framed, eighteenth-century print of Schloss Arlberg, a perfect plan of the entire castle — every walk, every strongpoint, all clearly defined.

The armory contained few surprises. Perhaps a dozen extra Schmeissers, twenty spare rifles, a couple of boxes of grenades, some plastic explosive. No heavy stuff at all.

"Plenty of ammunition, that's one good

thing," Canning said. He hefted a couple of Walther service pistols and said to the others, "All right, let's go and see the ladies."

They found Madame Chevalier warming herself in front of the log fire in the upper dining hall in the north tower. Canning said, "Where's Claire?"

"She went to her room. She was feeling the cold very badly. We stood outside too long."

Canning held up the Walther. "You know how to use one of these things?"

"I play a different instrument, as you well know."

"You'd better learn this one fast, believe me." He turned to Finebaum. "See if you can get the finer points across to Madame Chevalier in a fast five minutes, soldier."

"Anything you say, General."

Madame Chevalier looked him over, horror on her face, and Finebaum tried his most ingratiating smile. "They tell me you play piano, lady. You know 'GI Jive'?"

Madame Chevalier closed her eyes

momentarily, then opened them again. "If you could show me how the pistol works now," she said.

When Canning tried the handle on Claire's door, it was locked. He knocked and called her name. It was two or three minutes before the bolt was drawn back and she peered out at him. Her eyes seemed very large, the face pale.

"I'm sorry, Hamilton. Come in," she said.

He walked past her into the bedroom. "You don't look too good."

"As a matter of fact, I've just been thoroughly sick. I panicked down there when I heard that the SS had arrived."

Canning remembered how her husband had died. "It made you think of Etienne and what happened to him?"

When she looked up at him, her face was very pale. "No, it made me think of myself, Hamilton. You see, I'm a total physical coward and the very thought of those devils . . ."

He placed a finger on her lips and took the Walther from his pocket. "I've brought you a life preserver. You know how to use it, I believe.''

She took it from him, holding it in both hands. ''On myself,'' she said. ''Before I allow them to take me from this place.''

''Hush.'' Canning kissed her gently. ''Nobody's taking you anywhere, believe me. Now come down and join the others.''

Ritter had taken the print down from the wall and was examining it closely when Strasser entered.

''A useful find,'' Ritter told him. ''A plan of Schloss Arlberg.''

''Never mind that now,'' Strasser said. ''I've made an even more interesting discovery. Hoffer, bring friend Meyer in here.''

''What is it?'' Ritter inquired.

''It appears that a certain Dr. Paul Gaillard is actually on the premises. Meyer's boy broke a leg this morning.''

''You're sure of this?''

''Oh, yes, my informant is completely reliable.''

Ritter frowned. ''You've been on the

radio. Where to? The castle? You mean you've actually got an agent planted up there? I really must congratulate you, *Reichsleiter*. My apologies — Herr Strasser. That really is taking organization to the outer limits."

"I do like efficiency, you see, Major. A fatal flaw, if you like, all my life."

The door opened, and Hoffer ushered Meyer into the room. Strasser turned to him and smiled. "So, Herr Meyer, it would appear you have not been strictly honest with us."

A few moments later, Paul Gaillard, bending over the still-unconscious boy, heard footsteps on the stairs. They approached the door confidently. He hesitated, then withdrew into the dressing room and stepped into the closet.

There was a long period of silence — or so it seemed — a slight creaking, and then, quite unexpectedly, the closet door opened and light flooded in.

Ritter was standing there. He didn't bother to draw his pistol. Simply smiled and said, "Dr. Gaillard, I believe? Your patient seems to be reviving."

Gaillard hesitated, then brushed past him and went into the other room, where he found Strasser and Meyer bending over the boy, who was moaning feverishly.

Meyer turned in appeal to Ritter, his concern wholly for his son now. "When you first arrived, *Sturmbannführer,* we didn't know what to think, the doctor and I. And there was the boy to consider."

"Yes, I can see that," Ritter said. "How bad is he?"

"Not good," Gaillard said. "A badly broken leg, high fever. He needs constant attention, that's why I stayed. But I can't have you in here. You'll have to go."

Ritter glanced at Strasser, who nodded slightly. Gaillard was ignoring them, sponging the boy's forehead. "So you didn't manage to get into the castle, it would seem."

"We will, Doctor, we will," Ritter said. "I'll have to put a sentry in here, of course, but we'll leave you for now."

He nodded to Meyer, who went out. Gaillard said, "All right, if you must, I suppose." He glanced up, saw Strasser for the first time. His mouth opened wide; there was a look of astonishment on his face. "Good God, I know you."

"I don't think so," Strasser said. "My name is Strasser, of the Prisoner-of-War Administration in Berlin, as the major here will confirm."

Gaillard turned to Ritter, who smiled. "We'll leave you to your patient, Doctor." And he ushered Strasser outside and closed the door.

"Bormann," Gaillard whispered. "When was it we were introduced? Munich, 1935? *Reichsleiter* Martin Bormann. I'd stake my life on it."

And at the same moment, in the bunker in Berlin, Martin Bormann and General Wilhelm Burgdorf, Hitler's army adjutant, waited in the central passage outside the *Führer's* personal suite. Since he was the man who had delivered the poison with which Field Marshal Erwin Rommel had been obliged to kill himself after the July 20 plot, it might be thought that Burgdorf was used to such situations, but just now he looked terrified and was sweating profusely.

At three-thirty there was a pistol shot. Martin Bormann rushed into the *Führer*'s suite, followed by Hitler's valet, Heinz Linge, and Colonel Otto Günsche, his SS adjutant. The room reeked of the cyanide which Eva Hitler had used to take her life. The *Führer* sprawled beside her, his face shattered.

Dr. Stumpfegger, the *Führer*'s personal doctor, and Linge, the valet, carried his body up to the Chancellery garden, wrapped in a gray blanket. Martin Bormann came next, carrying Eva Hitler.

A curious incident then took place, for the *Führer*'s chauffeur, Erich Kempka, was reminded of the fact that, in life, Bormann had been Eva Hitler's greatest enemy. He stepped forward and took her body from the *Reichsleiter,* for it did not seem right to him to leave her in his charge.

The bodies were placed in a shallow pit, and fifty gallons of gasoline were poured over them and set on fire. As the flames cascaded into the sky, those present stood at attention, arms extended in a final party salute.

The Russians, at that point in time, were perhaps a hundred and fifty yards away from the bunker.

Twelve

Ritter sat at the desk in Meyer's office, going over the print of the ground plan of Schloss Arlberg yet again. Hoffer stood by the door, waiting quietly. Ritter put down his pencil and sat back.

Hoffer said, "Can it be done?"

"I don't see why not," Ritter said. "All it requires is good discipline and a little nerve, and I think our Finns aren't noticeably lacking in either."

The door opened, and Strasser entered. "Jackson is back."

"Ah, yes," Ritter said. "You sent him to Arnheim. May one ask why?"

"First tell me of your plan of attack."

"Very well." Ritter looked down at the print of the castle again. "I will wait until dark. In fact, well after. Say, midnight, when the defenders will already have been

296

on the alert for a considerable period of time, which means they will be tired. No use moving in with the half-tracks because we alert them the instant we start the engines.''

"So?"

"A force of, say, twenty men will approach the edge of the moat under cover of darkness. Two of them will cross the moat, climb the drawbridge, and set a couple of demolition charges. Very easy to make up from what we've got, and it won't need a particularly powerful charge to blow these chains. Another charge against the gate will be timed to explode at the same instant.''

"I see," Strasser said. "The drawbridge falls, the gate opens, and your shock troops rush across to take possession.''

"Backed up by the half-tracks, which start moving the instant they hear the explosion. What do you think?''

"Very good," Strasser said.

"Any weak points?''

"Only one. As it happens, there's an outside floodlight at the entrance. They turned it on about fifteen minutes ago.

I'm sure Sorsa will confirm that if you raise him on the field telephone."

Ritter leaned back. "You have an excellent and very immediate source of information."

"So it would appear," Strasser said, but made no effort to enlighten him. "Of course, you could have a sniper shoot out this floodlight."

"And immediately alert them to the fact that we were up to something."

"An excellent plan, however, and it could still work."

"How?"

"If we had someone able to do exactly the same thing from the inside." Strasser walked to the door and opened it. "All right," he said.

Earl Jackson entered the room, wearing a flying jacket with a sheepskin collar over the uniform of a captain in the United States Army Air Corps.

As Colonel Hesser and Schneider mounted the steps to the east wall, the wind dashed frozen sleet in their faces. It was bitterly cold, and the sergeant major adjusted his grip on Magda's leash.

"A bitch of a night," Hesser said. "Takes me back to 1942 and the Winter War. The kind of cold that eats into the brain."

He shuddered, remembering, and Schneider said, "I wouldn't think they'd bother us on a night like this."

"Isn't that what we used to say about the Russians?" Hesser said. "Until we learned better? And so, I presume, did Ritter. He's spent enough time on the Eastern Front, God knows."

The sentries were spread woefully thin — not that he could do much about that. There was one at the east watchtower. Hesser had a word with him, then leaned out of an embrasure in the wall and looked back toward the pool of light at the gate.

"I wonder how long it will be before one of them can't resist shooting that out? I almost wish they would. An end to this damned uncertainty."

"You think they'll come, then, *Herr Oberst?*" Schneider asked.

"You saw Ritter yourself, didn't you?

Did he look like the kind of man to just run away? And what about those ski patrols circling through the forest right up until dark. No, he's there, all right. And when he's ready, you'll know about it. Anyway, let's check the water gate."

They went down the watchtower steps. There was a small, damp tunnel blocked by a heavy iron grille. A corporal called Wagner stood guard there, a veteran of the Eastern Front, his left arm partially wasted away from bad shrapnel wounds. Just now, he was leaning against the gate, looking out, his Schmeisser ready in his right hand.

"Everything is in order here?" Hesser demanded.

"I'm not sure, *Herr Oberst*. I thought I heard something."

They stood, listening. Snow drifted through the grille, and Hesser said, "Only the wind."

And then Magda whined, straining forward on the leash. "No, *Herr Oberst,*" Schneider said. "He's right. Something moves."

He and Hesser drew their pistols. There

was a distinct slithering sound on the other side of the moat, snow falling into the water, and then a hoarse whisper in English. "Is there anyone there? Don't shoot. I'm an American officer."

Someone entered the water. Hesser said to Schneider, "Switch on your flashlight, a second only, then down on the ground."

There was a pause, then Schneider's flashlight picked Earl Jackson out of the darkness instantly. He was in the middle of the moat, swimming strongly, only his head and the sheepskin collar of his flying jacket showing above the water.

"Kamerad!" he called, gasping for breath. "American officer. I'm looking for General Hamilton Canning."

It was Finebaum, crouched in the shadow of the wall above the main gate, who spotted the momentary spot of light on his left. Below him, Howard and Hoover crouched against the wall, smoking cigarettes.

"Hey, Captain, there was a light down there, below the east watchtower, in the moat."

They were on their feet instantly. "You're certain?" Howard leaned out of the embrasure. "I can't see a thing."

"There was a light. Just for a minute."

"Okay, let's move it," Howard said and started along the wall.

When they entered the water gate tunnel, Jackson was on the other side from Hesser and his men, clutching the grille, knee-deep in water. "Let me in, for Christ's sake. I've got to see General Canning."

"What is it?" Howard demanded. "What's going on?"

Hesser switched on the flashlight without a word. Jackson blinked in the sudden light. He was soaked to the skin, water dripping from his uniform, teeth chattering. He tried to peer into the darkness at Howard.

"You an American, buddy? For Christ's sake, make these crazy bastards let me in. Another five minutes of this, and I'll die of exposure."

"Hey, he's right, Captain," Finebaum said. "He don't look too good."

"Who are you?" Howard demanded.

"Harry Bannerman's the name. Crash-landed this morning about ten miles from here in a P-47. Got picked up by an SS unit. They had me down in the village here until an hour ago. In an inn called the Golden Eagle."

"How did you get away?"

"The landlord helped me — a guy called Meyer. There was another prisoner there. He put him up to it. A Frenchman named Gaillard. He told me to get up here fast and see General Canning. I've got information about when the Krauts intend to hit this place." He rattled the grille ineffectually, his voice breaking. "Let me in, for Christ's sake — if you don't want to die, that is."

"Okay," Howard said to Hesser. "Open the gate and drag him in — but fast. And you, Finebaum, I make personally responsible for blowing his backbone in half if he makes a wrong move.

In the darkness among the trees on the far side of the moat, Strasser, Ritter, and Hoffer listened to the clang of the grille shutting.

"So he's in," Ritter said. "Let's hope they buy his story."

"I don't see why not," Strasser said. "Jackson's strength, as I said before, lies in the fact that he's a genuine American, not the ersatz variety that let Skorzeny down so badly in the Ardennes."

"So now we wait," Ritter said.

"Until it's time for my part in this rather interesting drama." Strasser smiled through the darkness. "You know, I'm really rather looking forward to it."

General Canning, Birr, Madame Chevalier, and Claire were having a late supper of sandwiches and coffee when Hesser and Howard entered, followed by Jackson, an army blanket draped around his shoulders. Finebaum was right behind him, the muzzle of his M1 no more than an inch away from Jackson's backbone.

"What have we here?" Canning demanded, rising to his feet.

"Swam across the moat to the water gate, General," Howard said. "Claims to be an Army Air Corps officer. No papers, no identification on him whatsoever. Not

304

even his dog tags."

"They took them off me," Jackson said. "Those damned SS stripped me of everything. I mean, how many times do I have to tell you?"

"What outfit?" Canning demanded.

"Five Hundred and Tenth Squadron, Four Hundred and Fifth Group, sir. Operating out of what was a *Luftwaffe* base at Hellenbach until we took it four days ago."

"What's your story?"

"My squadron was ordered to hit a panzer column on the other side of Salzburg from here. This morning it was, General. We dropped our bombs dead on target — no problem, there being no *Luftwaffe* to speak of in this area anymore. Then, on the way back, my battery went dead and I had to crash-land."

"What was your aircraft?"

"P-47 Thunderbolt, sir. I made it down in one piece in a clearing in the forest, then struck out for the main road. It's a pretty fluid situation in this area, General. There are plenty of our people around.

305

It's just a question of knowing where."

"And you say you were picked up by an SS unit?"

"That's right, sir. Mostly Finns, but there was a German officer in charge. A man called Ritter."

"And they've been holding you all day?"

"That's right, sir, at an inn called the Golden Eagle in Arlberg." There was a slight pause. He gazed around him wildly. "Say, what goes on here? What do you people think I am — a Kraut or something?"

"Well, I'll tell you, Captain," Finebaum put in, "because it's really funny you should say that. When we were in the Ardennes in 'forty-four — and it was snowing then, too, I might add — there was guys popping up all over the place, just like you, GI uniform, everything. Saying they'd lost their units, asking the way to Malmédy. Stuff like that. An interesting thing — they was all Krautheads."

"Any chance of you shutting this man up?" Canning inquired coldly.

Howard said, "Button it, Finebaum."

Canning said to Jackson, "We're in a hell of a position in here, Bannerman. We can't afford to take anything on trust — you understand?"

"He says he's met Dr. Gaillard, sir," Howard put in.

Claire said excitedly, "You've seen Paul?"

"Sure I've seen him."

"How is he?"

"He's looking after a sick kid down there at the inn. Son of the landlord, a guy named Meyer."

"And the SS have him?" Canning asked.

"Oh, yes. Major Ritter, the officer in command, lets him see to the kid regularly, but they had us locked up together for quite a while. Meyer brought our food, and Gaillard saw him quite a lot each time he went to see to the kid. He's in a pretty bad way."

"All right, how did you escape?"

"Well, it was mostly Meyer who made that possible. He overheard Ritter and some guy called Strasser — a civilian he

307

had with him — discussing their plans for an attack just before dawn. They're going to put some guys across the moat with explosives to blow down your drawbridge. When Gaillard heard that, he told me I'd have to get away somehow and come and warn you people."

"Which you seem to have managed without too much trouble," Birr said.

"That was Meyer again. He tipped me off he'd leave the back door near the kitchen unlocked. I asked to go to the john, gave the Finn who was escorting me a shove at the right moment, got the door open, and ran like hell."

There was a long and heavy silence now, in which everyone seemed to be looking at him. Jackson said, "General, I'm Captain Harry Bannerman of the United States Army Air Corps and when that drawbridge of yours is blown to hell and gone just before dawn tomorrow, you'll know I was telling the truth. Just now, I'd settle for a cup of coffee, dry clothes, and somewhere to lay my head."

Canning smiled suddenly and held out his hand. "I'll tell you something, son.

All of a sudden I've decided to believe you." He turned to Hesser. "Can you find him some dry clothes?"

"Certainly," Hesser said, "if the captain doesn't mind a German uniform. This way, if you please."

Jackson started to follow him, paused, and turned. "Hey, there's just one thing, General. Something kind of funny. It doesn't mean a damn thing to me. Maybe it does to you."

"What's that?" Canning asked him.

"This guy Strasser — the civilian I told you about?"

"Well?"

"It's just that he seems to swing a lot of weight. I mean, a couple of times there he acted as if he was in charge, and I heard Ritter call him *'Reichsleiter.'* That ring any bells with you?"

Hesser turned pale. "Bormann?" he whispered.

"That's it," Canning said excitedly. "I knew I'd seen that ugly face somewhere before. Martin Bormann, secretary to Hitler himself. I saw him just once on the stand at the Berlin Olympic Games in 'thirty-six.'' He turned on Hesser. "You didn't recognize him?''

"I've never laid eyes on Bormann in my life," Hesser said. "He's a man of the shadows — always has been.''

"Now we know why they wanted us so urgently," Canning said. "Hostages to bargain with in the hope he might save his rotten neck.'' He rubbed his hands together excitedly. "Good work, Bannerman. You've really earned your keep with that one. Take him away now, Max, and get some dry clothes on him.''

Hesser and Jackson went out. Madame Chevalier said, "What does this mean, General? I've heard of this man Bormann. A member of the inner circle, isn't that so?''

"Not a thing to worry about, I assure you," Canning said. "Now have some more coffee, sit down and take it easy, and I'll be back in a moment.''

He went out with Howard and Finebaum, closed the door behind him, and paused in the shadows at the head of the stairs.

"What do you think, sir?'' Howard asked.

Canning looked down at Finebaum. "Is he any good?"

"A sackful of medals. You see, he seems to have a talent for killing people, General."

"Okay, soldier," Canning said. "You watch Bannerman like a hawk. Not too close, but be around just in case."

"I'm your man, General." Finebaum went down the stairs into the shadows.

"You don't believe Bannerman, sir?" Howard asked.

"I had a Scottish grandmother, Captain, from the Isle of Skye, who used to say she had an instinct for things. No proof because there was no need. She just knew. I sometimes think some of it rubbed off on me. Now get back to that gate. I'll join you there as soon as I can."

He opened the door and went back into the dining hall.

When Howard climbed up to the ramparts above the gate, it was snowing hard — large flakes drifting down through the yellow glare of the spotlight spiraling in the slight wind. Hoover was up there with three Germans. Like them, the American was wearing a *Wehrmacht* winter-issue parka.

"Decided to change sides, I see," Howard said. "Kind of late in the war, isn't it?"

"The romantic in me," Hoover said. "My great-grandfather was in the Army of the Confederacy. We Hoovers just take to losing naturally, I guess. What about Bannerman?"

"He tells a convincing story. Says the opposition are going to hit us just before dawn. Slip a couple of guys across the moat with explosives and come running."

He explained the rest of it, and when he was finished Hoover said, "That last part doesn't make too much sense to me. I never even heard of this guy Bormann. Did you?"

"Somewhere or other," Howard said. "But I never thought he was particularly important. I mean not like Ribbentrop or Goebbels or one of those guys. Sending someone like him sure lays it on the line how much they want to get their hands on these people as hostages."

"Where's Finebaum?"

"Somewhere back there in the north tower, keeping an eye on Bannerman. General Canning's orders."

One of the sentries said quickly in German, "Something moves — out there."

He grabbed Howard's arm and pointed. A moment later, Ritter, Hoffer, and Strasser moved out of the darkness into the circle of light.

"Hello, the wall," Ritter called. "Is General Canning there?"

Howard stayed back in the shadows. "What do you want?"

"Herr Strasser would like a word with General Canning. He has a proposition to put to him."

"Tell me," Howard called.

Ritter shrugged. "If that is your attitude, then I can see we are wasting your time. Thank you and good night."

They turned to go, and Hoover whispered, "Sir, this could be important."

"Okay, Harry, okay." Howard leaned forward into the light. "Hold it. I'll see what he says."

A moment later, he was speaking to Canning on the field telephone. "It could be a trap, sir."

"I don't think so," Canning said. "They must know they'd be cut down in half a second at the first sign of trouble, and I don't think they'd make that kind of sacrifice — not if Strasser is who Jackson says he is. No, drop the drawbridge and let them in. Send Strasser up here to me. Keep Ritter with you."

A few moments later, the drawbridge started to descend with a rattle of chains. Ritter said softly, "So, the fish bite. Are you always so correct in your prophecies?"

"Only where matters of importance are concerned," Strasser said, and as the drawbridge thudded down into place, they walked across together, Hoffer following.

The judas door opened, and Howard peered through briefly. He stepped back, and they moved inside. As he closed the gate and barred it, Howard said to Hoover, "Take Herr Strasser up to the north tower. General Canning is waiting. You, Major," he continued to Ritter, "will have to put up with my company until he gets back, I'm afraid."

Strasser moved off without a word. following Hoover. Hoffer stood, back to the gate, stony-faced. Ritter took out his case, selected a cigarette, then offered one to Howard.

"I must warn you they're Russian — an acquired taste."

Howard took one and leaned back against the wall, the butt of his Thompson braced against his hip. "So here we are again," he said.

When Hoover knocked on the door and led the way into the upper dining hall, only Canning and Justin Birr stood by the fire. Strasser paused nonchalantly in the center of the room, hands in the pockets of his leather coat, slouch hat slanted over one ear.

"Good evening, gentlemen."

Canning nodded to Hoover. "You can wait outside, Sergeant. I'll call you if I need you."

The door closed. Strasser crossed to the fireplace and spread his hands to the blaze. "Nothing like a log fire to take the

315

chill off. It's cold out there tonight. The kind that eats into your bones like acid."

Canning glanced at Birr and nodded. Birr crossed to the sideboard, poured a generous measure of brandy into a glass, and returned.

"Just to show how humanitarian we are. Now what the hell do you want, Bormann?"

Strasser paused in the act of drinking some of the brandy. "Strasser, General. The name is Strasser."

"Strange," Canning said. "You look exactly like the man I saw in Berlin in 1936 standing on the rostrum behind Adolf Hitler at the Olympic Games. *Reichsleiter* Martin Bormann."

"You flatter me, General. I am, I assure you, a relatively unimportant official of the Department of Prisoner-of-War Administration."

"I have difficulty in imagining you as relatively unimportant. But go on."

"Let us consider your situation here. There are twenty-four of you in this garrison, twenty-six if we count the ladies. Most of your men are reservists who have never fought, or cripples who can barely lift a rifle.''

''So?''

''We, on the other hand, have almost forty battle-hardened shock troops to call upon. Men of the *Waffen*-SS, and whatever you may think, General, however much you disapprove, that means the best in the world.''

''Get on with it,'' Justin Birr said. ''Just what are you trying to prove?''

''That if we decide to move against you, the consequences will be disastrous — for you.''

''A matter of opinion,'' Canning said. ''But accepting that what you say is true, what do you suggest we do about it. I mean, that is why you're here, isn't it? To offer us some kind of alternative solution? I mean, before you try slipping a couple of men across the moat just before dawn to blow the drawbridge chains?''

''My goodness, somebody has been busy,'' Strasser said. ''All right, General, it's simple. We have Dr. Gaillard, whom we found at the Golden Eagle in Arlberg attending to the landlord's sick son. Sad, how good deeds can so often prove our undoing. However, if you and Colonel Birr will hand yourselves over, we'll be content with that and let the ladies go free."

"Not a chance," Canning said.

Strasser turned to Birr. "You agree?"

"I'm afraid so, old boy. You see, we don't really trust you — that's the truth of it. Terribly sorry, but there it is."

"And the ladies?" Strasser said. "They have no say in this?"

Canning hesitated, then went and opened the door. He spoke briefly to Hoover, then returned. "They'll be here directly."

He and Birr lit cigarettes. Strasser turned to survey the room and immediately saw the great silver bowl of scarlet winter roses on the piano.

"Ah, my favorite flowers." He was genuinely delighted and crossed the room to admire them. "Winter roses. Like life in the midst of death — they fill the heart with gladness."

The door opened, and as he turned, Claire de Beauville, Madame Chevalier, and Earl Jackson entered the room. Strasser smiled at the American. "We missed you at supper."

"Sorry I couldn't stay."

Strasser turned to Canning. "An explanation of one or two things which were puzzling me. I was beginning to think you were a wonder-worker. It's nice to know you're just a man like the rest of us."

"Okay," Canning said. "I've had just about enough for one night. You wanted a word with the ladies. Well, they're here, so make the most of it."

"I can't imagine what you could possibly have to say to me that I would be interested in hearing, *monsieur,*" Madame Chevalier said. "Thankfully, I can use the time to some advantage."

She sat down at the piano and started to play a Debussy nocturne. Strasser, not in the least put out, said, "I have offered you ladies your freedom — guaranteed it — on condition that the general and Colonel Birr come quietly and with no fuss."

Madame Chevalier ignored him, and

Claire simply walked across to the bowl of roses and buried her face in them.

Strasser said, "I should have known. Above all flowers, they need delicate hands and infinite patience in their rearing. Your work, *madame?*"

"Yes," she said. "So, as you can see, I am fully occupied and cannot leave at the present time."

Canning moved in. "You heard the lady."

Strasser selected one of the blooms, snapped the stem, and placed it in his buttonhole. "Ah, well, it was worth the trip. You like winter roses, General?"

"I like whatever Madame de Beauville cultivates."

"Good," Strasser said. "I'll remember that at your funeral. One gets so bored with lilies. A single scarlet winter rose should look very good. And now, I think, I will bid you good night. There is obviously nothing more for me here."

He walked to the door. Hoover glanced at Canning, who nodded. The sergeant led the way out.

There was a heavy silence, and Madame

Chevalier stopped playing. "I must be getting old. Suddenly I feel cold — very, very cold."

Strasser stepped through the judas door, followed by Hoffer. As Ritter moved out, Howard said softly, "I'll be seeing you."

"When?" Ritter said. "Under the elms at dawn? Six paces each way, turn and fire? You take it all too seriously, Captain."

He followed the others across. As they stepped onto the bank, the drawbridge lifted behind them.

"Are you satisfied?" Ritter asked Strasser softly.

"Oh, yes, I think so. Jackson should be well enough entrenched now. The rest is up to him."

He started to whistle cheerfully.

It was just after midnight, and in Berlin, at his office in the bunker, Bormann worked steadily, the scatching of his pen the only sound, the noise of the Russian shelling muted, faraway. There was a light tap on the door. It opened, and Goebbels entered. He looked pale and haggard, the skin drawn tightly over his face. A dead man walking.

Bormann put down his pen. "How goes it?"

Goebbels passed a flimsy across the desk. "That's the radiogram I've just dispatched to Plön."

GRAND ADMIRAL DÖNITZ
(Personal and Secret)
To be handled only by an officer. Führer died yesterday, 1530 hours. In his will, dated April 29, he appoints you as president of the Reich, Goebbels as Reich chancellor, Bormann as party minister. . . .

There was more, but Bormann didn't bother to read it. "Paper, Joseph. Just so much paper."

"Perhaps," Goebbels said, "but we must preserve the formalities, even at this desperate stage."

"Why?"

"For posterity, if nothing else. For those who will come after us."

"Nobody comes after us. Not here — not in Germany for many years to come. Our destiny lies elsewhere, for the time being."

"For you, perhaps, but not for me," Goebbels said, his voice flat, toneless.

"I see," Bormann said. "You intend to emulate the *Führer?*"

"No shame in ending a life which will have no further value to me if I cannot stand at his side. I have no intention of spending the rest of my life running around the world like some eternal refugee. Preparations are already in hand. The children will be given cyanide capsules."

"What, all six of them?" Bormann actually smiled. "Thorough and painstaking to the end, I see. And you and Magda?"

"I have already detailed an SS orderly to shoot us when the moment comes."

Bormann shrugged. "Then I can only wish you better luck in the hereafter than you've had here."

"And you?" Goebbels said.

"Oh, I'll try my luck in the outside

world, I think. We should be all right here for the rest of today. I'll make a run for it tonight with Axmann, Stumpfegger, and one or two more. We intend to try the underground railway tunnel. That should get us to Friedrichstrasse Station all right. Mohnke is still holding out there with a battle group of three thousand. SS, sailors, *Volkssturm,* and a whole batch of Hitler Youth. They seem to be holding their own.''

''And then?''

''With their help we'll try to cross the Weidendammer Bridge over the Spree. Once on the other side, we should stand an excellent chance. Not many Russians in the northwestern suburbs yet.''

''I can only wish you luck.'' Suddenly Goebbels sounded very tired indeed. He turned to the door, started to open it, and paused. ''What comes afterward — if you get away?''

''Oh, I'll make out.''

''Come to think of it, you always did, didn't you?''

Goebbels went out, closing the door. Bormann sat there, thinking about what he had said. *I have no intention of spending my life running around the world like some eternal refugee.* He shrugged, picked up his pen, and resumed his writing.

Jackson lay on the bed, waiting in the dark in the room they'd given him. He glanced at the luminous dial of his watch. It was twenty past midnight — ten minutes to go. He lit a cigarette and drew on it nervously. Not that he was afraid — simply keyed up. A brilliant suggestion of Strasser's, to tell them he was the *Reichsleiter.* Coupled with Strasser's personal appearance, it had effectively clouded the entire issue. He was certain they'd accepted him completely now.

He checked his watch again. Time to go. He got up and padded to the door, and when he opened it, the passageway was deserted, a place of shadows partially illuminated by a single small bulb at the far end. He caught a brief glimpse of himself in a full-length gilt mirror. He was wearing Hesser's best uniform, and it fitted rather well. He moved on, past one oil painting after another — blank, eighteenth-century faces staring down at him. He turned the stairs at the end, paused by the white door on the small landing, and knocked.

The door opened slightly and instantly, as if the occupant had been waiting. "Valhalla Exchange," Jackson whispered.

"Good — everything's ready for you," Claire de Beauville said.

Jackson stepped into the room. On the washstand were plastic explosive, detonators, and a Schmeisser. He put the explosive in one pocket, the detonators in the other, and picked up the machine pistol.

"Anything else?" she said. Her face was pale, unnaturally calm.

"Yes. Some sort of handgun. Can you manage that?"

"I think so."

She opened the drawer of the bedside table and produced a Walther. Jackson checked that it was loaded, then pushed it down into his waistband at the small of his back under the tunic.

"I like an ace-in-the-hole, just in case

things go wrong. Amazing how often even an expert search misses that particular spot. Have you spoken to him on the radio again since he was here?''

''Twenty minutes ago. Everything is arranged, exactly as planned. They wait on you. You'll need a greatcoat and a cap to get you across the square unnoticed. There are men working out there. The small staircase at the end of the passage takes you to the main entrance hall, you'll find a cloakroom at the bottom, and the room that houses the drawbridge mechanism is the first door on the left in the gate tunnel.''

''You've done well.'' Jackson grinned. ''Well, mustn't stand here gossiping. Once more into the breach, dear friends . . .'' And he picked up the Schmeisser and slipped out.

In the dining hall, Canning was standing alone in front of the fire when Hesser entered. ''Cold,'' the German said. ''Too cold. Schneider said you wanted a word.''

''Yes. Let's say that the drawbridge falls and the gate blows, what happens then?''

"They'll come in at full speed in those half-tracks, I should imagine."

"Exactly. Armored troop carriers, and we don't even have anything capable of blowing off a track unless someone gets lucky and close enough with one of your stick grenades."

"True, but you have some sort of solution, I think, or you would not be raising the matter."

"We've been together too long, Max." Canning smiled. "Okay — that cannon in the center of the square. Big Bertha."

Hesser said, "She hasn't been fired since the Franco-Prussian War."

"I know, but she could still have one good belt left in her. Get Schneider on the job. You can soon make up some sort of charge. Prise open a few cartridges to make touch powder. Stoke up the barrel with old metal, chains, anything you can find, then have the men haul her down to the tunnel. Say, twenty or thirty yards from the entrance. It could knock hell out of the first vehicle to come out of there."

"Or simply explode in the face of whoever puts a light to the touch hole."

"Well, that's me," Canning told him. "I thought of it, so I'll stick with it."

Hesser sighed, "Very well, *Herr General*, you command here, not I," and he went out.

Thirteen

Jackson went down the rear staircase quickly and paused at the bottom, staying well back in the shadows; but his caution was unnecessary, for the hall was quite deserted. He opened the door on his left, slipped inside, and switched on the light.

As Claire de Beauville had indicated, it was a cloakroom, and there was an assortment of coats and caps hanging on the pegs — even a couple of helmets. He hesitated, debating, then selected a field cap and heavy officer's greatcoat. He and Hesser were, after all, of the same build, and it was a reasonable assumption that in the darkness he would be mistaken for the colonel by anyone who saw him.

When he opened the front door, snow filtered through. He moved out quickly and paused at the top of the steps to get his bearings. Most of the courtyard was in darkness, but in the center a group of German soldiers supervised by Howard and Sergeant Hoover worked in the light of a storm lantern on Big Bertha.

Jackson went down the steps to the left and moved into the protecting dark, following the line of the wall toward the main gate. He paused at the end of the tunnel. It was very quiet, except for an occasional murmur of voices from the men in the middle of the courtyard, and a sudden, small wind dashed snow in his face.

It was as if he were listening for something — waiting, he wasn't sure what for — and he felt a shiver of loneliness. Suddenly, in one of those instant flashes of recall, he was once again the fifteen-year-old minister's son standing in a Michigan snowstorm at one o'clock in the morning, despair in his heart. Home late, and the door locked against him for the last time.

And from that to Arlberg — so much in between, and yet in some ways so little. He smiled wryly, moved into the tunnel.

First door on the left, Claire de Beauville had said. He held the Schmeisser ready and tried the handle of the iron-bound door. It opened gently; he pushed it wide and stepped inside.

The place was lit by a single bulb. Gunther Voss, Gaillard's erstwhile guard, sat in helmet and greatcoat on a stool by a small woodstove, his back to the door, reading a magazine.

"Is that you, Hans?" he demanded without turning around. "About time."

Jackson pushed the door shut with a very definite click. Voss glanced over his shoulder; his mouth gaped in astonishment.

"Just do as you're told," Jackson said, "and everything will be fine."

He stepped lightly across the room, picked up Voss's Mauser rifle, and tossed it on top of one of the bunks, out of the way.

"What are you going to do?" Voss asked hoarsely. He was absolutely terrified, sweat on his face.

"You've got it wrong, my friend. It's what you're going to do that counts."

A cold breeze touched him in the back

of the neck; there was the faintest of creakings from the door. Finebaum said, "That's it, hotshot — you're all through."

Jackson turned in the same moment, the Schmeisser coming up, and Finebaum shot him through the right arm just above the elbow. Jackson was knocked back against the table, dropping the Schmeisser. He forced himself up, clutching his arm, blood spurting between his fingers.

"What are you bucking for — a coffin?" Finebaum demanded, and he nodded to Voss. "Search him."

Voss went through Jackson's pockets and found the plastic explosive and the detonators. He held them up without a word, and the door was flung open and Howard and Hoover rushed in.

"What's going on here?" Howard demanded.

Finebaum took one of the packets of plastic explosive from Voss and threw it across to him. "Just like I said, Captain. The Ardennes all over again."

Claire de Beauville, waiting in the

darkness of her room, heard the shot. Her window looked out over the water garden, not the courtyard, so she couldn't see anything, yet the shot was trouble, whatever the cause. It meant that Jackson had failed. She lit a cigarette and sat on the bed in the dark, smoking nervously, but that wasn't any good. She had to know what had happened, there was no avoiding that fact. She opened the washstand door, took out another Walther automatic pistol, slipped it into her jacket pocket, and went out.

When she went into the dining hall, Madame Chevalier was already there with Canning, Birr, and Hesser.

"What's happened?" Claire said. "I heard a shot."

"Nothing to be alarmed about." Canning put an arm about her shoulders. "Everything's under control. I've just had Howard on the field telephone from the gate. It seems friend Jackson wasn't all he pretended to be. They're bringing him up now."

She turned away and moved to join Madame Chevalier by the fire. The door opened and Howard entered, followed by Jackson and Finebaum. Jackson was no longer wearing the greatcoat. A scarf was tied about his right arm, blood soaking through.

"Okay, what happened?" Canning demanded.

Howard held up the packets of plastic explosive. "He was going to blow up the drawbridge winding gear with this. Lucky for all of us, Finebaum was on the ball."

Canning turned to Jackson. "All right, Bannerman, or whatever your name is. Who are you? What are you?"

"Sorry, General," Jackson said. "I've been trying to work that one out for myself for the past thirty years, with a total lack of success."

Before Canning could reply, the door opened and Hoover looked in. "General, sir?"

"What is it?"

"The German sentry who was on duty in the winding-gear room, Private Voss, is out here asking to see you or Colonel Hesser. He says he has information about this man."

"Let's have him in, then."

Hoover snapped his fingers, and Voss stepped into the room. His army greatcoat and the helmet were too big for him, and he looked faintly ridiculous.

"He doesn't speak English," Hesser said. "I'll deal with this. You've got something to say, Voss?" he asked in German.

It poured out of Voss like a dam bursting, the words seeming to spill over themselves, and several times he gestured toward Jackson. He finally stopped, and Hesser turned, a frown on his face.

"What is it?" Canning demanded. "Good news or bad?"

Hesser looked at Jackson gravely. "He says he's seen this man before — yesterday at Arlberg, sitting in a field car with Strasser and Ritter when they first drove into the square.

"He was at that time wearing the uniform of a *Hauptsturmführer* in the SS."

"Now that," Canning said, "really is interesting. Where did you learn your English, Bannerman? I must congratulate you. They did a first-class job."

"I think you'll find he was raised to it," Hesser said. "You see, Voss noticed that the armshield on this — this gentleman's uniform was a Stars and Stripes."

There was a heavy silence. Canning glanced at Jackson, then turned back to Hesser incredulously. "Are you saying this man is a genuine American?"

"In the *Waffen*-SS, *Herr General,* there are what are known as the foreign legions. Units of volunteers raised from every country in Europe. There is even a *Britisches Freikorps* raised from English soldiers recruited from prisoner-of-war camps."

"And you're trying to tell me there are Americans who would sell out their country like that?"

"Not many," Hesser said gently. "A handful only. They are called the George Washington Legion."

Canning turned, his arm swinging, and struck Jackson backhanded across the face. "You dirty yellow bastard," he shouted.

Jackson staggered back, cannoning into Madame Chevalier. In a second he had an arm around her throat and produced the Walther from the waistband at his back.

"Okay, just stand clear — all of you."

Claire de Beauville remained where she was on his left, apparently frozen, hands thrust deep into the pockets of her jacket.

Jackson said, "It's a funny world, General. Not too long ago I was one of the gallant American boys flying for the Finns against the Russians. Remember that one? Then, all of a sudden, the Finns are allies of the Nazis and back fighting the Russians again. Now that kind of thing can be just a little confusing."

"You should have got out," Canning said hoarsely.

"Maybe you're right. All I know is I was flying with the same guys against the same enemy. Hurricanes, by the way, with swastikas on them. Can you beat that?"

"Just let her go," Canning said. "She's an old woman."

"I'm sorry, General. I can't do that. She's going to walk me right out of that front gate — aren't you, *Liebling?*"

Claire stepped in close; her right hand came out of her pocket, clutching the Walther. She rammed the muzzle into his side and pulled the trigger.

The sound seemed very loud, sending shock waves around the room. Jackson bucked, crying out in agony, and staggered back. She swung the Walther up, clutching it in both hands now, and pulled the trigger again and again until the gun was empty, driving him back against the wall beside the fireplace.

As his body slumped to the floor, she threw the Walther away from her and turned to Canning, her face contorted.

"Hamilton?"

He opened his arms, and she ran into them.

She lay on her bed in the dark, as Jackson had lain no more than an hour ago, waiting, afraid to move in case they came back. And then, finally, when all seemed quiet, she got up, went to the door, and shot the bolt.

She lifted the washbasin out of its mahogany stand and took out the small compact radio which was secreted inside. An S-phone, they had told her. A British invention, far in advance of any German counterpart, obtained when an OSS agent in France had been picked up by the Gestapo.

She pressed the electronic buzzer that processed the call sign automatically, and waited. Strasser's voice sounded in her ear almost instantly, clear and distinct.

"Valhalla here."

"Exchange. It didn't work. He was caught in the act."

"Dead?"

She hesitated, but only for a moment. "Yes."

"Very well. You'll have to do it yourself. You have sufficient materials left?"

"Yes." She hesitated again. "I'm not sure that I can."

"No choice. You know the consequences if you fail. You should stand a good chance. The Jackson affair will have taken the edge off things. They won't be expecting a similar move from inside. Why should they?" He paused, then said, "I repeat — you know the consequences if you fail."

"All right." Her voice was barely a whisper, a dying fall.

"Good. Valhalla out."

She sat there for a long, long moment, then got up slowly and took the S-phone back to the washstand. Then she got down on her knees, removed the bottom drawer, and took out the two packets of plastic explosive and detonators that remained from what she had stolen from the armory earlier.

Strasser, seated at the desk in Meyer's office, closed the lid of the case containing the radio and locked it. He sat there thinking for a moment, his face grave, then stood up and went out.

Ritter was seated by the fire in the bar, enjoying a late supper. Cheese, black bread, and beer. Hoffer lurked in the background as usual, in case of need.

As Ritter looked up, Strasser said, "Total failure, I'm afraid. He's dead."

Ritter said calmly, "What now?"

"The plan still stands. My agent will

341

make another attempt.''

Ritter selected a cigarette from his case and lit it with a twig from the fire. ''One thing puzzles me. Why didn't this contact of yours make the attempt in the first place? Why the elaborate charade with Jackson?''

''It's really very simple,'' Strasser said. ''You see, she's a woman.''

Meyer went up the stairs from the kitchen, carrying a tray containing sandwiches, a pot of coffee, and a cup. The big Finn at the door regarded him impassively — one of the few who didn't speak a word of German, as Meyer well knew. In fact, communication had proved impossible. Meyer spoke fair English, but that had provoked no response, nor had the few phrases of French that he knew. He raised the tray and gestured at the door. The Finn slung his Schmeisser, unlocked the door, and stood back.

Gaillard was sitting beside the bed, wiping Arnie's damp forehead. The boy, obviously still feverish, moaned, tossing and turning, clutching at the blankets.

"Ah, there you are, Johann," Gaillard said in German. "I'm about ready for that."

"How is he, *Herr Doktor?*"

"A little better, though you might not think it to look at him."

Meyer put the tray on the bedside table and started to pour the coffee. "I was in the passageway that leads from the bar to the kitchen just now," he said in a low voice. "Don't worry about this one. He can't understand me."

"So?"

"I heard Herr Strasser and Major Ritter talking. Something about the castle. Strasser said he had a contact in there. A woman."

Gaillard looked up at him in astonishment.

"Impossible. There are only two women in the place, Madame Chevalier and Claire de Beauville. Frenchwomen to the core, both of them. What are you saying, man?"

"Only what I heard, *Herr Doktor.* I think they're waiting for something to happen."

The Finn said something unintelligible, strode into the room, and grabbed Meyer by the shoulder. He shoved him outside quickly and closed the door.

Gaillard sat there, staring into space. Impossible to believe. Meyer must have got it wrong. Must have. The boy cried out, and Gaillard turned quickly, squeezed out his cloth in the bowl of water, and wiped the forehead gently.

Claire de Beauville paused in the shadows at the bottom of the back stairs, listening. All was still. She opened the door on her left gently and stepped into the cloakroom. When she slipped out a few seconds later, she was wearing a military greatcoat and a steel helmet, both far too large for her, but that didn't matter. In the darkness it was only the general impression that was important.

It was snowing lightly when she went outside, and the entire courtyard was shrouded in darkness, no one working on Big Bertha this time. She took a deep breath to steady her nerves, went down the steps, and started across to the gate.

There was a murmur of conversation up on the wall where the sentries talked in subdued voices. In the tunnel itself, silence. She hesitated at the door of the winding-gear room, then tried the handle gently. The door opened with a slight creak. It was dark in there. With a tremendous surge of relief, she stepped inside. Her groping hand found the switch, and she turned on the light.

Canning was standing there with Hesser and Birr, Howard and Finebaum against the wall. She stood there, very pale, looking suddenly like some little girl in a macabre game of dressing up that had gone wrong, lost in that ridiculous greatcoat and steel helmet.

"How did you know?" she said tonelessly.

"Well, I'll tell you, miss, you'll have to blame me for that." Finebaum slung his M1, crossed to her side, and searched her pockets, finding the explosive and detonators instantly. "You see, the general here, being highly suspicious of our old pal Bannerman, put me on his trail. I was watching his door when he came out and went to your room. The rest, as they say in the movies, you know. I didn't get a chance to tell the general about it right away because everything happened pretty fast after that.''

''That'll do, Finebaum,'' Canning said.

''Anything you say, sir.''

Finebaum moved away. She stood there, defenseless. Canning glared at her, eyes burning, agony on his face.

It was Hesser who said, strangely gentle, ''Strasser is Bormann, then?''

''I don't know. I've never met him. Remember the Gestapo security check on the castle two months ago, when we were all interviewed privately? I received my instructions then from that SS colonel, Rattenhuber. He said he was acting for Bormann. A special radio was secreted in my room. I was given times when I could expect messages.''

''The damage to our own radio spares,'' Hesser said. ''That was you?''

''Yes.''

''Why, for God's sake?'' Canning said harshly.

''It's really quite simple,'' she said.

"Remember my husband, Etienne?"

"Of course. Shot dead while trying to escape from SD headquarters in Paris."

"So I believed," she said, "until Rattenhuber was able to prove to me that wasn't true. Etienne is alive, Hamilton. Has been all along. An inmate of Mauthausen concentration camp."

"I see," Justin Birr said. "And the price of his continued existence was your cooperation."

"It wasn't enough," Canning cried. "You hear me? Not to excuse what you have done."

The rage, the anguish in him was personal, and obvious to everyone there. His hand came up, clutching his Walther.

"Shoot me, then, Hamilton, if you must," she said in the same flat voice. "It doesn't matter. Nothing matters any longer. Etienne is as good as dead now."

It was Finebaum who moved first, getting in front of her and facing Canning, his M1 still slung from his shoulder.

"General, I respect you — I respect you like hell — but this isn't the way, sir, and

I can't just stand by and let you do it."

Canning gazed at him wildly, the Walther shaking in his hand, and then something seemed to die inside him, the light faded, he lowered the pistol.

"Captain Howard."

"Sir."

"Lower the drawbridge, then open the gate."

"I beg your pardon, sir?"

"You heard me." Canning's voice was flat. "I don't want her here, you hear me? Let her go. She can't harm us now."

He brushed past her and went outside.

It was Sorsa, in the observation post the Finns had set up in the trees above the first bend, who noticed the drawbridge descending. Ritter had only just arrived from the village and was still in the field car on the road below.

Sorsa called softly, "Something going on up there at the gate. They're lowering the drawbridge."

Ritter scrambled up the bank to join him, and as he did so, the judas door opened and Claire de Beauville stepped into the light. She started across without hesitation, and the moment she reached the opposite side, the drawbridge lifted again behind her. She came on.

"You know who it is?" Sorsa demanded.

"Madame de Beauville, one of the *prominenti.*" Ritter lowered his night glasses. "Now I wonder what friend Strasser will have to say about this rather singular turn of events?"

As the drawbridge started to rise again, Canning went back into the winding-gear room. Finebaum and Hoover were turning the massive wheels by hand, Howard watching them. Hesser and Birr talked together in low voices.

Canning's face was white with fury. "Okay, that's it. I've had enough of hanging around and nothing happening. I'm going out there to see what the situation is."

"Good God, Hamilton, how on earth are you going to do that?" Birr demanded.

"Leave by the water gate. There's an

old skiff in the tunnel there. We can cross the moat in that. They'll be heavily occupied with the woman at the moment. They won't expect any move like this."

Birr shrugged. "All right, Hamilton. If that's how you want it, I'm your man."

"No, not you. You're needed here."

Howard said, "If you're looking for volunteers, sir . . ."

"Captain, in my entire career, I never asked anyone under my command to volunteer for anything. If I need a man, I tell him." He nodded at Hoover and Finebaum. "I'll take these two. You stay here to back up Colonel Birr. Any questions?"

Birr shrugged helplessly. "You give the orders, Hamilton. You're in command."

It was damp in the tunnel, and cold. They waited while Schneider got the water gate unlocked, and then the sergeant major and a couple of his men got the skiff into the water.

Hesser said, "It's in pretty rotten condition, *Herr General*. Careful your boot doesn't go through the bottom."

Howard handed Canning his Thompson. "Better take this, sir. You might need it."

"Thanks," Canning said. "We'll hit those trees as fast as we can, then work our way through and see if we can make out what's happening around that first bend in the road. In and out again, nice and fast. I'd say we should be back here in thirty minutes."

"We'll be looking for you," Birr called softly.

Hoover and Finebaum were already in the skiff. Canning joined them, sitting on the stern rail, and Howard gave them a strong push. The skiff glided across the moat, its prow bit into the snow of the other bank, and Finebaum was ashore in an instant. He knelt there, covering Hoover and Canning while they pulled the skiff up out of the water a little.

"Okay," Canning whispered, "let's go."

"Excuse me, General, but I figure we've got something to settle first."

"What in hell are you talking about, soldier?"

"You did say this was a reconnaissance mission, General?"

"Yes."

"Well, that's good because that's what Harry and me and the captain have been kind of specializing in for the past eighteen months — only I always take point, sir. I mean, I lead the way on account of I seem to have a nose for it and we all live longer. Okay, General?"

"Okay," Canning said. "Just so long as we get moving."

"Right. Just keep your mouth shut and follow my ass."

He was away in an instant, moving very fast, and Canning went after him, Hoover following. They reached the tree line, and Finebaum paused to get his bearings. In spite of the darkness, there was a faint luminosity because of the snow.

Finebaum dropped to one knee, his face close to the ground, then he stood up. "Ski tracks, so those mothers are still around."

He set off again, going straight up the slope through the trees at a speed which had Canning struggling for breath. From the top of the slope, the ground inclined to the east more gently, through pine trees whose branches were covered with snow. Finebaum was some yards ahead by now, and suddenly signaling them to halt, he went forward. He waved them on.

Finebaum was crouched beside a snow-covered bush in a small hollow on the ridge above the road. The Finns were encamped below, beside the three half-tracks and the field car. The scene was illuminated by a couple of storm lanterns, and in their light it was possible to see Sorsa, Ritter, and Claire de Beauville standing by the field car. The Finns squatted around portable field stoves in small groups.

"Hey, this could be a real turkey shoot," Finebaum said. "There must be thirty or thirty-five guys down there. We open up now, we could take half of them out, no trouble." He caressed the barrel of his M1. "On the other hand, that would probably mean the lady getting it, and you wouldn't like that, would you, General?"

"No, I wouldn't like it at all,"

Canning said.

Strange how different it seemed, now that they were apart. Standing down there in the lamplight, she might have been a stranger. No anger in him at all now.

"But when she moves out, General?" Finebaum said. "That would be different."

"Very different." Canning eased the Thompson forward.

Finebaum leaned across to Hoover. "You move ten yards that way, on the other side of the bank, Harry. Give us a better field of fire. I'll look after the general."

"And who'll look after you!" Hoover asked and wriggled away through the snow.

Finebaum took out a couple of German stick grenades and laid them ready in the snow. They were still talking down there by the field car.

Canning said, "What are you going to do when you get home, Finebaum?"

"Hell, that's easy, General. I'm going to buy something big — like maybe my own hotel in New York someplace. Fill

354

it with high-class women."

"And make a fortune out of them? Or maybe plunge in yourself?"

"That's where I can't make my mind up." They didn't look at each other, but continued to watch the group below. "It's a funny war."

"Is it?"

"If you don't know, who does, General?"

Claire got into the field car. Ritter climbed in beside her and nodded to Hoffer, who started the engine. "Beautiful." Finebaum breathed. "Just too beautiful. Get ready, General."

The field car moved into the night, the engine noise starting to dwindle. And then, as Canning and Finebaum eased forward in the snow to take aim at the men below, there was a sudden whisper in the night, like wings beating.

They both turned as a Finn in white winter uniform, the hood of his parka drawn up over his field cap, erupted from the trees and did a perfect stem turn, coming to a dead halt. Finebaum fired from the hip three times very fast, knocking him back among the bushes.

"Watch it you two!" Hoover yelled. "Three o'clock high!"

Canning swiveled in the right direction and found another Finn coming down the slope through the trees like a rocket. He started to fire the Thompson, snow dancing in fountains across the face of the slope, and the Finn swerved to one side and disappeared. There was uproar down below as Sorsa shouted commands, ordering his men forward in skirmish order. Someone started to fire from the trees above them, and then, below on the road, a big Finnish *Rottenführer* jumped into one of the half-tracks, swung the heavy machine gun, and let off a burst that cut branches from the trees above Canning's head.

"You wanted action, General — you got it," Finebaum said and called to Hoover, "Hey, Harry, get ready to move out, old buddy. One, two, three — the old routine. Understand?"

There was no reply. He emptied his rifle into the men and the road below, and shoved in another clip. "Okay, General, let's move it," he said and crawled through the bushes toward Hoover.

The sergeant was lying on his back, eyes open wide, as if surprised that this could happen to him after all this time. There was a large and very ragged hole in his throat where two machine-gun bullets had hit together.

Finebaum turned and started to crawl back to their original position. The Finns were halfway up the slope at the side of the road now. He picked up the first stick grenade and tossed it over. There was a deafening explosion and cries of anguish. He ducked as the *Rottenführer* in the half-track swung the machine gun in his direction, kicking a wall of snow six feet in the air.

"Good-bye, old buddy," Finebaum shouted and tossed the second grenade.

It seemed to drift through the night in a kind of slow motion. The *Rottenführer* ducked; it dropped into the half-track beside him. A second later, it exploded, lifting him bodily into the air.

Finebaum yelled, "Okay, General, let's get the hell out of here," and he got to his feet and ran up the slope, head down.

Canning lost contact with him almost instantly, but kept on running, clutching the Thompson gun across his chest with both hands, aware of the spotlight over the castle gate in the distance.

There was a whisper of skis somewhere up above him on his right among the trees, and he swung the Thompson and fired. There were two rifle shots in reply, and he kept on running, head down.

As he came out of the trees on the final ridge, there was a sudden swish of skis. He was aware of movement on his right, turned too late as the Finn ran straight into him. They went over the edge together, rolling over and over through deep snow, the man's skis tearing free.

Canning didn't relinquish his hold on the Thompson — not for a second — flailing wildly at the Finn as the man tried to get up, feeling the side of the skull disintegrate under the impact of the steel butt.

He could hardly breathe now, staggering like a drunken man across the final section of open ground, aware of the deadly swish of skis closing behind, but as he fell down the bank of the moat, Finebaum was there, giving them one burst after another.

"Come on, you mothers! Is that the best you can do?"

Canning lurched into the water, thrashing out wildly, the Thompson still in his right hand. He went under once, and then someone had him by the collar.

"Easy, General. Easy does it," Jack Howard was saying.

Canning crouched against the wall, totally exhausted, in real physical pain. Hesser and Birr leaned over him. The German forced the neck of a flask between his teeth. It was brandy. Canning didn't think anything had ever tasted quite so good in his life before.

He realized that he was still clutching the Thompson and held it up to Howard. "I lost your sergeant."

"Hoover?" Howard said. "You mean he's dead?"

"As a mackerel. Took two heavy-chopper rounds straight in the throat," Finebaum said as he squatted beside Canning. "Anyone got a cigarette?

Mine are all wet."

Hesser gave him one and a light. Howard exploded, "Goddammit, Finebaum, is that all you can say? That's Harry out there."

"What the hell do you expect me to do, recite the prayers for the dead or something?"

Howard walked away along the tunnel. Canning said, "You saved my skin out there, Finebaum, I won't forget that."

"You did okay, General. You did as you was told. That's lesson number one in this game."

"Game?" Canning said. "Is that how you see it?"

Finebaum inhaled deeply and took his time replying. "I don't know about that, General, but I'll tell you one thing. Sometimes at night I wake up frightened — scared half to death — and you know why?"

"No."

"Because I'm afraid it'll soon be over."

For the first time since Canning had known him, he didn't sound as if he were trying to make a joke.

Fourteen

Ritter and Claire de Beauville did not exchange a single word during the drive down to the village. When Hoffer finally braked to a halt in front of the Golden Eagle, she made no attempt to get out, simply sat there mute, staring into space, snowflakes clinging to her eyelashes.

"We will go in now, *madame,*" Ritter said gently as Hoffer opened the door for them.

He took her hand to help her down, and she started to shake. He put an arm about her shoulder. "Quickly, Erich — inside."

Hoffer ran ahead to get the door open. Ritter took her up the steps and into the bar. Meyer was tending the fire. A look of astonishment appeared on his face when he saw Claire. "Madame de Beauville —

are you all right?"

She was shaking uncontrollably now. Ritter said, "Where is Herr Strasser?"

"In my office, *Sturmbannführer.*"

"I'll take her there now. You get Dr. Gaillard. I think she's going to need him. Go with him, Erich."

They both went out quickly. Claire leaned heavily against Ritter, and he held her close, afraid that she might fall. He walked her across to the fire and eased her into the large armchair beside it. Then he went to the bar, poured brandy into a glass, and returned.

"Come on, just a little. You'll feel better, I promise you."

She moaned softly, but drank, and then she seemed to choke a little, her fingers tightening on his shoulder as she stared past him.

Strasser said, "What happened? What went wrong?"

Ritter turned to look at him. "She is not well, as you can see."

"This is not your department, so kindly keep out of it," Strasser told him coldly.

Ritter hesitated, then got to his feet and

moved a few paces away. Strasser said, "You were discovered?"

"Yes."

"Then how do you come to be here?"

"General Canning threw me out."

Strasser stood there, confronting her, hands clasped behind his back, a slight frown on his face. He nodded slowly. "Exactly the sort of stupidity he would indulge in."

"What happens now?"

"To you? A matter of supreme indifference to me, *madame.*"

He started to turn away, and she caught at his sleeve, shaking again now, tears in her eyes. "Please, Herr Bormann. Etienne — my husband. You promised."

"Strasser," he said. "The name is Strasser, *madame.* And in regard to your husband, I promised nothing. I said I would do what I could."

"But Colonel Rattenhuber . . ."

". . . is dead," Strasser said, "and I can't be responsible for the empty promises of a dead man."

There was horror and incredulity on her face now. "But I did everything I was asked to do. Betrayed my friends — my country. Don't you understand?''

From the doorway Gaillard said, in shocked tones, ''For God's sake, Claire, what are you saying?''

She turned on him feverishly. ''Oh, yes, it's true. I was the puppet — he pulled the strings. Meet my master, Paul. *Reichsleiter* Martin Bormann.''

''I really am growing rather weary of this,'' Strasser said.

''Would you like to know why I did it, Paul? Shall I tell you? Etienne wasn't killed escaping from SD headquarters in Paris, as we thought. He's alive. A prisoner at Mauthausen concentration camp.''

There was agony in Paul Gaillard's face, and an overwhelming pity. He took her hands in his. ''I know, Claire, that Etienne wasn't shot trying to escape from Avenue Foch. I've known for a long time. I also know they took him to Mauthausen.''

''You know?'' she whispered. ''But I don't understand.''

''Mauthausen is an extermination camp. You only go in, you never come out.

Etienne died there in the stone quarry two years ago, along with forty-seven American, British, and French fliers. There seemed no point in causing you needless distress when you already believed him dead."

"How did they die?"

Gaillard hesitated.

"Please, Paul, I must know."

"Very well. At one point in the quarry there is a flight of steps, a hundred and twenty-seven of them. Etienne and the others were made to climb them, carrying heavy stones. Seventy, eighty, ninety — even a hundred pounds in weight. If they fell down, they were clubbed and kicked until they got up again. By the evening of the first day, half of them were dead. The rest died the following morning."

Canning and Justin Birr had a plan of the castle open across the top of the piano. Claudine Chevalier sat opposite them, playing softly. The door opened, and Hesser and Howard entered, the German brushing snowflakes from the fur collar of his great coat.

Canning said, "I've called you together for a final briefing on what the plan must be in case of an all-out assault."

"You think that's still possible, sir?" Howard asked.

"I've no reason to believe otherwise. One thing is absolutely certain. If it comes at all, it must come soon. I'd say no later than dawn because the one thing Strasser or Bormann or whoever he is doesn't have, is time. An Allied column could cross this place at any moment. However" — he pulled the plan forward — "let's say they do attack and force the drawbridge. How long can you hold them before they blast that gate, Howard?"

"Not long enough, General. All we have are rifles, Schmeissers, and grenades — and one machine gun up there. They still have two half-tracks with heavy machine guns, and a lot more manpower."

"Okay — so they force the gates and you have to fall back. What about Big Bertha, Max?"

"She is in position thirty yards from the mouth of the tunnel and overflowing with scrap metal. However, I can't guarantee that she won't blow up in the face of whoever puts a light to her."

"That's my department," Canning told him. "I said it, I meant it. If it works, we dispose of the first half-track out of the tunnel and probably every man in it. That should even things up a little."

"Then what?" Howard demanded.

"We retreat into the north tower, get the door shut, and stand them off for as long as we can."

Justin Birr said mildly, "I hate to mention it, Hamilton, but that door isn't really much of a barrier."

"Then we retreat up the stairs," Canning said. "Fight them floor by floor — or has anybody got a better suggestion?" There was only silence. "All right, gentlemen, let's get moving. I'll see you on the wall in five minutes."

They went out. He stood there looking at the plan for a while, then picked up a German-issue parka and pulled it over his head.

"A long wait until dawn, Hamilton," Claudine Chevalier said. "You really think they'll come?"

"I'm afraid so."

"And Paul and Claire? I wonder what will happen to them."

"I don't know."

"Or care?"

"About Gaillard — yes." Canning buckled on his holstered pistol.

"How strange," she said, still playing, "that love can turn to hate so quickly — or can it? Perhaps we only delude ourselves."

Canning walked out, slamming the door.

When Sorsa went into the bar at the Golden Eagle, he found Ritter sitting by the fire, a glass in one hand. Sorsa beat the snow from his parka. Ritter didn't say a word, simply stared into the fire. The door from the kitchen opened, and Hoffer entered with coffee on a tray. He put it down on the side table without a word. Ritter ignored him, also.

Sorsa glanced at the sergeant major, then coughed. Ritter's head turned very slowly. He glanced up, a brooding expression in his eyes.

"Yes, what is it?"

"You sent for me, *Sturmbannführer.*"

Ritter stared up at him for a moment longer, then said, "How many did you lose up there?"

"Four dead, two seriously wounded. Three others scratched a bit. We brought the wounded back here for the doctor to deal with. One of the half-tracks is a complete write-off. What happens now?"

"We attack at dawn. Seven o'clock, precisely. You and your men are still mine until nine, remember?"

"Yes, *Sturmbannführer.*"

"I'll take command personally. Full assault. We'll use *Panzerfausts* on the drawbridge. Hoffer, here, was the best gunner in the battalion. He'll blow those chains for us — won't you, Erich?"

It was delivered as an order, and Hoffer reacted accordingly, springing to attention, heels clicking together. *"Zu Befehl, Sturmbannführer."*

Ritter looked up at Sorsa. "Any questions?"

"Would it make any difference if

I had?'' Sorsa asked.

"Not really. The same roads lead to hell in the end for all of us."

"A saying we have in Finland, also."

Ritter nodded. "Better leave Sergeant Major Gestrin and four of your best men down here to hold the fort while we're away. You get back to your camp now. I'll be up in a little while."

"And Herr Strasser?"

"I shouldn't imagine so, not for a moment. Herr Strasser is too important to be risked. You understand me?"

"I think so, *Sturmbannführer.*"

"Good, because I'm damned if *I* do." Ritter got to his feet, walked to the bar, and reached for the schnapps. "I've known a lot of good men during the past five or six years who are no longer with us, and for the first time I'm beginning to wonder why." There was a kind of desperation on his face. "Why did they die, Sorsa? What for? Can you tell me?"

"I'm afraid not," Sorsa said gently. "You see, I fight for wages. We belong to a different club, you and I. Was there anything else?" Ritter shook his head.

"Then I'll get back to my boys."

The big Finn gave him a military salute and went out. Ritter moved to the fireplace and stared into the flames. "Why, Erich?" he whispered. "What for?"

"What's this, Major Ritter?" Strasser said from the doorway. "A little late in the day for philosophy, I should think."

Ritter turned, the dark eyes blazing in the pale face. "No more games, *Reichsleiter*. We've gone too far for that now, you and I."

"Have we, indeed?" Strasser went behind the bar and poured himself a brandy.

"Is it Bormann in Berlin and Strasser here — or the other way about?" Ritter said. "On the other hand, does it really matter?"

"Speeches now?"

"I'd say I've earned the right, if only because I had to stand by and watch that sickening spectacle with the Beauville woman. You left her more degraded than a San Pauli whore. You left her nothing."

"I did what had to be done."

371

"For God, the *Führer,* and the Reich —
or have I got that in the wrong order?"
Ritter ignored the horror on Hoffer's face.
"Hundreds of thousands of young
Germans have died, the cream of our
nation, who believed. Who had faith and
idealism. Who thought they were taking
our country out of the degradation and
squalor of the twenties into a new age. I
now realize they died for nothing. What
they believed in never existed in the first
place. You and your kind allowed, for
your own ends, a madman to lead the
German people down the road to hell, and
we followed you with joy in our hearts."

Strasser said, "Listen to me, Ritter.
This is sentimental nonsense of the worst
kind — and from you, a man who has
served the Reich as few others have done.
Do you think we are finished? If so, you
are badly mistaken. We go on — only
now the *Kameradenwerk* begins, and there
is a place for you in this. A place of
honor."

Ritter turned to Hoffer. "We're leaving
now, Erich."

Hoffer went out. Strasser said,

"What do you intend?"

"I'm attacking at seven o'clock. Full assault. We'll use *Panzerfausts* to blow the drawbridge chains. It might work, but I can't guarantee it. I'm leaving Sergeant Major Gestrin and four men to look after things here."

Hoffer returned and handed him his parka and field cap. Strasser said, "Let me get my coat. I'll come with you."

"No!" Ritter said flatly. "I command, and I say you stay here."

As Ritter buttoned his parka, Strasser said, "As you so obviously feel as you do, why are you doing this?"

"Most of my friends are dead now," Ritter told him. "Why should I get away with it?" And he walked out.

Arnie was sleeping peacefully, and the only evidences of the ordeal he had passed through were the dark smudges like purple bruising under each eye. Gaillard placed a hand on the boy's forehead. It was quite cool, and the pulse was normal for the first time in twenty-four hours.

He lit a cigarette, went to the window

and opened it. It was quite dark, except for light spilling out from the kitchen window across the courtyard below. It was snowing, and he breathed deeply of the cold bracing air.

There was a knock at the door, and Meyer entered with coffee on a tray. The Finnish guard stayed outside. Gaillard could see him sitting on a chair on the other side of the corridor, smoking a cigarette.

"How is he, *Herr Doktor?*" Meyer asked as he poured coffee.

"Temperature down, pulse normal, fever gone, and sleeping peacefully, as you can see." Gaillard drank some of the coffee gratefully. "And now I must check on Madame de Beauville."

Meyer said softly, "They mount a general assault on Schloss Arlberg at seven."

Gaillard said, "Are you certain?"

"I overheard Major Ritter and Herr Strasser discussing it in the bar a short time ago. Major Ritter has already left for the castle."

"And Strasser?"

"There was trouble between them. Strasser wanted to go, but Ritter wouldn't have it. He stays here with five Finns to guard him."

Gaillard turned and leaned on the windowsill, considerably agitated. "If a general assault is mounted up there, they won't stand a chance. We must do something."

"What can we do, *Herr Doktor?* It's a hopeless situation."

"Not if someone could get out with news of what's happening here." There was new hope on Gaillard's face. "There must be many Allied units in the vicinity of Arlberg now. You could go, Johann." He reached out a hand and gripped Meyer's coat. "You could slip away."

"I am sorry, *Herr Doktor,* I owe you a great deal — possibly even my son's life — but if I went, it would be like leaving the boy to take his chances." Meyer shook his head. "In any case, it would be impossible to steal the field car with those Finns out in front, and how far could anyone hope to get on foot?"

"You're right, of course." Gaillard

turned back to the window dejectedly and saw something in the courtyard below that filled him with a sudden fierce hope. A set of skis propped against the wall beside the kitchen window.

He controlled himself with considerable difficulty. "Pour me another coffee before that sentry decides you've been here long enough, and listen. The skis down there — they are yours?"

"Yes, *Herr Doktor.*"

"You are right, my friend, you do owe me something, and now is your chance to repay. You will take those skis, an anorak, mittens, and boots and leave them in the woodshed at the top of the yard. That is all I ask. Getting out of here is my problem."

Meyer still hesitated. "I'm not sure, *Herr Doktor.* If they ever found out . . ."

"Not for me or my friends, Johann," Gaillard said. "For Arnie. You owe him that much, I think."

The Finn moved into the room, said something in his own language, and gestured to Meyer, motioning him outside. Meyer picked up the tray.

"I'm counting on you, Johann."

"I'll try, *Herr Doktor.*" Meyer looked distinctly unhappy. "I'll do my best, but I can't promise more than that."

He went out, and the guard made to close the door, but Gaillard shook his head. He picked up his doctor's bag, brushed past him, and went down the corridor to the next room. Claire de Beauville was lying down, and when the Finn tried to follow him in, Gaillard shut the door in his face.

She started to get up, and Gaillard sat on the edge of the bed. "No, stay where you are. How do you feel now?"

"A little better."

"Not if someone comes in, you don't. You feel very ill indeed."

"The sentry?"

"No, he's been rather more amenable since standing by and watching while I patched up two of his comrades in a room along the corridor. Casualties of some fracas up at the castle." He opened his bag and took out a stethoscope. "I haven't got long, so listen carefully. This man Strasser, or whoever he is — do you still wish to serve him?"

She shuddered. "What do you think?"

He glanced at his watch. "In less than an hour, they mount a general assault on Schloss Arlberg. Everything they've got. No holds barred."

Her eyes widened. "Claudine, Hamilton, and the others — they won't stand a chance."

"Exactly, so someone must go for help."

"But how?"

"Meyer is hiding skiing equipment for me in the woodshed behind the inn. Getting out is my own affair. Will you help?"

"Of course." Her hand tightened on his, and she smiled sadly. "If you want the help of someone like me."

"My poor Claire. We are all casualties of war to a greater or lesser degree. Who am I to judge you?" There were voices outside. She lay back hurriedly. The door opened, and Strasser entered.

"How is she?"

"Not very well," Gaillard said. "I'm afraid a total breakdown is quite possible.

She has, after all, gone through a lengthy period of intense stress. Add to this the trauma of more recent events. The news of her husband's death."

"Yes, all very sad," Strasser said impatiently. "However, I want to talk to you."

"It will have to wait. Madame de Beauville needs my full attention at the moment, and I would remind you that I have two badly wounded Finns along the corridor."

"Ten minutes," Strasser said. "That's all you can have. Then I want you downstairs in the bar." His voice was cold, incisive. "You understand me?"

"Of course, *Reichsleiter*," Gaillard told him calmly.

Strasser left, leaving the door open, the Finnish guard standing outside. "That's bad," Gaillard said. "It doesn't give us much time."

"If you don't go now, you won't go at all, isn't that how it stands?" she said.

"Very probably."

"Well, then, it's now or never."

She sat up and swung her legs down,

somehow managing to knock his bag to the floor. She reached to pick it up, clumsily disgorging most of the contents — instruments, pill bottles, and so on — onto the carpet.

"Now look what I've done."

The Finnish guard moved into the room and stood watching. She started to kneel, and Gaillard said, "It doesn't matter. 'I'll get them."

Claire turned to the Finn, trying to look as confused and helpless as possible, and he responded as she had hoped. He grinned, unslung his rifle, and put it on the bed, then dropped to one knee beside Gaillard.

She didn't hesitate. There was a cut-glass decanter half full of water beside her bed. She seized it by the neck and struck with all her strength at the base of the guard's skull. Glass fragmented, bone splintered, the Finn slumped on his face without a sound.

She froze for a few moments, listening, but all was quiet. She said, "Go now, Paul."

"And you?" he asked, standing up.

"Don't worry about me."

He put his hands on her shoulders, kissed her briefly, and hurried out. Claire stood there looking down at the Finn, surprisingly calm, drained of all emotion, and very, very tried. A drink, she thought, that's what I need. And she went out, closing the door behind her.

Gaillard went down the back stairs. As he reached the stone-flagged passage, the door to the courtyard opened and Meyer entered, stamping snow from his boots. He drew back in astonishment at the sight of Gaillard, who grabbed his arm.

"Have you done as I asked?"

"Yes, *Herr Doktor,*" Meyer stammered. "I've just come back."

"Good man," Gaillard said. "If Strasser descends on you when I'm gone, just play dumb."

He opened the door, stepped out, and closed it. The first pale luminous light of dawn was filtering through the trees. There was a slight ground mist, and it was snowing a little. Meyer's tracks were plain, and Gaillard followed them quickly across the yard to the woodshed. He got the door open and went inside.

He was excited now, more so than he had been for years, and his hands shook as he took off his shoes and pulled on the woolen socks and heavy ski boots Meyer had provided. The anorak was an old red one which had been patched many times, but the hood was fur-lined, as were the mittens. He pulled them on quickly, picked up the skis and sticks, and went back outside.

It was snowing harder now, cold, early-morning mountain snow, strangely exhilarating, and when he paused on the other side of the wall to put on the skis, he was conscious of the old familiar thrill again. The years fell away and he was in the Vosges, practicing for Chamonix — 1924 — the first Winter Olympic Games. The greatest moment of his life when he had won that gold medal. Everything afterward had always savored a little of anticlimax.

He smiled wryly to himself and knelt to adjust the bindings to his satisfaction. He pressed on the safety catch, locking his boot in position, then repeated the performance with the other ski. So, he was ready. He pulled on his mittens and reached for the sticks.

It was perhaps five minutes later that Strasser, sitting waiting for Gaillard in the bar, heard a cry from outside in the square. He went to the door. Gestrin and the four Finnish soldiers Ritter had left were standing by the field car. One of them was pointing up above the houses to the wooded slope of the mountain behind.

"What is it?" Strasser demanded.

Gestrin lowered his field glasses. "The Frenchman."

"Gaillard?" Strasser said incredulously. "Impossible."

"See for yourself. Up there on the trail."

He handed him the field glasses. Strasser hastily adjusted the lenses. He found the woodcutters' trail that zigzagged up through the trees, and came upon the skier in the red anorak almost instantly. Gaillard glanced back over his shoulder giving a good view of his face.

Two of the Finns were already taking aim with their Mauser rifles. Gestrin said, "Shall we fire?"

"No, you fool, I want him back," Strasser said. "You understand me?"

"Nothing simpler. In this kind of country, on skis, these lads are the best in the business."

He turned away, giving orders in Finnish. They all moved quickly to the field car and started to unload their skis.

"You go with them," Strasser told Gestrin. "No excuses, no arguments. Just have him back here within the hour."

"As you say," Gestrin answered calmly.

They had their skis on within a few minutes and moved away in single file, rifles slung over their backs, Gestrin in the lead. Strasser looked up the mountains to the last bend in the trail which could be seen from the square. There was a flash of red among the green, then nothing.

He hurried into the inn, drawing the Walther from his pocket. He went up the stairs two at a time and moved along the corridor. Arnie's door stood open. The boy slept peacefully. Strasser hesitated, then turned to Claire de Beauville's room. The Finnish guard lay where he had fallen, his face turned to one side. The back of the skull was soft, matted with blood. There was a trickle of red from the corner of his mouth. He was quite dead, and Strasser went out quickly.

"Meyer, where are you, damn you?" he called as he went downstairs.

Meyer emerged from the kitchen and stood there, fear in his eyes. In the same moment, Strasser saw that Claire de Beauville was behind the bar, opening a champagne bottle.

"Ah, there you are, *Reichsleiter*. Just in time to join me. Krug. An excellent year, too. Not as chilled as I would normally expect, but one can't have everything in this life."

Strasser ignored her and menaced Meyer with his pistol, beside himself with rage. "You helped him, didn't you? Where else would he obtain skis and winter clothing?"

"Please, Herr Strasser. Don't shoot." Meyer broke down completely. "I had nothing to do with this business. You are mistaken if you think otherwise."

Claire poured herself a glass of champagne, perched on one of the high stools, and sipped it appreciatively. "Excellent. Really excellent. And he's quite right, by the way. I was the one who helped Paul. I had the greatest of pleasure in crowning that SS man of yours."

Strasser glared at her. "You?" he said. "He's dead, the man you assaulted, did you know that?"

The smile left her face, but she replied instantly. "And so is Etienne."

"You bitch. Do you realize what you've done?"

"Ruined everything for you, I hope. There must be British and American troops all over the area by now. I'm sure Paul will run across one of their columns quite quickly."

"No chance," he said. "Gestrin and four of those Finns of his have just taken off after him. Probably five of the finest skiers in the German Army. You think it will take them long to run down a sixty-year-old man?"

"Who won an Olympic gold medal in

1924. The greatest skier in the world in his day. I would have thought that would still count for something, wouldn't you?'' She raised her glass. *"A votre santé, Reichsleiter* — and may you rot in hell.''

He fired several times as the black rage erupted inside him. His first bullet caught her in the right shoulder, knocking her off the stool and turning her around. His second and third shattered her spine, driving her headlong into the wall, the woolen material of her jacket smoldering, then bursting into flame. He moved forward, firing again and again until the gun was empty.

He stood looking down at her, and Meyer, his face contorted with horror, backed away quietly, then turned and rushed upstairs. When he reached Arnie's room, the boy was still asleep. He closed the door, bolted it, then dragged a heavy chest of drawers across it as an additional barrier.

He went into the dressing room, lifted the carpet in the corner, and removed a loose floorboard. Inside, wrapped in a piece of blanket, was his old sawed-off shotgun from the poaching days of his youth, and a box of cartridges, both hidden since before the war. He loaded both barrels and went back into the bedroom. He placed a chair in the center of the room facing the door, sat down with the gun across his knees, and waited.

It had been a long time, but some things you never forgot. Gaillard moved out of the trees and started onto a flat plateau perhaps two hundred yards across, more trees on the other side. He was using the sliding, forward stride much favored by Scandinavians, a technique he had picked up in his youth and which ate up the miles at a surprising rate.

If you were fit, of course — always that — though at the moment he felt better than he had for years. Free, yes, but more than that — the knowledge that they'd come to the end of something. That freedom was just around the corner for everyone.

But this was no time for such considerations. He needed a destination and didn't have one. On the other hand, it seemed reasonable to assume that the help he was seeking was more than likely to be found on the main roads, which meant climbing higher, traversing the eastern shoulder of the mountain, and then descending.

Something made him glance back, some sixth sense. The Finns were halfway across the plateau, moving in single file, Gestrin leading. He was not afraid, but filled with a fierce delight, and started into the trees, moving at a fast, loping rate. He was already a hundred feet up the side of the mountain when the Finns reached the edge of the trees and Gestrin called them to a halt.

"All right," he said, "The party's over. He's good, this one. Too good to play with. From now on, it's every man for himself, and remember — we want him alive."

He started up the slope, and they moved after him.

Ritter and Sorsa stood beside one of the two remaining half-tracks, drinking coffee and examining the ground plan of Schloss

Arlberg which the German had brought from the inn.

"Once we're in, they'll fall back to the north tower," Ritter said. "Nowhere else to go."

"And what's that going to be like?"

"According to Strasser, a heavy oak door opening in two sections. That shouldn't take long. Inside, a hall, then a broad stairway that diminishes in size, becoming a spiral at the higher levels. The dining hall, then a maze of passages and rooms right on up to the top."

"If they take it room by room, it could be nasty."

"Not if we keep after them, right from the word *go*. No hesitation, no letup."

The Finns were ready and waiting in the half-tracks, half a dozen with the *Panzerfausts*. Ritter moved closer to examine the ugly-looking antitank projectiles. "Are they good with these things?"

"We've had our successes. On target, one of these can open a T-Thirty-four like a can of meat."

"How many have we got?"

"Ten."

"Then we can't afford to take chances. I'm putting Hoffer in charge. Make that clear to your men. He's the finest gunner I know."

At that moment, Hoffer called from the field car, "Herr Strasser on the radio for you, *Sturmbannführer.*"

Ritter leaned into the car. There was no static, and Strasser's voice sounded clear and distinct. "You've not started the assault?"

"Any minute now. Why?"

Strasser told him. When he finished, Ritter said, "So we don't have too much time, that's what you're trying to say? You needn't have bothered, *Reichsleiter.* We've been a little short on that commodity from the beginning. Over and out."

He replaced the handmike and turned to Sorsa. "Trouble?" the Finn asked.

"Gaillard's managed to escape. He's taken to the mountain on skis. Strasser's sent Gestrin and his boys after him."

"No problem," Sorsa said. "They're the best in the business. They'll lay him

391

by the heels soon enough."

"I wouldn't count on it. He was an Olympic gold medalist at Chamonix in 1924. If he runs across a British or American column before Gestrin and his men get to him . . ."

Sorsa looked grave. "I see what you mean. So, what do we do?"

"Get this little affair over with as quickly as possible. We move out now."

He started toward one of the half-tracks, and Sorsa caught his arm. "A moment, *Sturmbannführer*. The first half-track through that tunnel is likely to have a hard time. I'd like to be in it."

"I command here," Ritter said. "I thought I'd made that clear."

"But these are my boys," Sorsa persisted. "We've been together a long time."

Ritter stared at him, a slight frown on his face, and then nodded. "I get the point. Very well, for this occasion only, you lead and I follow. Now let's get moving."

He turned and scrambled up into the second half-track.

Fifteen

Claudine Chevalier was sitting at the piano in the dining hall, playing "The Girl with the Flaxen Hair," by Debussy. It was one of her favorite pieces, mainly because the composer himself had taught her how to play it when she was twelve years of age.

There was a knock at the door, and Finebaum entered. His M1 was slung from his left shoulder, a Schmeisser from his right, and there were three stick grenades in his belt.

She kept on playing. "Trouble, Mr. Finebaum?"

"Well, I'll tell you, ma'am. General Canning, he thought it would be a good idea to have someone look out for you personally. You know what I mean?"

"You?" she said.

393

"I'm afraid so, ma'am. Mind if I smoke?"

"Not at all — and I couldn't be in better hands. What do we do?"

"I'll take you up to the top of the tower when the time comes — out of the way of things."

"But not now?"

"No need. They haven't even knocked at the gate yet. Say, my old lady used to play piano. Nothing like that, though. I learned the clarinet when she got one cheap from my Uncle Paul. He was a pawnbroker in Brooklyn."

"Did you enjoy it?"

"Well, I ain't Benny Goodman, but I made front row with Glenn Miller."

"But that's wonderful. Do you like this piece that I'm playing now?"

"No, ma'am. It makes my stomach feel cold. It worries me — I don't know why — and that ain't good because I've got enough to worry about."

"Ah, I see. Perhaps you would prefer something like this?"

She started to play "Night and Day." Finebaum moved around the piano to look down at the keys. "Hey, that's great. That's really something. I mean, where did you ever learn to play like that?"

"Oh, one gets around, Mr. Finebaum. Isn't that the phrase?"

"I guess so."

A roar of engines shattered the early-morning stillness. "Oh, my God," she whispered and stopped playing.

As Finebaum ran to the window, there was a sudden booming explosion and the rattle of machine-gun fire.

Gaillard, high in the woods now, on the upper slopes of the mountain, heard the echoes of that first outbreak of firing and paused to listen. His lungs were aching as he struggled for breath, leaning heavily on his sticks, and his legs were trembling slightly.

He was too old, of course. Too many years under his belt, and the truth was, he simply wasn't fit enough. When it came right down to it, the only thing he really had going for him was technique and the skill born of his natural genius and years of experience.

The Finns, on the other hand, were

young men, battle-hardened to endure anything, and at the peak of their physical fitness. He really didn't stand a chance — had not from the beginning.

He langlaufed across the small plateau that tilted gently upward, and paused on the ridge. On the other side, the snow slope was almost vertical, dropping into gray mist, no means of knowing what was down there at all.

He turned and saw the first of the Finns appear from the trees on the other side of the plateau, no more than thirty yards away. Gestrin was number three, and the big Finn waved his hand to bring the patrol to a halt.

He pushed up his goggles. "All right, Doctor. You've put up a wonderful show, and we admire you for it, but enough of this foolishness. Now we go home."

There were two more violent explosions somewhere in the mist below. The rattle of small-arms fire persisted. Gaillard thought of his friends — of Claudine Chevalier and of Claire de Beauville and what had happened to her.

He was filled with a fierce, sudden

anger and shouted down at the Finns, "All right, you bastards. Let's see what you're made of."

He went straight over the edge of the near-vertical drop, crouching, skis nailed together, and plunged into the mist. The Finns, as they reached the edge, followed, one after the other, without hesitation.

Canning, Birr, and Hesser were in the tunnel, Howard on the wall, when the engine's roar first shattered the morning calm. A few moments later, the half-tracks emerged into view and took up position. The Finns spilled out and started to deploy. Hoffer and the men under his personal command took up position to the left.

Howard trained his glasses on them, trying to make out what they were doing. In the moment of realization, there came a tongue of orange flame and, a second later, a violent explosion as the first *Panzerfaust* projectile struck the wall beside the drawbridge.

Everyone crouched. "What the hell was that?" Birr demanded.

"Panzerfaust," Hesser replied. "It's an

antitank weapon rather like your bazooka."

"So I see," Canning said grimly, ducking as another violent explosion rocked the drawbridge — a direct hit, this time.

"Obviously it's the chains they're after," Birr said. "I wonder how long it will take?"

Heavy machine-gun fire raked the top of the wall, bullets ricocheting into space. "Give them everything we've got," Canning cried. "Really pour it on."

Schneider opened up with the MG34, and the rest of the Germans backed him with their Mauser rifles, sniping from the embrasures in the wall. The Finns took refuge behind the half-tracks, one of which moved position slightly to cover the *Panzerfaust* group.

The fourth projectile, fired by Hoffer personally, scored a direct hit on the drawbridge just below the chain mounting on the left-hand side. The woodwork disintegrated, the chain coupling tore free, the drawbridge sagged.

"Strike one," Howard said. "Not long now."

Two more projectiles homed in, a third landing just below the top of the wall above the gate, its shrapnel killing Schneider and the other two men in the machine-gun crew instantly, hurling the MG34 on its side, battered and useless.

Canning crawled across to Howard, blood on his face. "Not long now." He turned to Birr and Hesser. "Justin, you and Howard stay up here as long as you can, with half a dozen men. Max, you drop back on the tower."

"And what about you?" Birr demanded.

"Big Bertha and I have business together. You make things as hot for those bastards as you can on the way in, then get off the wall and join Max in the tower."

Birr started to argue, but in the same moment there was another frightful explosion just below them. The remaining chain disintegrated; the drawbridge fell down across the moat with a resounding crash.

There was a general cheer from the Finns, and Ritter jumped from the half-track to join Hoffer.

"How many have you left?"

"Two, *Sturmbannführer*."

"Make them count, Erich. The gate this time." He ran to the other half-track, and Sorsa leaned down. "Hoffer is going to blast the gate," Ritter said. "You make your move as soon as you like. Smash straight in, and we'll cover you. Good luck."

Sorsa smiled, waved a gloved hand, and pulled down his panzer goggles. He shouted an order in Finnish, and a dozen men scrambled over the side and joined him in the half-track. He clapped his driver on the shoulder and, as they started to move forward, took over the machine gun himself.

The first of Hoffer's last two projectiles punched a hole through a massive gate and exploded at the end of the tunnel. The blast knocked Canning, standing beside Big Bertha, clean off his feet, showering him with dirt and tiny fragments of shrapnel.

There was more blood on his face, his own this time, and as he started to get up, Hoffer fired the remaining *Panzerfaust*. The left-hand side of the gate sagged and fell in.

The lead half-track was halfway there. Sorsa firing the machine gun furiously, his men backing him up, and Ritter followed in the second half-track, spraying the top of the wall with such a volume of fire that it was virtually impossible for the handful of defenders to reply.

Howard tossed a couple of stick grenades over at random as the lead half-track got close and Birr grabbed his arm. "Let's get out of here!"

Of the German soldiers who had stayed on the wall with them, only three were left on their feet. Howard beckoned to them now, and they all went down the steps on the run and started across the courtyard to where Hesser and seven of his men waited on the steps of the tower entrance.

Canning leaned heavily on the cannon, blood running into his eyes, and Howard swerved toward him. The general sagged to one knee, groping for the length of smoldering fuse he had dropped, as Howard joined him.

"Get the hell out of here!" Canning ordered.

But by then it was too late, for as Howard handed him the fuse, the lead half-track smashed what was left of the gate from its hinges. The half-track emerged from the tunnel, Sorsa firing the machine gun, and Canning touched the end of his fuse to the powder charge.

Big Bertha belched fire and smoke in a thunderous roar, rocking back on her solid wheels, disgorging her improvised charge of assorted metal fragments and chain at point-blank range, killing Sorsa and every man in the half-track instantly, hurling the vehicle over to one side and back against the wall.

Both Canning and Howard were thrown down by the force of the explosion. As the roar of Ritter's half-track filled the tunnel, Howard grabbed the general by the arm, hauled him to his feet, and urged him into a stumbling run.

Hesser and his men were firing furiously now, retreating up the steps and back through the door at the foot of the north tower, but continuing to give them covering fire. As Howard and Canning made it to the steps, the half-track emerged from the tunnel across the courtyard and its machine gun tracked them across the cobbles.

Hesser's men were already getting the doors closed when, as Howard urged Canning up the steps, the general stumbled and fell. Hesser and Birr ducked out through the narrow opening and hurried down the steps to help.

Howard and Birr got Canning between them and dragged him up the steps. Behind them, Hesser turned, firing a Schmeisser one-handed across the courtyard, catching in reply a full burst from the machine gun that drove him across the steps in a crazy dance of death, hursling him over the edge into the snow.

A second later, Howard and Birr staggered in through the narrowing gap with Canning, and the massive doors closed.

Gaillard's speed was tremendous as he hurtled down into the gray mist, yet he was entirely without fear. What lay ahead, it was impossible to say. He could be rushing straight to his death, his only consolation the knowledge that his pursuers would follow him.

And what good would that do? he asked himself, suddenly angry, and moved into a parallel swing, changing course, the right-hand edge of his skis biting into the snow.

The mist was thinning now, and he glanced over his shoulder and saw that the lead Finn was perhaps forty yards behind, closely followed by another. Gestrin and the other two were a little farther back.

Gaillard came out of an S-turn and went down vertically again, knees together, and suddenly a gust of wind dissolved the remaining shreds of mist in an instant, and below was the valley, an awesome sight, the present slope vanishing into infinity fifty yards farther on.

Gaillard didn't deviate, but held his course true, skis so close together that they might have been one. At the last possible moment, that edge which meant certain death rushing to meet him, he hurled himself into a left-hand christie. It came off beautifully, and he had a brief impression of the glacier far below as he skirted the ultimate edge.

His pursuers were not so lucky, for behind him the lead Finn went straight over the edge with a terrible cry, his companion following him.

Gaillard, out of the area of immediate danger, started to traverse the lower slope. Above him, Gestrin and his two remaining comrades changed course and went after him.

Canning had a deep cut on his forehead above the right eye, of a kind that would require five or six inches at least. Howard hastily bound a field dressing around it.

"Is he all right?" Birr asked.

"Sure I'm all right," Canning told him. "How many of us left?"

"Six Germans and us three. Finebaum upstairs, of course."

"Not so good."

He peered out through a spyhole in the

door. The remaining half-track had retreated into the tunnel. Nothing moved.

"I'd say they could walk in here anytime they chose," Howard said.

"Then we retreat upstairs, floor by floor, like I told you."

The half-track nosed out of the mouth of the tunnel and stopped. Its heavy machine gun, Hoffer firing, started to spray the door at the rate of 850 rounds per minutes. As Canning and the others went down, the door started to shake to pieces above them.

"This is bad," the general cried. "No good staying. Better get up those stairs now, while we still have a choice."

He called to the Germans, and they all started to drop back.

Gaillard was incredibly tired. His body ached, and his knees hurt. The amazing thing was that he hadn't fallen once, but now, as he went into a right-hand christie to make for the cover of some pine trees, he snarled a ski and took a bad tumble.

He slid for some considerable distance before coming to a halt, winded. His skis were still on and apparently undamanged, which was something. No broken bones in evidence. But God, how tired he was. Hardly enough strength to get up. He turned and saw Gestrin and his two comrades traversing the slope above him, terribly close now.

Suddenly the earth shook, there was a tremendous rumbling like an underground explosion, and above the Finns the snow seemed to boil up in a great cloud.

Avalanche. Not surprising, really, fresh snow having fallen so late in the season. But already Gaillard was on his feet and dropping straight down the slope, taking that vertical line again, for the only way to beat an avalanche was to stay in front of it, one of the first lessons he'd learned as a boy in the Vosges.

And the trees were not too far away — some sort of protection there. He moved to the right in a wide curve that took him into their shelter within seconds. He halted, turning to glance back.

The avalanche had almost overtaken the Finns. The enormous cloud of white smoke rolled over the one in the rear, enveloped him completely, but Gestrin and the remaining man rode the very edge, managing to run at the last minute, coming to a halt above the line of trees.

The rumble of the avalanche died away. Gestrin pushed up his goggles, searching for Gaillard, whose red anorak gave him away instantly. The Finns started down the slope at once, and the Frenchman turned and pushed himself forward and through the trees, every bone aching.

From the shattered great window of the upper dining room, Finebaum sniped down and across the yard at the half-track.

"What's happening, Mr. Finebaum?" Claudine Chevalier, crouched on the floor, asked him.

"Whatever it is, it ain't good, ma'am. I figure it's time maybe you and me made a move upstairs."

There was a burst of firing, and more of the window shattered above their heads, spraying them with glass. Amazingly, she showed no fear.

"Whatever you say, Mr. Finebaum."

"You're something special," Finebaum said. "You know that?"

He took her arm and helped her toward the door, and below, in the courtyard, the half-track surged forward.

For Gaillard, the sight of the road below was like a shot in the arm, and he dropped toward it with renewed hope, although his pursuers were closer than ever now, Gestrin trailing his companion, a young man called Salmi.

Gaillard glanced over his shoulder, aware that this couldn't go on, that he had been existing on willpower alone for too long. There was one final, suicidal chance, and he took it, dropping straight down through the trees like a bullet to the embankment at the side of the road below.

As he hit, he dug in his sticks at precisely the right moment, launching himself into space. The road flashed beneath him, he soared across, landing perfectly in soft snow on the other side, sliding broadside on in a spray of snow. At the last moment, the point of his left ski caught a branch hidden beneath the white blanket. As he crashed heavily to the ground, the ski splintered.

He lay there, winded, and Salmi soared through the air across the road, smashing straight into a pine tree with a terrible cry.

Gaillard sat up. There was no sign of Gestrin. He tore at the frozen bindings of his skis and got them off. When he rose to his feet, he was convinced for a moment that his limbs had ceased to function. He took a hesitant step forward and fell headlong over the embankment, sliding down to the road.

He picked himself up and started to walk, putting one foot in front of the other, a roaring in his ears, and Gestrin slid down the embankment about fifteen yards in front of him. He'd taken off his skis and was holding his rifle.

"No!" Gaillard said. "No!"

He turned away, and Gestrin shot him in the right shoulder. Gaillard lay on his back, the roaring in his ears louder, then pushed himself up on one elbow. Gestrin stood holding the rifle across his chest, and now he started to raise it.

The roaring became the sound of an engine, and a Cromwell tank came around the bend in the road. Gestrin swung to face it, raising his rifle. A burst of machine-gun fire hurled him back into a snowdrift at the side of the road.

Gaillard lay there, aware of footsteps approaching, his eyes closed, breathing deeply, hanging onto consciousness. He opened his eyes and saw to his astonishment that the man leaning over him in a tank officer's uniform wore a kepi.

"Oh, my God," Gaillard said in his own language. "Can it be true? You are French?"

"But of course, *monsieur.*" The officer dropped to one knee. "My name is Dubois. Captain Henri Dubois of the Second French Tank Division. We are at present pushing toward Berchtesgaden. But who are you?"

"Never mind that now," Gaillard said hoarsely. "You know Arlberg?"

"The next village, two miles along the road from here."

"Only two miles?" Gaillard said in

wonder. "I must have been running in circles up there." He pulled himself up and caught hold of Dubois by the front of his uniform. "Listen to me, my friend, and listen well, for lives depend on it."

When the half-track started across the courtyard, Ritter himself was at the wheel, a dozen Finns packed in behind him, Hoffer at the machine gun. The rest followed behind on foot.

In the tower, the defenders had already retreated up the main staircase and taken up position on the first landing, except for Howard, who stayed at the shattered door, peering out.

"Here they come!" he cried and started to fire his Thompson furiously.

Ritter gunned the motor, giving the half-track everything, roaring straight up the steps, hitting those shattered doors at full speed. Howard was already halfway up the marble stairs as the doors disintegrated, the half-track smashing through, sliding to a halt, broadside on.

The defenders immediately started to pour it on from the landing, Canning and

Birr firing Schmeissers between the pillars of the balustrade, Howard backing them up with the Thompson.

The Finns were caught badly, three or four of them going down as they scrambled from the half-track. Hoffer took a bullet in the shoulder that knocked him over the side, and Ritter, without hesitation, stood up and grabbed the handles of the machine gun.

He started to spray the landing expertly, shattering the windows behind the rows of marbles statues, an awesome figure crouched behind the gun, his face pale beneath the black cap. Howard let loose one burst after another, even standing up on occasion, all to no effect, for it was as if the German bore a charmed life.

The landing had become a charnel house, four of the Germans hit, one of them crying out continuously. Birr had taken a bullet through the right hand, and below, in the hall, at least nine of the Finns were down.

Canning pulled at Howard's sleeve, eyes wild. "This is no good — we'd better get out of here."

"Take Birr with you," Howard said. "I'll cover you."

He rammed another clip into the Thompson, and behind him the two surviving Germans got Birr by the shoulders and dragged him along the landing. Ritter stopped firing. He looked down and found Hoffer leaning against the side of the half-track, stuffing a field dressing inside his uniform blouse.

"All right, Erich?"

Hoffer nodded, his face twisted with pain, and from up above, in the smoke on the landing, Howard called, "What's keeping you, Ritter?"

Something flared in Ritter's eyes. He picked up a Schmeisser and vaulted to the floor. He did not say a word, gave no command, simply went up the stairs into the smoke, and the Finns went after him.

The curtains were on fire now, the wood paneling on the walls, smoke swirling, billowing along the landing, so that it was impossible to see more than a few feet. Howard fired blindly, moving back a step or two, then turned and started up the stone staircase.

He paused at the bend, slinging the Thompson over his shoulder, and took two stick grenades from his belt. He could hear voices below, stumbling steps on the stairs. He tossed the two grenades down into the murk, one after the other, went around the corner, and continued to climb without pause.

There was an explosion below, followed by another. Cries of pain. He could hardly breathe now, smoke everywhere, choking the landing outside the dining hall. He groped his way around the wall, found the entrance to the upper staircase, and started to climb to the top of the tower.

Had he but known it, the others had gotten no farther than the upper landing, Birr having collapsed completely, so that the two Germans had been compelled to drag him into the dining hall.

Canning crouched over him, almost overcome by smoke, waiting for the end that seemed inevitable now. He got to his feet, lurched across to the window, and smashed what glass remained in the lower half. The Germans dragged Birr across the floor, choking and coughing.

They all crouched at the window, drawing in deep lungfuls of fresh air. Canning cried, "The table — get it over."

They crouched behind it, waiting for the end.

On the landing at the foot of the stairs, Ritter rolled over, pushing a body away from him. There was blood on him — but not his own — and he pulled himself up and leaned against the wall. A hand reached out to steady him — Hoffer.

"Are you all right, *Sturmbannführer?*"

"Everything in perfect working order, or so it would seem, Erich." An old, bad joke between them, no longer funny.

A gust of wind blowing in through the shattered doorway below cleared the smoke from the landing. It was a charnel house — bodies everywhere, blood and brains sprayed across the walls.

There were perhaps a dozen Finns left alive and unwounded, crouched at the head of the stairs. Ritter glanced at his watch. It was almost eight-thirty.

"All right, damn you. You're still mine

for another thirty minutes. Still soldiers of the *Waffen*-SS. Let's get it done."

They made no move. It was not that there was fear there. Only emptiness, faces drained of all emotion, all feeling.

"It's no good," Hoffer said. "They've had enough."

As smoke swirled back into place again, the Finns retreated, simply melted away.

"So?" Ritter said, and he leaned down and picked up a Schmeisser.

As he turned, Hoffer caught his arm. "This is madness. Where are you going?"

"Why, to the top of the tower, old friend." Ritter smiled and put a hand to his shoulder. "We've come a long way together, but no more orders. It is over. You understand me?"

Hoffer stared at him, horror in his face. Ritter started upstairs.

When Howard lurched out of the smoke onto the roof, Finebaum almost shot him. Howard fell on his hands and knees, and Finebaum crouched beside him.

"Is he all right?" Claudine Chevalier demanded.

Howard answered her, struggling for breath. "All I need is a little air." He looked around him. "Where's the general?"

"No sign of him up here," Finebaum said. "What happened below?"

"It was bad," Howard told him. "The worst I've ever known." He got up on his knees. "I'll have to go back. See what's happened to them."

Madame Chevalier, who had gone to the parapet to look down, cried, "There are tanks coming. A whole column."

Finebaum ran to join her in time to see half a dozen Cromwells, several Bren-gun carriers and trucks moving toward the castle at full speed. The surviving Finns had just emerged from the entrance. As they started across the courtyard, the first Cromwell emerged from the tunnel and opened up with its machine gun. Two Finns went down; the rest immediately dropped their weapons and put up their hands.

Finebaum turned and found Howard leaning over the parapet beside him. "Did you ever see a prettier sight?" Finebaum demanded. Howard gazed down blankly, eyes remote, and Finebaum shook him roughly. "Hey, noble Captain, it's over. We survived."

"Did we?" Howard said.

And then Claudine Chevalier cried out sharply.

Ritter stood there at the head of the stairs, smoke billowing around him. He wore no cap. There was blood on his face, and the blond hair flashed pale fire in the morning light. The black panzer uniform was covered with dust, but the Knight's Cross with Oak Leaves and Swords still made a brave show at his throat.

"Captain Howard?" he called.

Finebaum turned, unslinging his M1, but Howard knocked it aside. "My affair — stay out of it."

He was smiling, his eyes full of life again. He leaned down slowly and picked up his Thompson.

Ritter said, "A firstrate show. My congratulations."

Howard fired then, a long burst that ripped the Iron Cross First Class from

Ritter's tunic, hurling him at the wall. The German rebounded, falling to his knees. He flung up the Schmeisser, arm extended, firing one-handed, driving Howard back against the parapet, killing him instantly. For a moment, the young German hung onto life on his knees there in the snow, and then he fell forward on his face.

Hoffer emerged from the smoke, a Walther in his good hand, and crouched beside him. Finebaum dropped to one knee by Howard. There was a pause, then the American's M1 came up.

It was Claudine Chevalier who ended it, her voice high on the morning air. "No!" she screamed. "Enough! Do you hear me? Enough!"

Finebaum turned to look at her, then back to Hoffer. The German threw down his Walther and sat back on his heels, a hand on Ritter's shoulder. Finebaum, without a word, tossed his M1 out over the parapet to fall through clear air to the courtyard below.

It was on the steps outside the main

entrance that Canning met Henri Dubois for the first time. The Frenchman, a pistol in one hand, saluted. "My respects, *mon général.* My one regret is that we couldn't get here sooner."

"That you got here at all is one small miracle, son."

"We must thank Doctor Gaillard for that."

"Paul?" Canning caught him by the arm. "You've seen him?"

"He escaped from the village this morning and skied across the mountains, hotly pursued by some of these Finnish gentlemen. It was only by the mercy of God that he came across us when he did. He is in the ambulance now, at the rear of the column."

"Thanks." Canning started down the steps and paused. "There was a man called Strasser in the village. He was in charge of this whole damn business. He had Madame Claire de Beauville with him. Did you get them?"

"We came straight through without stopping, *mon général.* Naturally, Schloss Arlberg was our main objective, but if this man Strasser is there, we'll find him."

"I wouldn't count on it."

He found Gaillard on a stretcher in the ambulance at the rear of the column, as Dubois had indicated. The little Frenchman lay there, a gray army blanket pulled up to his chin, eyes closed, apparently sleeping. A medical orderly sat beside him.

"How is he?" Canning demanded in French.

"He is fine, Hamilton, never better." Gaillard's eyes fluttered open. He smiled.

"You did a great job."

"And the others — they are safe?"

"Claudine is fine. Justin got knocked about a bit, but he'll be all right. I'm afraid the rest makes quite a casualty report. Max is dead, and Captain Howard. Most of the Finns. Ritter himself. It was quite a shooting match up there."

"And Strasser?"

"We'll get him — and Claire. Only a question of time now."

Gaillard's face was twisted with pain,

and yet concern showed through. "Don't let him get away, Hamilton. He is capable of anything, that one. What he did to that girl was a terrible thing."

"I know," Canning said soothingly. "You get some sleep now. I'll see you later."

He jumped down from the ambulance and stood there, thinking of Strasser, wanting only to get his hands on the German's throat. And then there was Claire. Suddenly he knew that she was by far the most important consideration now.

There was an empty jeep standing nearby. Without the slightest hesitation he jumped behind the wheel, gunned the motor, and drove out through the tunnel and across the drawbridge.

When he braked to a halt outside the Golden Eagle, the square was silent and deserted, everyone staying out of the way. There was an M1 in the rear seat of the jeep. He checked that it was loaded, then jumped out and kicked open the front door.

"Strasser! Where are you, you bastard?"

It was very quiet in the bar — too quiet. He saw the bullet holes in the wall, the blood on the floor, and the hair rose on the nape of his neck. A stair creaked behind him. He turned and found Meyer standing there.

"Where is he?"

"Gone, *Herr General*. After the Finns left to hunt Herr Gaillard, he moved their field car to the rear courtyard, where it was out of sight. When the French soldiers with the tanks came half an hour ago, they passed straight through without stopping. Herr Strasser drove away shortly afterward in the field car."

"And Madame de Beauville — he took her with him?"

Meyer's face was gray, his voice the merest whisper when he said, "No, *Herr General*. She is still here."

He stumbled along the hall, opened his office door, and stood back. She lay on the floor, covered by a blanket. Canning stood there, staring down, disbelief on his face. He dropped to one knee and pulled back the cover. Her face was unmarked and so pale as to be almost transparent, wiped clean of all pain, all deceit. A child asleep at last.

He covered her again very gently, and when he turned to Meyer, his face was terrible to see. "Do you know where he went?"

"I overheard them speak of it several times, *Herr General*. There is an abandoned airstrip at Arnheim, about ten miles from here. I understand there is an airplane waiting."

"How do I get there?"

"Follow the main road to the top of the hill east of the village. A quarter of a mile on, there is a turning to the left, which will take you all the way to Arnheim."

The door banged. A moment later, the engine of the jeep roared into life. Meyer stood there in the quiet, listening to the sound dwindle into the distance.

At Arnheim it was snowing again as the Dakota taxied out of the hangar. Strasser, standing behind Berger in the cockpit, said, "Any problems with the weather?"

"Nothing to worry about. Dirty enough to be entirely to our advantage, that's all."

"Good. I'll get out now and see to the Stork. I don't want to leave that kind of evidence lying around. You get into position for takeoff, and I'll join you in a few moments."

Berger grinned. "Spain next stop, *Reichsleiter.*"

Strasser dropped out of the hatch, skirted the port wing, and ran toward the entrance to the hangar as the Dakota moved away. He took a stick grenade from his pocket and tossed it through the entrance, ducking to one side. It exploded beneath the Stork, which started to burn fiercely.

He turned away, aware of the Dakota turning in a circle out there at the end of the runway, and then the jeep swung through the entrance from the road and braked to a halt about thirty yards away.

Canning saw the Dakota turning into the wind, thought for one dreadful moment that he was too late, and then the shock of the Stork's tank exploding turned his eyes to the hangar. He saw Strasser in front, crouching as he pulled a Walther from his pocket.

Canning grabbed for the M1, fired three or four shots, and it jammed. He threw it away from him and ducked as Strasser stood up, firing at him coolly, two rounds punching holes through the windshield.

Canning slammed the stick into gear, revving so furiously that his wheels spun in the snow and the jeep shot forward. Strasser continued to fire, dodging to one side only at the very last minute, and Canning slammed his boot on the brake, sending the jeep into a broadside skid.

He jumped for the German while the vehicle was still in motion, and they went over in a tangle of arms and legs. For a moment, Canning had his hands on the German's throat and started to squeeze, and then Strasser swung the Walther with all his force, slamming it against the side of the general's head.

Canning rolled over in agony, almost losing consciousness, aware of Strasser scrambling to his feet, backing away, the Walther pointing. Canning got to his knees, and Strasser took careful aim.

"Good-bye, General," he said and pulled the trigger.

There was an empty click. Strasser threw the Walther at Canning's head, turned, and ran along the runway toward the Dakota.

Canning went after him, forcing himself into a shambling trot, but it was hopeless, of course. Things kept fading, going out of focus, then back again. The one thing he did see clearly — and it was all that mattered — was Strasser scrambling up through the hatch, the Dakota's engine note deepening, and then it was roaring along the runway.

Canning slumped down onto his knees and knelt there in the snow, watching it flee into the gray morning like a departing spirit.

Sixteen

It was almost dawn in La Huerta when Canning finished talking. Rain still tapped against the window of the bar, more gently now, but when I got up and looked out, the square was quiet and deserted.

Canning threw another log on the fire. "Well, Mr. O'Hagan — what do you think?"

"Such a waste," I said, "of good men."

"I know. They were all that. Not Strasser, of course. He was the Devil walking, but Jack Howard, Ritter, Sorsa, and those Finns. . . ."

"But why?" I asked. "Why did they persist in going through with it? Why didn't they simply tell Strasser — or Bormann or whoever — to go to hell?"

"Well, Sorsa and his Finns are possibly

429

the easiest to understand. As he said, they were fighting for wages. They'd taken the gold — if you like to look at it that way — pledged their word, and stuck to it — until the final carnage, anyway.''

"And Ritter?"

"He was like a man in deep water, swept along by the current, able to go only one way. He and Jack Howard were a lot alike — opposite sides of the same coin. At the end of things, I believe now that they'd both had enough. After what they'd been through, the things they'd done for their separate countries, the future held nothing. Didn't exist, if you like."

"You mean they were looking for death, both of them?"

"I'm certain of it."

"And Strasser, or should I say Bormann?"

"That's the terrible thing — not being sure. Remember Berger, the pilot who brought them out of Berlin? The guy who flew the Dakota out of Arnheim in the end? I found him in Italy fifteen or sixteen years ago. Dying of cancer. He was in the kind of state where a man just doesn't give a damn."

"And?"

"Oh, he thought Strasser was Bormann, all right. Last saw him in Bilbao in June of 'forty-five. In the ensuing years, they gave him plenty of work to do, the *Kameraden*. They looked after him."

"I'm surprised he didn't get a bullet like the rest."

"Well, he was something special. A pilot of genius. He could fly anything anywhere. I suppose that had its uses."

"But all those facts," I said, "about what took place in the bunker. Where did they come from?"

"Erich Hoffer," he said simply. "He's still alive. Runs a hotel in Bad Harzberg, and when a Russian infantry unit checked out Eichmann's hideout, they found one of the assistants still alive, a man called Walter Koenig. He pulled through after hospital treatment and spent twenty years in the Ukraine. When he finally returned to West Germany he wasn't too strong in the head, so they didn't take much notice of his story at his interrogation. I heard about it from a contact in German Intelligence.''

''Did you go to see this Koenig?''

''Tried to, but I was just too late. He'd committed suicide. Drowned himself in the Elbe. But I managed to get a look at the report. The rest, of course, is intelligent guesswork.''

''So where does it all leave us?'' I asked.

''I don't know. Was it Strasser at Arlberg and Bormann in the bunker, or the other way around? That's what's plagued me all these years. Oh, I told it all to the Intelligence people immediately after the events.''

''And what did they say?''

''I think they thought I'd been locked up too long. As far as they were concerned, Bormann was in Berlin right to the bitter end. Strasser was something else again.''

''And what did happen to Bormann, then, according to history?''

''He left the bunker at one-thirty A.M. on May second. As far as we know, he didn't attempt to disguise himself. It seems he wore a leather greatcoat over the uniform of a lieutenant general in the SS. He met his secretary, Frau Kruger, by sheer chance on his way out. He told her there wasn't much sense in any of it now, but that he'd try to get through."

"And from that moment the myth began?"

"Exactly. Was he killed on the Weidendammer Bridge as Kempka, the *Führer's* chauffeur, said . . ."

"Or later, near Lehrter Station, where Axmann said he saw him lying next to Stumpfegger? Those two bodies, as I recall, were buried near the Invalidenstrasse by post-office workers."

"That's right, and in 1972, during building work, they found a skeleton which the German authorities insist is Bormann's."

"But wasn't that refuted by experts?"

"One of the greatest of them put it perfectly in perspective. He pointed out that Bormann couldn't be in two places at once — dead in Berlin, and alive and well in South America."

There was a long silence. Rain

continued to tap at the window. General Canning said, "As we know, that bizarre condition is only too possible. I need hardly point out that it would also explain a great many puzzling features of the Bormann affair over the years."

He went to the bar and poured himself another drink. "So, what now?" I asked him.

"God knows. All of a sudden I feel old. All used up. I thought I was close this time. Thought it would finally be over, but now. . . ." He turned on me, a surprisingly fierce expression on his face. "I never married, did you know that? Never could, you see. Oh, there were women, but I could never really forget her. Strange." He sighed. "I think I'll go home to Maryland for a while and sit by the fire."

"And Strasser — or Bormann?"

"They can go to hell — both of them."

"It would make a beautiful story," I said.

He turned on me, that fierce expression on his face again. "When I'm dead — not before. You understand me?" It was an order, not a request, and I treated it as such.

"Just as you say, General."

I hadn't heard the car draw up, but there was a quick step in the hall and Rafael entered. "They have sent the taxi for you from the airstrip, *Señor* Smith. Your pilot says it would be possible to leave now, but only if you hurry."

"That's for me." Canning emptied his glass and placed it on the bar. "Can I offer you a lift?"

"No, thanks," I said. "Different places to go."

He nodded. "Glad we met, O'Hagan. It passed a lonely night at the tail end of nowhere."

"You should have been a writer, General."

"I should have been a lot of things, son." He walked to the door, paused, and turned. "Remember what I told you. When I'm gone you can do what the hell you like with it, but until then . . ."

His steps echoed on the parquet floor of the hall. A moment later, a door slammed and the taxi drove away across the square.

I never saw him again. As the world knows, he was killed flying out of Mexico City three days later, when his plane exploded in midair. There was some wild talk of sabotage in one or two newspapers, but the aviation authority's inspectors turned over the wreckage and soon knocked that little story on the head.

They buried him at Arlington, of course, with full honors, as was only proper for one of his country's greatest sons. They were all there. The President himself, anybody who was anybody at the Pentagon. Even the Chinese sent a full general.

I was still in South America when it happened, and had a hell of a time arranging a flight out, so that I almost missed it, and when I arrived at Arlington, the high and the mighty had departed.

There were one or two gardeners about, no one else, and the grave and the immediate area were covered with flowers and bouquets and wreaths of every description.

It started to rain, and I moved forward,

turning up the collar of my trenchcoat, examining the sentiment on the temporary headstone they'd put up.

"Well, old man, they all remembered," I said softly. "I suppose that should count for a lot."

I started to turn away, and then my eye caught sight of something lying close to the base of the stone, and the blood turned to ice water inside me.

It was a single scarlet rose. What some people would call a winter rose. When I picked it up, the card said simply: *As promised.*